I0614228

SMITHSONIAN INSTITUTION

BUREAU OF AMERICAN ETHNOLOGY: J. W. POWELL, DIRECTOR

BULLETIN 27

TSIMSHIAN TEXTS

BY

FRANZ BOAS

WASHINGTON

GOVERNMENT PRINTING OFFICE

1902

CONTENTS

TSIMSHIAN TEXTS

NASS RIVER DIALECT

Recorded and translated by
FRANZ BOAS

INTRODUCTION

The following texts were collected in Kinkolith, at the mouth of the Nass river, during the months of November and December, 1894, while I was engaged in researches under the auspices of the British Association for the Advancement of Science. The principal object of these investigations was a study of the Athapascan tribe of Portland canal, and the following texts were collected incidentally only. The ethnologic results of these investigations were published in the reports of the Committee on the Northwestern Tribes of Canada of the British Association for the Advancement of Science.[1]

The texts are in the Nass River dialect of the Tsimshian language. The dialect is called by the natives Nîsqa'ᴇ. The texts were obtained from four individuals—Philip, Moses, Chief Mountain, and Moody. By far the greater number of them are myths of the tribe. Judging from similar myths which I collected in previous years among the Tsimshian proper,[2] they are only moderately well told.

Possibly the method of transcribing sounds is not quite satisfactory. I have not been able to determine definitely if there are one or two palatized l's. I consider it probable that there may be two; but in the present texts all the palatized l's are rendered by one character. There is also a certain inconsistency in my perception of the surds and sonants, the fortis, or the surd followed by a hiatus, very often sounding similar to the sonant. I have not endeavored to make the spelling throughout consistent, but have rather followed the transcription which seemed to me most appropriate at the time when I wrote the texts down.

FRANZ BOAS.

NEW YORK, *June, 1899.*

---

[1] Report of the 65th meeting of the British Association for the Advancement of Science, Ipswich, 1895, pp. 569–586.

[2] Franz Boas, Indianische Sagen von der nord-pacifischen Küste Amerikas, Berlin, 1895, pp. 272–305.

Alphabet

a, e, i, o, u	have their continental sounds (short).
ā, ē, ī, ō, ū	long vowels.
E	obscure e in flower.
ᵃ, ᵉ, ⁱ, ᵒ, ᵘ	vowels not articulated, but indicated by position of the mouth.
ä	in German Bär.
â	aw in law.
ô	o German voll.
ê	e in bell.
ai	i in island.
au	ow in how.
ʟ	posterior palatal l; the tip of tongue touches the alveoli of the lower jaw, the back of the tongue is pressed against the hard palate; generally surd. The occurrence of the corresponding sonant is doubtful. Possibly there is still another l, produced a little nearer the front part of the hard palate.
q	velar k.
g̣	velar g.
k	English k.
g·	palatalized g, almost gy.
k·	palatized k, almost ky.
x	ch in German Bach.
X	x pronounced at the posterior border of the hard palate.
x·	palatal x as in German ich.
s	pronounced with open teeth, therefore somewhat similar to English sh.
d, t / b, p / g, k	as in English, but surd and sonant more difficult to distinguish.
h	as in English.
y	as in year.
w	as in English, probably always aspirated.
l / m / n	as in English; as terminal sounds articulated but inaudible, unless followed by a word beginning with a vowel.
'	a pause; when following an initial or terminal mute, it tends to increase the stress of the latter.

Txä́'msem and Lôgôbolä́'

[1–5 told by Moses; 6–8, 2a, and 5a told by Philip]

1. There was a town in which a chief and chieftainess were living. The chieftainess had done something bad. She had a lover, but the chief did not know it. The young man loved the chieftainess very much. He often went to the place where she lived with the chief. Then the chieftainess resolved, "I will pretend to die." She pretended to be very sick, because she wanted to marry that man. After a short time she pretended to die. Then all the people cried. Before she died the chieftainess said, "Make a large box in which to bury me when I am dead." The people made a box and put her

---

Txä́'msem and Lôgôbolä́'

1. Hētkᵘʟ qal-ts'a'p. Nʟk·'ē k·'âlʟ sᴇm'â'g·it dē-k·'âlʟ sîg·idᴇmna'q. 1
   There stood / a town. / Then / one / chief / and one / chieftainess.

Nʟk·'ē sg·īʟ hwîlʟ sîg·idᴇmna'q. K·'âlʟ ʟgo-g·a'tg·ê, nʟnē t'an 2
   Then / had done something / the chieftainess. / One / little man, / he / who

lēlē'luksʟ sîg·idᴇmna'q. Nî'g·ît hwîlā'x·ʟ sᴇm'â'g·it. Sᴇm-sī'epᴇnʟ 3
   stole often / the chieftain- / ess. / Not / knew it / the chief. / Very / he loved

sîg·idᴇmna'q t'an qaqâ'ôdet aʟ dᴇd'ā't aʟ awa'aʟ sᴇm'â'g·it. Nʟk·'ē 4
   the chieftainess / who / went there often / to / she was / in proximity of / the chief. / Then

tgōnʟ sa-gâ'ôtkᵘʟ sîg·idᴇmna'q: "Āmʟ dᴇm nô'ôēᴇ aʟ dᴇm 5
   this / resolved / the chieftainess: / "Good / (fut.) / I am dead / and / (fut.)

sī-bē'ᴇkᵘsēᴇ." Nʟk·'ē ā'd'îkskᵘʟ dᴇm hwîl sī'epkᵘʟ sîg·idᴇmna'q. 6
   make / I lie." / Then / came / (fut.) / being / sick / the chieftain- / ess.

Nʟk·'ē wī-t'ē'sʟ ha-sī'epkᵘʟ aʟ sī-bē'kᵘstg·ê dᴇmt hwîla nak·skᵘʟ 7
   Then / was great / sickness / at / she a lie made / (fut.) / trying / she wanted to marry

k·'âlʟ g·at, qan hēt. Nî̂g·i nakᵘʟ sg·ēʟ sîg·idᴇmna'q, nlk·'ē 8
   one / man, / there- fore / she said so. / Not / long / lay / the chieftainess, / then

nô'ôt. Nʟk·'ē sig·a'tkᵘʟ txanē'tkᵘʟ qal-ts'a'p. Nʟk·'ē tgōnʟ hēʟ 9
   she was dead. / Then / cried / all the / people. / Then / this / said

sîg·idᴇmna'q: "Tsᴇ sī-laîsᴇm xpeîs tsᴇ hwîl lō-sg·i'eᴇ." ʟa nô'ôt, 10
   the chieftainess: / "Make / that large / a box / where in / I shall lie." / When she was dead,

nʟk·'ēt dzā'pdᴇʟ xpeîst. Nʟk·'ēt lō-ma'qdet lâ'ôt. Nʟk·'ēt 11
   then / they made / a box. / Then / in they put her / in it. / Then

into it. They put it on the branches of a tree in the woods. The chieftainess had a spoon and a fish knife in her box. She pretended to be dead. For two nights the chief went into the woods, and sat right under the box in which the chieftainess was lying. Then he ceased to cry. Behold, there were maggots falling down from the bottom of the box. Then the chief thought, "She is full of maggots." But actually the chieftainess was scraping the spoon with her fish knife, and the scrapings looked just like maggots. In the evening her lover went into the woods. He climbed the tree and knocked on the box, saying, "Let me in, ghost!" He said so twice. Then the chieftainess replied, "Ha-ha! I pretend to make maggots out of myself

---

1 q'aldîx·-ma'qdet   aL   g·île'lîx·.   NLk·'et   ma'qsaandēL   g̣an.
in the rear they put   at   in the woods.   Then   they put her on   a tree.
of the houses her

2 Ts'ō'sg·îm nak^u,   nLk·'ēt   lō-dā'mL   sîg·idEmna'qL   q'aldō'x·   qanL
A little, while,   then   in held in   the chieftainess   a spoon   and
                  her hands

3 ha-q'ō'L.   Bēk^uL   hwî'ltg·ê.   Nîg·idē   nô'ôt.   NLa   g·ē'lp·El   yu'ksa
a knife to   She lied   she did so.   Not she   was   (Perf.)   two   evenings
split salmon.   dead.

4 qa'nē-hwîla   q'aldîx·-iä'L   sEm'â'g·ît   aL   lôgôl-dEp-d'ā't   aL   laXL
always   to the rear went   the chief   under   he sat   at   under
   of the houses

5 hwîl   lē-sg·īL   xpē'îs   hwîl   lō-sg·īL   sîg·idEmna'q.   La   Lēsk^uL
where   on was   the box   where   in lay   the chieftain-   When   finished
                    ess.

6 wi-yē'tk^uL   sEm'â'g·ît,   gwinā'dēL,   smā'wun   qa'nē-hwîla   mak·t   aL
crying   the chief,   behold,   maggots   always   fell   at
                             down

7 bak^ut   aL   siä'nL   xpē'îst.   NLk·'ē   tgōnL   bēL   qâtL   sEm·â'g·ît:
came   at   the bottom   the box.   Then   this   said   the heart   the chief:
out of   of   of

8 "La   smā'wun   da."   Dē'yaL   qâ'ôtL   sEm'â'g·ît.   Tgōnl   hwîlL
"It is all maggots."   Thus said   the heart   the chief.   This   did
                     of

9 sîg·idEmna'qg·ê.   La'lbEl   q'aldō'x·   aL   ha-q'ō'L.   NLk·'ēt   hō'g·îgaL
the chieftainess.   She   the spoon   with   the fish   Then   like
            scraped   knife.

10 smā'wunL   Lā   q'am-Lā'lbEqskt   aL   q'aldō'x·.   NLk·'ē   huX   yu'ksa.
maggots   (perf.)   refuse of   scraping   at   the spoon.   Then   again   it was
                                     evening.

11 NLk·'ē   huX   q'aldîx·-iä'L   an-k'ō'oXt.   NLk·'ēt   mEn-hē't'EnL   g̣an.
Then   again   to the rear went   her sweetheart.   Then   up   he placed   a tree.
           of the houses

12 NLk·'ē   mEn-iä'L   g·a'tg·ê.   NLk·'ēt   nā-d'îsd·ē'st.   NLk·'ē   tgōnL
[Then   up went   the man.   Then   with   he   Then   this
                         his hand knocked.

13 hē'tg·ê: "Ts'ēnt'Enē,   lū'laq.   Ts'ē'ntEnē,   lū'laq."[1]   G·ē'lp·ElL
he said: "Let me   ghost.   Let me   ghost."   Twice
       enter,   enter,

14 hē'tg·ê.   NLk·'ē   dē'lEmExk^uL   sîg·idEmna'q: "Hähä,   algwâ'L
he said so.   Then   answered   the chieftain-   "Hähä,   therefore
                       ess:

15 qan   sîsqaxsā'ntg·ê."   NLk·'ēt   hux   q'angō'uL   La   hä'bEL   an-sg·ē'îst.
I pretend to make mag-   Then   again   she opened   the cover   the grave.
gots out of myself."   of

---

[1] These words are in Tsimshian dialect.

in your behalf." Then she opened the cover of the box, and the man lay down with her. He did so every night. Then she came to be pregnant. The man always went up to her. The chief did not know it, but one man found it out. He told the chief. Then the chief's nephews kept watch and killed the man, and also killed the woman. Now she was really dead, and her body was putrefying. Then her child came out alive. It sucked the intestines of its mother, and therefore its name was Sucking-intestines. The child grew up in the box.

One day all the children went into the woods, shooting with bows and arrows at a target. They were not far from this tree when they were shooting. Then Sucking-intestines saw them. He went down and took their arrows. Thus the children lost them again and again.

NLk·'ē huX lō-g·ä'êL g·at aL awa'at. Txanē'tkᵘL axkᵘL hwîlt. 1
Then again in lay the in her prox- Every night he did so.
down man imity.

NLk·'e La ä'd'îk·skᵘL dEm ō'bEnt. NLk·'ē ō'bEnt qa'nē-hwîla 2
Then (perf.) she came (fut.) pregnant. Then she was always
pregnant

bax-iä'L g·a'tg·ê. Nî'g·it hwîlä'x·L sEm'â'g·ît. Hwä'i! K·'âlL 3
up went the man. Not knew it the Well! One
chief.

g·a'tg·ê t'an lō-hwa't. NLk·'ēt ma'Ldet aL sEm'â'g·ît. NLk·'ēt 4
man who in found Then he told to the chief. Then
it.

lēLk·L guslî'skᵘL sEm'â'g·ît. NLk·'ēt dza'kᵘdēL g·a'tg·ê. NLk·'ē 5
watched the nephews the chief. Then they killed the man. Then
of

huX dza'kᵘdēL hana'qg·ê. NLk·'ē sEm-hō'm nô'ôt. Hwä'i! La 6
also they killed woman. Then really she Well! (Perf.)
the was dead.

lôqL lō'lEqg·ê. NLk·'ē k·saxL Lgo-tk·'ē'LkᵘL dEdē'lstg·ê. NLk·'ē 7
putrefy- her body. Then out came a little child alive. Then
ing was

d'âqL Lgo-tk·'ē'LkᵘL hāts nôxt. NLnêL qan hwa'dEs Anmâgôm 8
it sucked the child the in- of his Therefore its name Sucking-
little testines mother.

hā't. Hwäi! Lā wî-t'ē'sL Lgo-tk·'ē'Lkᵘg·ê aL lō-d'ā't aL 9
intes- Well! When great was the child at in was in
tines. little

ts'Em-xpē'îst. 10
in the box.

NLk·'ē q'aldîx·-qâ'ôdEL txanē'tkᵘL k'ōpe-tk·'ē'Lkᵘ wî-hē'lt 11
Then to the rear of they were all the little children many
the houses gone

yukL sg·äela'xkᵘdētg·ê aL ha-Xda'kL dô'qdēt qanL hawî'l. 12
while they shot at a with bows they took and arrows.
target

Wagait-dō' hwîl hētkᵘL gan. NLnēL gu'Xdēit. NLk·'ē g·ig·a'as 13
At a distance far where stood a tree. Then they shot. Then saw
them

Anmâgôm hā't. NLk·'ē huX d'Ep-iê'êt. NLk·'ēt huX dôqL 14
Sucking- intes- Then again down he Then again he took
tines. went.

ba-wî'l. NLk·'ē huX k'ut-gwâ'disîL txanē'tkᵘL k'ōpE-tk·'ē'Lkᵘ. 15
arrows. Then again about lost them all the little children.

Now, the children saw that the boy came from out of the grave, and they told the chief. He said, "Keep watch and try to catch him." The chief's nephews went, and, behold, he came down again. While he was walking about, they caught him and took him home. They took him to the chief's house. Now he grew up, and his name was Sucking-intestines.

2. Now he heard that there was a chief's daughter on the other side of the hole where the heavens meet. Sucking-intestines caught a bird and skinned it. He put its skin on and flew. Then he said, "G·ît g·ît g·ît g·însăăăă!" He came to a town, and there he met a person. Then he shot a wood-pecker. He skinned it, and the other person put it on. They flew on. The one bird cried, "G·ît g·ît g·ît g·însăăăă!" The wood-

---

1 NʟK·'ē   Lā   sī-gō'n,   nʟk·'ē   hwîlā'x·detg·ê   hwîl   g·ik·si-hwî'tkᵘʟ
   Then   when   a little   then   they knew   where   out   came from
             while,

2 ʟgō-tk·'ē'ʟkᵘ   aʟ   ts'ɛm-an-sg·ē'îst.   Nʟk·'ēt   ma'ʟdēit   aʟ   sɛm'â'g·ît.
   the   boy   from   in   the grave.   Then   they   to   the chief.
   little   told

3 Nʟk·'ē   a'lg·îxʟ   sɛm'â'g·ît: "Ām   mɛsɛm   lēʟk·t   sɛm-g·idi-gō'uʟ."
   Then   spoke   the chief: "Good   you   watch   very   right   take him."
                                            there

4 Nʟk·'ē   hwîʟʟ   guslî'skᵘʟ   sɛm'â'g·ît.   Gwinādē'ʟ,   ʟa   huX
   Then   they did so   the nephews   the chief.   Behold,   when   again
               of

5 d'ɛp-ā'd'îk·skᵘt,   nʟk·'ē   huX   k'uʟ-iä'êt.   Nʟk·'ē   sā-t-gō'udet.
   down   he came,   then   again   about he went.   Then   sud-   they took
                                                     denly   him.

6 Nʟk·'ēt   na-dē-iä'edet.   Nʟk·'ē   ts'ɛlɛm-ma'qdet   aʟ   awa'aʟ
   Then   out of with   they   Then   into   they   at   the prox-
         woods him   went.   put him   imity of

7 sɛm'â'g·ît.   Nʟk·'ē   wī-t'ē'st,   Anmâgôm   hā'ʟ   hwa'tg·ê.
   the chief.   Then   he was large,   Sucking-   intes-   was his name.
                                                tines

8   2.   Nʟk·'ēt   nɛxna'ʟ   hwîl   d'āʟ   ʟgō'uʟkᵘʟ   sɛm'â'g·ît   aʟ   an-dâ'ʟ
         Then   he heard   where   was   the daughter of   a chief   at   other side
                                                       of

9 hwîl   nanô'ôʟ   mɛsmā'ʟ   lax-ha'.   Nʟk·'ēt   gō'us   Anmâgôm   hā'ʟ
   where   the hole of   the meeting   the sky.   Then he   took   Sucking-   intes-
                      of   tines

10 g·îtg·însa'.   Nʟk·'ēt   tsa'adēt.   Nʟk·'ēt   lō-ʟô'otkᵘt.   Nʟk·'ē
   (a bird).   Then   he skinned   Then   in he put it on.   Then
                 it.

11 g·ebā'yukt.   Nʟk·'ē   a'lg·îxt: "G·ît g·ît g·ît g·însăăăă."   Nʟk·'ēt
   he flew.   Then   he   "G·ît   g·ît   g·ît   g·însăăăă."   Then
                    said:

12 hwaʟ   k·'ēlʟ   qal-ts'a'p.   Nʟk·'ēt   gōl   k·'âlʟ   g·at.   Nʟk·'ēt
   he   one   town.   Then   he met   one   person.   Then
   found

13 gu'Xdēʟ   hā'atkᵘ.   Nʟk·'ēt   tsa'adetg·ê.   Nʟk·'ēt   lō-ʟô'ôtkᵘʟ
   he shot   a wood-   Then he   skinned it.   Then   in he put it on
          pecker.

14 k·'âlʟ   g·at.   Nʟk·'ē   lēba'yukdet.   Nʟk·'ē   huX   a'lg·îxʟ   g·îtg·însa':
   one   person.   Then   they flew.   Then   again   spoke   G·îtg·însa':

15 "G·ît   g·ît   g·ît   g·însăăăă."   Nʟk·'ē   dē-g·ebā'yukʟ   ha'atkᵘ:
   "G·ît   g·ît   g·ît   g·însăăăă."   Then   with   flew   the wood-
                                                      pecker:

pecker accompanied him, crying, "How-how!" They flew upward.
Now they came to a town. There a person said, "Son of the ghosts,
you must go on farther if you want to find the place where the heavens
meet." Then Sucking-intestines, who had the bird skin on, said "G·ît
g·ît g·ît g·însäääǎ!" and the woodpecker said, "How-how!" after Sucking-intestines had spoken. They came to many towns, and the people
all said the same to them. They went on for a long time, and finally
came to the hole in the sky. At that time it was always dark. There
was no daylight. They found the hole, and the bird and the woodpecker flew through it. When they reached the inside of the sky,
Sucking-intestines took off the skin of the bird, and the woodpecker
also took off his skin. He sat down near the hole of the sky, while

"Haau	hâ."	K·'ē	sa'k·sdēt.	NLk·'ē	lē-yô'xkⁿLdet	lax-o'L	k·'ēlL	1
"Haau	hâ."	Then	they went.	Then	on they went	on top of	one	

qal-ts'a'p.	NLk·'ē	a'lg·îxL	k·'âlL	g·at:	2
town.	Then	said	one	person:

Q'ai-yim	al-sg·ä'	hwîl	hax-hak·'waxL	mɛs-mā'	dɛmt	qan	de-hwa'L	LgōⁿLk·ⁿL	lō-lɛ-qai	3
Close by	lies	where	close	the meeting of the heavens	(fut.)	for	finds	the child of	the ghost.

NLk·'ē	a'lg·îxL	g·îtg·însā'	lō-Lô'ôtkⁿs	Anmâgôm	hāt:	4
Then	said	the g·îtg·însā'	whom had on	Sucking-	intes-tines

"Tsinî't,	tsinî't,	g·ît,	g·ît,	g·ît,	g·însäääǎ	hē',"	5
"Tsinî't,	tsinî't,	g·ît,	g·ît,	g·ît,	g·însäääǎ	hē'."

dē'yaL	hā'atkⁿ	aL	La	LēskⁿL	a'lg·îxL	g·îtg·însā'.	6
thus said	the woodpecker	at	when	finished	saying	the g·îtg·însa'.

NLk·'ē	sa'k·skⁿdēt	wī-hē'ld	qal-ts'îpts'a'p.	Lō-yô'xkⁿdēt	7
Then	they went to	many	towns.	In they went

sagait-k·'ē'lt	hadā'lqdētg·ê,	Lā	nakⁿL	hwî'ldēt.	NLk·'ē	8
together one	which they said,	(perf.)	long	they did so.	Then

hwa'dēt	hwîl	qalk·si-nô'ôL	lax-ha'	aL	spagait-sq'ä'ɛxkⁿ	9
they found	where	through the hole of	the sky	at	in the dark

q'ap-hwîla	hwî'lt	g·i-k'ō'oL.	Nîg·îdi	ā'd'îk·skⁿL	dɛm	10
always	was so	in olden time.	Not	came	(fut.)

mɛsā'x·.	NLk·'ēt	hwa'dētg·ê.	NLk·'ē	qalk·si-g·eba'yukL	11
day.	Then	they found it.	Then	through flew

g·îtg·însa'	qanL	hā'atkⁿ.	NLk·'ēt	qalk·si-ax'a'qLkⁿdet	12
the g·îtg·însa'	and	the woodpecker.	Then	through they came

ts'ɛm-lax-ha'.	·NLk·'ēt	sa-ma'gas	Anmâgôm	hāt	La	anā'sL	13
into the sky.	Then	off put	Sucking-	intestines	(part.)	the skin of

g·îtg·însa'.	NLk·'ē	dē-t-sa-ma'gasL	k·'âlL	g·at	anā'sL	hā'atkⁿ.	14
g·îtg·însa'.	Then	also off put it	one	person	the skin of	the wood-pecker.

Sucking-intestines went on.   He came to a spring near the chief's house.   Then the chief's daughter went out, carrying a small basket in which she was about to fetch water.   She walked down to the spring in front of her father's house.[1]   Then Sucking-intestines transformed himself into the leaf of a cedar, and floated on the water.   The chief's daughter dipped it up into her basket and drank it.   Then she returned. She entered her father's house.   After a short time she was with child. Then she gave birth to a boy.   Then the chief and chieftainess were very glad.   They washed him regularly, and he began to grow up. Now he was beginning to creep about, and the chief smoothed and cleaned the floor of his house.   Now the child was strong.   He began

1 | NʟK‧'ē | d'āt | aʟ | lax-ts'ä'ʟ | hwîl | nanô'ôʟ | lax-ha'. | NʟK‧'ē
  | Then | he sat down | at | on the edge of | where | the hole of | the sky. | Then

2 | dā'uʟs | Anmâgôm | hāt. | D'āʟ | an-a'k·sʟ | sɛm'â'g·ît | aʟ | g·ä'u.
  | left | Sucking- | intes-tines. | There was | the well of | the chief | at | in front of the house.

3 | Gwa'nîk·sʟ | hwa'tg·ê. | NʟK‧'ē | k·saxʟ | ʟgō'uʟkuʟ | sɛm'â'g·ît.
  | Spring was | its name. | Then | went out | the child of | the chief.

4 | ʟgō-qo'q | yu'kdɛt | dɛm | ak·sku. | NʟK‧'ē | iaga-iē'êt | aʟ | qag·ä'us
  | A little basket | she held | (fut.) | to get water. | Then | down she walked | to | in front of the house of

5 | nɛguâ'ôdɛt. | NʟK·'ēt | gō'us | Anmâgôm | hāʟ | laqs. | NʟK‧'ē
  | her father. | Then | took | Sucking- | intes-tines | a spike of a cedar. | Then

6 | lō-ʟô'ôtkut. | NʟK‧'ē | lō-g·ig·â'ôk·st | aʟ | ts'ɛm-a'k·s. | NʟK·'e | g·apʟ
  | on he put it. | Then | in he floated | in | in the water. | Then | dipped up

7 | ʟgō'uʟkuʟ | sɛm'â'g·îʟ | qoq. | NʟK‧'ē | ak·st | sɛm-tqal-a'k·sdɛʟ | la'qsg·ê.
  | the child of | the chief | the basket. | Then | she drank | very in it she drank | the leaf.

8 | NʟK‧'ē | lō-ya'ltkut. | K·'ē | ts'ēnt | aʟ | hwîlps | nɛguâ'ôdɛt. | NʟK‧'ē
  | Then | she returned. | Then | she entered | in | the house of | her father. | Then

9 | āmʟ | qa-nā'guat, | nʟK·'ē | ō'bɛnt. | NʟK‧'ē | aqʟkuʟ | ʟgō-g·a't | ʟgō'uʟkuʟ
  | suffi-ciently | long, | then | she was with child. | Then | she gave birth to | a little man | her child

10 | ʟgo-wî'lk·sîʟku. | NʟK‧'ē | lō-ā'mʟ | qâʟ | wî-sɛm'â'g·ît | qanʟ | sîg·idɛmna'q.
   | the little princess. | Then | in good was | the heart of | the great chief | and | the chieftainess.

11 | NʟK·'ēt | qanē-hwîla | lō-mā'k·sdet | aʟ | ts'ɛm-a'k·s. | NʟK‧'ē | ä'd'îk·skuʟ
   | Then | always | in she put him | in | in water. | Then | became

12 | dɛm | hwîl | wî-t'ē's. | NʟK‧'ē | ʟā | k'uʟ-tqä'atkut. | NʟK‧'ē | sɛm-lō-sa-ā'mʟ
   | (fut.) | being | great. | Then | (perf.) | about he crawled. | Then | really in made good

13 | sɛm'â'g·ît | lō-ts'ä'wuʟ | hwîlp. | NʟK‧'ē | ʟā | dax-g·a'tʟ | ʟgō-tk·'ē'ʟku.
   | the chief | in the inside of | the house. | Then | (perf.) | strong was | the little child.

14 | NʟK‧'ē | wî-yē'tkut. | Tgōnʟ | hēt: | "Hamaxä', | hamaxä'." | NʟK·'ēt
   | Then | he cried. | Thus | he said: | "Hamaxä', | hamaxä'." | Then

<hr />

[1] From here on the relater seems to have confounded the stories of the birth of Txä'msɛm and of the origin of daylight.   See the correct version in Franz Boas, Indianische Sagen von der nord-pacifischen Küste Amerikas, Berlin, 1895, p. 272 et seq.

to cry all the time, "Hamaxä, hamaxä!" Then the chief called the people. He did not know what the boy wanted, nor why he cried; but he wanted the box that was hanging in the chief's house. This was a box in which daylight was kept hanging in one corner of his house. Its name was max. The child cried for it. Then the chief was annoyed. He called the people, and they entered. Then they heard the child crying aloud. They did not know what the child was saying. He cried all the time, "Hamaxä! hamaxä! hamax!" Now one wise man who understood him said to the chief, "He is crying for the max." The chief ordered it to be taken down, and a man took it down. They laid it down, and the boy sat down near it. He was now quite large. He stopped crying, for he was glad. Then he rolled

| gun-qâ'ôdEL | sEm'â'g·îL | qal-ts'a'p. | Nî'g·ît | hwîlā'x·dēL | hasa'qL | 1 |
| caused to go | the chief | the people. | Not | they knew | wanted | |

| Lgō-tk·'ē'Lkᵘ | qan | hēL | wī-yē'tkᵘt. | Hasa'qL | lō-ia'gat | aL | hwîlpL | 2 |
| the little boy | why | he said | he cried. | He wanted | in hung | in | the house of | |

| sEm'â'g·ît. | Lō-ia'qL | max | aL | amō'L | hwîlpL | sEm'â'g·ît. | 3 |
| the chief. | In hung | the max | in | the corner of | the house of | the chief. | |

| SEm-k·ā-Lōt'ŭ'gŭL | sEm'â'g·ît. | MaxL | hwas | gō'stg·ê. | NLnē'L | ā'wutL | 4 |
| Really | (?) | the chief. | Max was | the name of | that one. | Therefore | cried | |

| Lgō-tk·'ē'Lkᵘg·ê. | NLk·'ē | lō-wā'ntkᵘL | qâ'ôL | sEm'â'g·it. | NLk·'ēt | 5 |
| the little child. | Then | in annoyed was the | heart of | the chief. | Then he | |

| gun-qâ'ôdEL | qal-ts'a'p. | NLk·'ē | ts'ElEm-qâ'odEL | qal-ts'a'p. | NLk·'ē | 6 |
| caused to go | the people. | Then | into went | the people. | Then | |

| naxna'dēL | hwîl | wī-yē'tkᵘL | Lgō-tk·'ē'Lkᵘ | Lā | g'ap-wī-t'ē'st. | NLk·'ē | 7 |
| they heard | (verbal noun) | cried | the little child | (perf.) | really large. | Then | |

| nî'g·ît | hwîlā'x·L | qal-ts'a'p | qane-hwîla | hēL | Lgō-tk·'ē'Lkᵘg·ê | aL | 8 |
| not | knew | the people | (what) always | said | the little child | and | |

| wī-yē'tkᵘt. | TgōnL | hēt: | "Hamaxä' | hamaxä', | hamax." | Hwä'i! | 9 |
| it cried. | Thus | it said: | "Hamaxä', | hamaxä', | hamax." | Well! | |

| K·'âlL | hwîl | xô'ôsgum | g·at | t'an | hwîlā'x·t, | tgōnL | hēL | hwîl | xô'ôsgum | 10 |
| One | wise | | man | who | knew it, | this | said | | the wise | |

| g·at: | "Sem'â'g·ît | tgōsL | an-hä'et. | MaxL | haä'ut." | NLk·'ēt | 11 |
| man: | "Chief | that | what he says. | Max | he cries about." | Then he | |

| gun-sa-gō'udEL | sEm'â'g·ît. | NLk·'ēt | sā-gō'udEL | g·at. | NLk·'ēt | 12 |
| caused off take it | the chief. | Then | off took it | a person. | Then | |

| sg·'ē'det. | NLk·'ēt | k'uL-d'ā'L | Lgō-tk·'ē'Lkᵘ | Lā | g'ap-wī-t'ē'st. | NLk·'ē | 13 |
| they laid it down. | Then | about sat | the little boy | (perf.) | really large he was. | Then | |

| hā'wuL | wī-yē'tkᵘt, | lō-ā'mL | qâôtt. | NLk·'ēt | k'uL-lō-tgo-lax-lē'lb'Ent | aL | 14 |
| he stopped | crying, | in good was | his heart. | Then | about in around to and fro | he rolled it in | |

it about inside the house. He did so for four days. Sometimes he carried it to the door. Now the chief did not think of it. He quite forgot it. Then the boy really took the max. He put it on his shoulders and ran out with it. While he was running one man said, "The giant is running away with the max, ha!" Thus he received the name Giant. Then he ran away with it. He came to the hole of the sky, and, behold, his companion was sitting there. Then he took the skin of the bird. He put it on. His companion took the skin of the woodpecker, and they flew through the hole in the sky, the Giant carrying the max. At that time the world was always dark.

3. The Giant went on. It remained daylight. The darkness did not return. He wore something tied over his head. He arrived farther up the river. Then he put what he was wearing on his head under a stone in a steep cliff. It is there yet.

---

1 lō-ts'ä′wuL hwîlp. Lā lîg·i-txa′lpxL saL hwîlt. Wagait-didē-hwa′dEL
   in inside of / the house. / (Perf.) about / four / days / he did so. / Sometimes with it reached

2 Lgō-tk·'ē′Lkᵘ aL ā′dz'Ep. Lā t'ak·L sEm′â′g·ît hwiLL Lgō′uLkᵘL
   the child little / at / the door. / (Perf.) / he forgot / the chief / he did so / his child

3 sEm-t'ē′îskᵘL hwî′lpg·ê. SEm-gō′udEL Lgō-tk·'ē′LkᵘL ma′xg·ê.
   quite forgetful of / the house. / Really got / the boy little / the sun-box.

4 SEm-qô′ltsagat. SEm-ba′xt, k·si-dE-bā′yît. NLk·'ē baxt. NLk·'ē
   Quickly he put it on his shoulders. / Much he ran, / out with it he ran. / Then he ran. / Then

5 a′lg·ixL k·'âlL g·at: "K·si-dE-bā′is Wī-g·a′t max, hâ!" NLk·'ē
   said / one man: / "Ont with runs it / Giant / the sun-box, / hâ!" / Then

6 hwîlt gō′uL su-hwa′dēt as Wī-g·a′t. NLk·'ē dE-ba′xt. NLk·'ēt hwaL
   he took it / they called him / Giant. / Then with it he ran. / Then he found

7 hwîl nanô′ôL lax-ha′. Gwinā′dEL Lē stē′lt dē-d'ā′t. K·'ē hwîl k·'ēt
   (verbal nonn) / the hole of / the sky. / Behold! / (Perf.) his companion / also was there. / At once

8 gō′uL anā′sL g·îtg·insā′. NLk·'ē lō-Lô′ôtkᵘt. NLk·'ē dēt-gō′uL Lē
   he took / the skin of the / g·îtg·insā′. / Then on he put it. / Then also took

9 stēlL anā′sL bā′atkᵘt. NLk·'ē qalk·si-lēba′yukdet. Yu′kdEs
   his companion / the skin of / the woodpecker. / Then / through they flew. / He carried

10 Wī-g·a′t max. Qa′nē-hwîla sq'ä′Exkᵘl ha-lē-dzô′qsē aL g·i-k·ō′uL.
   Giant / the max (sun-box). / Always / dark was / the world / at / long ago.

11 3. NLk·'ē iä′s Wī-g·a′t. Lā mEsā′x·, nî′g·i huX sqä′Exkᵘ.
   Then / went / Giant. / (Perf.) it was daylight, / not / again / dark.

12 K'uL-hâ′yîL t'âl. NLk·'ēt hwaL g·ig·ä′nîx·. NLk·'ēt
   About he wore / something tied over his head. / Then / he reached / above. / Then

13 yōsL t'âlt aL ts'Em-lô′ôp, ts'Em-biā′qL hwaL lô′ôpg·ê.
   he put away / something tied over his head / at / in a stone, / in a bluff / the / the rock. / name of

14 Hwäi! Sîsg·ī′t aL gōn.
   Well! / It is there / yet.

4. The Giant did not know where his companion had gone. It was at the mouth of the Nass river where the Giant had come down, while Lôgôbolā' had come down in the darkness at the mouth of Skeena river. The Giant went to the mouth of Nass river. It was always dark, and he carried the max about with him. He went up the river, and ghosts whistled right before him. Then he was afraid. He returned, and therefore the waters of the river also turned back.

5. He continued to go up the river in the dark. A little farther up he heard the noise of people who were catching leaves in nets from their canoes. There was a loud noise out on the river, because they were working hard. The Giant, who was sitting on the shore, said: "Throw ashore one of the things that you are catching." And those on the water answered: "Where did you come from, you great

---

4. Hwäi!   Nî′g·ît   hwîlā′x·s   Wī-g·a′t   tsɛ   hwîl   d'ɛp-a′xkᵘt.   1
   Well!   Not he   knew   Giant   where   down he came.

Nʟk·'ē   nî′g·ît   hwîlā′x·ʟ   hwîl   dā′uʟʟ   stēlt.   Hwäi!   magâ′nʟ   2
Then   not he   knew   where   he left   his companion.   Well!   at the mouth of

Lē′sɛms   hwîl   d'ɛp-ā′qʟkᵘs   Wī-g·a′t.   Nʟk·'ē   magâ′nʟ   K·san   3
Nass river   where   down   came   Giant.   Then   at the mouth of   Skeena river

hwîl   dē-d'ɛp-a′qʟkᵘs   Lôgôbolā′   aʟ   spagait-sqä′ɛxkⁿ.   Nʟk·'ē   4
where   also down reached   Lôgôholā′   at   in the dark.   Then

g·îsi-iä′ês   Wī-g·ä′t   aʟ   magâ′nʟ   Lē′sɛms   aʟ   spagait-sqä′êxkᵘ   5
down went river   Giant   to   the mouth of   Nass river   at   in the dark

qanēt-hwîla   k'uʟ-yo′guʟ   max.   Nʟk·'ēt   hwaʟ   qa-g·ig·ä′nʟg·ê.   6
always   about he carried   the max.   Then he   found   a little above.

Nʟk·'ēt   lō-g·îtwî′nqʟ   llō′lɛq   ts'ä′ɛlt.   Tgōnʟ   hē′tg·ê: (Whistle.)   7
Then   in   whistled   ghosts   his face.   This   they said: (Whistle.)

Nʟk·'ē   xpetsa′Xt.   Nʟk·'ē   sa-lō-ya′ltkᵘt;   nʟqan   hwîlʟ   ak·s,   8
Then   he was afraid.   Then   from there   he returned;   therefore   it did so   the water,

huX   dē-lō-ya′ltkᵘʟ   a′k·sg·ê.   9
also   on its part   returned   the water.

5. Nʟk·'ē   huX   iä′êt   aʟ   spagait-sqä′êxkⁿ.   Nʟk·'ēt   hwaʟ   10
Then   again   he went   at   in the dark.   Then   he found

q'ai′yîm   g·ig·ä′nîx·.   Nʟk·'ēt   naxna′ʟ   hwîl   hahä′t   t'an   mokᵘʟ   11
close by   above.   Then   he heard   where   noise of   who   catching in net

ia′ns   aʟ   g·îksʟ   uks-xwilâ′gantkᵘ   aʟ   sɛm-saqalq'ē′lɛqʟt.   Nʟk·'ē   12
leaves   at   off shore from land to sea   roaring   and   they were working hard.   Then

d'ās   Wī-g·a′t   aʟ   g·île′lîx·.   Nʟk·'ē   a′lg·îxt: "Sɛm-tsagam-mâ′gaʟ   13
sat down   Giant   at   inland.   Then   he said: "Really   ashore   you throw

k·'ä′guʟ   an-hwunsɛ′mîst   lâyē′ɛ."   Nʟk·'e   tgōnʟ   hēʟ   g·î′ksg·ê: 14
one   what   you got   to me."   Then   this   said   those off shore:

liar?" They knew that it was the Giant, therefore they made fun of him. The Giant said again: "Throw ashore one of the things that you are catching." Then they scolded him. Then the Giant said, "I shall break the max;" and a person replied, "Ah, where do you come from, great liar, and where did you get what you are talking about?" The Giant repeated his request four times, but those on the water refused what he asked for. Therefore the Giant broke the max. It broke, and it was daylight. Behold, boxes floated on the water. The ghosts had been fishing in the dark. Then the Giant knew it. He did not see where they went.

6. Now Txä'msEm met his brother Lôgôbolā'. They were going to Nass river. They crossed the mouth of the river, and when they

---

1 "Dzā ndaL La hwîl huX wîtkᵘL wi-gwīx·-qala'mgaL," hät.
"Where when being again come from great telling fibs," he said.

2 Hwîlā'x·det net Wī-g·a't. NîLnē'L qan ansgwa'tkᵘdēt lâ'ôt.
They knew him he was Giant. Therefore they made fun of him.

3 NLk·'ē huX hēs Wīg·a't: "SEm-tsagam-mā'gaL k·'ä'guL
Then again said Giant: "Really ashore you throw one

4 an-hwunsE'mêst lâyē'ᴇ." NLk·'ēt tsagam-ha'k·sdēt. NLk·'ē
what you got to me." Then from sea they sculled Then
to land him.

5 tgōnL hēs Wī-g·a't: "Ha'onē bēsL max lâ'sEm." NLk·'ē
this said Giant: "Later on I tear the for you." Then
max

6 tgōnL hēL g·a'tg·ê: "Dzā nda LdEmt hwîl de-wî'tkᵘL
this said a person: "Where will have being coming from
been

7 wi-gwīx·-qalamga'L hä'tsEnL an-hē't." La txalpxL hēs Wī-g·a't
great telling fibs what talks what he (Perf.) four times said Giant
says."

8 aL nî'g·i hēL g·ī'k·sg·ê lu'XdēL an-hēs Wī-g·a't. NLqan
to not said those off shore they refused what said Giant. Therefore

9 tgōnL hwîls Wī-g·a't. BēsL max. NLk·'ē bēst. NLk·'ē
this did Giant. He tore the Then it tore. Then
sun-box.

10 mEsā'x·. Gwina'dēL qal-hē'nq k·'uL-g·îsi-lâ'k·sît aL lax-a'k·s.
it was Behold boxes about down floated at on the water.
daylight. river

11 Llō'lEq La hwîlt aL spagait-sqä'êxkᵘ. NLk·'ēt hwîlā'x·s
Ghosts (perf.) did so in in the dark. Then knew it

12 Wī-g·a't. Nî'g·îL g·a'at tsē hwîla s'ak·skᵘt.
Giant. Not he saw (uncer- where they went.
tainty)

13 6. Wagait tgōnL huX hwîl hwî'ls Txä'msEm ta tqal-hwa'L
So far now again he did so Txä'msEm against he met

14 wa'k·tg·ê, Lôgôbolā'L hwat. NLa dEmt lō-qâ'ôdēiL ts'Em-Lē'sEms.
his brother, Lôgôbolā' his name. (Perf.) (fut.) in they went in Nass river.

15 NLk·'ē La tsaga-ma'qskᵘdet aL saXL Lē'sEms, Lat hwa'dēL sēlkᵘL
Then (perf.) across they wen at the mouth Nass river. When they found the mid-
of dle of

reached the middle, a fog arose. Lôgôbolā′ had taken off his hat and put it upside down in his canoe. Then the fog lay on the surface of the water. Txä′msɛm lost his way and paddled about; but Lôgôbolā′ did not paddle, he just drifted. Then Txä′msɛm became afraid. He called his brother: "Dear Lôgôbolā′!" But Lôgôbolā′ did not answer. He called to him again, and he was nearly crying. He called him: "Oh, my good brother!" Then Lôgôbolā′ pitied him. He gathered the fog, took it off from the water, and put it in his hat; then he put the hat on, and the fog cleared away. Then they paddled across.

7. They camped at Graveyard point, intending to eat there. Txä′msɛm went to get fuel and to look for water. After they had eaten, Lôgôbolā′ said to his brother, "What are you going to drink,

---

ak·s,	nʟk·'ē	ā′d'îk·sku̲ʟ	ie′n.	Sa-gō′udɛs	Lôgôbolā′ʟ	qā′itt.	K·'ēt	1
the water,	then	came	fog.	Off	took	Lôgôbolā′	his hat.	Then

hasba′-sg·ît.	K·'ē	sg·iʟ	ie′n	aʟ	lax-a′k·s.	Nʟk·'ē	q′asba-k′uʟ-hwā′ax·s	2
upside down	he laid it.	Then	lay	fog on	on the water.	Then	astray about paddled	

Txä′msɛm.	Nʟk·'ē	nî′g·îdî	hwāx·s	Lôgôbolā′;	saxg·â′ôk·s.	K·'ē	3
Txä′msɛm.	Then	not	paddled	Lôgôbolā′;	he was floating.	Then	

ā′d'îk·sku̲ʟ	hwîl	alî′sku̲ʟ	qâ′ôts	Txä′msɛm.	Nʟk·'ēt	ētku̲s	Lôgôbolā′ʟ	4
came	being	weak	the heart of	Txä′msɛm.	Then	he	Lôgôbolā′ called	

wa′k·tg·ê:	"Nāt,	nāt,	Lôgôbolā′."	Ansegō′s	Lôgôbolā′.	K·'ē	5
his brother:	"My dear,	my dear,	Lôgôbolā′.	He paid no attention	Lôgôbolā′.	Then	

huX	hēt	aʟ	ä′êsku̲t.	Wu̲ʟdē	wi-yē′tku̲dēʟ	hēt.	At'ē′tku̲ʟ	ama′	6
again	he said	and	he called.	As though	crying	he spoke.	He called	good

wa′k·tg·ê.	K·'ē	si-gō′n,	k·'ē	q′ä′êʟ	qâ′ôts	Lôgôbolā′.	K·'ēt	7
his brother.	Then	after a while,	then	pity of	the heart of	Lôgôbolā′.	Then	

sē′wunʟ	ie′n	t-sa′-dôqt,	t-lō-d′ā′tɛlt	aʟ	qā′it.	K·'ēt	hatsɛk·sɛm	8
he gathered the fog in a bag	the fog	he off took it	he in put it	in	his hat.	Then	once more	

huX	hâx·s	Lôgôbolā′ʟ	qā′itt.	K·'ē	q′andā′uʟ	ie′n.	K·'ē	9
again	put on	Lôgôbolā′	his hat.	Then	opened	the fog.	Then	

hwā′x·dēʟ	tsaga-ma′qsdēt.		10
they paddled	across they went.		

7. K·'ē dzîxdzô′qdēt aʟ ʟgo-sgan-mē′lîk·st aʟ dɛm txâ′ôxku̲dēt. 11
Then they stayed at little tree crab-apple to (fut.) eat.
(Graveyard point)

K·'ēt q′amgait-g·a′as Txä′msɛmʟ ak·s aʟ he-yu′kʟ sɛ-âô′ʟku̲dēt aʟ 12
Then at the same time saw Txämsɛm water while beginning made firewood for

dɛm la′ku̲det. Nʟk·'ē la txâ′ôxku̲dēt. Nʟk·'ē hēt aʟ wak·t 13
(fut.) their fire. Then (perf.) they ate. Then he said to his brother

Lôgôbolā′g·ê: "Agō′ʟ dɛm an-a′k·sɛn Wî-g·ō′t; miä′n 14
Lôgôbolā′: "What (fut.) drink you Giant; at foot of

Giant? [Are you going to drink from the] roots of little alder trees?"
After they had eaten, he gave Txä′msEm his basket-cup. Txä′msEm
took it and went toward the water, but there was no water in the brook.
It was lost. Then Txä′msEm worried. He knew at once that
Lôgôbolā′ had caused the water to be lost. He returned. His voice
was almost choked by tears when he spoke: "Oh, dear Lôgôbolā′,
chief, please don't tease me. I am very thirsty." Then Lôgôbolā′
pretended to drink. He took the basket and he dipped water up himself. Then Txä′msEm drank. Then the flood tide set in.

8. Then they went up Nass river, each in his own canoe. When they
had gone up to the point where the current runs downward, Txä′msEm
said, "Let us gamble." Lôgôbolā′ agreed, though he did not care.
He asked Txä′msEm, "What game shall we play?" Txä′msEm

1 LGwa-lū′i?"[1]   NLk·′ē   La   LaxLä′Exkᵘdēt,   k·′ēt   g·inä′mL   qōkᵘ
  little alder?"   Then   when   they finished eating,   then   he gave   a basket

2 ha-a′k·sdēt.   K·′ēt gō′us Txä′msEm.   K·′ē Lat qâ′ôL awa′aL   ak·s.
  their cup.   Then took it Txä′msEm.   Then (perf.) he went the prox-   the
                                                        imity of   water.
                                                        to

3 NLk·′ē   ni̭′g·i̭   baxL   ak·s,   gwâtkᵘL   ak·s.   K·′ē   aba′g·askᵘs
  Then   not   ran   the water, it was lost the water. Then   was troubled

4 Txä′msEm.   K·′ēt   q′amgait-hwîlā′x·s Txä′msEm   Lôgôbolā′   qan
  Txä′msEm.   Then   at once   knew   Txä′msEm   Lôgôbolā′   on account
                                                                    of

5 gwâtkᵘL   a′k·sg·ê.   K·′ē   lō-ya′ltkᵘt.   K·′ē   lō-k·i̭lek·i̭lä′yîmxt   aL
  was lost   the water.   Then   he returned.   Then   in   he was choked   and
                                                                by tears

6 hē′tg·ê: "SEm′â′g·i̭t!   Wa′g·i   Lôgôbolā′!   Wâ′gal   huX   sEbEnä′yîn
  he spoke: "Chief!   brother   Lôgôbolā′!   don't   again   tease

7 nēE,   La   gwalkᵘL   qâ′ôdēE   aL   dEm   a′k·sēE."   K·′ē   hîs-a′k·skᵘs
  me,   (perf.) dry   my heart   for   (fut.) I drink."   Then   pretended to
                                                                        drink

8 Lôgôbolā′.   K·′ēt   gōL   qō′kᵘg·ê.   K·′ēt   lEp-g·a′ps   Lôgôbolā′.
  Lôgôbolā′.   Then   he took the basket. Then   self dipped   Lôgôbolā′.
                                                        it up

9 K·′ē   ak·s   Txä′msEm,   nLk·′ē   La   pta′lîk·s.
  Then   drank   Txä′msEm,   then   (perf.) the water
                                                  rose.

10 8. NLk·′ēt   La   lō-qâ′ôdet   ts·Em-Lē′sEms   mELag·udä′t   aL
    Then   when   in they went   in Nass river   one in each   in
                       (up river)

11 mmāl.   NLk·′ēt   hwa′dēL   g·ig·ē′nîx·   hwîl   g·îsi-ba′xL   ak·sEm
   a canoe. Then   they reached   up river   where   down   ran   the water
                                                          river   of

12 Lē′sEms.   NLk·′ē   hēs   Txä′msEmL   dEm   xsa′ndet.   NLk·′ēt
   Nass river. Then   said   Txä′msEm   (fut.) they gamble. Then

13 q′am-anâ′ôqs   Lôgôbolā′.   NLk·′ēt   g·ē′dExs   Txä′msEm;   agōL
   without agreed   Lôgôbolā′.   Then   asked   Txä′msEm,   what
   caring

14 dEm   hwîl   xsa′ndet.   "DEm   qammē′ntsnōm."   "Āmɛ   dzāpt."
   (fut.) (being) they play.   "(Fut.) we try archery."   "Good   make it."

replied: "Let us have a shooting match." Lôg̑ôbolā' consented. Then
Txä'msEm prepared a rock. He split it that they might shoot at it, and
said: "Whoever hits this crack shall win the game, either I or you. Let
us stake Skeena river against Nass river." Lôg̑ôbolā' agreed. It is
said that Lôg̑ôbolā' had a nice box for his quiver, but Txä'msEm just
made a bow and an arrow. Then he took two stones on which they sat
down. They talked to each other, and Txä'msEm wished to sit
nearest the water. He placed his grandchildren nearby. Lôg̑ôbolā'
placed the Canada Jays, his grandchildren, nearby. Now Lôg̑ôbolā'
said, "You shoot first, brother Giant." But the Giant replied, "No;
let us shoot at the same time." Then Lôg̑ôbolā' agreed. Txä'msEm
said to his grandchildren, the Crows, "Fly ahead! If my arrow should
not quite reach the aim, take it up and stick it into the stone, but pull

---

| NLk·'ēt | dzāps | Txä'msEm | lô'ôp. | Sa'g̑ant | aL | dEmt | lō-guXde'it. | 1 |
| Then | made | Txä'msEm | a stone. | He split it | to | (fut.) | in they shoot. | |

| "Lîg·'î-tnā' | dEm | t'an | lō-gu'Xt, | nēL | dEm | xstāt. | Lîg·'ît | nē'E, | 2 |
| "Anybody | (fut.) | who | in hit, | he | (fut.) | win. | Either | I, | |

| lîg·'ît | nē'En. | DEm | ndô'qdEmL | K·san | qanL | Lē'sEms." | NLk·'ēt | 3 |
| or | you. | (Fut.) | we stake | Skeena | and | Nass river." | Then | |

| q'am-anâ'ôqs | Lôg̑ôbolā' | hēt. | K·'ē | sg·'ī'-gaL | ama | xpē'isîs | 4 |
| without caring | agreed Lôg̑ôbolā' | he said. | Then | there is it is said | a good | box | |

| Lôg̑ôbolā' | xpē'isEm | anda-hawî'ltg·ê. | K·'ē | nē'êst | Txä'msEm. | 5 |
| Lôg̑ôbolā' | box | his quiver. | Then | none | Txä'msEm. | |

| Q'am-guld-q'al-ts'a'pdEL | ha-Xda'kᵘ | qanL | hawî'l. | NLk·'ē | dôqL | 6 |
| Only right away he made | how | and | arrow. | Then | he took | |

| lô'ôpg·ê | k·'ē'lp'Ei | dEm | ha-lē-hwa'ndēt. | NLk·'ē | Lā | lē-hwa'ndet. | 7 |
| stones | two | for | their seats. | Then | (perf.) | on they sat. | |

| NLk·'ē | hē-yu'kᵘL | g·'ax na-al'a'lg·îxdet. | K·'ēt | hōukstiyu'ks | 8 |
| Then | they began | only to they talked. each other | Then | moved on his seat toward the water | |

| Txä'msEm | dE-ha-lē-d'ā't. | NLk·'ē | Lat | huwa'ndEs | Txä'msEmL | 9 |
| Txä'msEm | his seat. | Then | (perfect) | they sat | Txä'msEm | |

| huXdā'g·întkᵘt. | NLk·'ē | dēt-hwa'ndîs | Lôg̑ôbolā'L | ts'āsgusguâ'c | 10 |
| his grandchildren. | Then | also they sat | Lôg̑ôbolā' | jays | |

| dē-buxdā'g·întkᵘt. | NLk·'ē | hēs | Lôg̑ôbolā': | "ĀmL | k·s-qâ'ôgan | 11 |
| on his part his grandchildren. | Then | said | Lôg̑ôbolā': | "Good | you first | |

| wa'g·i | Wī-g·'a't." | K·'ē | nî'g·ēs | Wī-g·'a't: | "ĀmL | dEm | 12 |
| brother | Giant." | Then | not he | Giant: | "Good | (future) | |

| sagaīt-k·'ē'lL | dEm | Xdā'gōEm." | K·'ēt | q'am-anâ'qs | Lôg̑ôbolā'L | 13 |
| together | (future) | we shoot." | Then | without caring agreed | Lôg̑ôbolā' | |

| hē'tg·ê. | La | g·'i-na'kᵘL | lō-dā'uL | a'lg·îxs | Txä'msEm | aL | 14 |
| he said. | (Perf.) | before long | in go | said | Txä'msEm | to | |

| huxdā'g·întgum | q'auq'ā'ō: | "DEm | q'ai'yîm | ōk·sL | dē | 15 |
| his grandchildren | the crows: | "(Fut.) | close by | drops | my | |

out Lôgôbolā''s arrow and put it away." They did so. They shot at the same time. As soon as the brothers shot, the Crows flew ahead. Lôgôbolā' saw clearly when his arrow struck the stone, but Txä'msEm said, "I hit it." But Lôgôbolā' said, "No; I hit it." "No; I hit it," said Txä'msEm. He was very happy while he was saying this, therefore he used the Tsimshian language. Then Lôgôbolā' said he knew that he had lost. He saw the Crows taking the arrow and putting it away, while they put Txä'msEm's arrow into the cleft. Lôgôbolā' said, "You have won, brother Giant. Now the olachen will come to Nass river twice every summer." And Txä'msEm said, "The salmon of Skeena river shall always be fat." Thus they

1	hawî'lEist	ha'e,	mEdzEsE'm	k·'ē	gō'ut,	mEdzEsE'm	k·'ē
	arrow	(exclam.),	you	then	take it,	you	then

2	lō-hē't'Ent	aL	ts'Em-lô'ôbEst.	MEdzEsE'm	k·'ē	k·si-sā'yiL
	in stick it	at	in the stone.	You	then	out pull

3	hawî'ls	Lôgôbolā'.	MEdzEsE'm	k·'ē	sa-ma'gat."	NLk·'ē	La
	the arrow of	Lôgôbolā'.	You	then	off put it."	Then	(perf.)

4	hwî'ldetg·ê.	Adīk·'ē'leL	lē'duXdēit.	Q'ai-hē-lē'duXdēit,	k·'ē
	they did so.	At the same time	they shot.	First beginning they shot,	then

5	lēba'yuku L	q'auq'ā'ō.	Q'amgait-g·a'as	Lôgôbolā'	thwîl	lō-gu'XL
	they flew	the crows.	Surely saw	Lôgôbolā'	where	in it struck

6	lô'ôpg·ê.	NLk·'ē	iagai-hē's	Txä'msEm	t māLt:	"LEp-nē'	t'an
	the stone.	Then	however said	Txä'msEm	he told:	"Myself	who

7	lō-gu'Xt."	NLk·'ē	hēs	Lôgôbolā':	"NēE	t'an	lō-gu'Xt."
	in struck it."	Then	said	Lôgôbolā':	"I	who	in struck it."

8	"A'yîn	nE'riō	t'în	lō-gō'ht."[1]	AL	hê'sgusg·ē'tku sEm	hē'tg·ê,
	"No	I	who	in struck it."	On account of	he was happy	saying this,

9	qan	hēt	hâx·L	a'lg·îgEm	Ts'Emsa'n.	NLk·'ē	a'lg·îxs
	therefore	he used	the language	Tsimshian.		Then	spoke

10	Lôgôbolā'	aL	Lat	hwîlā'x·L	hwîl	dz'aLt.	K'ē	g·ā'as
	Lôgôbolā	when	(perf.)	he knew	(verbal noun)	he lost.	Then	saw

11	Lôgôbolā'	thwîl	gō'uL	q'auq'ā'uL	hawî'ltg·ê.	K·'ēt	k·si-ma'gat.
	Lôgôbolā	(verbal noun)	took	the crows	the arrows.	Then	outside they put it.

12	K·'ēt	iagai-lō-Lô'ôdeL	hawî'ls	Txä'msEm.	NLk·'ē	a'lg·îxs
	Then	however in they put	the arrow of	Txä'msEm.	Then	said

13	Lôgôbolā':	"La	xstā'nîst	wa'g·i	Wî-g·a't.	DEm	g·ē'lb·El
	Lôgôbolā':	"(Perf.)	you won	brother	Giant.	(Fut.)	twice

14	dEm	ā'd'îk·sL	sāk·	aL	Lē'sEms	aL	sînt."	NLk·'ē	dē-a'lg·îxs
	(fut.)	come	olachen	to	Nass river	in	summer.'	Then	on his part said

15	Txä'msEm:	"DEm	max-t'Elt'ē'lx·	hân	aL	K·san."	K·'ē	hwîl
	Txä'msEm:	·(Fut.)	all fat	the salmon	at	Skeena."	At once	

[1] These words are in Tsimshian dialect.

divided what Txä'msEm had won at Nass river. Txä'msEm was again hungry. What should he eat? Then Lôgôbolā' went toward sunrise, while Txä'msEm went down to the ocean.

2a. He did still another thing. He heard that the daylight was hidden in a box called max. He went to get it. He transformed himself into a leaf of a cedar, and he wished that the chief's daughter should be thirsty. The chief's daughter went to fetch water, and drank the leaf. Then she was pregnant and had a boy. His grandfather was very glad. The child grew up very quickly. He crept about. Then he began to cry very much. His grandfather worried because the boy was crying all the time. He said, "Call an old man. Maybe he will understand what he says." The old man sat down.

---

k·'ē	ba'sîxkⁿdet	aL	La	xsdās	Txä'msEm	aL	Lē'sEms.	NL	1
	they separated	when	(perf.)	had won	Txä'msEm	at	Nass river.	Then

hwîl　k·'ē　k'u'ɪ.-Xdax·s　Txä'msEm　agōL　dEm　g·ē'bEt.　K·'ē　2
(going)　hungry　Txä'msEm　what　(fut.)　his food.　Then
about

La　dā'uLs　Lôgôbolā'　wa'k·tg·ê　aL　yaē-anō-hwîl　k·si-gua'ntkⁿL　3
(perf.)　left　Lôgôbola　his brother　to　toward　out　rises

Lôqsʟ　qâ'ôt.　K·'ē　ya'ē-lax-mô'ônʟ　dē-qâ'ôs　Txä'msEm.　4
the sun　he went.　Then　toward the ocean　also went　Txä'msEm.

2a. K·'ēlʟ　huX　hwîl　hwî'ls　Txä'msEm.　NExna'yiʟ　hwîl　lō-sg·i'ʟ　5
One　again　did　Txä'msEm.　He heard　where　in　lay

mEsā'x·　sE-hwa'tgut　aL　max.　K·'ēt　qâ'ôt.　NLk·'ē　huX　hwîl　6
the daylight　it is　name　of　max.　Then　he went for it.　Then　again
made

hwî'ltg·ê　aL　lō-Lô'ôtkⁿL　laqs.　K·'ēt　bôxL　Lgō'uLkⁿL　sEm'â'g·it　7
he did so　and　he transformed　the leaf　Then　he waited　the child of　the chief
himself into　of a cedar.　for

aL　dEm　nôôm-a'k·st.　K·'ē　hwîLL　Lgō-wî'lk·sîLgum　hana'q　8
to　(fut.)　desire to drink.　Then　did so　the　princess　woman
little

a'k·skⁿtg·ê.　K·'ē　tq'al-a'k·sL　laqs.　K·'ē　ō'bEnL　Lgo-wî'lk·sîLkⁿ.　9
she got water.　Then　with it　she　the leaf of　Then　was with　the　princess.
drank　a cedar.　child　little

K·'ēt　hwaL　Lgō-tk·'ē'Lgum　g·at.　K·'ē　lō-ā'mL　qâ'ôts　niyē'êt.　10
Then　she found　a　child　boy.　Then　in was　the heart of　his grand-
little　good　father.

K·'ē　lā'p'ElL　masL　Lgō-tk·'ē'Lkⁿ　La　k'uL-qä'Ek·ckⁿtg·ê,　wuL　11
Then　quickly　grew　the　child.　When　about　he crawled,
little

skwatguî'L　wī-yē'tkⁿt.　K·'ē　aba'g·askⁿs　niyē'et,　aL　hwîl　sî-　12
he began to　cry.　Then　was troubled　his grand-　because　anew
father,

k·'a-wi-yē'tkⁿsL　huxdā'g·înt.　NLqan　hē'tg·ê:　"Wô'ôL　k·'âlL　13
exceed-　cried　his grandson.　Therefore　he said:　"Invite　one
ingly　(man)

wī-d'ē'sEt　dEm　t'an　guXL　qan-hē'tg·ê."　K·'ē　d'āL　wī-d'ē'sEtg·î　14
old　(fut.)　who　guess　what he speaks."　Then　sat　the old man
for　down

Now the boy was crying, "Hamahā'" all the time. Then the old man said to the chief, "I thought it was difficult to understand what the prince says. He cries for the max." The box in which the daylight was kept hanging in the corner of the chief's house. The child stopped crying when he heard what the old man said. The chief took the box off and put it down near the child, who was Txä'msEm. Then he stretched out his hand and clapped the box in which the daylight was. Then his grandfather was glad. Now Txä'msEm was playing with the box and moved it about in the house. He made it run about in his grandfather's house. On the following morning Txä'msEm rose from his mother's bed. He took the box and played with it all day. He went out of the house and made it roll about on the street. He

---

1 aL hē'tg·ê: "Hamahā'!" Dēya'L Lgō-tk·'ē'Lkᵘ. Qa'nē-hwîla hē'tg·ê.
   and he said: "Hamaha!" Thus said the boy Always he said so.
                            little

2 NLk·'ē hēL wī-d'ē'stg·î aL sEm'â'g·it: "Qastē'i lig·î-qē'tkui qan
   Then said the old man to the chief: "I thought some- difficult how
                                                          what

3 hēL Lgō-wî'lk·sîLkᵘ," dē'yaL wuī-d'ē's·Et. "'Mā'xE an-hä'it sê!'"
   said the prince," thus said the old man. "'Sun receptacle' what he says!'"
        little

4 Dē'ya aL hwîl lō-sg·i'L mEsā'x· an-hē't. MEn-ia'gat aL amō'sL
   Thus he at where in lay the daylight what he Up it hung at the corner
   said   said.   of

5 sEm'â'g·it. K·'ē sa-gē'sxkᵘs Txä'msEm Lgō-tk·'ē'Lkᵘg·ê aL Lat
   the chief. Then sud- stopped Txä'msEm the child when (perf.)
               denly crying   little

6 nExna'L hēL wī-d'ē'sEt. K·'ēt sā-gō'udēL max hwîl lō-sg·i'L
   he heard what said the old man. Then off they took the max where in was

7 mEsā'x·. K·'ēt sg·ē'dēt aL awa'as Lgō-tk·'ē'Lkᵘg·ê Txä'msEm
   the daylight. Then they laid it in the proxim- the child Txä'msEm
                                        ity of little

8 hwî'lt. K·'ē Lō'ôdEL an'ô'nt; at g·ilgal-t'axt'ä'EL max hwîl lō-sg·i'L
   was. Then he stretched his hand; around he clapped the where in lay
         out   max

9 mEsā'x·g·ê. K·'ē lō-ä'mL qâ'ôts nîyē'it. WūL skwa'tguiL
   the daylight. Then in good the heart his grandfather. Then began
                       was of

10 LELā'ntkᵘL max. At-La'ndEs Txä'msEm aL an-qalā'qt lâEt.
   to move the max. He moved it Txä'msEm at what playing on it.

11 K·'ēt k'uL-lō-tgo-ba'ant aL hwîlps niyē'et. K·'ē huX yu'ksa;
   Then about in around he made in the house his grand- Then again night;
           it run   of father.

12 hē'Luk, k·'ē huX g·în-hē'tkᵘs Txä'msEm, wîtkᵘt aL awa'as
   in the morn- then again rose Txä'msEm, coming from the prox-
   ing,   from imity of

13 nôxt. K·'ē huXt qâ'ôL max, aL anb'El-qalā'qt lâ'ôt aL wī-sa'.
   his Then again he went the and he played with it at all day.
   mother.   after max,

14 Qasqâ'it dē-k·sa'xt aL an-g·a'lEq. At-k'uL-ba'ant läx-lē'lb'Ent
   In the very also he went to outside. He about made to and rolling
   beginning out   run fro it

only pretended to play with it. When he was outside, he took it and ran away with it. One man saw him and said, "Txä′msEm is running away with the sun-box!" Then Txä′msEm ran away. He had assumed his full size which he had when going about murdering. Then he ran.

5a. He came down the river and arrived at its mouth. It was dark there, and he heard the ghosts catching olachen at night. He said, "Give me one of the things you have caught." One man replied, "Who is talking there? That is the great Txä′msEm; ha, ha, tssî!" After a while Txä′msEm said again, "Give me one of the things you caught, or I will tear the sun-box." Then all the ghosts said, "Ha, great slave; you great Scabby-shin! Where did you obtain what you are talking about, great slave, great

---

aL   lax-qē′nEX.   His-huwî′ltkⁿst   yukL   hwîlt.   K·′ē   de-ba′xt.   **1**
on   on   the trail.   He pretended   while   he was doing. Then   with   he ran.
                          to do it   it

K·′ēt   g·a′aL   k·âlL   g·at,   hwîl   dE-ba′xt.   K·′ē   hēL   g·a′tg·ê: **2**
Then   saw him   one   man,   (verbal with   run-   Then   said   the man:
                                 noun)   it   ning.

"K·si-dE-ba′îs   Txä′msEm   ma′xEist,   hâ′u!"   K·′ē   baxs   Txä′msEm.   **3**
"Out with runs   Txä′msEm   the max,   hâu!"   Then   ran   Txä′msEm.

Ha′tsîk·sEm   huX   hō′g·igat   La   waLEu-wī-gêsgâ′ôt   aL   hē-yu′kL   **4**
Again   also   like   (perf.) formerly large size   while

wi-guî′x·-su-g·a′tg·e.   K·′ē   ba′xt.   **5**
great expert murdering.   Then   he ran.
in

5a.   K·′ē   La   g·isi-a′qLkⁿt   aL   saXL   Le′sEms   sq'äxkⁿ.   K·′ēt   **6**
      Then   when   down   he   at   the mouth Nass river in the dark. Then
             river arrived   of

nExna′L   hwîl   yu′kt   mokL   llō′lEq   sāk·   aL   a′xkⁿg·ê.   NLk·′ē   **7**
he heard (verbal they   catching ghosts olachen at   night.   Then
          noun)   did

bēt: "SEm   tsagam-mâ′gEL   k·′ä′guL   an-hwu′nsEmEst   lâmē′;"   **8**
he said: "You   from sea   take   one   what you get   to us;"
          to land

dēya′.   "Agō′L   hē′tsEn,"   dēya′L   k·âlL   g·at.   "La   huX   nēL   **9**
thus he   "What is this talking,"   thus said   one   man.   "(Perf.) again   he
said.

wī-Txä′msEm,   hä   hä′E   tssî."   ĀmL   qa-nā′gut,   k·′ē   huX   hēs   **10**
the Txä′msEm,   hä   hä′E   tssî."   A good   while,   then   again   said
great

Txä′msEm: "SEm   tsagam-mâ′gEL   k·ä′guL   an-hwu′nsEmEst   lâmē′.   **11**
Txä′msEm: "You   from sea   take   one   what you got   to us.
            to land

Hawinuē   bēsL   max   lâ′sem."   K·′ē   sagait-hē′L   llō′lEq   aL   **12**
Soon I   tear   the max for you."   Then   together said   the ghosts   and

hē′det: "Tsaē′   wī-xa′E   wī-wu′sEu-amalma′lgum   t'Em-Lâ′m.   **13**
spoke: 'Tsaē′   big slave   big   along   scabby   leg below knee.

Nda   mE   dEme′l   dE-wî′tkⁿL   an-hä′nîst   wi-xa′E,   wi-lē′luks?"   **14**
Where you   (fut.)   with   come   what you   great slave,   great   thief?"
                     it   from   say

thief?" And Txä'msEm was angry. He opened the sun-box a little and it became light. Behold, large boxes floated on the water and capsized. They were the canoes of the ghosts. Then he shut the box again, and the ghosts continued to catch olachen.

---

1 K·'ē   sī'Epk^uL   qâ'ôts   Txä'msEm.   K·'ēt   q'ā'gaL   max   ts'ōsk·t
  Then   sick was   the   Txä'msEm.   Then he   opened   the max   a little
                      heart of

2 q'ā'gaL   max.   K·'ē   mEsā'x·.   Gwinā'dēL,   qaxpē'ist
  he opened   the max.   Then   it was daylight.   Behold,   blanket boxes

3 k'uL-g·ī'ldEp-qaxā'igut   aL   qa-g·ī'Eksît   mmālL   llō'lEq.   K·'ēt
  about   upset   capsized   at   opposite him on   the   the ghosts.   Then
                              the water   canoes of

4 hā'tsîksEm   huX   hapL   ma'xg·ê.   K·'ēt   hā'tsîk·sEm   huX   hē-yu'kL
  once more   again   he shut   the box.   Then   once more   again   began

5 llō'lEq   aL   sE-sā'k·t.
  the ghosts   made olachen.

[1, 4, and 2a told by Philip; 2 and 3 by Moses]

1. He came to the house of a chief who was asleep. He stood in the doorway. The water was in the house of this chief. Then Txä′msem thought he would steal it. He tore off the bark of a rotten tree. He chewed it and made it look like excrements. Then he entered secretly after he had finished his work. The great chief was asleep. Txä′msem lifted his blanket and laid the excrements next to his anus. Then he waked him and said, "Chief, you soiled your blanket." Then the chief awoke and said, "When did that happen?" Txä′msem repeated, "You soiled your blanket while you

---

Txä′msem

1. HuX	hwa′iʟ	hwîlpʟ	k·'âlʟ	sem'â′g·it	huwô′qtg·ê.	K·'ē 1
Again	he found	the house of	one	chief	while he slept.	Then
ts'ɛlɛm-hē′tkᵘt	aʟ	ā′dz'ɛp	hwîl	lō-sg·ē′ʟ	ak·s	hwî′lptg·ê 2
into he placed himself	at	the door	where	in lay	the water	the house of
sem'â′g·ît	tgōst.	K·'ē	lō-a′lg·îxʟ	qâts	Txä′msem	aʟ 3
the chief	that.	Then	in said	the heart of	Txä′msem	to
dɛm	hwîl	lē′lukst.	K·'ēt	sā-bɛsbē′sʟ	māsʟ	waʟɛn-ga′n. 4
(fut.)	(verbal noun)	steal.	Then	off he tore	the bark of	an old tree.
K·'ēt	qē′ɛnt,	sagait-qē′ɛnt.	K·'ēt	dzāpt	aʟ	su-k'oa′tst. 5
Then	he chewed it,	together he chewed it.	Then	he made it	at	made excrements.
Sɛm-hâ′g·igant	hwîla	dzāpt.	K·'ē	q'a′mts'ɛn	ts'ēnt	aʟ 6
Much	like	being he did.	Then	secretly	he entered	when
ʟēskᵘʟ	dzāptg·ê.	Huwô′qʟ	wî-sɛm'â′g·ît.	K·'ēt	bātsʟ	gula′t. 7
he finished	his work.	While slept	·the great chief.	Then	he lifted	his blanket.
Nʟa	ʟēskᵘt	sg·it	aʟ	ts'ɛm-gō′ɛlʟ	sɛm'â′g·it.	Nʟk·'ēt 8
When	he finished	he lay	at	in	the anus of	the chief.	Then
gō′ksaant	aʟ	hē′tg·ê:	"Sɛm'â′g·it,	yô′goaɛl,	sīpā′nɛnsēʟa,"	dēya'. 9
he awoke him	and	said.	"Chief,	something has been done,	excrements,"	thus he spoke.
K·'ē	gōkskᵘʟ	sem'â′g·it	aʟ	hē′tg·ê:	"Â ndaʟ	hwîl	hwîlʟ 10
Then	he awoke	the chief	and	said.	Ah where is	(verbal noun)	happened
an-hä′nsɛnē?"	"Yū′goaʟ	sīpā′nɛn	aʟ	huwô′ganisʟa′ɛ,"	dēya's 11
what you said?"	"It has been finished	your excrements	at	while you are sleeping,"	thus said

were asleep. Shall I clean it?" Then the chief did not say a word. He was ashamed. "Do not stir; I will go and fetch some moss to wipe it off." Txä′msEm had already brought some moss for that purpose. He went immediately to the chief, lifted his blanket, and said, "Hm, what a smell that is!" He showed it to the chief after he had finished wiping the blanket. Then the chief saw it and believed that he had soiled his blanket while asleep. He was much ashamed. Then Txä′msEm carried it outside. He entered again and said: "Chief, I am very thirsty." The water was hanging in the corner of the chief's house. The chief spoke, "Go and get the water yourself." Then Txä′msEm arose, put his bear-skin blanket on, and opened the receptacle in which the water was kept. Then he poured it into his blanket.

#						
1	Txä′msEm. Txä′msEm.	"DEm "(Fut.)	k·si-d'a′Ldeîst out I put them	ana′?" heh?"	K·′ē Then	nîg·î not	xstaltkᵘL made noise
2	sEm'â′g·ît. the chief.	Dzâqt Ashamed he was	hwî′ltg·ê. at what he did.	"G·ilô′ "Don't	tsE | La′ntgun. move.	DEm (Fut.)
3	k·'ax-qâ′ôeL for a while go for	bEla′q moss	dEm (fut.)	ha-g·ē′mk·aaē." my wiping." means for	K·′ē Then	ia′gait-g·ē′ElL already he had picked
4	bEla′qtg·ê moss in order	aL (fut.)	dEmt | hâx·t. he uses it.	K·′ē At once	hwîl | k·′ē | hagun-iē′êt toward he went	aL he to
5	asa′ēL the feet of	sEm'â′g·it. the chief.	K·′ēt Then	bātsL he lifted	gula′t, his blanket,	aL and	hē′tg·ê: said:	"Hm! "Hm!
6	ÎskᵘL Stench	an-hwu′nL what he has got	sEm'â′g·it the chief	tgōn." this."	K·′ēt Then	k·'ax-gun-g·a′adEtg·ê for a while he showed it
7	aL when	LēskᵘL he fin- ished	t he	g·îmk·t. wiped.	K·′ēt Then	g·a′aL saw it	sEm'â′g·itg·ê. the chief.	Ia′gai-ne′t But yes
8	lEp-g·a′aL self saw it	sEm'â′g·itg·ê the chief	Le (perf.)	k·saXt his excre- ments	aL while	huwô′qt. he slept.	K·′ē Then
9	sEm-dzâ′qt. much he was ashamed.	K·′ēt Then	k·si-d'ä′Ls out put it	Txä′msEm. Txä′msEm.	K·′ē Then	huX again	ts'ēnt he en- tered	aL and
10	hē′tg·ê: said:	"La "(Perf.)	gwalkᵘL dry is	qâ′ôdē my heart	aL to	dEm (fut.)	a′k·sēE I drink	sē 	sEm'â′g·it." chief."
11	K·′ē Then	iax'ia′q hung	hwîl where	wî′tkᵘL came from	ak·s water	aL in	amô′st. the corner.	"Ā′m "Better	mE | dEm you
12	lEp-qâ′ôdEst," self go for it,"	dē′yaL thus said	sEm'â′g·itg·ê. the chief.	K·′ē Then	hētkᵘs stood up	Txä′msEm Txä′msEm	at to
13	tgu-sā′g·iL around he put	gula′t. his blanket.	Gwis-o′lL Blanket bear	gula′tg·ê. his blanket.	K·′ēt Then	q′ä′gat he opened	hwîl where
14	lō-ga′tsL in was poured	a′k·sg·ê. the water.	K·′ēt Then	lō-bE′lxsEm iu he put it down	qaq'ä′q'ant he opened	aL to
15	ts'Em-gwis-o′lt. in his bear. blanket	Hwîl Then	k·′ē | k·si-ba′xt out he ran	aL and	hē′tg·ê. said.	A′lg·îxL The talk of

Then he ran out and uttered the cry of the raven, "Qa, qa, qa, qa!" He carried the great water, and ran away with it. Then the great chief became angry and said, "Ahum! Great slave! Scabby-shin! He did it. He took all the water." Txä'msEm ran away. It was dark while he was running. He could not see ahead, but he heard the ghosts whistling near his face. He returned immediately because he was afraid. The water was all the time running down from his bear-skin, and therefore the water now always runs back to sea. Now he arrived at the mouth of Nass river. He was very glad. Therefore Nass river is now a very large river.

2. He went on and made a house of stone. Then he saw a gull flying about. He said, "Whee!" The gulls continued to fly about, crying, "Qâq!" The Giant ran about and made small sticks, intending

qāqʟ	hâyis	Txä'msEm	aʟ	baxt:	"Qa,	qa,	qa,	qa!" 1
the raven	used	Txä'msEm	while	running:	"Qa,	qa,	qa,	qa!"
Qanet-hwîla	yō'guʟ	wī-t'ē'sEm	ak·s	at	dE-ba'xt.		K·'ē	2
Always	carrying	the great	water	he	with ran. it		Then	
LēntxꞏH	wī-sEm'â'g·itg·ê,	aʟ	hē'tg·ê:	"Êhmm!	Wī-xa'ᵉ,			3
angry was	the great chief,	and	he said:	"Ehmm!	Great slave,			
wī-wusEn-amElma'lgum	t'Em-ʟā'm,	ʟa	huX	nē'daEʟ	hūwî'lt."			4
great along scabs	lower leg,	(perf.)	again	he	who did it."			
Txa-gō'dEʟ	wī-a'k·s.	K·'ē	baxs	Txä'msEm.	BEba'xt	k·'ē	sq'äxkᵘ.	5
All took he	the water. great	Then	ran	Txä'msEm.	While he ran	then	it was dark.	
K·'ē	nî'g·ît	g·a'aʟ	qâ'qtg·ê	as	bagait-sqä'xkᵘ.	SEm-g·itwî'nqʟ		6
Then	not	he saw	in front	at	among darkness.	Much	whistled	
lō'lEq	q'ai'yîm	ts'Em-ts'ā'alt:	"Hw."	SEm-lō-ya'ltkᵘt		aʟ		7
ghosts	close to	in his face:	"Hw."	Imme- he returned diately		he		
xbEts'a'Xt.	K·'ē	qanē-hwîla	k·si-ba'xʟ	ak·s	aʟ	gwis-o'ltg·ê.		8
was afraid.	Then	always	out ran	the water	from	his bear. blanket		
K·'ē	qanē-hwîla	hwîlʟ	a'k·sg·ê	gōn	ʟa	hwîl	gulîk·s-ba'xs	9
Then	always	does so	the water	now	(perf.)	when	back ran	
Txä'msEm.	K·'ē	g·îsi-a'qʟkᵘt	aʟ	Lē'sEms.	K·'ē	lō-ā'mʟ		10
Txä'msEm.	Then	down he river arrived	at	Nass river.	Then	in good was		
qâ'ôtt,	nʟqan	wī-t'ē's	Lē'sEms	gōn	se.			11
his heart,	therefore	is great	Nass river	now.				
2. NʟK·'ē	huX	iä't.	NʟK·'ēt	dzapʟ	hwîlpʟ	lô'ôp	tgō'stg·ê.	12
Then	again	he went.	Then	he made	a house of	stone	that.	
NʟK·'ē	tgōnʟ	hwîls	Wī-g·a't.	G·a'at	hwîl	k'uʟ-g·ebā'yukʟ	qē'wun.	13
Then	this	did	Giant.	He saw	(verbal noun)	about flew	a gull.	
NʟK·'ē	tgōnʟ	hēs	Wīg·a't:	Hūi	ʟā	nakᵘʟ	k'uʟ-lēba'yukʟ	14
Then	this	said	Giant:	Hūi	(perf.)	long	about they flew	
xs-qâ'ôqskᵘ.	NʟK·'ē	k'uʟ-ba'xt.	NʟK·'ēt	dzîpdzā'pʟ	sīsō'sEm	gan		15
crying qâôq.	Then	about ran he.	Then	he made	little	sticks		

to gamble.   Then the great Gull came.   They began to gamble.   Soon they began to quarrel, and the Giant said, "I guess this stick."   The Gull did not reply.   Therefore the Giant threw the Gull on his back and stepped on his stomach.   Then the great Gull vomited two olachens. The Giant took them, and the Gull flew away.

In the evening the Giant made a little canoe of elderberry wood. Then he started to gamble.   He went down the river and landed at the beach in front of the house of a great chief.   He took his gambling sticks and went up.   He entered, and many people were in the house.   They began to gamble.   Now, before the Giant landed he had rubbed the spawn of the olachen over the inside of his canoe and left the tails under the stern sheet.   Now he sat down among the gamblers.

---

1 aL   dɛm   xsant.   Nʟk·'ē   ā'd'îk·sk^uʟ   wi-qē'wun.   Nʟk·'ē   yukʟ
   for   (fut.) gamble.   Then   came   the gull.   Then   they
                                                                   great   began

2 xsa'ndēt.   Nʟk·'ē   na-xsē'nqdet.   Tgōnʟ   hēs   Wī-g·a't: "Tgōnʟ
   they gambled. Then   each   they   This   said   Giant: "This
                          other disbelieved

3 gōuî'st."   Nʟk·'ē   nî'g·i   hēʟ   qē'wun,   nîʟqan   hwîʟʟ   Wī-g·a't,
   I guess."   Then   nothing   said the gull, therefore did so Giant,

4 haspā-ō'yitʟ   qē'wun.   Nʟk·'ēt   ma'qsaans   Wī-g·a't   asîsa'it   aL
   on his   he   the gull.   Then   stood   Giant   his feet   on
   back   threw

5 banʟ   wī-qē'wun.   Nʟk·'ēt   xsē'dîʟ   wī-qē'wun   t'ɛpxā'tʟ   sāk·.
   the   the   gull.   Then   vomited   the   gull   two   olacher.
   belly of great   great

6 Nʟk·'ēt   dôqs   Wī-g·a't.   Nʟk·'ē   g·ebā'yukʟ   qē'wun.   Xʟk·'ē
   Then   took   Giant.   Then   flew   the gull.   Then he
             them

7 dā'nʟt.
   left him.

8 Nʟk·'ē   yu'ksa,   nʟk·'ēt   dzāps   Wī-g·a't   ʟgō-mā'lîm   sgan-lâ'ts.
   Then   evening, then   made   Giant   a little canoe of elderberry
                                                                      bush.

9 Nʟk·'ē   sî-g·â'tk^ut   dɛm   g·îtan-xsa'ntk^ut.   Hwä'i!   Nʟk·'ē
   Then   he started   (fut.)   started   to gamble.   Well!   Then

10 sî-g·â'ôtk^ut,   nʟk·'ē   g·îsā-hē'tk^ut.   Nʟk·'ē   g·â'ôt   aL   qa-g·ä'uʟ
    he started,   then   down he went.   Then   he was   at   in front of
                                river   the house of

11 hwîlpʟ   wī-sɛm'â'g·ît.   Nʟk·'ēt   gōʟ   anda-xsa'nt.   Nʟk·'ē   bax-iä'ēt.
    the house a   chief.   Then he   took   gambling-sticks. Then   up   he
    of   great   went.

12 Nʟk·'ē   ts'ent   hwîl   lō-hwa'nʟ   wī-hē'ldɛm   g·at.   Hē-yukʟ
    Then   he entered   where   in   were   many   people. They began

13 xsa'ndetg·ê.   Tgōnʟ   hwîls   Wī-g·a't   aL   hāô'n   g·ig·a'tsk^ut.
    they gambled. This   did   Giant   to   before   he landed.

14 Mɛnma'nt   ʟe   lānʟ   sāk·   aL   lō-ts'ä'wuʟ   mālt.   Nʟk·'ēt   lō-dô'xʟ
    He rubbed on (perf.) spawn   olachen at   inside of   his   Then   in were
                           of   canoe.

15 ʟa   qa-ʟā'tsxt   aL   laXʟ   qal-x·da'qs.   Nʟk·'e   d'āt   aL   hwîl
    (perf.) tails   at   under   the stern sheet. Then   he   at   where
                                                                  sat down

Then a person said, "Why don't you join us?" The Giant yawned, "I did not sleep all night. A certain person caught three canoe loads of olachen up the river." "La!" said one man, "how should olachen get there? It is not time yet. They will go up six months hence." They did not believe the Giant, and said, "You are a liar; you are a liar!" The Giant did not at first reply; then he said, "Well, look at the inside of my canoe. There are olachen tails under the stern sheets." The young men went down, and they saw that the whole inside of the canoe was full of olachen spawn; and when they lifted up the stern sheets they found two tails of olachen. Then the youths went up and said, "It is true." They showed the olachen tails. Then the great chief said, "Ask Little-captain-of-the-canoe, ask Dry-on-boxes-in-which-olachen-is-kept, and ask

lō-an-xsa′nt.	NLk·'ē	tgōnL	hēL	g·at:	"ĀmL dEm dō′-xsan."	1
in they gamhled.	Then	this	said	a person:	"Good (fut.) also gamble."	

NLk·'ē	q'âxs	Wī-g·a′t:	"Nî′g·î	wâ′goē	aL wī-a′xk^u. Gulā′l	2
Then	yawned	Giant:	"Not	I slept	at all night. Three	

mētk^uL	mā′la	sāk·	aL mokL	k·'âlL	g·at aL g·īg·ä′nîx·." "La!" Dē′yaL	3
full	canoes of olachen	ola- chen	and caught	one	per- at up river." "La!" Thus said	
				son		

g·a′tg·ê,	"Â,	aL	ndaL	dEm	hwîl wîtk^uL sak· dEm qan	4
a person,	"Ah,	at	where	(fut.)	(verbal noun) came from olachen (fut.) there- fore	

ā′d'îk·sk^uL.	Haō′n	g·idi-sīgō′tk^usL	lax-ha′	q'ai-q'â′lîL LôqS."	5
they come.	Before	it is not yet time	season	only six moons.'	

Xsē′nqdēt	Wī-g·a′t.	"Bē′gun,	bē′gun."	NLk·'ē nîg·i hēs	6
They disbelieved	Giant.	"You lie,	you lie."	Then nothing said	

Wī-g·a′t.	NLk·'ē	tgōnL	hēt:	"Adô′E sEm-g·a′aL lō-ts'ä′wuL	7
Giant.	Then	this	he said:	"Really look in the inside of	

mā′lêîst.	Lō-dô′xL	LatsxL	sāk·	aL laXL qal-x·da′qsîst."	8
my canoe.	In are	tails of	olachen	at under the stern sheet."	

NLk·'ē	iaga-sa′k·sk^uL	k'opE-tk·'ē′Lk^u.	NLk·'ēt	g·a′adēt	hwîl	9
Then	down went	the little children.	Then	they saw them	(verbal noun)	

lō-wusEn-mē′tk^uL	māl	aL	lānL	sāk·.	NLk·'ēt batsL	10
in along full	the canoe	of	spawn of	olachen.	Then lifted	

k'ōpE-tk·'ē′Lk^u	qal-x·da′qs.	NLk·'ēt	dô′qdEL	LatsxL	sāk·,	11
the little children	the stern sheet.	Then	they took	tails of	olachen	

t'Epxā′t.	NLk·'ē	bax-Lô′ôdēt.	NLk·'ē	tgōnL	hēL k'ōpE-tk·'ē′Lk^u:	12
two.	Then	up they went.	Then	this	said the little children:	

"ᵂSEm-hō′daast."	NLk·'ēt	gun-g·a′adēL	Lē	LatsxL	sāk·. NLk·'ē	13
"It is true."	Then	they caused them to see	(perf.)	the tails of the	olachen. Then	

tgōnL	hēL	wī-sEm'â′g·ît:	"Wô!	G·ē′dexL Lgo-mEn-xsiâ′ mēg·'ē	14
this	said	the great chief:	"Wô!	Ask Little-master-of-boat and	

Grease-that-is-sticking-to-the-stones-with-which-the-fish-are-boiled. See what they say." Then the person went to ask them. He was sent by the chief. They all agreed. Then the chief ordered the men who were standing in the four corners of his house to break the corners. They did so. Then the olachen jumped into the water. The Giant ran down to the water. He stepped into the water and shouted, telling the olachen to go into the river. He said, "Go up on both sides of the river." Then he came to a house. Many people were catching olachen. Then they gave fish to the Giant. He put the olachen on spits to roast them.

When they were done, a gull appeared over the Giant. Then the Giant called him: "Little Gull!" Then many gulls came, which ate all

---

1   g·ē′dExs   Lē-lerEnk·sîm   lax-nîsā′n,   mēg·′ē   g·ē′dExL   dza hēs
    ask   On-   dry-   box-for-keeping-   and   ask   what says
                                  olachen

2   Tq'al-lô′ôp.[1]"   NLk·′ē   iä′L   g·a′tg·ê.   Hē′dzîL   sEm'â′g·ît.   NLk·′ēt
    Against-stones."   Then   went   a person.   He sent him   the chief.   Then

3   anâ′qdētg·ê.   NLk·′ēt   gun-ia′tsL   sEm'â′g·ît.   MEn-hē′tk^ut   aL
    they agreed.   Then   he him   the chief.   Up he stood   at
                       caused to chop

4   amō′L   hwîlpt.   TxalpxL   amō′L   hwîlpt.   NLk·′ēt   ia′tsL   g·a′tg·ê.
    the   his house.   Four   corners of   his house.   Then   chopped   the man.
    corner of

5   NLk·′ē   XluXL   sāk·   aL   ts'Em-a′k·s.   K·′ē   iaġa-ba′xs   Wī-g·a′t.
    Then   burst   the   at   in the water.   Then   down ran   Giant.
            olachen

6   NLk·′ē   lō-hä′tk^ut   lō-yô′xguL   ak·s   aL   wī-amhē′t.   At   mā′LL
    Then   in- it   in   it went   the water   and   he shouted.   He   told
          side stood

7   La   k·si-hä′tk^uL   sāk·.   TgōnL   hēs   Wī-g·a′t: "Lāx-lō-liẏô′xk^utEst
    (perf.)   out   stood   the   This   said   Giant: "On both in   they go
                olachen.   sides

8   hâ′wu!"   NLk·′ē   lō-a′qLk^ut   aL   hwîl   hētk^uL   hwîlpt.   NLk·′ēt
    hâwu!"   Then   in he arrived   at   (verbal   stood   his house.   Then
                        noun)

9   mokL   wi-hē′ldEm   g·atL   sāk·.   Nîlnē′L   hwîl   xwāẏâ′msîs
    caught   many   people   olachen.   Therefore   (verbal   olachen that
                                           noun)   is given away

10   Wī-g·a′t.   NLk·′ē   dzāpL   gan-x-qanä′qt.   NLk·′ēt   lē-dô′xL   sāk·.
    Giant.   Then   he made   stick for first   Then   on he put   olachen.
                        olachen eaten.

11   NLk·′ēt   La   dEm   a′nuksL   sāk·.   NLk·′ēt   lē-liẏô′xk^uL   qē′wun
    Then   (perf.)   (fut.)   were done   the   Then   on   came   gulls
                           olachen.

12   lax-ō′s   Wī-g·a′t.   NLk·′ē   tgōnL   hēs   Wī-g·a′t.   Lō-se-hwa′deL
    on top of   Giant.   Then   this   said   Giant.   In   he called

13   Lgwa-ġagō′m.   NLk·′ē   ad'ā′d'îk·sk^uL   wī-hē′ldEm   qē′wun   t'an
    little   gull.   Then   came   many   gulls   which

---

[1] The chief's words are in Tsimshian dialect.

the Giant's olachen. They said while they were eating it, "Qanä', qanä', qanä', qanä'!" They cried so all the time while they were eating the Giant's olachen. Then he was sad. Therefore he took the gulls and threw them into the fireplace, and ever since that time the tips of their wings have been black.

3. He went on and met a deer. He killed it and skinned it. He put the skin on. Then he fastened pitch wood to the tail. Now he entered the house of a person, and when he saw the fireplace he ran toward it. The pitch wood at the end of the deer's tail began to burn. The name of the person was Qannēnē'lɛgulxlo. He was ice (?). Then the Giant sang as he entered, "? ? ?" Thus he spoke. When he had finished singing, he ran out. He ran about among the

---

dzaʟ	x-qanä'qs	Wī-g·a't.	Tgōnʟ	hēʟ	qē'wun	ʟat	g· î'pdet 1
ate all	the first olachen of the season of	Giant.	This	said	the gulls	when	they ate

x-qanä'qs	Wī-g·a't:	"Qanä,	qanä,	qanä,	qanä."	Hēltʟ hēʟ 2
the first olachen of the season of	Giant:	"Qanä,	qanä,	qanä,	qanä."	Much said

qē'wun	dza'ʟdeʟ	x-qanä'qs	Wī-g·a't.	Nʟk·'ē	sī'ɛpkuʟ	qâ'ôts 3
the gulls	they ate all	the first olachen of the season of	Giant.	Then	sick was	the heart of

Wī-g·a't.	Neʟ	qant	sagait-dô'qʟ	qē'wun.	Lō-d'a'ʟdet aʟ 4
Giant.	Therefore		together he took	the gulls.	In he put them at

ts'ɛm-an-la'ku;	nêʟ	qan	xʟîp-t'êst'ō'tskuʟ	qaq'ā'îx·ʟ	qē'wun. 5
in the fireplace;	therefore		at the ends are black	the wings of	the gulls.

3. Nʟk·'ē	huX	iä'et.	Nʟk·'ē	tq'al-hwa'deʟ	wan. Nʟk·'ēt 6
Then	again	he went.	Then	against he found	the deer. Then he

dzakut.	Nʟk·'ēt	tsâ'ôdet.	Nʟk·'ē	tq'al-da'k·ʟʟ	sg·înî'st	aʟ 7
killed it.	Then	he skinned it.	Then	against he tied	pitchwood	at

k'ō'ukt.	Nʟk·'ē	ts'ent	aʟ	hwîlpʟ	k·'âlʟ	g·a'tg·ê ʟät 8
his tail.	Then	he entered	in	the house of	one	person where he

hwaʟ	q'apʟ	laku.	Nʟk·'ē	tgo-ba'xt.	Nʟk·'ē mêʟʟ sg·înî'st 9
found	the end of	the fire.	Then	around he ran.	Then hurnt the pitch-wood

aʟ	k'ō'ukt.	Tgōnʟ	hwîlʟ	ā'dz'ɛpʟ	g·a'tg·ê. Qannēnē'lɛguʟxloʟ 10
at	his tail.	This	did	the door of	the person. Qannēnē'lɛguʟxloʟ

hwa'tg·ê,	dā'ut	gō'stg·ê.	Nʟneʟ	qan lē'mîx·s	Wī-g·a't aʟ ʟā 11
his name,	ice	was that.	Therefore	sang	Giant when (perf.)

ts'ent.	Tgōnʟ	lē'mîx·tg·e:	"G·îl-spagait-nê'êq g·îl-spagait-nē'êq," 12
he entered.	This	he sang:	(?) (?)

dēya'.	Hwä'i!	Nʟk·'ē	qâ'ô-deʟ	lē'mîx·tg·ê.	Hwä'i!	Nʟk·'ē 13
thus he said.	Well!	Then	was finished	his song.	Well!	Then

k·si-ba'xs	Wī-g·a't.	Nʟk·'ē	k'uʟ-ba'xt	aʟ spagait-ganga'n. 14
out ran	Giant.	Then	about he ran	at among trees.

trees and struck the tail against the butts of the trees.   Then the butts of the trees caught fire.   He went on after he had obtained the fire.

4. Now he came to a chieftainess, and they ate together.   He ate all the provisions of the chieftainess.   He was angry and threw away the salmon, and then all the salmon which he was going to eat ran away. After that his head became ugly, while it had been very nice when he first met the chieftainess.   After that it was ugly.[1]

2a. Txä′msEm did another thing.   He induced the olachen to come to Nass river.   He entered the house called Supernatural place or Tabued place.   There were many people inside gambling. Txä′msEm heard them.   He was very hung.y.   He found a small herring.   Then he squeezed out its roe and rubbed it all over the inside

---

1 NLk·′ēt   k'uL-hîsya′tsL   k'ō′ukt   aL   qamē′nL   ganga′n.   NLk·′ē
  Then   about   he struck   his tail   at   the foot of   the trees.   Then

2 mELmê′L   qamē′nL   ganga′n.   NLk·′ē   huX   iä′êt   aL   Lat
  burned   the foot of   the trees.   Then   again   he went   to   (perf.)

3 k·si-daa′qLkᵘL   lakᵘ.
  out he obtained   fire.

4 4. K·′ēt   hwaL   hwîl   d′āL   k·′âLL   sîg·idEmna′q.   NLk·′ē
  Then   he found   where   was   one   chieftainess.   Then

5 stik·′â′ôltkᵘt;   at   g·ipL   wunä′x·.   HuX   dzaLL   wunä′x·L
  they ate together;   he   ate   the food.   Again   he ate all   the food of

6 sîg·idEmna′q.   NLk·′ēt   am'ā′lEgaL   hâ′ng·ê.   NLk·′ē   k·si-hō′L
  the chieftainess.   Then   he threw away   the salmon.   Then   out   es-
                                    in anger   caped

7 hân   La   dEm   g·ē′îpdetg·ê.   NLk·′ē   ā′d′îk·s   hwîl   had′a′xkᵘL
  the   (perf.)   (fut.)   he ate them.   Then   came   being   had
  salmon

8 t′Em-qē′st.   K·′ē   La   k·'ax-ā′m-gaL   t′Em-qē′st   at   hē-hwa′L
  his head.   Then   (perf.)   before good it is   his head   when   begin- he
                                             said   ning   found

9 sîg·idEmna′qg·ê.   K·′ē   ha·ts'îk·sEm   had′a′xkᵘt   gōn.[1]
  the chieftainess.   Then   once more   it was had   now.

10 2a. HuX   k·′ēl   hwîl   hwî′ls   Txä′msEm   dāt   k·sōhō′kᵘsL   sāk·
   Again   one   did   Txä′msEm   when   he induced to   the
                                                                            come   olachen

11 aL   ts'Em-Lē′sEms.   K·′ē   ts'ēnt   aL   hwîlpL   SpE-nExnô′q.
   to   in   Nass river.   Then   he entered   aL   the house of   the   magic
                                                                                   place of power.

12 Spā-waLkᵘL   hwat.   K·′ē   lō-hwa′nL   hē′ldEm   g·at   lât.   Xsā′ndēt.
   Place tabu is   its name.   Then   in   were   many   people   in it.   They were
   of   gambling.

13 K·′ēt   naxna′s   Wî-g·a′t   aL   sEm-xda′x·t.   K·′ēt   hwaL   k·′ā′guL
   Then   heard   Giant   aL   very hungry.   Then   he found   one

14 Lgō-sg·a′n.   K·′ēt   k·sE-dä′mîk·sL   länt.   K·′ēt   lō-wusEn-mEnma′nt
   small herring.   Then   out he squeezed   its spawn.   Then   in- along   he rubbed it
                                                                           side

---

[1] This is an allusion to the legend about how the raven obtained the salmon. See Boas, Indianische Sagen von der nord-pacifischen Küste Amerikas, Berlin, 1895, pp. 160, 174, 209.

of his canoe. Now he arrived on the beach in front of Supernatural place, whêre the people were gambling. Then Txä'msɛm said, shaking his large blanket, which was all wet, "Ēhi-hi-hi! Water dropped on me from Txä'msɛm's bag net." Then the chief said, "Where does that come from that you are speaking of, Giant?" "Yes; the canoes are full. They caught olachen with their rakes last night." "Ah! Txä'msɛm is lying." "Go and look at my canoe." The young men went and saw what he had spoken of. Then they believed him. They saw olachen spawn in Txä'msɛm's canoe. Then the chief said, "What do these great fools, the olachen, come here for?" There were persons sitting in the corners of the house who held the strings of olachen. They took care of the olachen in the corners of Supernatural place. The chief said to them, "Let go what you

aL mālt. K·'ē k·'atskᵘt aL qa-g·ä'uL SpE-nExnô'qg·ê, hwîl 1
on his canoe. Then he landed at the beach in front of the house of the magic power, place of where

lō-d'ā'L xsant. NLk·'ē hēs Txä'msɛm LuXlā'wuL wī-gula't 2
in sat they gambled. Then said Txä'msɛm shaking his blanket large

txā-a'k·skᵘ. Hē'tg·ê: "Ē'hihihihi," dēya'. Lē-hē'tgut nēE 3
all wet. He said: "E'hihihihi," thus he said. On stood on me

q'am-k·sax-Lē'siL Txä'msɛm. K·'ē a'lg·îxL sɛm'â'g·it: "Â nda 4
only drippings of bag net of Txä'msɛm. Then said the chief: "Ah where

hwîl wîtkᵘL an-hä'nsɛn Wi-g·a't." "Â nēL mîx·mä'yîL 5
come from what you said Giant." "Oh, yes they are full (canoes)

qa-k·'edä't aL g·i-a'xkᵘ." "Ä, bēkᵘs Txä'msɛm." "Hwä'i! Adô', 6
those they raked at last night." "Ah, he tells a lie Txä'msɛm." "Well! Go,

sɛm g·a'aL mä'lɛist." K·'ē k·si-Lâ'ôL q'aima'qsit; at g·a'adet 7
you (plur.) see my canoe." Then out walked the youths; they saw

an-hē's Wī-g·a't. K·'ē sɛm-hō'tkᵘsdēt. G·a'adeL länL sāk· aL 8
what said Giant. Then they believed him. They saw spawn of olachen in

māls Wī-g·a't. NLqan a'lg·îxL sɛm'â'g·it aL hē'tg·ê: 9
the canoe of Giant. Therefore spoke the chief and said:

"TsE nā-'gat g·ē'ɛn aL wud'a'x ax-qagâ'odɛtg·ê aL g·îtwuyā'n 10
"To whom he says give food the great fools of early olachen

as huwî'lt." NLk·'ē a'lg·îxt aL g·at lō-mɛn-hwa'nt aL amō'st, 11
they did so." Then he said to the people in up sitting in the corner,

t'an dɛxdô'qL dêxdä'ɛdɛL sāk·, mɛLi-k·'â'lL g·at t'an habâ'ɛlL 12
who held the strings of the olachen, each one man that took care of

sāk·. Lō-mɛn-hwî'lt, aL ax·'amō'sL SpE-nExnô'q. NLqan 13
the olachen. In up they did it, in the corners of the magic place of power. Therefore

hē'tg·ê sɛm'â'g·it tgōst: "Qalix·lē'L an-hwu'nsɛmɛst," dēya'. 14
said the chief that: "Let go what you have," thus he said.

are holding." Then these men did so. Four of them were sitting in the corners of the house. As soon as Txä'msEm heard him say "Let go," he ran out to his little canoe. He paddled, and took his olachen rake. He said, "They go up on both sides of the river." He was very glad. Then he went to eat olachen. His canoe was quite full. He had not used his rake, but the whole shoal of olachen had jumped into his canoe, so that it was full.

Then he camped at Crab-apple place. He clapped on the stone until it was quite smooth, that the olachen should not disappear. Then he was very glad. He stayed a little farther up Nass river. He made a spit for roasting olachen in order to prepare them for his meal. When the olachen were almost done, he said to the gull that was sitting opposite him, "Come, Little Gull." The gull came and ate

---

1 | K·'ē | huwî'lɪ | g·a'tg·ê. | Txalpxdâ'ɛlg·ê | lō-mɛn-hwa'nt | aɪ
| Then | they did so | the people. | Four persons | in up were | in

2 | ax·'amō'st. | ɪguthē' | nɛxna's | Txä'msɛm | t'êɪxs: | "Qale't," | hwîl | k·'ē
| the corners. | Immediately | heard | Txä'msɛm | shout: | "Let go," | | at once

3 | baxt. | At | qâ'ôɪ | ɪgō-mä'lt; | hwîl | k·'ē | hwāx·t. | At | gō'uɪ
| he ran. | He | went to | little his canoe; | then | | he paddled. | He | took

4 | ha-k·'ēdā'tg·ê. | K·'ē | hē'tg·ê: | "Hōu, | lāx-lō-lîô'xkᵘtɛst | hâ'wu
| the rake for olachen. | Then | he said: | "Hōu, | on in they go both sides | hâ'wu

5 | dē'ya | aɪ | hîsgusg·ē'tkᵘst. | K·'ēt | qâ'ôɪ | dɛmɪ | hwîl | g·îpɪ
| thus he said | and | he was glad. | Then | he went to | (fut.) | being | eating it

6 | sā'ak·ɪ | lō-mē'tkᵘt | aɪ | ts'ɛm-mä'lt. | Nîg·ît | k·ax-hâ'x·ɪ | ha-k·'ēdā'
| olachen | in full | in | in his canoe. | Not | he used | the rake

7 | lɛp-lō-qē'nɛxkᵘɪ | an-g·â'saa | ɪgo-mä'lt. | K·'ē | mētkᵘt | aɪ | sāk·.
| self in falling | a shoal | little canoe. | Then | it was full | of | olachen.

8 | K·'ē | ɪa | dzôqt | aɪ | ɪgō-sgan-mē'lk·st, | nɪ | hwîl | hwî'lt, | t'axt'a'aɪ
| Then | when | he stayed | at | little crab-apple tree | then | | he did so, | he clapped

9 | lô'ôp. | K·'ē | sɛm-ia'ɪkᵘɪ | lax-ō'ɪ | lô'ôp | ōp | tsɛ | g·utg·wâ'ôtkᵘɪ
| the stone. | Then | very slippery | the top of | the stone | that | should not | be lost

10 | sāk· | qan | hwî'lt. | T'axt'a'aɪ | lô'ôp, | nɪqan | hēt | aɪ | lō-dā'uɪt
| the olachen | there-fore | he did so. | He clapped | the stone, | therefore | he said | where | in he went

11 | aɪ | ts'ɛm-Lē'sɛms. | K·'ē | sɛm-lō-ā'mɪ | qâ'ôtt. | Nɪk·'ē | huX | dzôqt
| to | in Nass river. | Then | very in good was | his heart. | Then | again | he stayed

12 | aɪ | g·ig·ē'nix· | aɪ | Lē'sɛms. | K·'ē | dzäpɪ | gan-x·qanä'qtg·ê | aɪ
| at | up the river | at | Nass river. | Then | he made | a stick for roasting olachen | to

13 | dɛm | hwîl | a'nuksɪ | sāk· | dɛm | g·ē'bɛt. | K·'ē | ɪa | dɛm | ā'nuksɪ
| (fut.) | being | cooked | the olachen | for | his food. | Then | when | (fut.) | cooked

14 | sāk·, | k·'ē | hē'tg·ê | aɪ | qē'wun | qa g·î'ik·sît: | "Lō-sɛ-hwä'ldē
| the olachen, | then | he said | to | the gull | opposite him: | "In do I

one olachen. He cried, "Qanä', qanä', qanä', qanä'!" Then many
gulls came and ate all the olachen. Now Txä'msEm was sad. He
took the gulls and threw them into the fireplace. Thus it happens
that their wings are black.

| Lgwa-gagū'm."[1] | K·'ē ā'd'îk·sk^uL | qē'wun. | K·'ēt hā'ts'îL k·'ä'guL | 1 |
| little seagull." | Tnen came | the gull. | Then he bit one | |

| sāk·; at g·ēîpt. | "Qanä', qanä', qanä', qanä'." | K·'ē ā'd'îk·sk^uL | 2 |
| olachen; he ate it. | "Qanä', qanä', qanä', qanä'." | Then came | |

hē'ldEm qē'wun.	K·'ē dzaLL hē'ldEm sāk·.	K·'ē sī'Epk^uL	3
many gulls.	Then they ate many olachen.	Then sick was
	it all		

qâ'ôts Wī-g·a't.	K·'ē dôqL qē'wun.	K·'ēt lō-qalu'ksL	4
the heart of Giant.	Then he took the gulls.	Then in he threw
			them

ts'Em-an-la'k^u; nLqan t'Est'ō'tsk^uL qaq·ā'ix·L qē'wun; hwîl hwî'ltg·ê.	5
in the fire- therefore black are the wings of the gulls; it happened so.	
place;	

---

[1] These words are in Tsimshian dialect.

[1-17 told by Philip; 18 to 20 and 3a told by Moses]

1. There was a chief who had a daughter who swallowed a leaf of a cedar when drinking water. Then she had a pretty child, a boy. The child was able to walk, but he did not eat. Then his grandfather worried. He called two old men to chew some food for the child. The two old men did so. They chewed some salmon and grease, and one of them scratched a scab from his shin. He put it among the salmon that he had chewed. Then the child ate what the old man had chewed; he ate very much. In the evening he ate one salmon in the house of his grandfather. He was hungry all the night, after the two old men who

---

Txä′msem

1 1. K·'âⱢ sɛm'â′g·it, nⱢk··′ē Lgō′uⱢgum hana′q t'an tqal-a'k·sⱢ
   One   chief,   then   a child   female   who   drank

2 laqs, nⱢk··′ē Ⱡa ā′d'îk·sk^{u}t dɛmt hwîl hwaⱢ ama Lgo-tk··′ē′Ⱡk^u.
  a leaf of a then (perf.) came (fut.) where she finds a   boy.
  cedar,   good

3 NⱢk··′ē Ⱡat hwa′tg·ê. NⱢK··′ē Ⱡa k'uⱢ-iē′Ⱡ Lgo-tk··′ē′Ⱡk^u. k·'ē
  Then (perf.) she found it. Then (perf.) about went the boy,   then

4 nî′g·i yō′ôxk^{u}Ⱡ Lgo-tk··′ē′Ⱡk^u. K·'ē sɛmgal aba′g·ask^{u}Ⱡ niē′et.
  not   ate   the boy.   Then   much   was troubled his grand-
                                          father.

5 NⱢk··′ēt huwô′ôⱢ bagadē′lⱢ wud'ax-g·ig·a′t dɛm t'an qē′ɛndɛxⱢ
  Then   he invited   two   old men   (fut.) who chewed for

6 Lgo-tk··′ē′Ⱡk^u. NⱢk··′ē Ⱡa hwîⱢⱢ t·êst'ē′stg·ê. NⱢa yukt qē′ɛndēⱢ
  the boy.   Then (perf.) they the old men. When begin- they chewed
                    did so   ning

7 hâ′ng·ê, tqal-qē′ɛndet aⱢ t·ēlx·. NⱢk··′ēt sa-t·â′qⱢ ama′lgum
  salmon,   with it they chewed of grease.   Then   off he   a scab of
                                          scratched

8 t'ɛm-Ⱡā′mt k·'â′ltg·ê. NⱢk··′ē tqal-hu′ksaant aⱢ qē′ɛnt hântg·ê.
  his leg below one man. Then with it placed of he his salmon.
  the knee   with it   chewed

9 K·'ēt g·ē′îpⱢ Lgo-tk··′ē′Ⱡk^u. NēⱢ sɛm-k·s-qâ′gum qē′ɛntg·ê.
  Then ate it   the boy.   That very first   he chewed.

10 K·'ē hwîl k·'ē yō′ôxk^{u}t aⱢ wî-t·ē′sɛm yō′ôxk^{u}t. DzaⱢⱢ k·ä′guⱢ
     At once   he ate and   greatly   he ate.   He ate all one

11 hân aⱢ hēyu′ksa. Hwîl hwî′ltg·ê aⱢ hwîⱢps niē′êt. NⱢk··′ē
  salmon in the evening. He did so at the house his grand- Then
                                 of   father.

12 Xdax·t wî-a′xk^u Ⱡa k·si-sa′k·sk^{u}Ⱡ t·êst'ē′stg·ê t'an qē′ɛndaxt.
  he was all night when out started the old men who chewed
  hungry   for him.

had chewed for him left the house. Then he did not sleep, but he ate until the day broke. Now his grandfather was glad; but the boy ate all day, and after a short time all the food was gone. Then he ate all the provisions in another house, and he ate all the provisions of the whole village. Then his grandfather was troubled. He wanted to get rid of him because he knew that the boy had done wrong. He said, "My grandchild has eaten scabs of Wâ'sᴇ, therefore I will get rid of him. Go, slave, and tell the tribe." The slave ran out and said, "Great tribe, you shall move to-morrow morning." On the following morning the people moved. They deserted the prince.

2. What was he to eat? He went toward the beach searching for some food, but he did not find anything. Behold, there was a fish in

---

K·'ē·	hwîl	k·'ē'	q'amgait-nîg·i	wôqt	aʟ	yō'ôxkᵘt. K·'ē **1**
At once		more	not	he slept	and	he ate. Then

wagait	hwîl	mᴇsā'x·,	k·'ē	lō-ā'mʟ	qâts	niē'êt. K·'ē **2**
until	being	daylight,	then	in good	heart	his grand- father. Then

yō'ôxkᵘt	aʟ	txanē'tkᵘʟ	sa,	aʟ	t'ē'sᴇm	yō'ôxkᵘt. K·'ē nî'g·i **3**
he ate	at	all	day, and	much		he ate. Then not

laltkᵘʟ	wunä'x·,	k·'ē	qâ'ôdᴇt.	K·'ēt	q'al-bā'ʟ	wunä'x·ʟ **4**
slowly	food,	then	he finished it.	Then he ate in other houses		the food of

qal-ts'a'p.	K·'ē	ha'tsîk·sᴇm	alî'skᵘʟ	qâ'ôts	niē'êt.	Nʟk·'ē **5**
the people.	Then	once more	was weak	the heart of	his grand- father.	Then

hasa'qs	niē'êt	dᴇmt	sa-mā'gat	aʟ	at	hwîlā'x·ʟ hwîl **6**
he desired	his grand- father	(fut.)	off he put him	at	he	knew being

had'a'xkᵘʟ	hwî'ltg·ê:	"X-ama'lgwaxdᴇʟ		Wâ'sᴇ	huxdā'k·ᴇnēᴇ, **7**
had	he did:	"Eating scab of		Wâ'sᴇ	my grandson,

qan	hwîlt.	Wagait	dᴇm	sa-ma'qdēᴇ	gōn.	Adô', xa'ᴇ! **8**
there- fore	he does so.	Until (?)	(fut.)	off I put him	now.	Go, slave!

ma'ʟᴇʟ	aʟ	qal-ts'a'p."	Nʟk·'ē	k·si-ba'xʟ	xa'ᴇg·ê:	"Tsᴇ lōkᵘ- **9**
tell	to	the people."	Then	out ran	the slave:	"To move

gat	nē'sᴇm	ts'ēt'aʟa'kᵘ,	wī-tsâ'p	q'am-hē'ʟukᵘ."	K·'ē	lukᵘʟ **10**
he says	ye	to-morrow,	great people	only morning."	Then	moved

ts'ap.	K·'ᴇt	kᵘsta'qsdēʟ	ʟgo-wî'lk·sîʟkᵘ.	K·'ē	g·ina-d'ā't. **11**
the peo- ple.	Then	they deserted	the prince.	Then	behind he was.

2. Agō'ʟ	dᴇm	g·ē'bᴇt?	K·'ē	k'uʟ-iē'êt	aʟ	qa-g·ä'uʟ **12**
What	(fut.)	his food?	Then	about he went	at	in front of the houses of

qal-ts'a'p,	aʟ	k'uʟ-g·ig·ē'ᴇʟ	dᴇm	g·ē'bᴇt.	K·'ē	nî'g·it hwat. **13**
the town,	to	about he searched	(fut.)	his food.	Then	not he found it.

Gwinā'dēʟ,	lō-hwî'lᴇm	ts'ᴇm-a'k·sʟ	g·a'at,	hwîl	am-g·â't. **14**
Behold,	in being (a fish)	in water	he saw,	where	it lay in water.

the water. It was not moving. Then he called it ashore to talk to it. The fish came toward the shore. Its name was Bullhead. The prince thought he would kill it. Now it was almost within reach, but it swam back into the water. Then the prince was much depressed because he was hungry. The fish knew his intentions. It swam back from the shore saying, "Do you think I do not know you, Giant?" Then he acted as though he were taking hold of the image of the fish, and, stretching out his hand, said, "You shall have a thin tail. Only your head shall be thick." Then it became the Bullhead. The Bullhead used to be remarkably stout. Txä'msɛm cursed it, and therefore it is thin at one end.

3. Then the prince put on his grandfather's dancing blanket. He went on, not knowing where he went. He tore his dancing blanket and was

---

1 Nᴌk·'ē   tsagam-wô'ôt   aᴌ   dɛm   dɛdā'lɛqt.   Nᴌk·'ē   tsagam-yu'kᴌ
   Then   ashore he called   to   (fut.)   with talk.   Then   ashore   came
                  it

2 lō-hwî'lɛm   ts·ɛm-a'k·sg·ê.   Mas-q'ayā'iᴌ   hwat.   Nᴌk·'ē   hēᴌ
   in   being   in   water.   Bullhead   was its name.   Then   said
      (the fish)

3 qâ'ôtt   dɛm   dza'k"tg·ê.   Nᴌk·'ē   ʟa   yukᴌ   dɛmt   gō'ut.
   his heart   (fut.)   he killed it.   Then   (perf.)   he   (fut.)   he took it.
                                                           began

4 K·'ē   sa-uks-ts'ɛn-x·k·'ä'xk"t.   Nᴌk·'ē   sɛmgal   gwä'ɛl   qâᴌ
   Then   off out leaving   it escaped.   Then   very   poor was   the
      to sea   heart of

5 ʟgo-wî'lk·sîʟk"   aᴌ   Xdax·t   qan   hwî'ltg·ê.   Nᴌk·'ēt   hwîlā'x·ʟ
   the   prince   on ac-   his hunger   there-   he was so.   Then   knew
   little   count of   fore

6 lō-hwî'lɛm   ts'ɛm-a'k·sg·êᴌ   qâ'ôdɛtg·ê.   K·'ē   sa-uks-lō-ya'ltk"t
   in   being   in water   his heart.   Then   off out   it returned
      (the fish)   to sea

7 aᴌ   a'lg·îxtg·ê: "Nā   t'an   ax-hwîlā'yîn.   Wī-g·a't!"
   and   said: "Who   who   not knows you,   Giant!"

8 K·'ē   hwîl   k·'ēt   pɛlɛm-gō'dɛl   ʟa   ha'yukt   aᴌ   na'k"stg·ê.
   At once   he acted   he took   the image   by   stretching out
            as though   his hand.

9 "Hoō'ksyō'gunē   as   gōst,   tsɛ   k·'ē   lō-g·igî'sk"ʟ   au-qalā'nɛm.
   "Out to   while you   to   there,   then   small at one end   hind end.
   sea   go

10 K·sax-wī-an-t'ɛm-qē'sɛn   tsɛ   dɛd'ā't."   K·'ē   hwîlʟ   mas-q'ayā'itg·ê.
   Only   great   your head end   is."   Then   it was   the bullhead.

11 Lîks-g·a't-gaʟ   wî-t'ô'Xʟ   mas-q'ayā'itg·ê.   K·'ē   hwîl   had'ā'gam
   Remarkably   it is   stout was   the bullhead.   Then   being   bad
      said

12 a'lg·îxs   Txä'msɛm   lât,   qan   hwîʟʟ   lō-g·igî'sk"t.
   the word of   Txä'msɛm   to it,   there-   being   small at one end.
                              fore

13 3. K·'ē   iē'êt.   gulā'iʟ   guîs-halai'ts   niē'êtg·ê.   K·'ē   iē'êt;
   Then   he went,   he put on   blanket shaman's   his grand-   Then   he went;
                              of   father.

14 q'asba-sa-k'uʟ-iē'êtg·ê.   Nᴌk·'ē   sɛm-gwä'ɛl   hwîlt   aᴌ   ʟa   gwasʟ
   astray off about   he went.   Then   very   poor   he was   and (perf.)   he tore

very poor. Then he caught a number of ravens, and used any means
he could invent to kill them. He took their skins and tied them
together, and put on the raven blanket. Then he went about dressed
up nicely. Now he saw a good dancing blanket like the one he had
worn before. At once he tore his raven blanket and took the dancing
blanket that hung before him. Behold it was no dancing blanket;
there were only lichens on the trees. Now he saw that there were
nothing but lichens. He sat down weeping. He took his raven
blanket, tied it together again, and walked on, hungry and weeping.

4. Now he wanted to go to war. He met a pretty slave whose name
was K·'ixō'm. He took him along, and they came to the house of a
chief. The chief called to him, "Come in, my dear, if it is you who
ate the scabs of Wâ'sE." Then he was ashamed. He entered with his

guîs-halai'tg·ê.	NLk·'ēt	g·îdi-dô'qL	qāq.	Lîg·i-lEp-agō't hwîla	1
his blanket shaman's.	Then	he caught	ravens.	Anything (he used)	
ia'tsL	qāq.	K·'ē dôqL	annā'sL qāq.	K·'ēt an-dē-ts'Epts'ē'bEt,	2
to kill	ravens.	Then he took	the skins of the ravens.	Then what with he tied them,	
at	gula'L	guîs-qā'qtg·ê.	NLa SEm-ā'DIL k'uL-iē'êt,	t g·a'aL	3
he	put on	blanket his raven's.	Then when very well about he walked,	he then he saw	
ama'	guîs-halai't	hwîl	La gula'tg·ê.	NLk·'ēt ha'tsîk·sEm	4
a good	blanket shaman's	where	(part.) he put it on.	Then once more	
bîsbē'sL	guîs-qā'qt.	NLk·'ēt	gō'uL guîs-halai't	sqa-ia'gat aL	5
he tore	his raven blanket.	Then	he took the shaman's blanket	sideways it hung at	
qâqt.	Gwinā'dēL!	nîg·idi nēL	guîs-halai't.	MElax'â'EstL gan.	6
his front.	Behold!	not it	a blanket shaman's.	Lichens of a tree.	
NLk·'ēt	hwîlā'x·L	hwîl	mElax'â'Est.	NLk·'ē d'āt aL	7
Then	he knew it	being	lichens.	Then he sat and	
wī-yē'tkᵘt.	K·'ēt	gō'uL gwîs-qā'aqt	at an-dē-ts'Epts'ē'bEt.	K·'ē	8
cried.	Then	he took blanket raven	and what with he tied them.	Then	
ha'tsîk·sEm	huX	k'uL-iē'êt aL	k'uL-wī-yē'tgum	Xdax·t.	9
once more	again	about he went and	about crying	his hunger.	
4. NLk·'ē	La	hasa'qt	dEm k'uL-su-g·a'tt.	K·'ēt tq'al-hwa'L	10
Then	(perf.)	he desired	(fut.) about murdering.	Then against he found	
ama'	xa'E.	K·'ixō'mL	hwat.	K·'ēt k'uL-stē'Elt. K·'ēt	11
a good	slave.	K·'ixō'm	his name.	Then about he accompanied him. Then	
hwa'deL	hwîlpL	k·'âlL	sEm'â'g·it.	K·'ē ts'ElEm-wô'ôL	12
they found	the house of	one	chief.	Then into invited them	
sEm'â'g·it:	"Ts'ē'nēn	nāt,	tsEdat nē'En,	La x-ama'guaxdEL	13
the chief:	"Come in,	my dear,	if it is you,	(part.) eating scabs of	
Wâ'sE."	K·'ē	sEm-lō-dz'â'qL	qâ'ôdEtg·ê.	K·'ē ts'ēnt qanL	14
Wâ'sE."	Then	very in ashamed was	his heart.	Then he entered and the	

slave, and they sat down. The chief (a small bird) fed them. First they ate salmon, then the waiters served crab apples mixed with grease. When Txä′msεm saw this he became very desirous of eating it; therefore with a low voice he said to his slave, "Tell them that I like to eat what they have there." The slave said, "Oh, chief! he says he does not like to eat what you have there," and the slave ate it all alone, and Txä′msεm sat there looking on. He did not eat anything. After they had finished eating, they went out, Txä′msεm first.

5. Then they came to a deep canyon. He took the dried stem of a skunk-cabbage (?) and laid it across. He made a bridge. Then he himself went across, and after he had done so he called K·′ixō′m (that was the name of his slave) to come across; but the slave was afraid to follow Txä′msεm. After a while, however, he followed him, and when he

---

1 xa′E.   K·′ē   hwa′ndet.   SEm′â′g·idεm   x-mō′gut   hwîl   ts′ē′ntg·ê.
   slave.   Then   they sat down.   Chief   eating ripe   where   he entered.
                                                   (a bird)

2 K·′ē   ʟa   hēyu′kt   yō′ôg·ant.   K·s-qâkʟ   hân   at   g·ē′îpt,   nʟk·ēt
   Then   (perf.)   he began   he fed them.   First   salmon   he   ate it,   then

3 ʟuwā′iʟʟ   t′êlg·a′dεtg·ê   ʟayi   môk".   K·′ē   tsεda   ʟat   g·a′as
   mixed the   waiters   crab   ripe.   Then   when   (perf.)   he saw
              apple

4 Txä′msεm   dεm   g·ē′bεt,   k·′ē   sεmgal   abā′gask"t.   Nʟqan
   Txä′msεm   (fut.)   his food,   then   much   he was   Therefore
                                              troubled.

5 hēt   aʟ   xa′Eg·ê   aʟ   q′amtsεn   hē′t: "Mā′ʟtsεn   gwîx·-g·ē′îpʟ
   he   to   the slave   at   secretly   he said: "Tell   fond of eating
   said

6 an-hwî′ns   gōst."   K·′ē   hēʟ   xa′Eg·ê: "Â,   sεm′â′g·it!   nē′gat
   what they do   that."   Then   said   the slave: "Oh,   chief!   not he
                                                                            says

7 g·idet   gwîx·-g·ē′îpʟ   sεm′â′g·it   tgōn   an-hwî′nεn."   Nʟk·′ē
   fond of   eating   the chief   this   what you do."   Then

8 lεp-nē′ʟ   xa′Eg·ê   t′an   g·ē′îpt   q′am-k·′â′l.   K·′ē   k·ax-d′ä′s
   him-   he   the slave   who   ate it   only one.   Then   only there
   self   sat

9 Txä′msεm.   Nî′g·i   yō′ôxk"t.   Nʟk·′ē   k·si-Lô′ôdet   aʟ   ʟa
   Txä′msεm.   Not   he ate.   Then   out they went   at   (perf.)

10 ʟaxʟä′xk"det.   Nʟk·′ē   k·s-qâ′ôqs   Txä′msεm.
   they finished   Then   first (went)   Txä′msεm.
   eating.

11 5. Nʟk·′ēt   hwa′dεʟ   hwîl   iaga-lō-ʟa′pʟ   lô′ôp.   Nʟk·′ēt   gō′uʟ
      Then   he found   where   down in deep   rock.   Then   he took

12 gwa′lk"xanεm   hōk",   k·′ēt   tsaga-sg·i′t.   At   sE-gā′ndet.   K·′ēt
    dry   (a plant),   then   across he laid   He made a stick.   Then
                                  it.

13 lεp-tsaga-yô′xk"t.   At   ʟēsk"ʟ   hwîlt,   k·′ēdεt   gun-tsaga-ic̆′ês
    him-   across   he went.   He   finished   he did so,   then   he   across to go
    self   caused

14 K·′ixo′m.   K·′ixo′m   hwaʟ   xa′Eg·ê.   K·′ē   xpεtsa′Xʟ   xa′Eg·ê
    K·′ixo′m.   K·′ixo′m   was the   the slave.   Then   was afraid   the slave
                            name of

15 aʟ   dεm   dē-yô′xk"ʟ,   ʟô   yôxk"s   Txä′msεm.   Si-gō′εn,   k·′ē
    of   (fut.)   also to go,   (perf.)   went   Txä′msεm.   After a while,   then

reached the middle of the bridge it broke. He fell down into the canyon, and his belly burst. When Txä′msεm saw what had happened, and saw the food of which he had not been able to partake, then he flew to the bottom of the canyon and ate the contents of the slave's stomach. He simply took the food with his hands. When he had finished eating, the slave arose and said, "He eats excrements." Then Txä′msεm was ashamed. The slave recovered and parted company with Txä′msεm.

Thus the slave found out that it was Txä′msεm. When the latter went about murdering he heard himself called very bad names. First the Bullhead called him Giant, and then the chief called him Eating-scabs-of-Wâ′sε. He was again very hungry.

---

uks-iē′t;	ʟat	hwaʟ	sē′lukʟ	gan,	k·'ē	hēʟā′gaʟ	gan. 1
toward he water went;	when	he found	the middle of	the stick,	then	broke	the stick.
K·'ē	t'ogwā′ntkᵘʟ	xa′ɛg·ê.	K·'ē	sɛm-bē′siʟ	bant.	K·'ē	2
Then	fell down	the slave.	Then	much tore	his belly.	Then	
tsεda	ʟat	g·a′as	Txä′msεm	hwî̂l	hwî̂′ltg·ê,	k·'ēt	g·a′aʟ 3
when	(part.)	saw it	Txä′msεm	what happened,		then	he saw
wunä′x·	ʟa	ax-g·ē′bɛtg·ê	aʟ	hwî̂l	xʟuXt	aʟ	ts'ä′wuʟ 4
the food	(perf.)	not he had eaten	at	when	burst	at	inside
xa′ɛg·ê.	Nʟk·'ē	hwî̂l	k·'ē	g·ig·ɛbā′yukt	aʟ	lō-d'ɛp-qâ′ôʟ 5
the slave.	At once			he flew	at	in down he went to
ts'ɛm-tsâ′ɛg·ê.	K·'ēt	g·ē′îpʟ	lō-hwî̂′lt	aʟ	qalâ′sʟ	xa′ɛg·ê.	6
in the cleft.	Then	he ate it	in was	in	the stomach of	the slave.	
At	ksax-d'ô′qt	aʟ	an'o′nt	at	g·i′ptg·ê.	K·'ē	ʟa ʟä′ɛxkᵘt, 7
He	only took	with	his hands	he	ate it.	Then	when he finished eating,
k·'ē	haldɛm-ba′xʟ	xa′ɛg·ê.	K·'ē	bēt:	"Si-gō′nʟ	dē-hwî̂′lt	8
then	arose	the slave.	Then	he said:	"Now	also he does so	
at	x-gwats."	K·'ē	dzâqʟ	qâ′ôts	Txä′msεm.	K·'ē	ha′tsîk·'sɛm 9
he	eats excrements."	Then	was ashamed	the heart of	Txä′msεm.	Then	once more
mâ′ôtkᵘʟ	xa′ɛg·ê.	K·'ē	ba′sîxkᵘdet	qans	Txä′msεm.		10
was well	the slave.	Then	they separated	and	Txä′msεm.		
Nɛʟ	hwî̂l	wîtkᵘʟ	alō-d'ā′ʟ	hwî̂l	Txä′msεmt	hwî̂l 11
That	where	came from	evidently he was	being	Txä′msεm	being
su-g·a′ttg·ê	ʟat	lɛp-naxna′ʟ	qabē′iʟ	huwa′m	had'a′xkᵘtg·ê. 12
murdering	when	himself he heard	several	names	bad.
T Wîg·a′tʟ	k·s-qâ′gum	ētkᵘʟ	mas-qayā′it.	Nʟk·'ē	sɛm'â′g·idɛm 13
Giant	first	called him	the bullhead.	Then	chief
x-mō′gut	t'an	sa-hwā′dɛt	aʟ	X-ama′lgwaxdɛʟ	Wâ′sε.	Nʟa 14
(eating ripe)	who	made name	of	Eating- scabs-of-	Wâ′sε.	Then
nēʟ	hwî̂l	k'nʟ-Xda′x·t.				15
he was	being	about hungry.				

6. Then he arrived at another village, and saw little children playing at the end of the town. They were throwing pieces of seal blubber at one another. He stepped among them and ate the blubber. He ate all the blubber which the children were throwing at one another. Then they wondered what had become of it. Txä′msEm asked them, "Where do you get that blubber?" And they told him where they got it. They said, "We climb up a tree and throw ourselves down. When we strike the ground, we open our eyes and say, 'High piles of our blubber,' and immediately there are high piles of blubber." Therefore Txä′msEm also climbed the tree. He threw himself down, saying, "High." Then the children looked and saw that he

---

1 6. NLk·′ē   nā-ba′xt   aL   huX   k·′ēlL   qal-ts′a′p.   NLk·′ēt
      Then   out of he ran   to   again   one   town.   Then
                woods

2 g·a′aL   hwîl   qalā′qL   k′ōpE-tk·′ē′Lkᵘ   aL   q′apL   ts′a′pg·ê.
   he saw   where   played   little children   at   the   the town.
                                                      end of

3 Max-hē′m   ēlxL   ha-hwî′ldet.   Nē-is′ia′tst   aL   hēx·L   ēlx.
   All fat   seal   they used.   Each they   with   fat of   seal.
                                   other struck

4 NLk·′ē   dē-lō-spagait-hō′kskᵘt   lâ′ôt.   K·′ēt   qa′ne-hwîla   g·ē′îpL
   Then   also in among he was   with   Then   always   he ate
                          with them   them.

5 ēlx.   NLk·′ē   La   qâ′ôdEL   hēx·L   ēlx,   La   ha-ni-ya′tsL
   the   Then   when was finished the fat of the (perf.) what each to
   seal.   the   seal,   used other strike

6 k′ōpE-tk·′ē′Lkᵘ,   nLk·′ē   wôxwa′xdet   atse   hwî′l   hwîlL   ēlx.
   the children,   then   they wondered   if   where   was   the
   little   seal.

7 NLk·′ēt   g·ē′dExs   Txä′msEm   tsEt   hwîl   dE-wî′tkᵘdet.
   Then   asked   Txä′msEm   (dubita- where   they get it
                                    tive)   from.

8 NLk·′ēt   ma′Ldet   hwîl   wî′tkᵘtg·ê: "MEn-Lô′ônōm   aL   lax-ga′n,
   Then   they told   where   they got it   "Up   we go   at   on tree,
                                 from:

9 k·′ē   gulîk·s-d′Ep-t′a′Lgōm.   NLk·′ē   La   ō′k·sEm   aL   lax-dz·ä′dz·îk·s,
   then   selves   down we throw.   Then   when   we drop   at   on   ground.

10 k·′ē   q′ā′axL   ts′ā′lEm.   K··ē   'GE-g·îpg·a′psL   hwîl   daxdô′xt   gōn
    then   open   our eyes.   Then   'High   piles   now

11 aL   hēEm   g·apk·s,'   dEp   hē′idEnōm.   K·′ē   gE-g·îpg·a′psL
    at   fat   high,'   we   say.   Then   high

12 hwîl   daxdô′xL   hēx·   tgōn."   NLqan   hwîls   Txä′msEm   huX
    piles of   fat   this."   Therefore   he did   Txä′msEm   also
                                         so

13 dē-mEn-iē′t   aL   lax-ga′n.   NLk·′ē   dē-gulîk·s-d′Ep-ma′qst   aL
    also up he   at   on tree.   Then   also himself down he threw   and
    went

14 hē′tg·ê: "G·apk·s."   K·′ē   Lat   g·a′aL   k′ōpE-tk·′ē′Lkᵘ   hwîl
    said: "High."   Then   when   saw it   the   children   where
                                                   little

was dead. They laughed at him and left him. After a while Txä′msEm opened his eyes. He did not find anything to eat.

7. Txä′msEm found another house which belonged to Chief Cormorant. The house was full of provisions, and he sat down and ate. Then he asked the Cormorant to join him in catching halibut. Txä′msEm did not catch anything, while Chief Cormorant caught a great many. Then Txä′msEm went up to him in the canoe. He took a louse from the Cormorant's neck, held it up to him, and said, "Open your mouth and I will put your louse into it." The Cormorant replied, "No! Put it overboard into the water." "You will not catch anything if I put it into the water." Txä′msEm urged him, "Put out your tongue and let me put it on." Then the Cormorant did so.

nô′ôt, he was dead,	k·′ēt then	kᵘsta′qsdēt they left him	aL and	halā′yîxdet. laughed.	NLk·′ē Then	La de-q'ā′axL 1 (perf.) also opened
ts'ā′lîst his eyes	Txä′msEm, Txä′msEm,	k·ē then	nî′g·it not	hwaL he found	lîg·î-ago′L anything	dEm g·ē′bEt. 2 (fut.) his food.

7. K·′ē　　La t　　huX　　hwas　　Txä′msEm　　hwîlpL　　sEm'âg·idEm　3
　　Then　　(perf.)　again　　found　　Txä′msEm　　the house of　　chief

hā′uts. cormorant.	HēlL Much	wunä′x· food	aL in	hwî′lptg·ê. his house.	NLk·′ē Then	lō-d′ā′t lâ′ôt 4 in he sat in it down
aL and	yō′ôxkᵘt. ate.	NLk·′ē Then	Lat (perf.)	huX again	sä′lix·t he asked him to go with him	aL dEm ig·a′t 5 to (fut.) fish halibut
dEmt (fut.)	mu′kdēL they catch	txōx· halibut.	NLk·′ē Then	nî′g·idê nothing	môks caught	Txä′msEm, 6 Txä′msEm,
ksax-sEm'â′g·idEm only chief		hā′uts cormorant	hē′ldEL many	mukt. caught.	NLk·′ē Then	La si-gō′n, 7 (perf.) a little while,
nLk·′ē then	wusEn-iä′s along went	Txä′msEm Txä′msEm	aL in	ts'Em-mā′l. in the canoe.	NLk·′ēt Then	gō′uL 8 he took
ts'ēskᵘ a louse	aL from	t'Em-lā′nîx·L the neck of	hā′uts. the cormorant.	K·′ē Then		dEx-yō′gutg·ê: 9 he held it:

"Q'ā′gan　　dEm　　lō-ma′qdēEL　　ts'ē′sgun　　aL　　ts'Em-ā′gan."　　K·′ē　10
"Open　　(fut.)　in　　I put　　your louse　　in　　in　　your　　Then
　　　　　　　　　　　　　　　　　　　　　　　　　mouth."

"Nî′g·î,"　　hēL　　hā′utsg·ê.　　"T'uks-ma′gaL　　ts'Em-a′k·s."　　"Nî′g·î 11
"No,"　　said　　the cormorant.　　"Out put it　　in the water."　　"Not

dEm　　mō′gun,　　tsE　　ndā　　t'uks-ma′gat　　ts'Em-a′k·s."　　K·′ē　12
(fut.)　you catch,　　if　　someone　　out puts it　　in water."　　Then

g·ap·hä′q'als　　Txä′msEm.　　"K·si-Lô′ôdEL　　dē′lEn　　dEm　　lē-sgē′ist 13
much urged him　　Txä′msEm.　　"Out put　　your tongue　　(fut.)　on I lay it

lâ′ôt."　　NLk·′ē　　hwîlL　　hā′utsg·ê.　　K·si-Lô′ôdEL　　dē′lîxt. 14
on it."　　Then　　did so　　the cormorant.　　Out he put　　his tongue.

He put out his tongue. Txä'msEm seized it and tore it out. Then the
chief was dumb. They returned to the shore and quitted fishing.
The Cormorant's wife went down to the beach, and Txä'msEm said to
her, "The chief fainted, and lost his speech." But Chief Cormorant said, "Gogogo!" "Now you hear he says that he caught all this
halibut, but I caught it." Yet he had not caught it. In this way
the Cormorant lost his speech. Then they carried up the halibut,
and Txä'msEm told how the chief had lost his speech.

8. Txä'msEm did another thing. He came to a chief, who called
him into his house. His name was TEnō'kᵘLEnx. The house stood

---

1 NLk·'ēt   gō'us   Txä'msEm   dē'lîxtg·ê.   K·'ēt   k·si-mā't'Ent.
Then   took   Txä'msEm   his tongue.   Then   ont   he tore it.

2 K·'ē   nî'g·i   a'lg·îxL   sEm'â'g·it.   NLk·'ē   tsagam-lō-ya'ltkᵘdet.
Then   not   spoke   the chief.   Then   from sea to land   they returned.

3 Hāul   Lē   ig·am   txō'x·dēitg·ê.   NLk·'ē   La   iaga-iē'êt
They stopped   (perf.)   fishing halibut   their halibut.   Then   when   to beach went

4 nak·sL   hā'utsg·ê,   k·'ē   a'lg·îxs   Txä'msEm: "Guldā'uL
the wife of   the cormorant,   then   said   Txä'msEm: "Fainted

5 sEm'â'g·it   tgōna?   GwâtkᵘL   La   a'lg·îxt."   NLk·'ē   a'lg·îxL
the chief   this?   It is lost   (past)   his speech."   Then   spoke

6 sEm'â'g·idEm   hā'uts,   aL   hē'tg·ê: "Gôgôgô."   "Wô,   naxna'L!
the chief   the cormorant,   and   he said: "Gō, gô, gô."   "Now,   hear!

7 gul-ganēL   mō'gudEL   txō'x·,   tgōn   dēya'L   hē'tsē.   ALk·'ē'
all   he caught   halibut,   this   thus said   he said.   But

8 nē'e   t'an   mukL   an-hē't.   Q'amgai't-nî'g·idi   mukL   sEm'â'g·it
I   who   caught   what he said.   Still   not   caught   the chief

9 tgōn.   Nda   aL   nēL   dEm   gwâ'ôtkᵘL   La   a'lg·îxt   qan   ax-mu'kt."
this.   He   it is   who   (fnt.)   he lost   his speech   therefore   not he caught."

10 NLk·'ē   La   yukt   bax-dô'qdEL   txōx·.   NLk·'ē   hēs   Txä'msEm
Then   (perf.)   began   up   they took   halibut.   Then   said   Txä'msEm

11 aL   sEm'â'g·ît,   La   yukt   ma'LEL   hwîl   hwî'lL   sEm'â'g·ît   qan
to   the chief,   (perf.)   begin   he told   what did   the chief   and

12 gwâtkᵘL   a'lg·îx,   aL   nak·st   hwîl   hē'tg·ê.
it was lost   the speech,   to   his wife   when   he said.

13 8. Ha'tsîk·sEm   huX   k·'ēlL   hwîl   hwîls   Txä'msEm.   K·'ēt
Once more   also   one   did   Txä'msEm.   Then

14 hwaL   hwîl   lo-d'ā'L   sEm'â'g·it.   K·'ē   hē'tg·ê   dEm   lō-d'ä't
he found   where   in was   a chief.   Then   he said   (fut.)   in sit down

15 lâ'ôt.   TEnō'kᵘLEnxL   hwat.   Alō-hehē'tkᵘL   hwî'lptg·ê.   K·'ē
in it.   TEnō'kᵘLEnx   his name.   Alone   stood   his house.   Then

all alone.   Txä′msEm was very glad because he saw much food there.
He ate there all the time.   Then he saw TEnō′kᵘLEnx's club.   It hung on
the house post and was inlaid with abalone shell.   Txämsem said, "He
acts like a bad slave."   He saw that the chief had large teeth.   The
chief arose and took the club, intending to kill Txä′msEm, but he ran
out of the house.   Then Txä′msEm spoke kindly, "I said you are
acting nicely, Chief."   TEnō′kᵘLEnx said, "No, you said, 'He acts like
a bad slave.'"   "I shall not say so again, Chief.   Let me sit near you."
Then TEnō′kᵘLEnx agreed.   Txä′msEm reentered the house and stayed
there a long time.   Now Txä′msEm went into the woods near the
house.   He made a club of rotten wood.   He pounded mussel shells
and inlaid the rotten wood with it.   Then he took TEnō′kᵘLEnx's club

---

sEm-tq'al-sī′Ep′Ens	Txä′msEm	nē′tg·e	aL	hwîl	g·a′aL	wunä′x·, 1
much against liked him	Txä′msEm	him	because	he saw		food,

qan hēt.	K·′ē	qanē-hwîla	yō′ôxkᵘt	lât.	K·′ēt g·a′aL	ha-q'alā′X. 2
there- he said fore so.	Then	always	he ate	in it.	Then he saw	a club.

MEn-ia′gat	aL	daganē′sL	hwî′lptg·ê,	txa-bElā′da.	K·′ē 3
Up it hung	at	the house post of	his house,	all abalone shell.	Then

lō-a′lg·îxL	qâ′ôts	Txä′msEm	t	hwîl	g·ā′aL	wī-wē′nL	sEm′â′g·it. 4
in	said	the heart of	Txä′msEm	he	when	he saw	the tooth of great the chief.

K·′ē	haldEm-ba′xL	sEm′â′g·it,	at	gō′uL	ha-q'alā′X	aL dEmt 5
Then	arose	the chief,	he	took	the club	to (fut.)

dzakⁿs	Txä′msEm.	K·si-ba′xs	Txä′msEm.	K·′ē ama	a′lg·îxs 6
kill	Txä′msEm.	Out ran	Txä′msEm.	Then well	said

Txä′msEm:	"ĀmL	hwî′lEnEst	sEm′â′g·it.	Dēya′L	qâ′dEE." 7
Txä′msEm:	"Good	you do so	chief.	Thus said	my heart."

K·′ē	"Nî′g·i,"	hēs	TEnō′kᵘLEnx.	"'Had'a′xkᵘL	hwîL xa′E′ 8
Then	"No,"	said	TEnō′kᵘLEnx.	"'Bad	did the slave

mē′yaanîst."	"Nî′g·î dEm huX hēE, sEm′â′g·it.	DEm g·ap-k'uL-d'ā′nē 9
you said thus."	"Not (fut.) again I say, chief.	(Fut.) really about I sit

awa′an."	K·′ēt anâ′qs	TEnō′kᵘLEnxL	hē′tg·ê.	K·′ē ha′tsîk·sEm 10
your proximity."	Then he agreed	TEnō′kᵘLEnx	he said.	Then once more

huX	ts′ēns	Txä′msEm.	K·′ē	nakᵘL lō-d'ā′t.	K·′ē k'uL-iē′s 11
again	entered	Txä′msEm.	Then	long in he was.	Then about went

Txä′msEm	aL	g·îlē′lîx.	K·′ē	dzäpL ha′îx aL	sE-qawā′x·t 12
Txä′msEm	at	inland.	Then	he made rotten at wood	he club made a

sEl-hwîl-g·a′t′Ent.	K·′ēt	kᵘLē-ax·′ô′x·L	qam-g·a′lis.	K·′ēt 13
to- being he made gether it be.	Then	all he pounded over	mussel shell.	Then

sE-bElā′dEL	qawā′x·.	K·′ēt	sE-dä′xt,	k·′ēt gō′uL	qawā′x·s 14
he abalone made on it	the club.	Then	he it made fast,	then he took	the club of

and hung in its place the club of rotten wood which looked like it. Then he hid TEnō′kⁿLEnx's club, and sat down, and said again, "How bad acts that slave to whom I came!" Then TEnō′kᵘLEnx rose. He took his club, and Txä′msEm ran out of the house. As soon as TEnō′kⁿLEnx came outside he struck Txä′msEm on the head, who said, "My brother is using a rotten wood club to kill me." Then he took TEnō′kⁿLEnx's own club and killed him. He threw the body on the beach. He stayed in the house and ate all of TEnō′kⁿLEnx's food.

9. Another time Txä′msEm came to the house of the Seal. The Seal invited him in. He was eating salmon. He took a dish and placed it near the fire; then he held up his hands near the fire so that they grew warm. Then grease dripped from his fingers and ran into the

1 TEnō′kⁿLEnxt.   K·'ēt   ia′gai-lē-ia′qL   lEp-qawā′ɣîm   ha′îxt
   TEnō′kᵘLEnx.   Then   however on hung   his   club   rotten wood
   (his own)

2 sEl-hwîl-g·a′t'Ent.   K·'ēt   ia′xL   qawā′x·s   TEnō′kⁿLEnxt.   ɴLk·'ē
   to- being made   Then   be hid   the club of   TEnō′kᵘLEnx.   Then
   gether to be.

3 hē′tg·ê   aL   k·'ē′l   huX   d'āt: "Had'a′xg·îL   wāLL   xaE
   he said   (when)   once   again   he sat down: "Bad   did   slave

4 dēn wâ′in."[1]   K·'ē   haldEm-ba′xs   TEnō′kⁿLEnxt.   At gō′uL   qawā′x·.
   whom found you."   Then   rose   TEnō′kᵘLEnx.   He took   the club.

5 K·'ē   k·si-ba′xs   Txä′msEm.   Lat   hwaL   g·alq,   k·'ēt   ia′tss
   Then   out ran   Txä′msEm.   When he reached   outside,   then   struck

6 TEnō′kⁿLEnx   t'Em-qē′st.   K·'ē   hē′tg·ê: "Qawā′ɣîm   hā′ya
   TEnō′kᵘLEnx   his head.   Then   he said: "Club   rotten

7 t hwilā′akⁿdet   hwa′tsēE."   K·'ēt gō′uL   lEp-qawā′x·s   TEnō′kⁿLEnxt.
   what used on me   my brother."   Then he took   own club of   TEnō′kᵘLEnx.

8 K·'ēt   ia′tss   TEnō′kⁿLEnxt,   k·'ē   sg·it   nô′ô.   K·'ēt   iaga-ma′gat
   Then   he struck   TEnō′kᵘLEnx,   then   he lay   dead.   Then   down he put him

9 aL   g·ä′u.   K·'ē   lō-dzô′qs   Txä′msEm   aL   hwîlpt.   At g·ē′îpL
   in   front of the house.   Then   in he stayed   Txä′msEm   in   the house.   He ate

10 wunä′x·.   Lō-dza′LL   wunä′x·s   TEnō′kⁿLEnxt.
    the food.   In he ate all   the food of   TEnō′kᵘLEnx.

11 9. HuX   hwā′is   Txä′msEm   hwîlpL   ēlx.   K·'ē   wô′ôtkᵘL   ēlx
    Again   found   Txä′msEm   the house of   the seal.   Then   invited   seal

12 lâ′ôt.   HânL   g·ē′îpt.   K·'ēt   gō′uL   ts'ak·,   k·'ēt   sg·it   aL
    in it.   Salmon   he ate.   Then   he took   a dish,   then   he laid it   at

13 lax-ts'ä′L   lakⁿ.   K·'ēt   mEn-dô′qL   an'ô′nt   aL   gō′unt   aL   lakⁿ.
    on the edge of   the fire.   Then   up he held   his hand   to   hit it   at   fire.

14 K·'ē   ä′d'îk·skᵘL   t'ē′lx·   aL   qats'uwunê′tt.   K·'ē   lō-ma′qskᵘL
    Then   came   grease   from   his fingers.   Then   in it ran

[1] This sentence is in Tsimshian dialect.

dish.   He gave it to Txä′msEm to dip the salmon in the grease.
Txä′msEm ate the salmon with the seal blubber.   He ate very much, and
was satiated.   Then he left.   Now Txä′msEm made a house.   He
finished it and invited the Seal to visit him.   The Seal entered, and sat
down in the rear of the house, and Txä′msEm took a dish.   He placed
it near the fire and held up his hands so that they grew warm, but his
hands were scorched.   Then Txä′msEm turned back secretly, crying,
"Mmmmmm!"   When the Seal saw that Txä′msEm was crying, he
rose.   There was no grease in the dish.   Then he said, "He tries
to imitate what I do."   Txä′msEm was ashamed.   He put pitch on
his hand because it hurt.   Then he said, "You ought not to try such
things.   You would better get food for me that I may eat."   He was

---

| t'ēlx· | aL | ts'Em-ts'a′k·, | dEm | wutxs | Txä′msEm | aL | hân. | 1 |
| grease | toward | in the dish, | (fut.) | to dip in grease | Txä′msEm | (at) | salmon. | |

| K·'ēt | g·ē′îps | Txä′msEmL | hân. | Qan-g·ē′îpdeL | t'ē′la | ēlx. | 2 |
| Then | ate | Txä′msEm | salmon. | With it he ate | the fat of | seal. | |

| K·'ē | hĕlL | wunä′x· | huX | g·ē′bEt. | K·'ē | ts'ä′x·tg·ê. | K·'ēt | 3 |
| Then | much | food | again | he ate it. | Then | he was satiated. | Then | |

| kᵘsta′qsêt. | K·'ē | dē-dzä′ps | Txä′msEmL | hwîlp | aL | wagai-dō′u. | 4 |
| he left him. | Then | also made | Txä′msEm | a house | at | ar. | |

| K·'ē | La | LēskᵘL | dzäpL | hwîlp, | k·'ē | dēt-wô′ôL | ēlx. | K·'ē | 5 |
| Then | when | he finished | he made | the house, | then | also he invited | the seal. | Then | |

| dē-ts'ē′nL | ēlx. | K·'ē | d'ät | aL | q'alä′n. | K·'ē | dēt-gō′us | 6 |
| also entered | the seal. | Then | he sat | at | in the rear of the house. | Then | also took he | |

| Txä′msEmL | ts'ak·. | K·'ē | dēt-sg·it | aL | awa'aL | lakᵘ. | K·'ē | 7 |
| Txä′msEm | a dish. | Then | also laid he it | at | the proximity of | the fire. | Then | |

| dēt-haL-dô′qL | an'ô′nt. | K·'ē | Lat | guxL | lakⁿ | an'ô′ns | Txä′msEm, | 8 |
| also along he held | his hands. | Then | (perf.) | struck | the fire | the hands of | Txä′msEm, | |

| k·'ē | ts'Ex·ts'ä′LkⁿL | an'ô′nt. | K·'ēt | tgo-ya′ltkᵘs | Txä′msEm | 9 |
| then | it scorched | his hands. | Then | around turned | Txä′msEm | |

| q'a′mts'En | wi-yē′tkᵘt: | "Mmmmm," | dēya′. | K·'ē | haldEm-ba′xL | 10 |
| secretly | he cried: | "Mmmmm," | thus he said. | Then | rose | |

| ēlx, | Lat | g·a′aL | hwîl | wi-yē′tkᵘs | Txä′msEm. | Nî′g·i | lō-g·ä′nL | 11 |
| the seal, | when | he saw | (verbal noun) | cried | Txä′msEm. | Not | in was | |

| t'ēlx· | aL | ts'ä′k·g·ê. | K·'ē | a′lg·îxt: | "DEm | dē-yô′xkᵘt | La | 12 |
| grease | in | the dish. | Then | he said: | "(Fut.) | also he follows | (perf.) | |

| hwä′lēE." | K·'ē | dzâqs | Txä′msEm. | K·'ēt | sEnt-sg·a′ndEL | 13 |
| what I do." | Then | was ashamed | Txä′msEm. | Then | he put pitch on | |

| an'ô′ntg·ê | aL | sEmgal | aba′g'askᵘt. | K·'ē | lEp-hē′tg·ê: | "Se | ä′mL | 14 |
| his hand | for | very | he was troubled. | Then | himself he said: | "You do well | |

| gwîx·-txä′kᵘsEm | dadī | yô′ôxguē | aL | ld'ä′gEsEm." | Aba′g'askᵘt | 15 |
| to be always | eating you | when | I eat | you eat fast." | He was troubled | |

greatly troubled, therefore he said so.　He spoke to his hand.　For that reason the hands of man are bent (in old age) to this day.

Txä′msEm went on, and came to a nice house.　There he found Chief Ts′Enk′oa′ts, who had stores of provisions.　The chief invited in Txä′msEm, who sat down.　Then he ate salmon, good salmon. After he had eaten he drank water.　Ts′Enk′oa′ts took a nice dish, and stretched his foot out over the dish; then he took a stone, struck his ankle, and pulled out fish roe.　He placed it before Txä′msEm, who ate it.　He was very glad.　He left the house of Ts′Enk′oa′ts when he had eaten enough.　Then Txä′msEm thought he would invite his friend to visit him.　He made a house and invited in Ts′Enk′oa′ts, who sat down.　Then Txä′msEm took a dish and stretched his foot out

1	qan	hē′tg·ê,	an′ô′nL	qan	hē′tg·ê.	NLqan	hwîlL	hwîl
	there-fore	he said so,	his hand	on account of	he spoke.	Therefore	they are	(verbal noun)
2	hîxiLa′LaganL		an′ô′nL	g·at	gō′Ensē.	DElda′lbîk·sk"		gōn.
	bending		the hands of	man	now.	They shrink (his hands)		now.
3	K·′ē	huX	iē′s	Txä′msEm.	HuX	hwa′itg·ê	ama	hwî′lpg·ê.
	Then	again	went	Txä′msEm.	Again	he found	a good	house.
4	HuX	sEm-k·′a-hē′lL		wunä′x·L	sEm′â′g·it.		Ts′Enk′oä′tsL	
	Again	very exceedingly		much food of	the chief.		(A little bird)	
5	hwa′tg·ê.	K·′ē	wô′ôtk"L	Ts′Enk′oä′ts	as	Txä′msEm.		Ama
	his name.	Then	invited	Ts′Enk′oä′ts	to	Txä′msEm.		Well
6	d′ä′tg·ê.	K·′ē	x-hâ′ônt,	ama	hân,	Läxk"t.	K·′e	a′k·stg·ê.
	he sat down.	Then	he ate salmon,	good	salmon,	he finished eating.	Then	he drank.
7	K·′ēt	gō′uL	Ts′Enk′oä′ts	ama	ts·a′k·g·ê.	K·′ēt		uks-Lô′ôdEL
	Then	took	Ts′Enk′oä′ts	a good	dish.	Then		toward the fire he stretched
8	asa′ēt.	K·′ēt	gō′uL	lô′ôp.	K·′ēt	na-ô′yîL		k·′ôqō′Ltg·ê.
	his foot.	Then	he took	a stone.	Then	so that it breaks		he struck it his ankle.
9	K·′ēt	k·si-sa′g·îL	lān,	txa-k·′ē′Eltgum	lān.	Wī-hē′ltg·ê.		K·′ēt
	Then	out he pulled	spawn,	a whole one	spawn.	It was much.		Then
10	sg·it	as	Txä′msEm.	K·′ēt	g·ips	Txä′msEm.	Hē-yu′kt	g·ips
	he laid it	to	Txä′msEm.	Then	ate it	Txä′msEm.	He was	eating it
11	Txä′msEm,	k·′ē	Lū	yukL	yō′ôxk"s	Txä′msEm,	k·′ē	lō-ä′mL
	Txä′msEm,	then	(perf.)	while	was eating	Txä′msEm,	then	in good
12	qâ′ôtt.	K·′ēt	k"sta′qstg·ê	gwatsîks-tsä′ix·	aL	hwîlps	Ts′Enk′oä′ts.	
	heart.	Then	he left	very satiated	at	the house of	Ts′Enk′oä′ts.	
13	K·′ē	huX	dē-a′lg·îxL	qâts	Txä′msEm	aL	dEmt	wô′ôL
	Then	again	also said	the heart of	Txä′msEm	to	(fut.)	invite
14	an-sī′EpEnsk"t.	K·′ē	dē-dza′pL	hwîlpt.	K·′ē	dē-wô′ôL		Ts′Enk′oä′ts.
	his friend.	Then also	he made	a house.	Then also	he invited		Ts′Enk′oä′ts.
15	K·′ē	d′äL	Ts′Enk′oä′tsg·ê.	K·′ēt	gō′us	Txä′msEm		ts·ak·.
	Then	sat down	Ts′Enk′oä′ts.	Then	took	Txä′msEm		a dish.

over the dish. He took a stone and struck his ankle. He fell down backward, and said, "Oh! I am dead; I am almost dead." Ts'ɛnk'oa′ts said, "He tries to imitate me," and left the house. Then Txä′msɛm was ashamed. His foot was swollen.

He went on, not knowing which way to turn. He came to the house of Salmon-berry-bird, who invited Txä′msɛm in. Then he ate salmon. When he had finished eating, he drank. Now, Salmon-berry-bird took a nice dish. He wiped it out. Then he rose and said, "Miyâ′! Miyâ′!" He said so very often. Then the dish was full of salmon-berries. Txä′msɛm saw them and ate. Then he thought he would do the same. Secretly he took an unripe salmon-berry and put

---

| K·'ē | dē-t'uks-Lô′ôdɛL | asa′ēt | aL | ts'ɛm-ts'a′k·. | K·'ēt | gō′uL | lô′ôp. | 1 |
| Then | also out he put | his foot | to | in the dish. | Then | he took | a stone. | |

| K·'ē | dēt-ô′x·L | k·'ôq'ō′Lt. | K·'ē | haspa-Lâ′ôt | aL | hē′tg·ê: | 2 |
| Then | also he struck | his ankle. | Then | upside down he fell | and | said: | |

| "Haɛ! | Nô′ôē | gōn." | Q'am-ts'ō′sk·L | dɛm | wagait-nô′ôt | gōn. | 3 |
| "Ha! | I am dead | now." | Only a little | (fut.) | until he was dead | now. | |

| Hwî̇l | hux | hwî′ltg·ê. | K·'ē | a′lg·ixL | Ts'ɛnk'oā′ts | aL | hē′tg·ê: | 4 |
| He | again | imitated. | Then | spoke | Ts'ɛnk'oā′ts | and | said: | |

| "Dɛm | dē-yô′xᵘt | hwä′lēɛ." | Dēya′ | aL | k·sa′Xtg·ê. | K·'ē | 5 |
| "(Fut.) | also he goes after | what I do." | Thus he said | and | he went out. | Then | |

| dzâqs | Txä′msɛm. | G·î̇tkᵘs | asa′ētg·ê. | | | | 6 |
| was ashamed | Txä′msɛm. | It was swollen | his foot. | | | | |

| K·'ē | huX | iä′t | qasbasa-k'uL-iē′t. | HuX | hwa′yî̇L | hwî̇lpL | 7 |
| Then | again | he went | astray about he went. | Again | he found | the house of | |

| sɛm'â′g·it. | x-smiyâ′tkᵘsî̇L | hwa′tg·ê. | K·'ē | huX | wô′ôtkᵘt | 8 |
| a chief. | (Bird) | his name. | Then | again | he invited | |

| as | Txä′msɛm. | K·'ē | Lat | g·eî̇pL | hâ′ng·ê. | K·'ê | Lä·ɛxkᵘt, | 9 |
| to | Txä′msɛm. | Then | (perf.) he | ate | salmon. | Then | he finished eating, | |

| k·'ē | a′k·stg·ê. | K·'ēt | gō′uL | x-smiyâ′tkᵘsî̇L | ama | ts'ak·. | K·'ēt | 10 |
| then | he drank. | Then | took | x-smiyâtkᵘs | a good | dish. | Then | |

| lō-g·î̇′mk·t. | K·'ē | dē-hē′tkᵘt | aL | hē′tg·ê: | "Miyâ′, | miyâ′." | 11 |
| in he wiped it. | Then | also he stood up | and | said: | "Miyâ′, | miyâ′." | |

| Hēlʟ | hē′tg·ê | aL | x-smiyâ′tkᵘst. | K·'ē | mētkᵘL | ts'ak· | aL | 12 |
| Much | he said | and | said miyâ′. | Then | it was full | the dish | of | |

| mēg·â′ôqstg·ê. | K·'ēt | g·a′as | Txä′msɛm. | K·'ēt | sg·i′tg·ê. | 13 |
| salmon-berries. | Then | saw it | Txä′msɛm. | Then | he laid it down. | |

| Hē-yu′kt | g·ē′ips | Txä′msɛm. | K·'ē | huX | dē-lō-a′lg·ixL | qâ′ôtt | 14 |
| He was | eating it | Txä′msɛm. | Then | again | also in spoke | his heart | |

| aL | dɛm | dē-hwî̇′ltg·ê. | Q'amgait | q'a′mts'ɛn | dâ′gôL | hwî̇l | 15 |
| to | (fut.) | also he does so. | Before | secretly | he took | being | |

it into his hand. He left the house. Then he made a house and invited in Chief Salmon-berry-bird. He imitated him. He arose after having placed the unripe salmon-berry in his dish. Then he stood there and said, "Miyâ'! Miyâ'!" He said so very often, but there remained just as many unripe salmon-berries in the dish as he had put in. He placed the dish before Chief Salmon-berry-bird, who rose, saying, "He tries to imitate me." Then Txä'msEm was ashamed. He did not imitate any more.

10. He went on, not knowing which way to turn. Behold, he came out of the woods to a large town. There were poople in front of the town fishing for halibut. Txä'msEm thought, "They have much bait, and I will eat it." He dived, and he saw the bait. He took it from

---

1 ax-dē-mîx·môkᵘʟ   mēg'â'qst   lō-dâ'yit   ts'ɛm-an'ô'ntg·ê.   K·ē
   not also ripe   salmon   in he laid in   his hand.   Then
                       berries   them

2 k·saXt   aʟ   hwî'lpg·ê.   HuX   dē-dzā'pʟ   hwî'lpg·ê.   K·ēt
   he went   of   house.   Again also he made a house.   Then
   out

3 huX   wô'ôʟ   sɛm'â'g·idɛm   x-smiyâ'tkᵘs.   K·ē   dēt-hō'g·îxʟ
   again he invited   the chief   x-smiyâ'tkᵘs.   Then   also he did
                                                               the same as

4 x-smiyâ'tkᵘs   aʟ   huX   dē-hē'tkᵘtg·ê.   Ia'gait-lō-dâ'ɣiʟ
   x-smiyâ'tkᵘs   and   again also he stood   Already in he had
                                      up.   put

5 ax-mîx·mô'gum   mēg'â'ôkst   aʟ   ts'ɛm-ts·a'k·tg·ê.   K·ē
   not   ripe   salmon berries at   in   his dish.   Then

6 dē-hē'tkᵘt   aʟ   hē'tg·ê: "Miyâ'   miyâ'."   Wī-hē'ld   hē'tg·ê   aʟ
   also he stood and   said: "Miyâ'   miyâ'."   Much   he said   and
   up

7 x-smiyâ'tkᵘst.   Qanē-qabē'iʟ   ax-mîx·mô'gum   mēg'â'ôqst   aʟ
   said   miyâ'.   All   as many not   ripe   salmon berries at

8 ts'ɛm-ts'â'k·g·ê.   K·ē   dēt-sg·'ē't   aʟ   sɛm'â'g·idɛm   x-smiyâ'tkᵘst.
   in   dish.   Then   also he laid   be-   the chief   x-smiyâ'tkᵘs.
                              it   fore

9 K·ē   haldɛm-ba'xʟ   sɛm'â'g·it.   A'lg·îxtg·ê: "Dem   dē-ɣô'xkᵘt
   Then   rose   the chief.   He said: "(Fut.) also he wil'
                                                                  go after

10 La   hwä'lēɛ."   K·ē   dzâqs   Txä'msɛm;   qâ'ôdɛʟ   hwîl   hwî'ltg·ê.
   (perf.) what I do." Then   he was   Txä'msɛm;   it was   what he did.
                              ashamed   finished

11 10.   K·ē   huX   qa'sbɛsa-k'uʟ-iē'ɐt.   Gwinā'dēʟ,   wī-ts·a'p
          Then   again not knowing about he   Behold,   a   town
                        where   went.   large

12 hwîl   na-ba'xt.   Gwinā'dēʟ,   māl   aʟ   gî'ikc   qa-ig·a't   dɛp-
   where   out of he ran. Behold,   a canoe   at   front of the fishing   (plural)
           woods   village   halibut

13 gō'stg·ê   dɛm   mô'kdeiʟ   txox·.   K·ē   lō-a'lg·îxʟ   qâ'ôts
   those   (fut.)   they eatch   halibut. Then   in   said   the heart
                                                                      of

14 Txä'msɛm: "Hē'ldɛm   aʟ   naxs   dɛp-gō'st   an   dɛm   g·'ē'îpt."
   Txä'msɛm: "Mueh   at   bait   those   for   (fut.)   to eat."
                                                       me

15 Nʟqan   hwî'ltg·ê.   Sō'uqskᵘt   ts'ɛm-a'k·s.   Gwinā'dēʟ,   naxʟ   g·a'at.
   There-   he did so.   He dived   in   the   Behold,   the bait he saw it.
   fore   wa

the hook and ate it. He went from one hook to the other, eating all
the bait. Then the bait of all the fishermen had disappeared, but they
did not know how it had happened. Finally one of the men caught
Txä′msEm's jaw. His jaw was caught on one of the hooks. Then the
fisherman pulled. Txä′msEm was pulled up, although he was resist-
ing. He could not take the hook out of his mouth. He held on to the
rocks at the bottom of the sea. Then he was hauled up with the fish
line. The fishermen came together and they all hauled the fish line.
Txä′msEm said to the rocks at the bottom of the sea that they should
help him, and finally he said to his jaw, "Break off, jaw! I am
getting tired." Then his jaw broke off. When the fishermen saw
the great jaw with a long beard, some of them laughed, but others
were scared. They went ashore, and all the people assembled in the

K·′ē At once	hwîl	k·′ēt he took it,	gō′ut, 	at he	g·ē′îpt. ate it.	SEm-dōx′ä′bEL Really he went from one to the other	hō′ldem much	1

nax,   at g·ē′îpt. K·′ē sagat-qâ′ôdEL naxL qa-ig·a′t. K·′ē 2
bait, he ate it. Then entirely was the bait the fishermen. Then
                finished of

gawaxwa′xdēit aL hwî′ltg·ê. SEm-mô′k^{u}I k·′âlL g·at x·pä′us 3
they wondered what happened. Really caught one man the jaw of

Txä′msEm. Lō-hō′ksk^{u}L ig·a′ aL x·pa′us Txä′msEm. 4
Txä′msEm. In it was the halibut at the jaw of Txä′msEm.
          with it hook

SEm-dä′mgant. K·′ē g·îdi-qä′k·sk^{u}s Txä′msEm. Aqt-hwîla 5
Strongly he pulled. Then trying was dragged Txä′msEm. With- (verbal
        to be stopped   out noun)

k·sE-gō′uL ig·a′ aL ts′Em-ä′qtg·ê, at hwîl iaga-dô′qL 6
off he took the hook at in his mouth, he being down he held
                            to

lEplô′ôp aL ts′Eō′yuX aL qan-LEmâ′mtg·ê. La k·′ē 7
the rocks at the bottom of sea for means helping. (Perf.) then
                of

dä′mgansk^{u}L lax-ha′ye aL môo′lk^u. K·′ē sagait-iē′L qa-ig·a′t 8
he was pulled on top at the fish line. Then together went the fishermen

at dä′mgandēL môo′lk^u. K·′ē dē-hwî′ls Txä′msEm aL 9
they pulled the line. Then on his did so Txä′msEm at
                part

ts′Eō′yuX at dExdô′qL lEplô′ôp qan-LEmâ′mtg·ê. K·′ē hēs 10
the bottom of he holding the stones means helping. Then said
the sea   of

Txä′msEmg·ê aL k·pa′ôt: "K·si-bē′sEn k·pa′ô La dEm 11
Txä′msEm to jaw: "Out tear jaw (perf.) (fut.)

gwâtk^{u}L qâ′ôdēE." K·′ē sa-bē′sîL x·pä′ut. K·′ēt g·a′aL 12
lost my heart." Then off tore his jaw. Then saw

qa-ig·a′L wī-k·pä′o wī-max-iē′mq. K·′ēt halä′g·îxdēit. Lagats′ō′ut 13
the the jaw great all heard. Then they laughed. Some of them
fishermen great

laxbēits′ē′wut. K·′ē tsagam-ho′uL qa-ig·a′t. K·′ē sagait-iē′L 14
were scared. Then ashore escaped the fishermen. Then together went

chief's house. There they looked at the great jaw. Txä′msEm went ashore, coming out of the water. He was greatly worried. Then he repented and said, "I am always doing this to myself." He arrived at the town while the people were looking at the great jaw in the chief's house. Txä′msEm entered and sat down near the door. He saw the people looking at the great jaw. He held his blanket over his mouth to cover his lost jaw. When he saw his own great jaw he stretched out his hand, saying, "Give it to me." He took it and looked at it, turning it over and over, examining it. Then he put it on and ran out, and the people said, "That is Txä′msEm, the cheater!" Then Txä′msEm was well again.

11. Txä′msEm went on. He was very hungry, and he saw a steelhead salmon jumping in the river. Then he devised a plan. He

---

1 g·at   aL   hwîlpL   sEm′â′g·it,   at   g·a′adEL   wi-k·pā′o.   K·′ē
   the   to   the house   the chief.   they   they saw   the   jaw.   Then
   people   of   great

2 spi-iä′s   Txä′msEm   aL   ts′Em-a′k·s.   Aba′g·ask^ut   aL   hwî′ltg·ê.
   ashore went Txä′msEm   out   in   water.   He was troubled   about   what he did.
                           of

3 SEm-gulîk·s-ē′tk^usL   qâ′ôtt   aL   hē′tg·ê: "Lep-nē′E   qane-hwîla
   Very   self   called   his heart and   said: "Self I   always
   (repented)

4 gōn."   K·′ē   na-ba′xt   aL   qal-ts′a′p.   La   he-yu′kt   g·a′aL   g·atL
   this." Then   out he ran to the town.   Then they began to see it the
                  of woods   people

5 wi-x·pa′o   aL   hwîlpL   sEm′â′g·it.   K·′ē   dē-ts·ē′ns   Txä′msEm   lâEt.
   the jaw   at   the house of the chief.   Then also entered   Txä′msEm   in there.
   great

6 K·′ē   dē-d′ā′t   aL   ā′dz′Ep.   K·′ēt   g·a′aL   hwîl   ā′lg·aLL   g·at
   Then   also he sat at the door.   Then   he saw   (verbal examined it the
          down   noun)   people

7 wi-x·pā′ot.   MEn-Lô′ôdEs   Txä′msEm   gula′t   at   ia′XL,   hwîl
   the   jaw.   Up   pushed   Txä′msEm   his blanket to   hide it,   being
   great

8 ax-k·pā′ntg·ê.   K·′ēt   q′am-Lô′ôdEL   an′ô′ntg·ê,   aL   Lat   hwaL
   with- his jaw.   Then   just he stretch- his hand,   when (perf.) he found
   out   ed out

9 wī-Lep-x·pā′o   aL   awa′at.   "Ndä′e,"   dēya′.   At   gō′ut.   K·′ēt
   his own jaw   at   his   "Give it to he said. He   took it.   Then
   great   proximity.   me,"

10 k′wa′ts·ik·s-tgo-ma′gat;   at   lā′ag·alt.   Sā-lō-d′ē′st   aL   Lep-k·pā′ut.
   much   around   he   he   examined it. Sud- in he   on   own his jaw.
          turned it;   denly pushed it

11 Hwîl   k·′ē   k·si-ba′xt.   Hwîl   k·′ē   hēL   hē′ldEm   g·a′tg·ê: "La
   Then   out he ran.   Then   they   many   people: "(Perf.)
                                      said

12 huX   nē′d   as   Txä′msEm,   gwîx·-iä′mq·asgu′t."   K·′ē   mâtkc
   again it is he as Txä′msEm,   the cheater."   Then   he was
                                                                 well

13 Txä′msEm.
   Txä′msEm.

14   11. La   iē′s   Txä′msEm.   K·′ē   sEmgal   Xdax′t.   K·′ēt   g·a′aL
          (Perf.) he   Txä′msEm.   Then   very   he was.   Then   he saw
                   went   hungry.

15 hwîl   gōksL   mElē′t.   NLk·′ē   sE-wusEn-xô′ôsk^ut.   NLk·′ēt
   where jumped a steel-head Then   he   up his mind.   Then
                  salmon.   made

kicked a rock and made a deep hole. He said with a loud voice,
"Steel-head salmon, hit my heart." After he had said so he sat down
quietly. The steel-head salmon hit his heart, and Txä'msɛm lay there
dead. After a little while he opened his eyes and he saw that the
salmon had jumped over the hole that he had made. Then he kicked
the rock a second time, and he again told the salmon to hit his heart.
He sat down again and the same was repeated. He told the salmon
to hit his heart, and it did so. Again he was dead. After a while
he opened his eyes and saw the salmon lying in the hole near the
water. He rushed down to catch it, but he could not reach it. He
kicked the rock a third time, and sat down again. Then he told the
salmon to hit his heart. It did so, and again he was dead. His heart

---

1 g·îdi-k·ʟa′qsʟ / lô′ôp. / Nʟk·′ē / wī-lō-ʟa′pʟ / lô′ôp. / Nʟk·′ē
   right there he kicked / a stone. / Then / great in deep / stone. / Then

2 a′lg·îxtg·ê. / Wī-amhē′t: / "Däqskᵘʟ / qâ′ôdēᴇ, / mɛlē′t!"[1] / ʟēskᵘʟ
   he spoke. / He shouted: / "Hit / my heart, / steel-head salmon!" / He finished

3 hēt, / k·′ē / ama / d′ā′t. / K·′ēt / guXʟ / mɛlē′tʟ / qâ′ôdᴇt. / K·′ē
   he said / then / well / he sat down. / Then / hit / the steel-head salmon / his heart. / Then

4 nô′ôt. / K·′ē / ʟa / q′ā′axʟ / ts′a′ᴇlt / aʟ / hwîl / nô′ôt. / K·′ēt / g·a′aʟ
   he was dead. / Then / (perf.) / he opened / his eyes / at / where / he was dead. / Then / he saw

5 mɛlē′t / ʟa / t′uks-da′uʟt. / K·′ēt / huX / g·îdi-k·ʟa′qsʟ / lô′ôp,
   the steel-head salmon / (perf.) / out had gone. / Then / again / right there he kicked / the stone,

6 k·′ē′lbᴇlt. / K·′ē / ha′ts·îk·sᴇm / huX / hē′tg·ê / at / gun-gō′oʟ / qâ′ôdᴇt
   a second time. / Then / once more / again / he said / he / caused to hit / his heart

7 aʟ / mɛlē′t. / K·′ē / huX / ama / d′ā′t. / HuX / hō′g·igat / ʟa
   at / the steel-head salmon. / Then / again / well / he sat down. / Again / like / (perf.)

8 waʟen-hwî′lt. / Nʟk·′ē / huX / a′lg·îxt / at / gun-gō′uʟ / qâ′ôdᴇt / aʟ
   formerly he did. / Then / again / he spoke / to / cause to hit / his heart / to

9 mɛlē′t. / K·′ē / huX / hwîlʟ / mɛlē′t. / K·′ē / huX / nô′ôt. / K·′ē
   the steel-head salmon. / Then / again / he did so / the steel-head salmon. / Then / again / he was dead. / Then

10 ʟa / ha′ts·îk·sᴇm / huX / q′ā′axʟ / ts′a′ᴇlt, / nʟk·′ē / ʟa / lō-sg·ī′t / aʟ
    when / once more / again / he opened / his eyes, / then / (perf.) / in he lay / in

11 lō·ks-g·ē′wît. / At / g·a′at, / hwîl / k·′ē / iaga-hē′tkᵘt / aʟ / dᴇmt
    in the lowest hole. / Then / he saw it, / at once / down to the water rushed / he / to / (fut.)

12 gō′ut. / K·′ēt / sq′ōk·st / aʟ / dᴇmt / gō′ut. / K·′ēt / huX
    take it. / Then / he was out of reach / at / (fut.) / he took it. / Then / again

13 g·îdi-k·ʟa′qsʟ / lô′ôp. / Nᴇʟ / gulā′alt. / K·′ē / huX / d′āt; / k·′ē
    right there he kicked / the stone. / Then / the third time. / Then / again / he sat down; / then

14 huX / hēt / at / gun-gō′uʟ / qâ′ôdᴇt. / K·′ē / huX / hwîlʟ / mɛlē′t.
    again / he said / to / cause to hit / his heart. / Then / again / did so / the steel-head salmon.

---

[1] This sentence is in G·itkcan dialect.

was swollen. Then he opened his eyes again, and saw the salmon which lay right in the middle of the rock. He went down slowly and caught it.

12. Now he did not know how to prepare his food. So he sat down and defecated. Then he asked his excrements, "What shall I do, my excrements?" They said, "Steam it in a hole." Then he cut wood, but while he was doing so he forgot what he was to do. Then he sat down again and defecated. Only a little came out. He asked, "What shall I do, my excrements?" They said, "Steam it in a hole." They spoke in a low voice. Now Txä'msEm gathered stones, and he said all the time, "Steam it in a hole." He said it as though he was singing.

---

1 K·'ē   huX   nô'ôt.   La   g·itkuᴸ   qâ'ôdɛt   aᴸ   hwî'ltg·ê.   K·'ē
   Then   again   he was   (perf.) it swelled his heart   at   he did so.   Then
                   dead.

2 huX   hwîᴸᴸ   mɛlē't,   huX   gō'yiᴸ   qâ'ôdɛt.   K·'ē   huX   q'ā'axᴸ
   again   did so   the steel   again   he hit   his heart.   Then   again   he opened
                   head salmon,

3 ts'a'ɛlt,   k·'ēt   g·a'aᴸ   mɛlē't.   Lō-sg·ī't   aᴸ   lo-ks-sē'lgut   lô'ôp.
   his eyes,   then   he saw   the steel   In it lay   at   in middle-most   stone.
                            head salmon.

4 K·'ē   iaga-iä'êtg·ê.   Hagul-hwî'ltg·ê.   K·'ēt   gō'uᴸ   mɛlē't.
   Then   down he went.   Slowly he did so.   Then   he took   the steel
                                                                  head salmon

5 K·'ē   iä'êt.
   Then   he
           went.

6 12.   K·'ē   aqt-hwîla   dzā'bɛt   aᴸ   dɛmt   g·ē'îpt.   Nᴸk·'ē   d'āt
          Then   with- being to make   to   (fut.)   his food.   Then   he sat
                  out   it   down

7 aᴸ   sipa'ntg·ê.   K·'ēt   g·ē'daxᴸ   sipa'nt: "Agō'ᴸ   dɛm   hwî'lēᴇ
   to   he defecated.   Then   he asked   his   "What   (fut.)   I do
                                             excrements:

8 ʟᴇ,   g·uā'tsēᴇ?"   K·'ē   a'lg·îxᴸ   sipa'ntg·ê: "Sā'lɛbɛʟ!"   K·'ē
   (perf.), my excre-   Then   spoke   his excrements: "Steam it in a   Then
             ments?"   hole."

9 sa-â'ʟkutg·ê.   Hē-yukt   sa-â'ôʟkut,   k·ē   t'ak·ʟ   dɛm   hwî'ltg·ê.
   he   firewood. Beginning he fire-   then   he   (fut.)   he did.
   made   made wood,   forgot

10 K·'ē   lîg·i-k'uᴸ-d'ā't.   K·'ē   ha'ts'îk·sɛm   huX   d'āt.   K·'ē   huX
   Then   any- about he   Then   once more   again   he sat.   Then   again
           where   sat.

11 ā'd'îk·skuᴸ   k·saXt;   ʟgo-ts'ō'osk·ʟ   k·saXt.   K·'ē   huX
   came   out it went; little small   it went out.   Then   again

12 hēt: "Ndaᴸ   dɛm   hwî'lēᴇ   ʟᴇ,   g·ua'tsēᴇ?"   K·'ē   ʟgo-a'lg·îxᴸ
   he said: "What   (fut.)   I do   (perf.),   my excre-   Then   little it spoke
                                             ments?"

13 ʟᴇ   g·ua'tst: "Sā'lɛbɛl."   Ts'ōsk·ʟ   a'lg·îxt.   K·'ēt   sagait-dô'qs
   his excre-   "Steam it in a   Little   it spoke.   Then   together took
   ments: hole."

14 Txä'msɛm   lô'ôp.   K·'ē   qa'ne-hwîla   a'lg·îxt: "Sā'lɛbɛl!"   K·'ē
   Txä'msɛm   stones.   Then   always   he spoke: "Steam it in a   Then
                                                            hole!"

He made a song of the words, "Steam it in a hole." When the hole was hot he went to gather leaves of the skunk-cabbage to cover it. Then he cut the salmon lengthwise and put it on top of the leaves in the hole. A stump lay near the hole. Then he took part of the salmon out and said to the stump, shaking the salmon, "I am sure you envy me, Stump." Then he went to get some more leaves which were to serve as his dish. After he had left, the Stump moved and sat down on top of the hole. Now Txä′msᴇm returned to eat. Behold, the Stump was sitting on the hole. Then he opened his mouth and cried on account of his food. He took a long lever and turned the Stump over. Behold, it had eaten all the salmon. Then he hit the Stump with stones, and turned it all over with his lever until the Stump was broken. It was quite rotten. He found a few small

---

hō′g·igat lē′mᴇdēl hē′tg·ê, aʟ hwîl k·′ē′ an-mᴇ-lē′mx·t aʟ 1
like singing he said, at being then making a song of

"sä′lᴇbᴇʟ!" K·′ē ʟa g·amʟ an-dâ′lᴇptg·ê, k·′ē sᴇ-hina′qt 2
"steam it in a hole." Then when hot the hole for steaming, then he made leaves of skunk-cabbage

aʟ dᴇm hâ′yaᴇm sä′lᴇpt. K·′ēt hadîx·-qō′tsʟ mᴇlē′t. K·′ē 3
to (fut.) use of steaming. Then lengthwise he cut the steel-head salmon. Then

txa-lē-ba′ʟt aʟ lax-ō′ʟ an-sä′lᴇp. Q′ai′yîm d′āʟ an-sä′lᴇpt 4
all on he spread on on top of hole for steaming. Close by was the hole for steaming

aʟ awa′aʟ am-hä′ts'. K·′ēt k·si-gō′uʟ q′apʟ mᴇlē′t. K·′ē 5
at the proximity of a stump. Then out he took the end of the steel-head salmon. Then

hē′tg·ê aʟ am-hä′ts': "Nō′mdzîk·s, hāts';" dēya′, at sä′wuʟ 6
he said to the stump: "You must envy me, stump;" thus he said, he shook

mᴇlē′t. K·′ē huX iē′êt aʟ sᴇ-hina′qt aʟ dᴇm wâ′ôst. Nʟ 7
the steel-head salmon. Then again he went to make leaves of skunk cabbage to (int.) his dish. That

qalä′nt, k·′ē lē-gä′îksguʟ am-hä′ts' aʟ an-sä′lᴇpʟ mᴇlē′t. 8
after, then on crawled the stump on the hole for steaming the steel-head salmon.

K·′ē lō-ya′ltkᵘt aʟ dᴇm yō′ôxkᵘt. Gwinä′dēʟ, lē-d′ä′ʟ 9
Then he returned to (fut.) eat. Behold, on sat

am·hä′ts' aʟ lax-an-sä′lᴇpt. K·′ē q′aqt (aʟ) wī-yē′tkᵘt hwîl 10
the stump at on the hole for steaming. Then he opened his mouth with crying

hwî′lʟ dᴇm g·ē′îpt. K·′ēt gō′uʟ gan, k·′ēt qē′mᴇgant 11
he did so (fut.) his food. Then he took a stick, then he turned over with lever

wī-am-hä′ts'. Gwinä′dēʟ, dzaʟ am-hä′ts' dᴇm g·ē′îptg·ê. K·′ēt 12
the great stump. Behold, he ate all the stump (fut.) his food. Then

kᵘʟē-ax·′o′x·ʟ am-hä′ts'g·ê aʟ lô′ôp qanʟ k′uʟ-qam-qē′mᴇgant. 13
all over he hit the stump with stones and about only he turned it over with lever.

K·′ē g·usgwa′ᴇʟ ga·ng·ê am-hä′yîx. K·′ēt hwîthwa′ʟ k′ōpᴇ- 14
Then was broken the stick well rotten. Then he found small

pieces of fresh salmon.   He put these into his mouth and he was very
hungry while doing so.

13. He went on toward the sea and entered the house of the Grizzly
Bear.   He asked him to join him in catching halibut, but the Grizzly
Bear said that he had no bait.   Txä′msEm replied, "We will use our
own bodies as bait; we will use our testicles."   He carried the tail of
the steel-head salmon.   Txä′msEm went down to the water and took
the canoe of the Grizzly Bear.   While he was doing so, the Bear rose
and went into the canoe, and they started for the fishing bank.   Now
they reached it, and Txä′msEm pretended to cut off his penis and to
tie it on to his hook for bait.   The Grizzly Bear saw the act, but was
afraid to do the same.   He was surprised at what he saw Txä′msEm
doing.   The latter urged him, saying, "Go on, do the same;" but the

1   gatEptē′tgum   k·sa-hâ′n.   K·′ēt   lō-d′ā′tElt   aL   ts′Em-ā′qt   aL
       pieces of   fresh salmon.   Then   in he put it   at   in   his   and
                                                                                                        mouth

2   sEm-Xda′x·t   aL   hwî′ltg·ê.
       very hungry   and   he did so.

3   13. K·′ē   ha′ts′îk·sem   huX   iē′êt   aL   anō-lax-mô′ônL   qâ′ôt.
             Then   once more   again   he went   to   toward on   sea   he went.

4   K·′ē   ts′ēnt   aL   hwîlpL   lig·′ē′Ensk".   K·′ēt   sä′lîx·L   lig·′ē′Ensk"
      Then   he entered   at the house of the grizzly bear.   Then   he bade   the grizzly bear

5   aL   dEm   ig·a′t.   "AqL-nā′Em,"   dēya′L   lig·′ē′Ensk".   "DEm
       to   (fut.)   catch   "With-   bait we,"   thus said   the grizzly bear.   "(Fut.)
                         halibut.   out

6   lEp-hwa′yîmL   dEm   nā′Em,"   dēya′s   Txä′msEm.   "DEm   nā′Em
       selves   we find   (fut.)   our bait,"   thus said   Txä′msEm.   "(Fut.)   our bait

7   g·a′lpnōm."   K·′ē   k′uL-yu′kdēL   wī-La′tsxL   mElē′tg·ê.   NLk·′ē
       our testicles."   Then   about he carried   the   tail of   the steel-head   Then
                                                        great   salmon.

8   siyâ′ôtk"s   Txä′msEm   at   iaga-gō′uL   māLL   lig·′ē′Ensk".
       started   Txä′msEm   to   down take   the canoe of   the grizzly bear.
                                          to sea

9   K·′ē   haldEm-ba′xL   lig·′ē′Ensk"   aL   hwîls   Txä′msEm.   K·′ē
      Then   rose   the grizzly bear   at   he did so   Txä′msEm.   Then

10   uks-hē′tk"dēt   aL   an-ī′g·a.   K·′ē   La   lē-g·a′ôdēt,   k·ēt   sa-q′ō′tsL
       out to they stood   to   the place of   Then   (perf.) on   they were   then   off he cut
       sea   halibut fishing.   there,

11   lEp-gan-dEdē′lîst   lEp-sma′x·tg·ê.   K·′ēt   lē-da′k·LL   naxt,   k·ēt
       his   penis   his   flesh.   Then   on he tied   his bait,   then
       own   own

12   g·a′aL   lig·′ē′Ensk".   K·′ē   xpEdz′a′Xt   aL   dEm   dē-hwî′lt.
       saw it   the grizzly bear.   Then   he was afraid   at   (fut.)   also he does
                                                                                              so.

13   Lō-sanā′Lk"t   hwîls   Txä′msEm.   K·′ē   hä′q′als   Txä′msEm:
       He was astonished   he did so   Txä′msEm.   Then   urged him   Txä′msEm:

14   "Gwô′ôm,   laô′n   dē-hwî′lEn!"   K·′ē   sEmgal   xpEdz′a′xL
       "Go ahead,   to you   also   do it!"   Then   very   afraid was

Grizzly Bear was afraid to do so. Then Txä′msEm pushed his knife along the canoe, handing it to the Bear. Now the Bear cut off his penis, and he fainted. When he felt that he was dying, he made a rush at Txä′msEm, trying to kill him, but Txä′msEm jumped into the water and dived. He clung to the bow of the canoe, and when he knew that the Bear was dead, he boarded the canoe again. He went ashore and stepped up to the Bear's wife.

He put stones into the fire and told the female Grizzly Bear to swallow the hot stones. He said that the wives of those who do not catch anything must do so, and she was to do so, because her husband had not caught any halibut. The chieftainess trusted him. Txä′msEm took up the stones with tongs. He told her to open her

---

lig·′ē′Ensk^{u}g·ê	aL	dEm	dē-hwî′lt.	K·′ēt	wusEn-ma′gas	1
the grizzly bear	at	(fut.)	also he does so.	Then	along put	

Txä′msEm	ha-LEbē′îsk^u	aL	dEm	dē-hwî′lL	lig·′ē′Ensk^u	La	2
Txä′msEm	a knife	to	(fut.)	also do so	the grizzly bear	(perf.)	

hwî′ltg·ê.	K·′ē	dēt-q′ō′tsL	lig·′ē′Ensk^{u}L	La	gan-dEdē′lîst.	K·′ē	3
he did so.	Then	also cut	the grizzly bear	(past)	his penis.	Then	

nô′ôL	lig·′ē′Ensk^u.	Lat	baqL	dEm	hwîl	nô′ôt,	k·′ē	4
he was dying	the grizzly bear.	When	he felt	(fut.)	being	he dies,	then	

wusEn-hē′tk^{u}t	aL	dEm	dzak^{u}s	Txä′msEm.	K·′ēt	uks-sō′ôksk^{u}s	5
along he rushed	to	(fut.)	kill	Txä′msEm.	Then	out of canoe dived	

Txä′msEm	ts′Em-a′k·s.	K·′ēt	g·îldEp-da′lbîk·sk^{u}L	g·its′ä′gaL	6
Txä′msEm	in water.	Then	under he clung	the bow of	

māl.	K·′ē	Lat	hwîlā′x·L	hwîl	nô′ôL	lig·′ē′Ensk^u,	k·′ē	7
the canoe.	Then	when	he knew	being	dead	the grizzly bear,	then	

ha′ts′îk·sEm	huX	maxk^{u}t	aL	ts′Em-mā′l.	K·′ē	tsagam-hē′tk^{u}t.	8
once more	again	he boarded	at	in the canoe.	Then	to shore he stood.	

K·′ē	bax-iä′êt	aL	awa′aL	nak·sL	lig·′ē′Ensk^u.	9
Then	up he went	to	the proximity of	the wife of	the grizzly bear.	

K·′ē	txä′ldEL	lô′ôp.	K·′ē	hēt	dEmt	g·ē′ipL	hana′gam	10
Then	he put into the fire	stones.	Then	he said	(fut.)	eats	the female	

lig·′ē′Ensk^u	g·a′mg·îm	lô′ôpg·ê.	K·′ēt	māLt	g·ap-hwîla	11
grizzly bear	hot	stones.	Then	he told	really	

hwî′lL	nak·sL	ax-mō′gut,	aL	hwîl	ax-mō′k^{u}L	nak·sL	12
does so	the wife of	not catching,	because		not caught	the husband of	

hana′gam	lig·′ē′Ensk^u.	K·′ē	ax′iä′ksk^{u}L	sîg·idEmna′qg·ê.	13
the female	grizzly bear.	Then	trusted	the chieftainess.	

K·′ēt	hāk^{u}Ls	Txä′msEm	lô′ôpg·ê	aL	gant.	K·′ēt	gun-q′a′kL	14
Then	took up with tongs	Txä′msEm	stones	with	sticks.	Then	he caused her to open	

mouth and he put the hot stones into it. Then she tumbled about, and Txä′msEm hit her all over while she was doing so until she was dead. He walked down at once and took the Bear that he had killed first out of the canoe. He cut him first, and then his wife. Both the Bears were dead. He stayed there for many days eating. When he had eaten all the provisions of the Bear, he left again, not knowing where he went.

14. Then he went out of the woods and came to a house, the house of Little Pitch, who was rich, and lived there with his wife. Then Little Pitch invited him in and he ate. When he was satiated, he slept. Then he said that they would go to catch halibut. Little Pitch was willing, and said to him, "It is not good for me to be out after sunrise.

---

1 sig·idEmna′qg·ê. K·′ēt lō-ma′gaL g·a′mg·îm lô′ôp. K·′ē
the chieftainess.   Then   in he put   hot   stones.   Then

2 k′uL-qaba′ksk°L sîg·idEmna′qg·ê. K·′ēt k°Lē-ia′tss Txä′msEm,
about tumbled,   the chieftainess.   Then   all hit her over   Txä′msEm,

3 La k′uL-qaba′ksk°t. K·′ē nô′ôt. Hwîl k·′ē iaga-iē′êt.
while about she tumbled.   Then   she died.   At once   down he to sea went.

4 NLk·′ēt uks-gō′uL wī-lig·′ē′Ensk°L Lē k·s-qâ′gum dza′k°det.
Then   out he took   the great grizzly bear   (perf.)   first   he had killed.

5 K·′ē bELba′Lt, qanL huX k·′ä′guL. T′Epxä′tL lig·′ē′Ensk°
Then   he spread them,   and   also   one.   Two   grizzly bears

6 gul-gadä′wut. K·′ē nak°L yō′ôxk°t, at g·ē′îpt aL wī-hē′ldEL
both were dead.   Then   long   he ate,   he   ate it   for   many

7 sa. K·′ē dzaL wunä′x·L lig·′ē′Ensk°g·ê. K·′ēt huX ksta′qsît;
days.   Then   he ate all   the food of   the grizzly bear.   Then   again   he left;

8 q′asbasa-iä′êt.
astray   he went.

9 14. K·′ē huX na-ba′xt aL k·′ēlL hwîlp; hwîlps Lgo-sg·a′n.
Then   again   out of woods ran he   to   one   house;   the house of   little pitch.

10 Ama hwî′l qanL nak·st lō-bagadē′l. K·′ē hē-yukL
Rich   was he   and   his wife   inside two.   Then   began

11 wô′ôtk°s Lgo-sg·a′n lâ′ôt aL ama yō′ôxk°tg·ê. K·′ē ts·äx·t.
invited   little pitch   to him   at   well   he ate.   Then   he was satiated.

12 K·′ē lō-wâ′gôt lâ′ôt. K·′ē hēL dEm ig·a′t aL dEmt
Then   in he slept   in it.   Then   he said   (fut.)   to fish halibut   at   (fut.)

13 mōk°L txôx·. K·′ē saxk°s Lgo-sg·a′n. K·′ē k·s-qâ′gum
catch   halibut.   Then   was willing   little pitch.   Then   first

14 a′lg·îxs Lgo-sg·a′n as Txä′msEm: "Nîg·i ä′mē atsEda
said   little pitch   to   Txa′msEm: "Not good   I   when

I must return while it is still chilly. I shall have enough by that time."
Txä′msɛm replied, "I shall do whatever you say, Chief." Little
Pitch said, "Well!" Then they started for the fish bank. They
fished all night. When the sun rose Little Pitch wanted to go ashore,
but Txä′msɛm said, "I enjoy the fishing. Lie down in the bow of
the canoe and cover yourself with a mat." Little Pitch did so. Then
Txä′msɛm said, "Little Pitch!" "Heh!" he replied. After a while
Txä′msɛm called again, "Little Pitch!" He answered again in a loud
voice. After some time Txä′msɛm called again. Then Little Pitch's
voice was weak. Now Txä′msɛm hauled up his line and paddled home.
He pretended to paddle strongly, but he put his paddles into the water

k·si-gwa′ntkᵘʟ	Lôqs.	Q'aē-gugunä′gamk·s,	k·'ē	huX	k·'a′tsguē.	1
ont	rises	the sun. Still	chilly,	then	again	I land.

Āmʟ	qapē′iʟ	mâ′guēɛ."	K·'ē	a′lg·îxs	Txä′msɛm:	"Lîg·i-agō′ʟ	2
A good	number	I catch."	Then	said	Txä′msɛm:	"Whatever

dɛm	hē′nîst,	sɛm'â′g·ît,	dɛm	hwî′lēɛ."	K·'ē	hēs	Lgo-sg·a′n:	3
(fut.)	you say,	chief,	(fut.)	I do."	Then	said	little pitch:

"Ām!"	K·'ē	sig·â′ôtkᵘdet	aʟ	ig·a′det	dɛm	dɛ-mu′kdel	4
"Well!"	Then	they started	to	fish halibut	(fut.)	they fished

txōx·.	K·'ē	hwî′ldet	aʟ	wî-sa′.	K·'ē	k·si-yu′kʟ	Lô′qsg·ê,	5
halibut.	Then	they did so	at	all day.	Then	out	rose	the sun,

k·'ē	hēs	Lgo-sg·a′n	dɛm	tsagam-g·'ā′ndet.	K·'ē	nîg·i	hēs	6
then	said	little pitch	(fut.)	ashore they go.	Then	no	said

Txä′msɛm:	"Q'aē-hē-yu′kʟ	a′k·sdaʟ	mō′guēɛ.	Q'am-lō-g·ä′ɛʟɛn	7
Txä′msɛm:	"Still beginning	sweet	I catch.	Only in lie down

aʟ	g·ilä′nɛst.	Qōlk·skᵘʟ	sqā′naɛ."	K·'ē	hwîls	Lgo-sg·a′n.	8
in	the bow.	Cover yourself with	a mat."	Then	did so	little pitch.

K·'ē	hēs	Txä′msɛm:	"Lgo-sg·a′n!"	"Gwō!"	Sî-gō′ɛn	9
Then	said	Txä′msɛm:	"Little pitch!"	"Heh!"	After a while

k·'ē	huX	hēs	Txä′msɛm:	"Lgo-sg·â′n!"	K·'ē	huX	10
then	again	said	Txä′msɛm:	"Little pitch!"	Then	again

gwâ′ôtkᵘs	Lgo-sg·a′n;	ama	gwâ′ôtkᵘt.	K·'ēʟ	huX	ä′êskᵘs	11
answered	little pitch;	well	he answered.	Once	more	called

Txä′msɛm.	K·'ē	alî′skᵘʟ	hēs	Lgo-sg·a′n.	K·'ēt	sa′g·îs	12
Txä′msɛm.	Then	weakly	said	little pitch.	Then	hauled up

Txä′msɛmʟ	ig·a′t.	Hwîl	k·'ē′	hwäx·t.	Tsagam-hwā′x·t.	13
Txä′msɛm	his hook and line.	At once	he paddled.	Ashore he paddled.

K·'ē	nî′g·i	hō′g·îxʟ	hwäx·t,	haʟi-g·â′ôt'ɛntʟ	hwäx·t.	Aʟ	14
Then	not	really	he paddled,	edge-ways he put	his paddle.	At

sɛm-dax-g·a′dɛm	hwäx·t,	k·'ē	bēkᵘʟ	hwî′ltg·ê.	K·'ēt	15
very strongly	he paddled,	then	he lied	he did so.	Then

edgewise. Again he called, "Little Pitch!" "Heh!" Little Pitch replied, but his voice was very weak. Then Txä′msEm knew that Little Pitch was dying. Behold, pitch came out and ran over the halibut where Little Pitch died. Therefore the halibut is black on one side.

That is the end of another adventure of Txä′msEm. He always ate all the food of the chiefs. He killed two chiefs, Grizzly Bear and Little Pitch.

15. He did another thing. He found the town of the air. He saw houses, and heard people saying, "The chief is coming," but he did not see anyone. A man said to him, "Enter the house of the chief." Then he entered. He walked proudly and erect. Behold, a mat was being spread for him on one side of the house. Txä′msEm sat down on it. Behold, a box opened of itself and salmon came out

---

1 ētkᵘs   Lgo-sg·a′n: "Lgo-sg·â′n!"   "Gū!"   ts′ōsk·L   am-hē′t.   K·′ēt
   he   little piteh: "Little pitch!"   "Heh!"   little   voice.   Then
   called

2 hwîlā′x·s   Txä′msEm   La   nô′ôs   Lgo-sg·a′n.   Gwinā′dē,   sg·an
   knew   Txä′msEm   (perf.) dead   little pitch.   Behold,   pitch

3 La   ā′d′îk·skᵘt   aL   lax-ō′L   txōx·,   La   nô′ôs   Lgo-sg·a′n.
   (perf.)   came   at   on top of   the   when   died   little pitch.
                                                       halibut,

4 NLqan   hwîlL   txōx·   stEx-t′ō′tskᵘL   an-stô′ôt   gō′Entsē.
   Therefore   is   halibut   half black   its one side   now.

5 HuX   sa-ba′xL   k·′ēlL   hwîls   Txä′msEm.   Q′am-dzîdza′LL
   Again   the end of   one   did   Txä′msEm.   Only   he ate all

6 wunē′x·L   sEmg·ig·a′t   an-hwî′ntg·ê.   La   bagadē′lL   sEmg·ig·a′t
   the food   the chiefs   what he did.   (Perf.)   two   chiefs
   of

7 ia′tstg·ê;   lig·′ē′Enskᵘ   qans   Lgo-sg·a′n.
   he killed;   the grizzly   and   little pitch.
                 bear

8 15. HuX   k·′ēlL   hwî′ltg·ê.   K·′ēt   hwaL   ts′apL   ha.   K·sEX-
       Again   one   he did.   Then   he found   the town   the   Only
                                                                  of   air.

9 huwî′lp,   qanL   al′a′lg·îxL   g·at.   Naxna′yît: "A′d′îk·skᵘL
   houses,   and   they   people.   He heard: "There comes
                         talked

10 sEm′â′g·idEst,   hâ′u."   K·′ē   nî′g·ît   g·a′aL   g·aL   hē′tg·ê   lâ′ôt:
    the chief,   hâu."   Then   not   he saw   the man   who   to him:
                                                                                   said

11 "ĀmL   dEm   ts′ēnt   aL   hwîlp,   sEm′â′g·idEst."   K·′ē   ts′ē′ntg·ê.
    "Good   (fut.)   he en-   at   the house,   the chief."   Then   he entered.
                        tered

12 "G·ī,   sEm′â′g·it,   g·ī."   K·′ē   ā′dzîk·sEm   iä′tg·ê.   At   g·ap-hē′t′EnL
    "This   chief,   this   Then   proudly   he walked.   He   really   put up
    way,   way."

13 ts′ā′Eltg·ê.   Gwinā′dēL,   sqā′naE   La   ba′Lt   an-stô′ôL   hwîlp.
    his face.   Behold,   a mat   (perf.)   spread   on the one   the house.
                                                                         side of

14 K·′ē   lē-d′ā′s   Txä′msEm   lâ′ôt.   Gwinā′dēL,   hân,   gwa′lgwa   hân
    Then   on sat   Txä′msEm   on it.   Behold,   salmon,   dried   salmon

of it. A dish walked to the fire all by itself. Txä′msɛm was much astonished. It lay down in front of him. He thought about it while he was eating. When he had finished, he drank. Then cranberries mixed with grease and water came from the corner of the house and placed themselves in front of him. Then a spoon came to him. He took the handle of the spoon, but nobody was holding it. Then he ate. The dish was very small, and he thought (?) (?) (?). Thus thought Txä′msɛm. Then he heard many women laughing near the wall of the house. They said, ''The Giant thinks (?) (?) (?).'' He heard his own name, Giant, mentioned. He rose from the place where he was eating and went to where the women were speaking,

---

| Lᴀ | ā′d′îk·skᵘt. | Lɛp-q′a′qkᵘsL | qal-hē′nɛqg·ê | hwîl | wî′tkᵘL | hân | 1 |
| (perf.) | came. | Self   opened | a box | where | came from | the salmon | |

| qanL | ts′a′k·g·ê. | K·′ē · | t′ɛm-iä′êt | aL | lax-ts′ä′L | lakᵘ | aL | 2 |
| and | a dish. | Then | toward   he the middle walked | at | on edge of | the fire | at | |

| lɛp-gulik·s-haLā′ɛltkᵘtg·ê. | | K·′ē | sɛmt-lō-sanā′aLkᵘs | Txä′msɛm. | 3 |
| by   for itself   working. itself | | Then | very   astonished was | Txä′msɛm. | |

| K·′ē | Lᴀ | sg·it | aL | qa-sä′Xt, | k·′ē | a′lg·îxL | qâ′ôttg·ê. | K·′ē | 4 |
| Then | (perf.) | it lay | in | front of him, | then | spoke | his mind. | Then | |

| Lᴀ | yukt | g·ē′îptg·ê. | K·′ē | Läxt | g·ē′ipt, | k·′ē | ak·st. | K·′ē | 5 |
| (perf.) | he began | he ate it. | After | he finished | eating, | then | he drank. | Then | |

| ā′d′îksL | Lᴀ′yix | amo′ost, | huX | ts′ɛm-qal-hē′nɛq | hwîl | 6 |
| came / | cranberries mixed with grease and water | from the corner, | also | in   box | where | |

| wî′tkᵘtg·ê. | K·′ē | Lᴀ | sg·it | aL | qa-sä′Xt. | K·′ēt | g·i-lɛp-ā′d′îk·skᵘL | 7 |
| it came from. | Then | (perf.) | it lay | in | front of him. | Then | by itself   came | |

| hâ′bix· | aL | awa′as | Txä′msɛm. | K·′ēt | g·ilwul-dā′mL | an-dâ′L | 8 |
| a spoon | to | the proximity of | Txä′msɛm. | Then | beyond he held | the other side of | |

| hâ′bîx·. | K·′ē | nî′g·ît | hwaL | lîg·i-ago′. | K·′ē | yō′ôxkᵘtg·ê | sɛm-Lgō′-gat | 9 |
| the spoon. | Then | not | he found | anything. | Then | he ate | very small considering | |

| ts′ak· | hwîl | ts′ō′osk·t. | NLqan | hētL | qâ′ôtt: | ''Dɛm | 10 |
| the dish | being | too small. | Whereupon | said | his heart: | ''(Fut.) | |

| lîg·î-qak·smā′tēisɛn | nɛ-wā′nt,''[1] | dēya′L | qâts | Txä′msɛm. | NLk·′ē | 11 |
| ·(?) | what you have,'' | thus said | the heart of | Txä′msɛm. | Then | |

| hēL | wi-hē′ldɛm | hanā′q | naxna′yît | aL | g·itsâ′ɛn: | ''Hä+ | hä+.'' | 12 |
| said | many | women | he heard them | at | toward the wall: | ''Ha | ha.'' | |

| ''Dɛm | lîg·î-qak·smā′tē | nɛ-wā′n | sg·ɛgua′sga, | dēya′sɛnL | qâ′ts | 13 |
| ''(Fut.) | (?) | what you have | (?) | says | the heart of | |

| Wī-g·a′t.''[1] | K·′ēt | nɛxna′L | lɛp-hwa′dɛs | Wī-g·a′tg·ê. | K·′ē | 14 |
| Giant.'' | Then he | heard | his   name of own | Giant. | Then | |

| haldɛm-ba′xt | aL | hwîl | yō′ôxkᵘt; | at | qâ′ôL | hwîl | hēL | hā′naq. | 15 |
| he rose | at | where | he was eating; | he | went to | where | spoke | the women. | |

---

[1] This sentence is in Tsimshian dialect.

but he did not find anyone, although they were speaking right in front of him. He did not see them. He went back to the fire and sat down. He was quite out of breath. Then he thought, "I will take these things and eat them outside." He rose and took a bundle of salmon. He ran out of the house, but when he came to the door they dragged him back, and he almost fell down. Then he heard someone saying, "Sit down, Chief Giant." Txä'msEm sat down again. He was quite out of breath. He rose again and dragged the box from which the berries had come toward the fire. Then he was attacked and beaten with sticks, although he did not see a person. The sticks moved of themselves, hitting his body, his head, his hands, and his feet. Then he felt very badly. He went on, not knowing which way to turn.

---

1. K·'ē   nî'g·ît   hwaL   lîg·î-ago'.   Q'ai'yîm   lō-al'a'lg·îxL   ts'ā'Elt.
   Then   not   he found   anything.   Close by   in speaking   face.

2. K·'ē   nî'g·ît   g·a'at.   K·'ē   huX   t'Em-iē'êt.   K·'ē
   Then   not   he saw them.   Then   again   to the middle he walked.   Then

3. huX   d'āt   aL   hwîl   d'ā't.   SEnā'Lqt   aL   hwî'ltg·ê.   K·'ē
   again   he sat down   at   where he had   sat.   He was out of breath   on account of   he did so.   Then

4. lō-a'lg·îxL   qâ'ôts   Txä'msEm: "DEm   ksE-dE-ba'ē   dEm   g·ē'bee,"[1]
   in   spoke   the heart of   Txä'msEm: "Shall   out with I run   (fut.)   I eat,"

5. dē'yaL   qâ'ôt.   Hwîl   k·'ē   haldEm-ba'xt.   At   gō'uL   hwîl
   thus said   his heart.   At once   he rose.   He   took

6. xLEm-da'k·Lk·uL   hē'ldEm   hân.   At   k·si-dE-ba'xt   La   dEm
   a bundle of   many   salmon.   He   out with ran   (perf.)   (fut.)

7. k·si-a'qLk·ut   aL   ā'dz'Ep.   K·'ēt   gulîk·s-q'ä'qdēt.   K·'ē
   out he arrived   at   the door.   Then   back they dragged him.   Then

8. mâdzE-sg·is   Txä'msEm.   K·'ē   huX   hēL   a'lg·îxL   naxna'yit:
   almost lay   Txä'msEm.   Then   also   saying   speaking   he heard:

9. "ĀmL   dEm   d'ā'nEst   sEm'â'g·it   Wî-g·a't."   K·'ē   huX   d'ās
   "Good   (fut.)   sit down   chief   Giant."   Then   again   sat down

10. Txä'msEm,   aL   sEnā'Lqtg·ê.   K·'ē   huX   haldEm-ba'xt.   At
    Txä'msEm,   and   he was out of breath.   Then   again   he rose.   He

11. qâ'ôL   hwîl   lō-d'ā'L   La'yîx   Le   g·ē'bEtg·ê.   At   t'Em-q'ä'qLt.
    went to   where   in lay   berries   he   was eating.   He   toward dragged the middle it.

12. K·'ē   hwîl   sagait-hā'p'aaL   t'an   k·uɪē-hîsya'tst   aL   ganga'n,   aL
    Then   all   together they rushed after him,   who   all over hit him   with   sticks,   and

13. nî'g·ît   g·a'aL   g·at.   Q'am-ba'gait-bEbEsba'tsk·uL   ganga'n   t'an
    not   he saw   a person.   By themselves they were lifted   sticks   which

14. hîsya'tsL   LEpLa'nt,   t'Em-qē'st,   qa-an'ô'nt,   asEsa'et.   K·'ē
    hit   his body,   his head,   his hands,   his feet.   Then

15. sEm-pLa'k·sk·ut   aL   hwî'ltg·ê.   K·'ē   dä'uLt.   Q'asbasa-k'uL-iē'êtg·ê.
    much he was tired   on account of   what he did.   Then   he left.   Astray   about   he went.

---

[1] This sentence is in Tsimshian dialect.

16. Txä′msEm did still another thing. He came to the house where the Deer was living with his wife. There were two persons in the house. Then Txä′msEm sat down and said, "Let us go and cut wood." He called the Deer his brother-in-law. The Deer trusted him, and they went to cut wood. While they were splitting the wood the wedges jumped out all the time. Txä′msEm said to the Deer, "Hold the wedges." He did so. Txä′msEm struck the wedges with his hammer, and said to the Deer, "Come a little nearer to the wedges, friend!" The Deer was afraid; but Txä′msEm again asked him to come nearer, because the wedges were always jumping out. Txä′msEm sang while splitting wood, because he was very glad: "Hôho, hôho,

16. HuX	k·′ēʟ	hwîls	Txä′msEm.	K·′ēt	hwaʟ	hwîlp	hwîl	1
Again	one thing	did	Txä′msEm.	Then	he found	a house	where	

dzôqʟ	wan.	Nak·sʟ	wa′ng·ê	lō-bagadē′lt	aʟ	hwîlp.	K·′ē	2
camped	the deer.	The wife of	the deer	in two persons were	in	the house.	Then

huX	lō-d′ā′s	Txä′msEm	lâ′ôt.	K·′ē	hēs	Txä′msEm,	3
also	in sat down	Txä′msEm	in it.	Then	said	Txä′msEm,

a′lg·îxtg·ê:	"Āmʟ	dEm	sE-â′ʟgum,"	dēya′,	aʟ	xs-q′aʟā′ntkᵘst	4
he spoke:	"Good	(fut.)	we make	firewood,"	thus he said,	and he called him	brother-in-law

aʟ	wan.	K·′ē	ax′iâ′kskᵘʟ	wan.	K·′ē	hwî′ldet,	sE-â′ʟkᵘtg·ê.	5
to	the deer.	Then	trusted	the deer.	Then	he did so,	he firewood, made

K·′ē	ʟa	yukt	guXgu′Xdēʟ	lakᵘ,	k·′ē	gwa′nEm-k·si-gEsgō′sʟ	6
Then	(perf.)	while	splitting	firewood,	then	always out jumped

lēt.	Nʟqan	hēs	Txä′msEm	aʟ	wa′ng·ê:	"Ām	mE	dEm	7
the wedges.	Therefore	said	Txä′msEm	to	the deer:	"Good	you	(fut.)

dExdô′gôʟ	lēt,"	dēya′	aʟ	wan.	K·′ē	hwîʟʟ	wan,	8
take hold of	the wedges,"	thus he said	to	the deer.	Then	did so	the deer,

dExdô′gôʟ	lēt.	K·′ēt	ôx·s	Txä′msEmʟ	lēt	aʟ	hē′tg·ê:	9
taking	the wedges.	Then	struck	Txä′msEm	the wedge	and	he said:

"Txal-sgE′ren	damxʟ."[1]	K·′ē	xpEdz′a′Xʟ	wa′ng·ê.	K·′ē	hēs	10
"Against it	lie	friend."	Then	was afraid	the deer.	Then	said

Txä′msEm.	At gun-tq′al-sg·i′tg·ê	aʟ	hwîl	gwa′nEm-k·si-gEsgō′sʟ	11
Txä′msEm.	He made against	lie	because	always out jumped

lēt.	Hēs	Txä′msEm	aʟ	hē-yu′kʟ	tguXʟ	lakᵘ.	Lîst	aʟ	12
the wedges.	He said	Txä′msEm		while	splitting	wood.	Singing accompanying work

lō-ama	qâ′ôtt:	13
in good	his heart:

Hô	hō	hô	hō	hî	hî	14

Clapping.

_____

[1] This sentence is in Tsimshian dialect.

hîhî!" When he had said so, he hit the Deer's head. "O, my poor
brother-in-law!" he said when the Deer died. Then he took the Deer
into his canoe. He broke some mussel shells and stuck them into his
body, saying that they were arrowheads. Then he paddled back to
the village singing (?) (?) (?). Then the Deer's wife went down,
and Txä′msem showed her where the arrow points were sticking in
the Deer's blanket. The woman believed him. They carried up the
Deer which Txä′msem had murdered. Then he killed the Deer's wife
also. He stayed at the house and ate them. He had killed them for
this purpose.

17. Then he came to the house of Smoke-hole. The house was at
the foot of a mountain. He entered. The chief said to his grand-

---

1 Sa-ba′xʟ   hē′tg·ê,   k·′ēt   ia′tsʟ   t′ɛm-qē′sʟ   wan.   "Aiawa′s
  It was finished he said,   then he   hit   the head of   the deer.   "Oh,

2 q′aʟā′nēē   gua′!"   dēya′   aʟ   ʟa   nô′ôʟ   wa′ng·ê.   K·′ēt   lôgôm-gō′ôʟ
  my brother- Oh, poor he said at (perf.) died   the deer.   Then   into   he took
  in-law!   one!"

3 wa′ng·ê   aʟ   ts′ɛm-mā′l.   K·′ē   dôqʟ   q′am-g·usgua′sɛm   hā′gun.
  the deer   in   in the   Then   he took only   broken   large mus-
                canoe.   sels.

4 Kᵘʟē-ax·′â′yit.   K·′ēt   lō-ma′ksaant   aʟ   ʟɛpʟa′nt.   Ma′ʟdɛl   hawu′l
  All he struck it. Then   in he stuck it   in   his body.   He told that arrows
  over   were

5 lâ′ôt.   K·′ē   hwāx·t   aʟ   lō-ya′ltkᵘtg·ê: " Max-Lig·itwä′ltkᵘ
  in it.   Then   he   while he returned: "All
                paddled

6 t′ēn   wulä′kdɛm   qans   dā′nɪxʟē.   Hē′i,   hi′i,   hi′i.¹"   K·′ē
            and   my   Hē′i,   hi′i,   hi′i."   Then
                      friend.

7 iaga-iē′ʟ   nak·sʟ   wa′ng·ê.   K·′ēt   gun-g·a′adɛs   Txä′msɛm
  down went   the wife the deer.   Then   made   her see   Txä′msɛm
             of

8 hwîl   lō-ma′qskᵘʟ   wun   hawu′l   aʟ   gula′s   lɛp-nē′tg·ê.
  where in   struck   the   arrows   in   his blanket himself.
                       points of

9 K·′ē   sɛm-hō′tkᵘsʟ   hana′qg·ê.   K·′ē   bax-gō′dɛʟ   wa′ng ê.   ʟa
  Then   believed him   the woman.   Then   up they took the deer.   (Perf.)

10 su-g·a′dɛs   Txä′msɛm.   K·′ē   huX   dē-dza′kᵘʟ   na′k·stg·ê.   K·′ē
   murdered   Txä′msɛm.   Then   also he killed   his   Then
                                                  wife.

11 huX   tq′al-lō-dzô′qst   aʟ   hwî′lpg·ê,   aʟ   yō′ôxkᵘt,   qan
   also   against in he stayed at   the house,   and   he ate,   there-
                                                             fore

12 hwî′ltg·ê.
   he had done
   it.

13   17. HuX   hwā′iʟ   hwîlps   Am′ala′.   Hētkᵘʟ   hwî′lpg·ê   aʟ
        Again   he found the house Smoke-hole. It stood   the house   at
                        of

14 dēp-sqanē′st.   K·′ē   ts′ēnʟ   lâ′ôt.   K·′ē   hē′tg·ê: "Qâ′ôʟ,   qâ′ôʟ,
   the of a   Then   he   in it.   And   he spoke: "Go for   go for
   foot mountain.   entered   him,   him,

---

¹ This sentence is in Tsimshian dialect.

children, "Attack him, because he steals all the good things he sees."
Txä′msEm took off the bark of an alder and chewed it.   Then he entered
the house of Smoke-hole, intending to steal his bow, which was ornamented with abalone shells.   He transformed himself into a raven and
took the bow.   Smoke-hole said to his door, "Shut, Door!"   Then
Txä′msEm was unable to leave the house.   They tried to catch him,
intending to kill him.   He cried, "Qa, qa, qa, qa!"   Smoke-hole said
to his smoke hole, "Shut!" and the smoke hole caught Txä′msEm's
neck.   He was dead, and his body was hanging in the smoke hole.
Txä′msEm pretended to be dead.   Then Smoke-hole made a fire.   Then
Txä′msEm took his own voice and put it in the woods, in a bluff behind
Smoke-hole's house.   There it made an echo, crying, "Miserable chief,
what are you doing?   You are a chief and you eat the excrements of a

dEm	lē′lukst	aL	am′ā′ma	lîg·i-hwî′lL	g·a′atg·ê.″	NLk·′ē 1
(fut.)	he steals	of	good	things	he sees.″	Then he
k·s-qâ′ôqt	sā-gō′dEl	māsL	lōx·,	at	qē′Entg·ê.	NLk·′ē huX 2
first	off took	the bark of	alder	and	chewed it.	Then again
ts′ēnt	aL	hwîlps	Am′ala′.	K·′ēt	k·si-dE-ba′xL	ha-Xda′k^u 3
he entered	at	the house of	Smoke-hole.	Then he	out with ran	the bow
txa-bElā′da.	K·′ēt	lō-Lô′ôtk^uL	qāk,	Lat	gō′uL	ha-Xda′ks 4
all abalone shell.	Then he	transformed himself into	the raven,	he (perf.)	took	the bow of
Am′ala′g·ê.	"Hā′k′waxan,	ā′dz′Ep!"	dēya′s	Am′ala′.	NLk·′ē 5
Smoke-hole.	"Shut so that it can not be moved	door!″	thus said	Smoke-hole.	Then
aqL-k·si-yô′xk^us	Txä′msEm.	K·′ē	hwî	k·′ē	lō-tk′o-yô′xk^ut aL 6
with- out to go out	Txä′msEm.	At once		in around	he in followed
hwî′lptg·ê	aL	dEm	dzak^ut.	K·′ēt	lō-Lô′ôtk^us	Txä′msEm qāq 7
his house	to	(fut.)	kill him.	Then	transformed himself	Txä′msEm raven
aL	hē′tg·ê:	"Qa,	qa,	qa,	qa."	K·′ē a′lg·îxs Am′ala′: 8
and	said:	"Qa,	qa,	qa,	qa."	Then said Smoke-hole:
"Ha′k^uwaxan,	gan-ala′!"	K·′ēt	hā′tsEL	t′Em-lā′nîx·s	Txä′msEm 9
"Shut,	boards smoke of hole!"	Then	hit	the neck of	Txä′msEm
gan-alā′g·ê.	K·′ē	nô′ôs	Txä′msEm.	Lō-d′Ep-iax′ia′qL	g·a′dEt aL 10
the boards of the smoke hole.	Then	was dead	Txä′msEm.	In down hung	his body in
ts′Em-ala′.	Hîs-nô′ôtk^uL,	hwî′ltg·ê	Txä′msEm.	K·′ēt	sE-mē′Ls 11
in the smoke hole.	He pretended to be dead,	he did	Txä′msEm.	Then	he burn made
Am′ala′L	lak^u.	K·′ēt	gōs	Txä′msEm	lEp-a′lg·îxt.	K·′ēt 12
Smoke-hole	a fire.	Then	took	Txä′msEm	his speech. own	Then
qaldîx·-ma′gat	aL	ts′Em-biā′qL	qaq′alā′ns	Am′ala′g·ê.	At 13
to the rear of the house he put it	at	in bluff	behind the house of	Smoke-hole.	He
sE-gul′ā′datg·ê:	"Qâ′gEm	tsE	dē-lEbElt-hwî′lEnEstä′,	tEdē 14
made echo:	"Miserable	when	also against you do,	when

raven!" Then Smoke-hole was ashamed.   Therefore he said to his
smoke hole, "Open!"   It opened, and Txä'msᴇm flew away, crying,
"Qa, qa, qa, qa!"   He was almost dead.   He let the chewed alder juice
run out of his mouth, pretending that blood was coming out of it.
When Smoke-hole saw the alder juice he really believed that it was
blood, and then he told his smoke hole to open entirely.   He said,
"Be ashamed of yourself, Txä'msᴇm, great slave!   You were trying
to steal again."   Txä'msᴇm could not steal this time.

18. He went on, and came to a house where a man lived, near the
beach.   Then the Giant said: "I am your friend."   The person replied,
"That is good."   The beach in front of the house was full of seals.
The Giant ate them all during two nights.   Then he killed his friend.
He finished all the seals in front of the house, and he ate them all.

---

1 sᴇm'â'g·idᴇn   aʟ   x-k'wa'dzᴇm   qāq."   K·'ē   dzâqʟ   qâts   Am'ala'.
   you are a chief   eat- excrements   raven."   Then   was   the   Smoke-hole.
                        ing   ashamed heart of

2 Nʟqan   hē'tg·ê: "Q'ā'gan,   gan-alâ'."   K·'ē   q'aqʟ   ala'.   K·'ē
   Therefore he said: "Open,   board smoke   Then   opened   the   Then
                                     of hole."   smoke hole.

3 g·ᴇba'yuqs   Txä'msᴇm   aʟ   hē'tg·ê: "Qa,   qa,   qa,   qa."
   flew   Txä'msᴇm   and   said: "Qa,   qa,   qa,   qa."

4 Mâdzᴇ-nô'ôt.   K·si-yô'xkᵘʟ   iʟä'ᴇʟ   ts'ᴇm-ā'qt.   Hîs-huwî'ltst
   Almost he was   Out   went   blood   in   his   He pretended
   dead.   mouth.

5 hwî'ltg·ê.   K·'ēt   g·a'as   Am'ala'   iʟä'êg·ê,   k·'ē   sᴇm-hō'tkᵘst.
   he did so.   Then   saw   Smoke-hole the blood,   then   he believed.

6 Nʟqan   hēt   gun-q'ā'kʟ   ala'g·ê.   "Dsâgan,   wi-xa'ᴇ,   ʟa   dᴇm
   Therefore he said caused to open the   "Shame you, great slave, that   would
                                smoke hole.   (perf.) (fut.)

7 huX   lē'lukst."   Qō'sᴇs   Txä'msᴇmʟ   dᴇm   lē'lukst.
   again   steal."   Could not Txä'msᴇm   (fut.)   steal.

8   18. Nʟk·'ē   huX   iä'êt.   Nʟk·'ēt   hwaʟ   hwîlp   tsē   dzôqʟ
       Then   again   he went.   Then he   found   a house where   lived

9 g·at   aʟ   lax-ts'ä'ʟ   ak·s.   Nʟk·'ē   hēs   Wī-g·a't: "Dᴇm
   a man   at   on the   the   Then   said   Giant: "Will be
            edge of   water.

10 an-dā'mqʟguē   nē'ᴇn."   Nʟk·'ē   tgōnʟ   hēʟ   g·a'tg·ê: "Ām,"
   my friend   you."   Then   this   said   the person: "It is
                                                                    good."

11 dē'yaʟ   g·a'tg·ê.   Mētkᵘʟ   qa-g·ä'uʟ   g·at   aʟ   ēlx.   Nʟne'ʟ
   thus   the person.   Full was   the front of   the   of   seal.   That
   said   the house of   person

12 huX   g·ē'îps   Wī-g·a't.   G·'ē'lp'ᴇʟ   axkᵘ,   nʟk·'ēt   dzaʟt.   Nʟk·'ēt
   again   ate it   Giant.   Two   nights,   then   he ate it   Then he
                                                                  all.

13 sᴇ-g·ā'dᴇs   Wī-g·a't   an-dā'mqʟk"t.   Sᴇm-qû'ôdᴇʟ   ēlx   dât   aʟ
   murdered   Giant   his friend.   Very he finished   the   that   at
                                                               seal   was

14 hwîlpʟ   g·a'tg·ê.   Dzäls   Wī-g·a't.   Nʟk·'ē   a'd'îk·skᵘʟ   dᴇm   hwîl
   the house the person. He ate it Giant.   Then   he came   (fut.)   being
   of   all

Now he was hungry again, and he used the canoe of the person whom
he had killed. Only the man's canoe and harpoon remained. The Giant
used them. Then he speared seals, and caught four. He returned
and went ashore. He took the seals out of the canoe, and began cutting wood. Then he built a fire, and placed stones in it in order to
heat them. Then he put the seals on a pile of hot stones. He cooked
the four seals, and covered them with skunk-cabbage leaves. The
Giant then raised the cover and took out a seal, which he ate
when it was cooked. Then he stretched out his hand and took out
another seal. There was a stump of a tree near by. The Giant held
the seal in his hands and said to the stump, "Don't you envy me,
Stump?" Then he went into the woods. Meanwhile the Stump rose
and sat down on the hole in which the seals were steaming. The seals

---

| Xdax·s | Wī-g·a′t. | NʟK·′ēt | hâx·ʟ | māĴʟ | g·a′tg·ê | ʟa | g·i-nô′ôʟ | 1 |
| hungry | Giant. | Then | he used | the canoe of | the person | (perf.) | already dead | |

| g·a′tg·ê. | K·sax-mā′lʟ | g·îna-g·â′ôt | qanʟ | sgan-dā′pxʟt. | NʟK·′ēt | | 2 |
| the person. | Only his canoe | behind was | and the | shaft of his harpoon. | Then | | |

| hâx·s | Wī-g·a′t. | NʟK·′ēt | lɛp-g·a′ʟkᵘʟ | ēlx. | Txalpx | daa′qʟgut. | 3 |
| used it | Giant. | Then he | him-self | speared | seals. Four | he got. | |

| NʟK·′ē | lō-ya′ltkᵘt. | NʟK·′ē | k·′atskᵘt. | NʟK·′ēt | uks-dô′qʟ | 4 |
| Then | he return-ed. | Then | he landed. | Then | out he took | |

| ēlx. | NʟK·′ē | yukʟ | sa-â′ʟkᵘt. | NʟK·′ē | dâ′ʟept. | ʟa | 5 |
| the seals. | Then | he began mak-ing | fire-wood. | Then | he built a fire of stones and sticks. | When | |

| lɛmla′mk·ʟ | lô′ôp, | nʟK·′ēt | lē-d·ā′ʟʟ | ēlx | aʟ | lax-an-sā′lɛp. | 6 |
| hot the | stones, | then | on he laid | the seals | on | on the pile of hot stones. | |

| TxalpxʟL | ēlx | sā′lɛpdētg·ê. | Yîna′qʟ | lē-ha′-baxt. | NʟK·′ē | ʟa | 7 |
| Four | seals | he cooked. | Skunk-cab-bage was | on for cover. | Then | (perf.) | |

| lē-d·ā′t. | NʟK·′ē | tgōn | hwîls | Wī-g·a′t, | ba′tsdɛʟ | ha′-baxtg·ê. | 8 |
| on it was. | Then | this | did | Giant, | he lifted | his cover. | |

| NʟK·′ēt | k·si-gō′ʟ | ēlx. | NʟK·′ēt | g·îpt | ʟa | a′nukst. | NʟK·′ēt | 9 |
| Then | out he took | a seal. | Then | he ate it | (perf.) | done. | Then | |

| huX | nakᵘst. | NʟK·′ēt | huX | gōʟ | k·′ēlʟ | ēlx. | D·āʟ | 10 |
| again | he stretched out his hand. | Then | again | he took | one | seal. | There was | |

| am-hā′ts′ | aʟ | awa′at. | ʟā | k·uʟ-yo′gus | Wī-g·a′t | k·′ēlʟ | ēlx, | 11 |
| a stump | in | his proximity. | When | about he carried | Giant | one | seal, | |

| tgōnʟ | hēt | aʟ | am-hā′ts′g·ê: | "No′mdzîk·s | hāts′. | Nô′mdzîk·s | 12 |
| this | he said | to | the stump: | "Envious | stump. | Envious | |

| hāts′." | NʟK·′ē | iä′êt | ʟā | qalā′nt. | NʟK·′ē | g·în-hē′tkᵘʟ | am-hā′ts′. | 13 |
| stump." | Then | he went | to | the rear of the house. | Then | rose | the stump. | |

| NʟK·′ē | lē-d·ā′tkᵘʟ | an-sā′lɛps | Wī-g·a′t. | Tq′al-k·slaXʟ | ēlx. | 14 |
| Then | on he sat | the hole for steaming of | Giant. | Against it was under him | the seal. | |

were right under him. Now the Giant returned, carrying leaves of
the skunk-cabbage. When he saw the Stump sitting on his seals, he
cried. He was very much troubled, because he was hungry. Then
he took a stick and dug the ground. He cried while he was digging.
He found a little bit of meat and ate it. He was crying all the time
because he was hungry. He could not do anything.

19. He went on and came to the shore of the sea. There he built a
house. Then he made up his mind what to do. After he had finished
his house, he dressed himself, put up his hair, and fastened his blanket.
He took coal and rubbed it all over his face. He made a dagger and
tied it to his hand. Then he rose, and ran out, saying, " I am sad."
Thus he spoke while he was walking down to the beach. There he saw

---

1 NLk·'ē   lō-ya'ltkᵘs   Wī-g·a't.   Dô'gôL   yîna'q.   NLk·'ēt   g·a'at.
   Then   returned   Giant.   He took   skunk-   Then   he saw it.
                                                  cabbage.

2 K·'ē   wi-yē'tkᵘt   aL   aba'g·askᵘt   aL   Xdax·t.   NLk·'ēt
   Then   he cried   and   he was troubled be-   he was   Then
                                                       cause   hungry.

3 gōL   gan.   NLk·'ēt   wôqL   dz'ä'dz'îk·s.   at   dē-wi-yē'tkᵘL
   he   a stick.   Then   he dug   the ground,   while also crying
   took

4 wôq·'ē·'skᵘt.   NLk·'ēt   huX   hwaL   qasqâ'ô   tgōn.   Ts·ōsk·L
   he was   Then   again   he   a little bit this.   A little
   digging.   found

5 hwa'yît.   K·'ēt   huX   g·îpt   aL   qa'nē-hwîla   wi-yē'tkᵘt.
   he found   Then   again   he ate it at   always   he cried.
   it.

6 Aba'g·askᵘt   aL   Xdax·t.   NLk·'ē   aqL-hwî'lt.
   He was troubled be-   he was   Then   without doing
                   cause   hungry.   anything.

7 19. NLk·'ē   huX   iä'êt.   NLk·'ē   hwaL   lax-ts·ä'L   mô'ôn.
       Then   again   he went. Then   he   on the   the sea.
                                                 found   edge of

8 NLk·'ēt   dzapL   hwîlp.   NLk·'ē   sa-qâ'tkᵘL   qâ'ott   aL   dEm
   Then   he made   a house. Then   he   mind   to   (fut.)
                                            up his
                                            made (mind)

9 hwîl   hwî'lt   La   LēskᵘL   hwîlp,   nLk·'ē   nō'ôtkⁿt.   MEn-dô'gôL
        what   when   he   the house, then   he dressed. Up   he took
        to do   finished

10 qēst.   NLk·'ēt   sag·ait-da'k·Lt.   NLk·'ēt   sag·ait-da'k·L   gula't.
   his hair. Then   together he fast-   Then   together he   his
                      ened it.   fastened   blanket.

11 NLk·'ē   gō'nL   q·am-t'ō'uts.   NLk·'ēt   qä'êlt.   NLk·'ē   d·ä'Lt
   Then   he took   coal.   Then he   rubbed it.   Then   he put it

12 aL   ts·ä'Elt.   NLk·'ēt   dzāpL   t·ontskt.   NLk·'ē   tq·al-da'k·Lt   aL
   on   his face.   Then he   made   a knife.   Then   against he tied it to

13 an'ô'nt.   NLk·'ē   hētkᵘt.   NLk·'ē   k·si-ba'xt.   TgōnL   hē'tg·ē:
   his hand. Then   he stood. Then   out he ran.   This   he said:

14 "Lō-sī'EpkᵘL   qâ'ôdeîst."   Dēya'   aL   iag·a-ba'xt   aL   g·ä'u.
   "In   sick is   my heart."   Thus he while down he ran   to   in front of
                                 said   the house.

a stump. He took it and said, "I caught you." Then he returned.
He entered and put the little stump down in his house.

20. The Giant was sad all the time, because he was hungry and there
was no food in the house. Therefore he resolved what to do.
Early next morning he ran out of the house. Behold, there were
ripples on the water. Salmon and halibut and bullheads and porpoises were swimming about in the water. There were all kinds of
salmon. When the Giant saw this, he said, "Alâ! alâ! alâ! guts'ē'ekᵘ."
Then the salmon said, "Hm!" There was one chief among the
salmon who commanded all the others. He said, "I can not hear what
the chief on shore there is saying;" thus he said to the Giant. Then

---

G·a'at	hwîl	d'āʟ	am-hā'ts'.	NîL	gō'udɛt;	tgōnʟ	hēt	1
He saw	(verbal noun)	there was	a stump.	Then	he took it;	this	he said:	

"Gōdēᴇ	nēnîsdäē,	gōdēᴇ	nēnîsdäē."	Nʟk·'ē	lō-ya'ltkᵘt.	2
"I take	you,	I take	you."	Then	he returned	

NʟK·'ē	ts'ɛnt.	Sg·ī'îL	ʟg·o-am-hā'ts'	aʟ	ts'ɛm-hwî'lpt.	3
Then	he entered.	It lay	the little stump	at	in his house.	

20. Qa'nē-hwîla	sī'ɛpkᵘʟ	qâ'ôts	Wī-g·a't	aʟ	Xdax·t,	qan	4
Always	sick was	the heart of	Giant	on account of	hunger,	there-fore	

hēt	nî'g·i	sg·îL	dɛm	g·ē'bɛt.	NʟK·'ē	sa-gâ'ôtkᵘt	aʟ	dɛm	5
he said	not	there was	(fut.)	his food.	Then	he resolved	to	(fut.)	

hwîla	hēt.	NʟK·'ē	sɛm-hē'ɛʟuk,	k·'ē	k·si-ba'xs	Wī-g·a't.	6
being	say so.	Then	very	early,	then	out ran	Giant.	

Gwinā'dɛʟ,	lax-a'k·s	hwîl	ʟakᵘʟ	ak·s	sagait-qâ'ôdîʟ	hân	7
Behold,	on the water	where	was rippled	the water	together were	salmon	

qanʟ	txox·	qanʟ	mas-q'ayā'it	qanʟ	dzīX.	Wī-hē'lt,	hwîl	8
and	halibut	and	bullhead	and	porpoise.	Many,	all	

lîk·s-g·ig·a'ʟ	hân.	NʟK·'ēt	g·a'as	Wī-g·a't.	Tgōnʟ	hēs	9
kinds of	salmon.	Then	saw it	Giant.	This	said	

Wī-g·a't:	"Alâ',	alâ',	alâ',	guts'ē'ekᵘ,	alâ',	alâ',	alâ',	10
Giant:	"Alâ',	alâ',	alâ',	guts'ē'ekᵘ,	alâ',	alâ',	alâ',	

guts'ē'ekᵘ."	NʟK·'ē	huX	xs-mē'mɛxkᵘʟ	hân:	"Hmm!"	K·âlʟ	11
guts'ē'ekᵘ."	Then	again	said "Hm!"	a salmon:	"Hm!"	One was	

mēnʟ	hâ'ng·ê,	t'an	a'lg·igaʟ	txanē'tkᵘʟ	hwîl	lîk·s-g·ig·a'ʟ	12
the chief of	the salmon,	who	commanded	all	all	kinds of	

hân.	NʟK·'ē	tgōnʟ	hēʟ	sɛm'â'g·idɛm	hân:	"Gwanɛm-nîg·în	13
salmon.	Then	this	said	the chief	salmon:	"Always not I	

naxna'ʟ	hahä'ʟ	sɛm'â'g·ît	g·îlē'lîx·,"	dēya'	as	Wī-g·a'tg·ê.	14
hear	what says	the chief	inland,"	thus he said	to	Giant.	

he called Little Porpoise, saying, "You will be able to hear what the chief on shore is saying." Little Porpoise swam ashore. He was not very large. Then the Giant ran out again and cried, "Alâ! alâ! alâ! guts'ē'ekᵘ." Then the chief of the salmon understood it, because Little Porpoise had told him. He said, "The chief ashore tells us what to do. He says that we salmon shall all swim together." Then the chief of the salmon repeated it, and all the salmon went ashore together. Then all the halibut were left dry on the beach. The Giant ran out of his house carrying a stick. He clubbed them and carried them up to the house. Then he dried some of them and ate others. He was eating all the time. He was a great eater. He ate them all and then he went on.

3a. Now he was very poor. He had no blanket. He was quite

---

1 NʟK·'ēt wô'ôʟ ʟgo-dzī'X: "Nēn dɛm t'an naxna'ʟ häʟ sɛm'â'g·it
Then he | called | little porpoise: | "You | (fut.) | who | hears | what the chief says

2 aʟ g·îlē'lîx·t Wī-g·a't," an-hä'ʟ hâ'ng·ê. NʟK·'ē hagun-g·â'ʟ
at | inland | Giant," | what said | the salmon. | Then | toward was

3 ʟgō-dzī'X. Nî̂g·î wī-t'ē'st. NʟK·'ē huX k·si-ba'xs Wī-g·a't:
little porpoise. | Not | it was large. | Then | again | out ran | Giant:

4 "Alâ', alâ', alâ', guts'ē'ekᵘ, alâ', alâ', alâ', guts'ē'ekᵘ."
"Alâ', | alâ', | alâ', | guts'ē'ekᵘ, | alâ', | alâ', | alâ', | guts'ē'ekᵘ."

5 NʟK·'ē naxna'ʟ sɛm'â'g·idɛm hân ʟät maʟʟ ʟgō-dzī'X:
Then | heard him | the chief | salmon | (perf.) | he told | little porpoise:

6 "Tgōn-gaʟ dɛm hwîlɛm dɛm alâ'tkᵘ-gat nōm."
"This he says | (fut.) | we do | (fut.) | swim in a shoal he says | we will."

7 NʟK·'ē a'lg·îxʟ mēnʟ hân. NʟK·'ē alâ'tkᵘʟ hân. Hwä'i!
Then | spoke | the chief of | the salmon. | Then | swam in a shoal | the salmon. | Well!

8 K'uʟ-g·îna-dô'xt aʟ g·îlē'lîx· txanē'tkᵘʟ txox·. NʟK·'ē k·si-ba'xs
About left they were | at | inland | all | the halibut. | Then | out ran

9 Wī-g·a't yu'kdɛʟ gan. NʟK·'ē q·ax·q·ayā'ant. NʟK·'ēt
Giant | he carried | a stick. | Then | he clubbed them. | Then

10 sagait-wî'lgat lîk·s-g·a'ʟ qabē't. NʟK·'ē gwa'lgus Wī-g·a't
together he carried them | a strange | number. | Then | dried | Giant

11 ʟa qats'ō'ot. NʟK·'ēt g·îpʟ huX qats'ō'ot. Qa'nē-hwîla
some of them. | Then | he ate | again | some. | Always

12 yō'ôxkᵘt, sɛm-ga'lg·a lîk·s-g·a'ʟ q'alga'nt. NʟK·'ē ʟa wi-hē'ʟʟ
he ate, | very | he was a strange | eater. | Then | (perf.) | many

13 saʟ hwîlt. NʟK·'ēt huX dzaʟt. NʟK·'ē qâ'ôdɛt.
days | he did so. | Then | again | he ate it all. | Then | they were finished.

14 3a. NʟK·'ē ā'd'îk·skᵘʟ sɛm-hwîl gwä'êt. Nî̂'g·i gula't
Then | he came | very being | poor. | None | his blanket

naked.　Then he was ashamed.　He took a root and killed many ravens.　After he had caught them he fastened their skins together and put them on.　He went for a long time, and then he saw a dancing blanket hanging in front of him.　He was very glad; he took off his raven blanket and tore it to shreds.　He threw it down and went to take the dancing blanket, but behold, there was nothing but old, withered leaves.　Then the Giant was troubled.　It was no dancing blanket at all, and he cried with a loud voice.　He returned and found the shreds of his raven blanket.　He cried while he was gathering them up.　Then he repaired the raven blanket, making a small blanket out of it, which he put on.

---

sᴇm-k·sax-tsax'ō′tkⁿ.	Nʟk·'ē	dzâqt.	Nʟk·'ēt	k·si-gō′ʟ	hwîst.	1
very　only　he was naked.	Then	he was ashamed.	Then	out　he took	roots.	

Nʟk·'ēt	hukⁿgusîʟ	qāq.	Nʟk·'ē	daa′qʟkᵘʟ	wī-hē′ltt.	Nʟk·'ēt	2
Then	he caught	ravens.	Then	he got	many.	Then	

nē-dē-ts'îpts'ē′ᴇbᴇʟ	annā′st.	Nʟk·'ēt	gulā′t.	Nʟk·'ē	iä′êt;	3
together　he fastened	their skins.	Then	he put it on.	Then he	went;	

ʟa	nakᵘʟ	hwîl	iä′êt,	nʟk·'ēt	g·a′aʟ	hwîl	sqa-iax'ia′qʟ	4
(perf.)	long	(verbal noun)	he went,	then	he saw	(verbal noun)	across the way　hung	

gwīs-halai′t.	Nʟk·'ē	sᴇm-lō-ā′mʟ	qâ′ôtt.	Tgōnʟ	hwîls	Wī-g·a′t.	5
blanket dancing.	Then	very　in good was	his heart.	This	did	Giant.	

Sā-gō′dᴇʟ	gwīs-qā′qt.	Nʟk·'ēt	kᵘʟē-bêsbē′st.	Nʟk·'ē	sā-d'a′tᴇlt.	6
Off he took	blanket raven.	Then	all over he tore it.	Then	off he put it.	

Nʟk·'ē	iä′êt	aʟ	awa′aʟ	gwīs-halai′t.	Gwīnā′dēʟ,	maʟax'â′st.	7
Then	he went	into	the proximity of	blanket dancing.	Behold,	withered old leaves.	

Nʟk·'ē	aba′g·askᵘs	Wī-g·a′t.	Nîg·idē	gwīs-halai′ts	gō′stg·ê.	8
Then	was troubled	Giant.	No	blanket dancing was	this.	

Nʟk·'ē	wī-amhē′s	Wī g·a′t	aʟ	wi-yē′tkⁿt.	Nʟk·'ē	lō-ya′ltkᵘt.	9
Then	shouted	Giant	and	he cried.	Then	he returned.	

K·'ēt	hwaʟ	hwîl	dôxʟ	q'am-bîsbē′sʟ	gwīs-qā′qt.	Nʟk·'ē	10
Then	he found	where	was	only	the torn	blanket raven.	Then	

sagait-dô′qt	qa′ne-hwîla	k'uʟ-wi-yē′tkⁿt.	Nʟk·'ē	yuk	hak·sᴇm	11
together he took it	always	about　he cried.	Then	he began	again	

nē-dē-ts'ᴇpts'ē′ᴇbᴇt.	Nʟk·'ē	huX	ā′d'îk·skⁿt	hwîl	ʟgō-wît'ē′st.	12
together	to make it.	Then	again	it came	where	a little　large.	

Nʟk·'ē	hatsᴇmt	huX	gulā′t.	13
Then	once more	again	he put it on.	

THE STONE AND THE ELDERBERRY BUSH

[Told by Moses]

A little before the Stone gave birth to her child, the Elderberry Bush gave birth to her children. For that reason the Indians do not live many years. Because the Elderberry Bush gave birth to her children first, man dies quickly. If the Stone had first given birth to her children, this would not be so. Thus say the Indians. That is the story of the Elderberry Bush's children. The Indians are much troubled because the Stone did not give birth to her children first, for this is the reason that men die quickly.

LÔ′ÔP QANL SGAN-LÂ′TS

THE STONE AND THE ELDERBERRY BUSH

1 Q'ai-be-yu′kʟ dɛm aqʟkᵘʟ lô′ôpg·ê. Nʟk·'ē aqʟkᵘʟ sgan-lâ′ts.
A little before (fut.) gave birth the stone. Then gave birth the elderberry bush.

2 Nʟk·'ē hwîl k·'ē g·î-k·si-d'ā′t, aʟ hwîl k·s-qâ′ôqʟ aqʟkᵘʟ
At once out it stuck, because first gave birth

3 sgan-lâts. Nɛʟnc′ʟ qan hwîʟʟ alō-g·ig·a′t. Nî′g·i hē′lʟ k·ō′oʟ
the elderberry bush. Therefore do the Indians. Not many years

4 dɛldē′lst aʟ hwîl k·s-qâ′gum aqʟkᵘʟ sgan-lâ′ts. Nîʟ qan hwîʟʟ
they live because first gave birth the elderberry bush. Therefore do

5 g·at t'ēlʟ daXt. K·'ē nîg·iʟ dɛm dē-hwîlt atsɛ lē k·s-qâ′gum
men quickly they die. Then not (fut.) also they do so if (perf.) first

6 aqʟkᵘʟ lô′ôp, dē′yaʟ a′lg·îxʟ alō-g·ig·a′t. Nʟne′ʟ dē-adā′wuqdēt
had given birth the stone, thus says the saying of the Indians. That is the story

7 hwîl sgan-lâ′tsʟ ʟg·ît lâ′ôdet. Nʟk·'ē sɛm-abaxbā′g·askᵘdēt aʟ
about the elderberry bush the children to them. Then much they are troubled

8 hwîl ax-lô′ôp tsɛ k·s-qâ′gum aqʟkᵘt. Nɛʟ qan t'ēlʟ da′Xdēt.
because not the stone first gave birth. Therefore quickly they die.

72

The Porcupine and the Beaver

[Told by Moses]

The Porcupine and the Beaver were friends. They loved each
other. The Beaver used to invite the Porcupine to his house all the
year round. The Porcupine went and entered the Beaver's house.
The house of the Beaver was in the middle of a great lake. The
Beaver liked the water very much, but the Porcupine could not go
into the water because he could not swim; he was afraid he might
perish if his stomach should get full of water. Therefore the Beaver
went to the shore and called the Porcupine. The Beaver came up
twice when going to the place where the Porcupine was sitting on the

---

AX̂T QANL TS'EMĒ'LÎX·

PORCUPINE AND BEAVER

An-dā'mqʟkᵘʟ	aX̂ʟ	ts'Emē'lîx.	Nʟk·'ē	nE-sEpsī'Ep'Endēt.	1
The friend was	the porcupine of	the beaver.	Then	each other they loved.	

Nʟk·'ē	txanē'tkᵘʟ	k'ō'uʟ	hwîl	hwî'ldēt.	Wô'ôʟ ts'Emē'lîx·	2
Then	all	year	they	did so.	It invited the beaver	

aX̂t.	Nʟk·'ē	iä'êʟ	aX̂t,	nʟk·'ē ts'ent	aʟ hwîlpʟ ts'Emē'lîx·.	3
the porcupine.	Then	went	the porcupine,	then he entered	at the house of the beaver.	

Wī-lax-t'a'xg·ê,	nʟk·'ē	sEm-bagait-sē'lukʟ	t'ax	hwîl d'āʟ	hwîlpʟ	4
Large on lake,	then	very right there	on the middle of	the lake where was	the house of	

ts'Emē'lîx·.	NEʟ	q'ap-dē-anâ'gôʟ	ts'Emē'lîx·ʟ	ts'Em-a'k·s.	Nʟk·'ē	5
the beaver.	Then	really on his part liked	the beaver	in the water.	Then	

aqʟ-uks-hwî'lɪ	a'X̂tg·ê,	aʟ hwîl	nî'g·idēt	hwîlā'x·ʟ	dEm ha'dîk·st.	6
no way from land to sea to do	the porcupine,	because	not he knew		(fut.) to swim.	

Nʟne'ʟ	qan	xpets'a'xʟ	a'X̂tg·ê	aʟ ōp tsE nô'ôt,	tsE mē'tkᵘʟ	7
Therefore	was afraid	the porcupine	that else he might die,	if was full of	

ak·s	aʟ	bant	aʟ hwîl	nî̂g·idēt	hwîlā'x·t. Nʟqan tgōnʟ	8
water	in	belly	because	not he knew it.	Therefore this	

hwîlʟ	ts'Emē'lîx·:	tsagam-qâ'ôʟ	aX̂t	ʟē wô'ôtg·ê. Q'am-g·'ē'lpEl	9
did	the beaver:	from sea to land he went to	the porcupine	(perf.) he invited him. Only twice	

hwîl	g·a'bEnʟ	ts'Emē'lîx·	aʟ hwîl	houks-d'ā'ʟ	aX̂t. Nʟk·'ē	10
	emerged	the beaver	to where	at the shore sitting	the porcupine. Then	

73

shore. Now he came ashore. He said to the Porcupine, "I will carry you. Hold on to my neck." Then the Beaver turned round, but the Porcupine was afraid to be carried across the water. He said to the Beaver, "I might perish." But the Beaver said, "You are not going to die," and after a while the Porcupine climbed on the Beaver's back. The Beaver said, "Now, hold tight to my neck." The Porcupine did so, and the Beaver started across the lake. After a little while he dived; then the Porcupine was much troubled. He broke wind because he did not know how to swim. The water is the Beaver's home, while the Porcupine's home is between the mountains. The Beaver came up twice before he reached his house in the middle of the lake. The Porcupine was very much afraid that he would perish in the water.

---

1 tsagam-a′qʟkᵘt. Nʟk·′ē hēt aʟ aXt: "Dem hwa′lēᴇ nēᴇn,
from sea to land / he got. / Then / he said / to / the porcupine: / "(Fut.) / I carry / you,

2 tsᴇ sᴇm-g·it dä′mdᴇnʟ t'ᴇm-lä′nēᴇ. Dᴇm hwa′lēᴇ nēᴇn."
fast / hold / my neck. / (Fut.) / I carry / you."

3 Nʟk·′ē tgō-ya′ltkᵘʟ ts'ᴇmē′lîx·. Nʟk·′ē xpets'a′Xʟ aXt aʟ
Then / around turned / the beaver. / Then / was afraid / the porcupine / to

4 dᴇm hwîlt, lō-dē-yô′xkᵘt ts'ᴇm-a′k·s. "Ōp tsᴇ nô′ôēᴇ,"
(fut.) / to do so, / in also he went / in the water. / "Else / I might / die,"

5 dēya′ʟ aXt aʟ ts'ᴇmē′lîx·. Nʟk·′ē tgōn hēʟ ts'ᴇmē′lîx·:
thus said / the porcupine / to / the beaver. / Then / this / said / the beaver:

6 "Nîg·i dᴇm dē-nô′ôn." Sī-gō′n k·'ē mᴇn-iä′êʟ aXt aʟ lax-
"Not / (fut.) / on your part you die." / After awhile / then / up went / the porcupine / at / on

7 hak·'â′ôʟ ts'ᴇmē′lîx·. Nʟk·′ē a′lg·îxʟ ts'ᴇmē′lîx·: "Sᴇm-g·ît dä′mʟ
the back of / the beaver. / Then / said / the beaver: / "Really / hold

8 t'ᴇm-lä′neîst." Nʟk·′ē hwîlʟ aXt. Nʟk·′ē ha′dîk·sʟ ts'ᴇmē′lîx·
my neck." / Then / did so / the porcupine. / Then / swam / the beaver

9 aʟ lax-a′k·s. Nî′g·i nakᵘʟ hwîl ha′dîk·st. Nʟk·′ēt dē-sō′uqskᵘt.
at on the water. / Not / long it was / (verbal noun) / he swam. / Then he / with / dived.

10 Nʟk·′ē sᴇm-aba′g·askᵘʟ aXt. Ts'ᴇm-q·â′ᴇlt k·si-yô′xkᵘʟ ʟē näʟqt,
Then / much troubled was / the porcupine. / In his anus / out went / the wind,

11 aʟ hwîl nî′g·idit hwilä′x·ʟ dᴇm dē-hä′dîk·st. Q'ap-lᴇp-ts'a′pʟ
because / not / he knew / (fut.) / on to swim. his part / Really own / the country of

12 ts'ᴇmē′lîx· ts'ᴇm-a′k·s. K·'ē spagait-sqanē′st dē-ts'a′pʟ aXt.
the beaver / in the water. / Then / among mountains / on the coun- his part try of / the porcupine.

13 G·'ē′lp'ᴇlʟ hwîl g·a′bᴇnʟ ts'ᴇmē′lîx·. Nʟk·′ē uks-a′qʟkᵘt aʟ ʟē
Twice it was / (verbal noun) / emerged / the beaver. / Then / from land he to sea reached / at

14 ts'a′pt. Sᴇm-sē′lukᵘʟ wi-t'a′x hwîl g·ig·â′k·sʟ hwî′lptg·ê. Sᴇmgal
his town. / Very great / middle of / the lake / where / floated / his house. / Really

15 wī-t'ē′s hwîl k'ōpᴇ-aba′g·askᵘʟ aXt aʟ dᴇm nô′ôt aʟ ts'ᴇm-
much / (verbal noun) / a little / troubled was / the porcupine / at / (fut.) / he die / at / in the

Now he entered the Beaver's house, and ate the food the Beaver gave him. Sticks were the food at the Beaver's feast. Now the Porcupine was really troubled because he had to eat sticks, but he ate them.

Another day the Beaver said to the Porcupine, "My dear, let us play." Then he told him how they would play. He said, "I will carry you on my back, and four times I will come up." Then the Porcupine thought, "Now I surely must die," but he agreed. The Beaver carried the Porcupine on his back and said, "Hold on to my neck and put your nose close down to my nape." Now the Porcupine was really ready to die. The Beaver dived, but before he did so he struck the water with his tail. Then a little water splashed into

---

a'k·s.	NLk·'ē	ts'ent	aL	hwîlpL	ts'Emē'lîx·.	NLk·'ē	yō'ôxk^ut.	1

a'k·s. water. — NLk·'ē Then — ts'ent he entered — aL in — hwîlpL the house of — ts'Emē'lîx·. the beaver. — NLk·'ē Then — yō'ôxk^ut. he ate. **1**

TgōnL This — g·atk^uL had for food in the feast — ts'Emē'lîx·g·ê; the beaver; — ganL sticks — g·a'tk^utg·ê. were the food for his feast. — NLk·'ē Then **2**

sEm-aba'g·ask^uL really troubled was — aXt the porcupine — aL at — dEmt (fut.) — hwîl where — g·ē'îpL he eats — ga'ng·ê. stick. **3**

NLk·'ēt Then — g·ē'îpL ate — aXt the porcupine — ga'ng·ê. the stick. **4**

Hwäi! Well! — La When — k·'ē'ElL one — sā, day, — nLk·'ē then — hēL said — ts'Emē'lîx· the beaver — aL to — aXt: the porcupine: **5**

"DāmqLk^u, "Friend, — dāmqLk^u, friend, — dEm (fut.) — qalā'qnōm." we play." — NLk·'ēt Then he — ma'LEL told **6**

dEm (fut.) — hwîl being — qalā'q: they will play: — "DEm "(Fut.) — hwa'lēE I carry — nē'En. you. — TxalpxL Four times it is — dEm (fut.) **7**

hwîl (verbal noun) — g·ā'bEnēE." I emerge." — NLk·'ē Then — tgōnL this — hēL said — qâtL the heart of — a'Xtg·ê: the porcupine: — "La "(Perf.) **8**

āmL good — nô'ôēE," I die," — dē'yaL thus said — qâ'ôtL the heart of — a'Xtg·ê. the porcupine. — NLk·'ē Then — saxk^ut. he agreed. — NLk·'ē Then **9**

hwîlL did so — ts'Emē'lîx·. the beaver. — NLk·'ēt Then — hwa'lîx·L he carried on his back — aXt. the porcupine. — TgōnL This — hēL said **10**

ts'Emē'lîx· the beaver — aL to — a'Xtg·ê: the porcupine: — "DEm "(Fut.) — sEm-g·it strongly — dax-yu'kdEnL hold to fast **11**

t'Em-lā'ṇēE. my neck. — NL (Fut.) — dEm then — k·'ē right on — kwa'ts'îk·s against — tq'al-sg·în lie — aL at **12**

ts'Em-dē'bElēE." my nape." — NLk·'ē Then — gwaldEm was ready — qâ'dîL the heart — qâtL the heart of — aXt the porcupine — aL at **13**

dEm (fut.) — q'ap-nô'ôt. really he dies. — NLk·'ē Then — sō'uqsk^uL dived — ts'Emē'lîx·. the beaver. — TgōnL This — hwîlL did **14**

ts'Emē'lîx· the beaver — aL at — qâ'ôqL before — dEm (fut.) — sō'uqsk^ut. he dived. — Lē-ia'tst On he struck — lax-a'k·s on the water **15** the Porcupine's face, and he gasped.   The Beaver stayed under water a long time.   The Porcupine was almost dead and his stomach was full of water.   Three times the Beaver came up.   Once more he went down, and when he came up again the Porcupine was almost dead. Now he returned and put him ashore.

The Porcupine went back to his tribe.   When he arrived, he invited the people to his house.   When his guests entered, he told them what the Beaver had done on the large lake when he had invited him to come to see him.   He said, "My friend almost killed me."   Then his people said, "Invite him in and play with him in your turn."

---

1   aL   Lē   waqᴌt.   Nʟk·'ē   k·s-qâqʟ   k'ōpɛt-lō-qabu'Xʟ   ak·s   aʟ
with   the   his tail.   Then   he first   a little   in   splashed   water   into

2   ts'a'ɛlʟ   ʟgō-a'Xt.   Nʟk·'ē   sɛm-lō-d'ɛp-dā'uʟ   Lē   nāʟqt.
the face of   the porcu-   Then   very   in   down   went   his breath.
              little pine.

3   Nʟk·'ē   sō'uqsk\u{u}ʟ   ts'ɛmē'lîx·.   K·'ē   nak\u{u}ʟ   g·ē'ukst.   Nʟk·'ē
Then   dived   the beaver.   Then   long   he was under   Then
                                                water.

4   ts'ōsk·   dɛm   hwîl   nô'ôʟ   aXt.   Qalā'iʟ   bant   tgōn   aʟ
a little   (fut.)   being   dead   the   As large   his belly   this   with
                                porcupine.

5   ak·s.   ʟā   gulā'alʟ   hwîl   dē-g·ā'bɛnt.   Q'am   huX   k·'ēlʟ
water.   When   three times   (verbal   with   he   Only   more   once
              it was   noun)   him   emerged.

6   mānt.   Nʟk·'ē   huX   sō'uqsk\u{u}ʟ   ts'ɛmē'lîx.   ʟa   tsō'usk·t
remain-   Then   again   dived   the beaver.   When   a little
ed.

7   dɛm   hwîl   nô'ôʟ   aXt,   nʟk·'ēt   lō-dē-ya'ltk\u{u}t.   Mâtsɛ-nô'ôʟ
(fut.)   (verbal   dead   the   then   in with   he   Almost   dead
          noun)   was   porcupine,   him   returned.   was

8   aXt.   Nʟk·'ē   dē-lō-ya'ltk\u{u}t;   tsagam-ma'qdɛt.
the por-   Then   with   he returned;   from sea   he put him.
cupine.   him   to land

9   Nʟk·'ē   dā'uʟʟ   aXt   aʟ   Lē   ts'apt.   Nʟk·'ē   ʟa
Then   left   the   to   his   Then   when
              porcupine   town.

10   gulîk·s-a'qʟk\u{u}t,   nʟk·'ē   wô'ôʟ   Lē   ts'apt.   Nʟk·'ē   ts·ɛlɛm-qâ'ôdɛʟ
back   he   then   he invited   his   Then   in   went
    reached,   town.

11   aXt   Lē   wô'ôtg·ê.   Nʟk·'ēt   ma'ʟɛʟ   hwîl   hwîlā'guʟ
to the   the invited ones.   Then   he told   what   had done
porcupine

12   ts'ɛmē'lîx·   aʟ   wī-lax-t'a'x.   ʟpēyō'·îʟ   aXt   Lē   ts'ap
the beaver   at   the   on   lake.   He told them   the   the   people
              great   porcupine

13   aʟ   hwîl   hwîlā'guʟ   ts'ɛmē'lîx·ʟ   t'an   wô'ôt: "Q'am-mâ'tsɛ-
abo t   what had done   the beaver   who   invited   "Only   almost
                              him;

14   nó'ōᴄᴇ   at   hwîlā'k\u{u}dēt   dā'mqʟguēᴇ."   Nʟk·ē   hēʟ   Lē   ts'a'ptg·ê:
I was   he   did to me   my friend."   Then   said   his people:
dead

15   "Ām,   mᴇ   dē-wô'ôt.   Dɛm   dē-sɛl-qalā'q·an."
"Good,   you   also invite   (Fut.)   also with   play."
              him.   him

Then the Porcupine did so. He invited the Beaver to his house. When the messenger who had invited the Beaver returned, the Beaver went up the valley in which the Porcupine lived. When the Beaver entered the Porcupine's house, the latter struck the fire with his tail, so that it burned. Then he was going to play with the Beaver. After he had struck the fire with his tail, his tail was burning. Then the Beaver made a song, as follows: "The little tail of the little Porcupine is burned in the middle, pâ! The little tail of the little Porcupine is burned in the middle." The Porcupine ran about in front of the Beaver, with whom he intended to play. After he had done so, the Porcupine gave food to his friend the Beaver.

Nᴌk·'ē　hwîlʟ　aXt,　dĕ-wô'ôʟ　ts'ɛmē'lîx·　an-dā'mqʟk^ut. 1
Then　did so　the　also he　the beaver　his friend.
　　　　　　porcupine,　invited

Nᴌk·'ē　dĕ-dā'uʟ　t'an　wô'ôʟ　ts'ɛmē'lîx·.　Nᴌk·'ē　lō-ya'ltk^ut 2
Then　also he　who　invited　the beaver.　Then　returned
　　　　went

t'an　wô'ôt.　Nᴌk·'ē　iä'ʟ　ts'ɛmē'lîx·　aʟ　ts'ɛm-t'ē'n.　Nᴌk·'ē 3
who　invited　Then　went　the beaver　to　in the　Then
　　　him.　　　　　　　　　　　valley.

bax-iä'êt.　Tgōnʟ　hwîlʟ　a'Xtg·ê.　Nʟa　ts'ēnʟ　ts'ɛmē'lîx· 4
up he　This　did　the porcupine.　When　entered　the beaver
went.

aʟ　hwîlpʟ　aXt,　nʟk·'ē　tgōnʟ　hwîlʟ　a'Xtg·ê.　Lē-ia'tsʟ 5
in　the house　the　then　this　did　the porcupine.　On he
　　of　porcupine,　　　　　　　　　　　　　struck

lax-an-la'k^u　aʟ　k'ō'uk^ut.　Nᴌk·'ē　mē'ltg·ê.　Nᴌk·'ē　yu'kdet 6
on　the fire-　with　his tail.　Then　it burnt.　Then　he began
place

sîl-qalā'qʟ　ts'ɛmē'lîx·　nîʟnē'ʟ　qan　hwîlt.　ʟa　ʟēsk^ut 7
with to play　the beaver　therefore　he did so.　When　he finished

lē-ia'tsʟ　aXt　k'ō'uk^ut　aʟ　lax-an-la'k^u,　nʟk·'ē　mēʟ 8
on struck　the　his tail　on　on the fire-　then　burnt
　　　porcupine　　　　　　　place,

k'ō'uk^uʟ　a'Xtg·ê.　Nᴌk·'ē　tgōnʟ　hē'tg·ê.　Sē-lē'mx·dîtg·ê: 9
the tail of　the porcupine.　Then　this　he said.　He made　a song:

"Lē-g·a-xtsɛ-mē'ʟ　ʟgo-k'ō'uk^uʟ　ʟgo-a'Xt.　Pâ!　Lē-g·a-xtsɛ-mē'ʟ 10
"In　middle burnt　the　tail of　the porcu-　Pâ!　In　middle burnt
　　　　　　　little　　　little pine.

ʟgo-k'ō'uk^uʟ　ʟgo-a'Xt."¹　Aʟ　lō-tgo-ba'xt　aʟ　qa-sä'êXʟ 11
the　tail of　the porcu-　While　in around he　at　in front of
little　little pine."　　　　　ran

ts'ɛmē'lîx·　aʟ　dĕt-sɛl-qalā'qs　dāmqʟk^ut.　Nᴌk·'ē　ʟa　qâ'ôdɛʟ 12
the beaver　to　also with　play　his friend.　Then　when　was finished

hwîlʟ　a'Xtg·ê,　nʟk·'ē　dĕ-dza'pʟ　wunä'x·　ʟā　dɛm 13
what did　the porcupine,　then　on his he　food　(perf.)　(fut.)
　　　　　　　　　part made

dĕ-yō'ôxk^uʟ　ts'ɛmē'lîx·.　Nᴌk·'ē　tgōnʟ　hwîlʟ　aXt,　ʟE 14
on his　eat　the beaver.　Then　this　did　the　ʟE
part　　　　　　　　　　　porcupine,

¹ Spoken very slowly, and accompanied by very rapid beating of time with a stick.

He gave him the bark of a tree and some needles of the spruce. Then
the Beaver was afraid to eat them; but the Porcupine said to his
friend the great Beaver, "Eat fast, friend," and the Beaver did so.
Then he said to the Beaver, "Friend, let us play to-morrow morning.
There is a tree on a grassy slope. That is my playing ground," and
when they were going to lie down to sleep, the Porcupine sang,
"When I walk along the edge (?) (?) (?) my shooting star
drops out." Then the Porcupine spoke to the sky, and it cleared up,
and in the morning the ground was covered with ice.

Now he gave another feast to the great Beaver; and when he had
finished, the Porcupine said, "Now let us play, friend. My playing

1 māsʟ   ganʟ   dē-g·a′tkᵘt   qanʟ   ʟē   la′qsʟ   gan.   Nʟk·′ē   dē-
  bark of   tree   on his food for   and   leaves of   a tree.   Then   on
                           his part feast   his part

2 xpets'a′Xʟ   ts'Emē′lîx·   aʟ   dEm   dēt-g·e′îpt.   Nʟk·′ē   tgōnʟ
  was afraid   the beaver   to   (fut.)   on food.   Then   this
                                                              his part

3 hēʟ   aXt   aʟ   an-dā′mqʟkᵘt   wî-ts'Emē′lîx·:   "T'ä′gan,
  said   the porcu- to   his friend   the   beaver: "Eat fast,
              pine   great

4 dāmqʟkᵘt.   T'ä′gan,   dāmqʟkᵘt."   Nʟk·′ē   hwîʟ   ts'Emē′lîx·.
  friend.   Eat fast,   friend."   Then   did so   the beaver.

5 Nʟk·′ē   a′lg·îxʟ   aXt: "Dāmqʟk",   dē′ya   aʟ   ts'Emē′lîx·.
  Then   said   the   "Friend,"   thus he said to   the beaver.
                               porcupine:

6 "DEm   qalā′qnōm   qans   nē′En   atsE   hē′ʟuk   ts'Et'a′ʟakᵘ.
  "(Fut.)   we play   and   you   when   morning   to-morrow.

7 Hētkᵘʟ   gan   aʟ   lax-sō′ukst.   Nêʟne′ʟ   an-qalā′qaîst."   Nʟk·′ē
  There   a tree   on   on a grassy   There is   my playground."   Then
  stands   slope.

8 ʟā   dEm   wâ′wôqdēt.   Nʟk·′ē   huX   lēmx·ʟ   aXt: "DEm
  (perf.)   (fut.)   they slept.   Then   again   sang   the   "(Fut.)
                                                                                  porcupine:

9 hwîl   haʟ-iä′ēE   gō,   aʟ   dEp   siō′wâl   k·si-t'îʟt'ō′ʟ   nEwînōlī
  being   along l   edge walk   at   walk   out drops

10 wīai.   Hak·sū   hadā′mgwa,   k'wōdzō   pia′lsdō."[1]   Nʟk·′ē   tgōnʟ
   excrements   my star."   Then   this

11 a′lg·îxʟ   aXt   aʟ   ts'Emē′lîx·.   A′lg·îxʟ   aXt   aʟ   lax-ha′.
   said   the   to   the beaver.   It spoke   the   to   heaven.
                   porcupine   porcupine

12 Nʟk·ē   hwîʟʟ   lax-ha′.   Nʟk·′ē   ä′d'îk·skᵘʟ   hwîl   q'andā′uʟ
   Then   it did so   the heaven.   Then   it came   (verbal   clear
                                                                                 noun)

13 lax-ha′.   Nʟk·′ē   dā′uʟ   dz'ä′dz'îk·s   aʟ   hē′ʟuk.
   the sky.   Then   ice was   the ground   in   the
                                                                           morning.

14 Nʟk·′ē   huX   wô′ôtkᵘʟ   aXt   aʟ   wî-ts'Emē′lîx·.   Nʟk·′ē   ʟā
   Then   again   sent an   the   to   the beaver.   Then   (perf.)
                            invitation   porcupine   great

15 ʟē′êxkᵘʟ   ts'Emē′lîx·,   nʟk·′ē   a′lg·îxʟ   aXt: "DEm   qalā′qnōmîst,
   finished   the beaver,   then   said   the   "(Fut.)   we play,
   eating   porcupine:

---

[1] This sentence is in Tsimshian dialect.

ground is yonder." It was very cold in the morning. There was a place where water was running down. It was slippery because the water was frozen. The Beaver followed the Porcupine across the place. Then the Beaver was troubled because his feet were slippery, but the Porcupine had long claws. Then he returned to see what the great Beaver was doing, and he said to him, "Come, do it, friend," but the Beaver could not cross the place on account of the ice on the mountain. Then the Porcupine returned, and took the Beaver by the hand and led him across. Thus the Beaver got across. The Porcupine was going to play with him; just once he did so. Then they walked on, and came to the place where the tree was standing. The Porcupine said to the Beaver, "Now climb this tree." The Beaver

dāmqʟkᵘ.	Hētkᵘʟ	an-qalā′gaēE	aʟ	dā′u."	Nʟk·′ē	ā′d'îk·skᵘʟ 1
friend.	There stands	my playground	at	yonder."	Then	came
hē′ʟuk.	Nʟk·′ē	sEnɪgal	saqʟ	gunä′ᵡkᵘ.	Dā′uʟ	dz·ä′dz'îk·s. Tgōnʟ 2
the morning.	Then	very	sharp was	the cold.	Iee was	the ground. This
hwîʟʟ	iaga-qâ′ôʟ	a′k·sg·ê.	Hîʟia′ʟkᵘʟ	hwîl	dā′utg·ê.	NeʟnE′t 3
it was	down ran	water.	Slippery	where	ice.	There
tsaga-dē-yô′ᵡguʟ	aᵡt	ts'Emē′lîx·.	Nʟk·′ē	huᵡ	aba′g·askᵘʟ 4	
across also followed him	the porcupine	the beaver.	Then	again	troubled was	
ts'Emē′lîx·,	gwa′nEm	hîʟia′ʟkᵘʟ	an'ô′nt.	K·′ē	tgōn	hwîʟʟ 5
the beaver,	always	slippery were	his hands.	Then	this	did
a′ᵡtg·ê.	Nēnē′lukᵘʟ	ʟē	ʟaqst.	Nʟk·′ē	huᵡ	lō-ya′ltkᵘʟ aᵡt 6
the porcupine.	Long were	(perf.)	his claws.	Then	again	returned the porcupine
at	g·a′aʟ	hwîʟʟ	wī-ts'Emē′lîx·.	Nʟk·′ē	a′lg·îxʟ	a′ᵡtg·ê: "Sa! 7
to	see	what did	the great beaver.	Then	said	the porcupine: "Come!
āmʟ	hwî′lEn,	dāmqʟkᵘ!"	Dē′yaʟ	aᵡt	aʟ	wī-ts'Emē′lîx·. Qō′sEl 8
good	do,	friend!"	Thus said the porcupine	the	to great	the beaver. He could not
ts'Emē′lîx·	dEm	tsaga-a′qʟkᵘt	aʟ	hwîl	dā′uʟ	sqanē′st. Nʟk·′ē 9
the beaver	(fut.)	across he reached	because	ice was	the mountain.	Then
lō-ya′ltkᵘʟ	aᵡt.	Nʟk·′ē	tgōnʟ	hwîlt;	gō′udEʟ	an'ô′nʟ 10
returned	the porcupine.	Then	this	he did;	he took the	hands of
ts'Emē′lîx·;	nʟk·′ē	tsaga-dê′entkᵘt.	Nʟk·′ē	tsaga-a′qʟkᵘt.	ʟā 11	
the beaver;	then	across he led him.	Then	across he got.	(Perf.)	
hē-yu′kt	dēt-sEl-qalā′qʟ	aᵡt	ts'Emē′lîx·	q'ai-k·'ē′Elt	hwîl 12	
he was going	also with to play him	the porcupine	the beaver	just once		
dē-hwî′lt.	Nʟk·′ē	ʟô′ôdet.	Nʟk·′ēt	hwa′dEʟ	hwîl	hētkᵘʟ gan. 13
also he did so.	Then	they went.	Then	they reached to	where	stood the tree.
Nʟk·′ē	tgōnʟ	hwîʟʟ	a′ᵡtg·ê:	"Āmʟ	dEm	mEn-iē′ên," dēya′ 14
Then	this	did	the porcupine:	"Good	(fut.)	up go," thus he said

was much troubled. He was afraid. The Porcupine continued, "Now you shall see how I do it."

The Porcupine climbed up, and reached the very top of the tree. Then he let go, and dropped down. While he was falling down through space he said (?) (?) and he struck on a rock. Then he rose. He was not dead. He said to the Beaver, "Did you see, friend? That is not difficult." And the Porcupine carried the Beaver up the tree. He said to him, "Now hold on to my neck;" and the Beaver did so. He clung to the neck of the Porcupine, who climbed the tree. When they came near the top, the Porcupine put the Beaver on a branch of the tree. The Beaver was much afraid because

1　aʟ　ts'Emē'lîx·.　Nʟk·'ē　sEm-aba'g·askuʟ　ts'Emē'lîx·.　Sē'lk'unt.
　　to　　the beaver.　　Then　　very　troubled was　the beaver.　He was timid.

2　"Hwä'i!　DEm　g·a'an!"　Dē'yaʟ　aXt.
　　"Well!　(Fut.)　see!"　Thus said　the porcupine.

3　Nʟk·'ē　aXt　mEn-k·s-qâ'ôg̣ôt.　Nʟk·'ē　mEn-a'qʟkut　aʟ　Lē
　　Then　the porcupine　up　first.　Then　up　he got　to　the

4　sEm-ts'ēwî'nt.　Hwîl　wîtkuʟ　aXt　qalē'deʟ　ts'ēwî'nʟ　gan.
　　very　top.　Where　he came from　the porcupine　he let go　the top of　the tree.

5　ʟgotē-qalē't,　nʟk·'ē　tg̣ōnʟ　hēʟ　aXt　aʟ　dē-d'Ep-yu'kt
　　As soon as he dropped,　then　this　said　the porcupine　while　with down coming

6　aʟ　lax-qal-bē'is:　"Andabɛlâ'q,　andabɛlâ'q."　Nʟk·'ē　ok·st　aʟ
　　at　on the space:　(?)　(?)　Then　he　at dropped

7　lax-lô'ôp.　Nʟk·'ē　g·în-hē'tkut;　nîg·i　nô'ôt.　Nʟk·'ē　hēʟ　aXt　aʟ
　　on the stone.　Then　he rose;　not　he was dead.　Then　said　the porcupine　to

8　ts'Emē'lîx·:　"G·a'aʟ,　dāmqʟku!　Nî'g·idē　qaqē'tkut."　Nʟk·'ēt　mEn-
　　the beaver:　"See,　friend!　Not　it is hard."　Then　up

9　wa'lx·ʟ　aXʟ　ts'Emē'lîx·　aʟ　lax-ga'n.　Nʟk·'ē　dē-dē'lEmExkuʟ
　　carried　the porcupine　the beaver　to　on the tree.　Then　on his part　answered

10　aXt　aʟ　ts'Emē'lîx·:　"SEm-g·it　dē-yō'guʟ　t'Em-lā'nêîst."
　　the porcupine　to　the beaver:　"Very fast　hold　my neck."

11　Nʟk·'ē　hwîlʟ　ts'Emē'lîx·.　SEm-g·it　dEx-yu'kdēt　t'Em-lā'nîx·ʟ　aXt.
　　Then　did so　the beaver.　Very fast　he held　the neck of　the porcupine.

12　Nʟk·'ē　mEn-iä'êt　aʟ　lax-ga'n.　Nʟk·'ēt　hwaʟ　Lē　ham-ts'ēwî'nt.
　　Then　up he went　to　on the tree.　Then he　reached　(fut.) near　the top.

13　Nʟk·'ēt　lē-d'ä'deʟ　ts'Emē'lîx·　aʟ　lax-ānē'st.　Nʟk·'ē　wī-t'ē's　hwîl
　　Then　on he put　the beaver　to　on the branch.　Then　greatly was　(verbal noun)

14　xpEts'a'xʟ　ts'Emē'lîx·　aʟ　hwîl　nî'g·idi　tq'al-ā'mʟ　an'ô'nt　aʟ
　　afraid　the beaver　on account of　not　against good　his hands　at

his hands were not able to hold on to the tree. Only the Porcupine knows how to do that, because his claws are long.

Now the Porcupine said, "Hold on to the tree, friend. I will go down first." The Beaver did so, clinging round the branch with his arms. Then the Porcupine let go of the tree and fell down. He said again (?) (?) and he struck the rock, but he was not dead.

Now the great Beaver was much troubled, holding on to the branch. He was afraid to let go; but the Porcupine ran about at the foot of the tree, and looked up to his friend. He said, "Oh, friend, that is not difficult. Look at me. I am not dead, although I fell down." Then the Beaver let go of the branch, and when he fell through space, he

---

dɛm	dēt-dîx·-yō′guʟ	gan.	K·sax	aXt	t'an	hwîlā′x·t	aʟ hwîl	1
(fut.)	on his fast hold part	the tree.	Only	the porcupine	who	knows	because	

nēnē′luk^{u}ʟ	ʟa′qstg·ê.	2
long its	claws.	

Nʟk·'ē	tgōnʟ	hēʟ	a′Xtg·ê:	"Sɛm-g·it	dîx·-yō′guʟ,	dāmqʟk^u. 3
Then	this	said	the porcupine:	"Really	fast hold,	friend.

Dɛm	d'ɛp-k·s-qâq	nēē′st	lân."	Nʟk·'ē	hwîlʟ	ts'ɛmē′lîx·. 4
(Fut.)	down first	1	thee."	Then	did so	the beaver.

Txā-xʟɛnɪ-d'a′ʟdîʟ	an'ō′nt.	Nʟk·'ēt	qalē′ʟ	aXʟ	ga′ng·ê, lax- 5
All around were	his hands.	Then	let go	the porcupine	the tree, on

qal-bē′îs	yō′xgutg·ê.	Nʟk·'ē	huX	tgōnʟ	hēt:	"Andɛbɛlâ′q, 6
space	he went.	Then	again	this	he said:	(?)

andɛbɛlâ′q."	Nʟk·'ē	ha′k·sɛm	huX	ōk·st	aʟ	lax-lô′ôp.	Nʟk·ē 7
(?)	Then	once more	again	he dropped	on	on the stones.	Then

nî′g·i	nô′ôt. 8
not	he was dead.

Tk·'ē	sɛm-lō-ha′xk^{u}ʟ	qâ′otʟ	wī-ts'ɛmē′lîx·	at	lō-dā′mʟ	anē′st 9
Then	very in troubled was	the heart of	the beaver great	he	in held	the branch

aʟ	aba′g·ask^u	aʟ	dɛm	tgwantk^{u}t.	Nʟk·'ē	k'uʟ-ba′xʟ aXt aʟ 10
and	he was troubled	to	(fut.)	to fall.	Then	about ran the porcupine at

mēnʟ	gan.	Nʟk·'ēt	mɛn-g·a′aʟ	hwîl	lē-d'ā′ʟ an-dā′mqʟk^{u}t. 11
the foot of	the tree.	Then	up he looked	where	on was his friend.

Nʟk·'ē	tgōnʟ	hēʟ	a′Xtg·ê:	"Gwôm, dāmqʟk^u!	Nîg·îdi qaqē′tk^{u}t. 12
Then	this	said	the porcupine:	"Go on, friend!	Not it is hard.

G·a′as	nē′e;	nî′g·i	nô′ôēɛ,	aʟ	hwîl	tgwantk^u." Nʟk·'ēt qalē′ʟ 13
Look	at me;	not	1 am dead,	because	I fell."	Then let go

ts'ɛmē′lîx·ʟ	anē′st.	Tgōnʟ	hēʟ	ts'ɛmē′lîx·	aʟ	ʟa tgwantk^{u}t aʟ lax- 14
the beaver	the branch.	This	said	the beaver	at	(perf.) he fell at on

cried, "Rock, rock!" Then he struck the rocks. He lay on his back, and his belly burst. He was dead.

---

1 qal-bē'is: "Lô'ôp   lô'ôp,"   ts'ᴇmē'lîx·ʟ   hē'tg·ê.   Nʟk·'ē   ōk·st   aʟ
  space: "Stone,   stone,"   the beaver   said.   Then   he   at
                                                                    struck

2 lax-lô'ôp.   Sᴇm-hasbā'-sg·it.   Nʟk·'ē   sᴇm-xʟu'xʟ   bant.   Nʟk·'ē   nô'ôt.
  on the stones.   Very on his he   Then   very   burst   his   Then   he was
                    back lay.   belly.   dead.

The Wolves and the Deer

[Told by Moody]

The Wolves had a feast on a prairie at the mouth of Skeena river. They invited the chiefs of the Deer to the feast. The Deer who had been called came. Then they sat down on the prairie face to face with the Wolves. The Wolves said to the Deer, "You on the opposite side begin to laugh." But the Deer did not agree. They said, "You shall laugh first." The Wolves replied, "Now we will laugh. Ha, ha, ha, ha, ha! Now you must laugh, you on the other side." Then the Deer laughed: "M, m, m, m, m! Now you laugh again,

---

The Wolves and the Deer

Lē′lyitxaʟ	kˑebō′al	aʟ	lax-amā′uksal	aʟ	saXʟ	Ksan.	1
They had a feast	the wolves	at	on a prairie	at	the mouth of	Skeena river.	
Nʟkˑ′ēt	wô′ôʟ	kˑ′ebō′ʟ	txanē′tkⁿsʟ	sɛm-gˑigˑa′dɛm	wan.		2
Then	invited	the wolves	all the	chief	deer.		
Nʟkˑ′ē	hwîl	kˑ′ē	ad′ā′d′îkˑsʟ	wô′ôm	wan.	Nʟkˑ′ē hwîl kˑ′ē	3
At once			came	the invited	deer.	At once	
wī-ama	hwa′ndet	aʟ	lax-amā′uks	nagalaxde′lt	qanʟ	kˑebō′.	4
very well	they sat down	at	on the prairie	face to face	and	the wolves.	
Nʟkˑ′ē	hwîl	kˑ′ē	hēʟ	kˑebō′gˑê	aʟ	wan: "Kˑ′ax-hîsqaā′qsɛsɛm	5
At once			said	the wolves	to	the deer: "Only laugh ye	
aʟ	an-dâ′sdaas."	Kˑ′ē:	"Nîˑ′gˑi,"	hēdet,	"kˑ′ax-nē′sɛmʟ		6
at	the other side."	Then:	"No,"	they said,	"only ye		
kˑs-qâ′gôm	hîsqaā′qsɛt,"	dē-hē′deʟ	wan	aʟ	kˑebō′.	Kˑ′ē	7
first	laugh,"	on their part said	the deer	to	the wolves.		
hwîl	kˑ′ē	hēʟ	kˑebō′gˑê:	"Hwä′i!	D′ē′ɛn	dɛm	hîsqaā′qs	8
At once		said	the wolves:	"Well!	(Fut.)		laugh	
nō′mɛst.	Hwä′i!	Hā,	ha,	ha,	ha,	ha!	Hwä′i!	Gôp	9
we.	Well!	Ha,	ha,	ha,	ha,	ha!	Well!	Go on	
dē-lâ′sɛm.	Kˑ′ax-dē-hîsqaā′qsɛsɛm	aʟ	an-dâ′sdaas."	"Hwä′i!	10
also to you.	Only also laugh ye	at	the other side."	"Well!"	
D′ē′ɛn,"	dē′yaʟ	wan.	"Hwä′i!	M—,	m,	m,	m,	m.	Hwä′i!	11
	said	the deer.	"Well!	M—,	m,	m,	m,	m.	Well!	
Gôp	dē-lâ′sɛm,	kˑebō′.	Kˑ′aX	huX	dē-hîsqaā′qsɛsɛm.	12
Go on	also to you,	wolves.	Only	again	also you laugh.	

83

Wolves." Then the Wolves laughed again: "Ha, ha, ha, ha, ha!"
Now the Deer were afraid when they saw the large teeth of the Wolves.
The Wolves said, "Now, you on the other side, you shall laugh again.
Don't keep your mouths closed when you are laughing. Nobody
laughs like that. You must open your mouths as far as possible when
you are laughing. Now do so. Try as hard as you can. Don't be
afraid to open your mouths." Thus spoke the Wolves. "Now
laugh." Then the Deer laughed again: "Ha, ha, ha, ha, ha!" They
opened their mouths wide. They had no teeth. When the Wolves
saw that they had no teeth they attacked them, and they bit them all

---

1 Hwä'i!   D'ē'ɛn."   Hwîl   k'ē   huX   dē-hîsqaā'qsʟ   k'ebō':
  Well!"   At once   again   also   laughed   the wolves:

2 "Hā,   ha,   ha,   ha,   ha!"   K'ē   hwîl   k'ē   sɛm-lexpēts'ē'Xʟ
  "Hah, ha,   ha,   ha,   ha!"   At once   much   afraid
                                                              were

3 txanē'tkⁿsʟ   wa'ng·ê,   hwîl   ʟat   g·a'aniʟ   wud'ax   qa-wē'nʟ
  all   the deer,   when   (part.)   they saw   the great teeth of

4 k·ebō'g·ê.   Hwä'i!   K·'ē   huX   dē-hē'ʟ   k·ebō'g·ê: "Gôp!
  the wolves.   Well!   Then   again   also said   the wolves: "Go on!

5 huX   dē-hîsqaā'qsɛsɛm   aʟ   an-dâ'sdaas.   G·ilâ'ʟ   sɛxsā'mɛxsɛmɛs
  again   also   laugh ye   at   the other   Do not   keep your mouths
                                        side.   closed

6 aʟ   da-hîsqaā'qsɛsɛms.   Nî'g·ide   hwîʟʟ   hîsā'qsɛt,"   dē'yaʟ
  at   also   you laugh.   Not   he does   he laughs,"   thus said
                                              so

7 k·ebō'.   "Q'ap-sɛm-lō-gâ'dɛʟ   hwîl   q'aqʟ   ts'ɛm-ā'gam
  the   "Really very in go   where   open   in mouth
  wolves.

8 da-hîsā'qsɛm,"   dē'yaʟ   k·ebō'   aʟ   wan.   "Hwä'i!   Gôp
  (when) you laugh," thus said   the   to   the deer. "Well!   Go on
                                  wolves

9 q'ai-hwî'lsɛm   sɛm-lō-qâ'dɛnsksɛm   aʟ   hîsqaā'qsɛsɛm.   G·ilâ'ôl
  so far do you   very in (as hard as   at   you laugh.   Do not
                          you can)

10 lexpēts'ē'xsɛm   aʟ   mē'dɛmsɛm   q'ā'axʟ   qats'ɛm-ā'qsɛms,"   dē'yaʟ
   be afraid you   at   you   open   your mouths,"   thus
                                                                             said

11 k·ebō':   "Hwä'i!   D'ē'ɛnsɛm   hîsqaā'qsɛsɛm."   Hwîl   k·'ē'   huX
   the wolves: "Well!   Now you   laugh you."   At once   then

12 dē-hîsqaā'qsʟ   wa'ng·ê: "Hā,   ha,   ha,   ha,   ha!"   Dē'yaʟ   wan
   also laughed   the deer: "Hah, ha,   ha,   ha,   ha!"   Thus said the deer

13 aʟ   lō-qa-lā'iʟ   qa-ts'ɛm-a'qdet.   K·'ē   nî'g·i   qa-wē'ndet.   Hwä'i!
   at   in   great   their mouths.   Then   not   their teeth.   Well!

14 Q'am-g·a'aʟ   k·ebō'g·ê   hwîl   nî'g·i   qa-wē'nʟ   wa'ng·ê.   K·'ē
   Only   saw   the wolves   where   not   teeth   the deer.

15 hwîl   k·'ēt   ha'p'adet.   K·'ē   hwîl   k·'ē't   kⁿʟē-hatsha'tsdɛʟ
   At once   they attacked   At once   all over   bit them
                      them.

over. Then they devoured the Deer. Only a few of the Deer succeeded in escaping. For this reason the Deer are afraid of the Wolves.

---

k·ebō′g·ê.   K·'ē   hwîl   k·'ē′t   g·ē′pdeʟ   wa′ng·ê.   Q'am-ʟɛbō′ʟ   1
the wolves.   At once   they ate   the deer.   Only   few

wanʟ   nda′aqkᵘʟ   hō′det.   Nʟnē′ʟ   qan   an-xpɛtsa′xʟ   wan   aʟ   2
deer   succeeded   escaped.   Therefore   the fear of   the deer   of

k·ebō′   gōn.   3
the wolves   now.

THE STARS

[Told by Moses]

There was a town. One evening a man went out of the house, and his son accompanied him. They sat down on the beach. After they had been sitting there for some time, the boy looked up to the sky and said to a star, "Poor fellow! You little twinkler, indeed, you must feel cold." Thus spoke the boy to the Star. The Star heard it, and one evening when the boy went out, the Star came down and took him up to the sky.

When day broke, the people found that the boy was lost. They

PELî'ST

THE STARS

1. **Hētkᵘʟ** (There was) **qal-ts'a'p.** (a town.) **Nʟk·'ē** (Then) **yu'ksa.** (it was evening.) **Nʟk·'ē** (Then) **k·si-ʟô'ôʟ** (out went) **g·at** (a man)

2. **k·si-stē'lʟ** (out accompanying) **ʟgō'uʟkᵘt,** (his child,) **tk·'ē'ʟgum** (a child) **g·at** (man) **ʟgō'uʟkᵘt.** (his child.) **Nʟk·'ē** (Then)

3. **hwandē't** (they sat down) **aʟ** (at) **g·ä'u.** (in front of the town.) **Lā** (When) **nakᵘʟ** (long) **hwa'ndēt,** (they sat,) **k·'ē** (then) **mɛn-g·a'askᵘʟ** (up looked)

4. **ʟgō-tk·'ē'ʟkᵘ** (the little boy) **aʟ** (to) **lax-ha'.** (the sky.) **Nʟk·'ē** (Then) **tgōnʟ** (this) **hēt** (he said) **aʟ** (to) **pɛlî'st:** (a star:) **"Q'äa,** ("Poor fellow,)

5. **g·ä'aʟ** (look) **k'opɛ-hwîla** (little being) **dā'us** (twinkler) **gōst.** (that,) **k'opɛ-xs-gumä'qs** (little feeling cold) **sa'ɛ!"** (indeed!") **Dē'yaʟ** (Thus said)

6. **ʟgō-tk·'ē'ʟkᵘ** (the little boy) **aʟ** (to) **pɛlî'st.** (the star.) **Nʟk·'ēt** (Then) **naxna'ʟ** (heard it) **pɛlî'st.** (the star.) **La** (When) **huX** (again)

7. **k·'ē'ɛlʟ** (one) **sa,** (day,) **nʟk·'ē** (then) **Lā** (it was evening,) **yu'ksa,** **nʟk·'ē** (then) **k·saxʟ** (went out) **ʟgō-tk·'ē'ʟkᵘ.** (the little boy.)

8. **K·'ē** (Then) **d'ɛp-ä'd'îk·skᵘʟ** (down came) **pɛlî'st.** (the star.) **Nʟk·'ēt** (Then) **gō'ut.** (he took him.) **Nʟk·'ēt** (Then) **mɛn-dē-** (up with him)

9. **dā'uʟt** (he went) **aʟ** (to) **lax-ha'.** (the sky.)

10. **Nʟk·'ē** (Then) **mɛsā'x·.** (it was daylight.) **Nʟk·'ē** (Then) **gwâtkᵘʟ** (was lost) **ʟgō-tk·'ē'ʟkᵘ.** (the little boy.) **Nʟk·'ē** (Then)

86

looked for him everywhere. They asked all the tribes, but they could
not find him. Then the people stopped, but his father and his mother
longed for him. They were crying all the time. They did so many
days.

One day the man was walking about crying. When he stopped crying, he looked up a mountain, and, behold, smoke came out of it. He
went up, and when he came near, he saw a woman. She asked the man,
"Do you know who took your child?" "No," said the man. "The
Star took your child. He tied him onto the edge of his smoke-hole.
The child is crying all the time. He is almost dead, because the sparks
the fire are burning his body." Thus she spoke. Then she said,

---

g·etk·sL	qal-ts'a'p.	Txanē'tkⁿL	lig·î-nda'	k'uL-g·ig·î'ɛldēt.	1
looked for him	the town.	All	everywhere	about they looked.	

Txanē'tkⁿL	saL	hwî'ldēt;	nî'g·ît	hwa'dēt.	La	gwâ'tkⁿdet.	2
Every	day	they did so;	not	they found him.	(Perf.)	they lost him.	

NLk·'ē	ha'udēt;	txanē'tkⁿL	qal-ts'îpts'a'pL	g·ē'daxdēt.	K·'ē	3
Then	they stopped;	all	the people of various towns	they asked.	Then	

qa'nē-hwîla	aba'g·askⁿL	nɛguâ'ôdɛt	qanL	nôxt.	Qa'nē-hwîla	4
always	was troubled	his father	and	his mother.	Always	

sīg·a'tkⁿdēt.	Wī-hē'lL	saL	hwî'ldēt.		5
they cried.	Many	days	they did so.		

Lā	huX	k·'ēlL	sa,	k·'ē	huX	k'uL-iē'êL	g·a'tg·ê	aL	6
When	again	one	day,	then	again	about went	the man	at	

k'uL-wī-yē'tkⁿt.	NLk·'ē	Lā	ha'wuL	wī-yē'tkⁿt,	k·'ēt	bax-g·a'aL	7
about	he cried.	Then	when	he stopped	crying,	then	up he saw	

lax-sqanē'st,	gwīnā'dēL,	mēyē'ên	k·si-hē'tgut	aL	lax-sqanē'st.	8
on a mountain,	behold,	smoke	out stood	at	on the mountain.	

NLk·'ē	bax-iä'L	g·a'tg·ê	lât.	NLk·'ē	hagun-a'qLkⁿt.	Gwīnā'deL,	9
Then	up went	the man	to it.	Then	toward he reached.	Behold,	

hana'q.	NLk·'ē	tgōnL	hēL	hana'qg·ê.	G·î'daqL	g·a'tg·ê:	10
a woman.	Then	this	said	the woman.	She asked	the man:	

"Hwîlā'yîn	t'an	gō'uL	Lgō'uLgunā'?"	"Nē',"	dē'yaL	g·a'tg·ê.	11
"Do you know	who	took	your child?"	"No,"	thus said	the man.	

"Pɛlî'st	t'an	gō'uL	Lgō'uLkⁿ.	Lax-ts'ä'L	ala'	t hwîl	lē-d'ā'dɛt	12
"The stars	who	took	the child.	On the edge of smoke-hole	the	where	on they put it	

tq'al-dē-da'k·Ldēt	lâ'ôt.	NLk·'ē	qa'nē-hwîla	wi-yē'tkⁿt.	NLk·'ē	13
against they tied it	to it.	Then	always	he cries.	Then	

La	dɛm	nô'ôt,	qanā'lɛguL	lakⁿ	t'an	mē'LL	Lîpla'nt."	14
(perf.)	(fut.)	dead,	sparks	fire	which	burns	his body."	

Dē'yaL.	Ma'LaaskⁿL	hana'qg·ê.	NLk·'ē	tgōnL	hēL	hana'qg·ê:	15
Thus she said.	He was told by	the woman.	Then	this	said	the woman:	

"Go on. Make many arrows, that you may have a great many quickly." The man went down and came to his town. There he made four bundles of arrows. He saw a very long mountain, which he climbed. He stood on top of it, took his bow, and took an arrow and shot at the sky. The arrow hit the edge of the hole of the sky, and stuck there. He shot another arrow, which hit the nock of the first one. He shot again, and continued to do so for many days. Then the arrows came down, and reached to him. The man was carrying tobacco, red paint, and sling-stones. Then he went up, climbing the arrows. He reached the sky, and met a person who said, "Your

1   "Adô',   dzāpʟ   wī-hē'ldɛl   hawî'l   dɛm   wī-hē'lt;   āmʟ
   "Go on,   make   many   arrows   (fnt.)   many;   good

2   sɛm-t'ē'ldɛn!"   Nʟk·'ē   iaga-iē'êl   g·a'tg·ê.   Nʟk·'ēt   hwaʟ
   very   quickly do it!"   Then   down went   the man.   Then   he found

3   qal-ts'a'p.   Nʟk·'ē   dzapʟ   wī-hē'ldɛl   hawî'l.   Txalpxt   hwîl
   the town.   Then   he made   many   arrows.   Four

4   lɛm-dîx·da'k·ʟt.   Nʟk·'ēt   g·a'aʟ   sɛm-k·'ā-wī-na'guʟ   sqanē'st,
   bundles.   Then   he saw   very exceedingly   great long   a mountain,

5   nîʟnē'ʟ   hwîl   mɛn-iä'êt.   Nʟk·'ē   lō-hē'tk·t   lâ'ôt.   Nʟk·'ēt
   that   where   up he went.   Then   on he stood   on it.   Then

6   gō'uʟ   ha-Xda'k.   Nʟk·'ēt   gō'uʟ   hawî'l.   Nʟk·'ēt   guXʟ
   he took   his bow.   Then   he took   an arrow.   Then   he shot at

7   lax-ha'g·ê.   Nʟk·'ē   hwîl   hwî'lʟ   hwîl   nānô'ôʟ   lax-ha'
   the sky.   Then   doing so   where   the hole of   the sky

8   nʟhwîl   lō-hē'tk·ʟ   hawî'l,   lē   lax-ts'ä't.   Sɛm-g·ît   lo-hē'tk·t
   there   in hit   the arrow,   on   its edge.   Strongly   in it stood

9   sɛm-lō-ts'ē'pk.   Nʟk·'ēt   huX   Xdak·ʟ   k·'ēlt.   Nʟk·'ēt   lō-gu'Xʟ
   very in   strong.   Then   again   he shot   one.   Then   in he hit

10   g·apʟ   lō-hē'tgutg·ê.   Nʟk·'ēt   huX   Xdak·t.   Nʟk·'ēt   huX
   the end of   in it stood.   Then   again   he shot.   Then   again

11   xʟîp-gu'Xʟ   ʟa   g·ap.   Wī-hē'lt   saʟ   hwîlt.   Nʟk·'ē   d'ɛp-a'qʟk·t
   at the end   he hit   the end.   Many   days   he did so.   Then   down it reached

12   aʟ   awa'at.   K'uʟ-iu'kdɛl   g·a'tg·ê   ʟa   hwîndô'ô   qanʟ   mîs-a'ust
   to   his proximity.   About carried   the man   tobacco   and   red paint

13   qanʟ   Xts'a.   Nʟk·'ē   mɛn-iä'êt.   Mɛn-iô'xgut   lax-hawî'l.
   and   sling shot.   Then   up he went.   Up he went   on the arrows.

14   Nʟk·'ē   mɛn-a'qʟk·t   aʟ   ts'ɛm-lax-ha'.   Nʟk·'ē   iä'êt.   Nʟk·'ēt
   Then   up he came   to   in the sky.   Then   he went.   Then he

15   hwaʟ   hwîl   hwî'lʟ   k·'âlʟ   g·at.   Nʟk·'ē   tgōnɪ   hēʟ   g·a'tg·ê:
   found   where   was   one   man.   Then   this   said   the man:

child is about to die. He is crying all the time because his body is being burned. Carve a piece of wood so that it will look just like your child." He gave to this person tobacco, red paint, and sling-stones in return for his advice. Then the person was very glad. The man made a figure of spruce, one of hemlock, one of balsam fir, and one of red cedar, and one of yellow cedar, all as large as his boy. Then he made a great fire. He built a pyre of slender trees, which he placed crosswise, and placed fire underneath. He hung his wooden images to a tree over the fire. He poked the fire, so that the sparks burned the body of the wooden figure. Then the latter cried aloud, but after a short time it stopped. Then he took it off, and took another one. It did the same. The figure stopped crying after a short time. He

---

"Lā dEm nô'ôL Lgō'uLgun. Qanē-hwîla ayawā'tkᵘt aL hwîl 1
'(Perf.) (fut.) dies your child. Always he cries because

meL Lîpla'nt. Ām mE dEm dzāpL gan dEm sE-g·a'dEn dEm 2
burns his body. Good you (fut.) make a (fut.) mak- a man (fut.)
stick ing

hō'g·îgat Lgo-tk·'ē'Lkᵘ." NLk·'ē g·inā'mL g·a'tg·ê hwindô'ô 3
like a child." Then gave him the man tobacco
little

qanL mEs-a'us qanL Xts'a. NLk·'ē sEmgal lō-ā'mL qâ'ôtL 4
and red paint and sling Then much in good heart
shot.

g·at tq'al-hwa'tg·îtg·ê. NLk·'ēt dzapL gan. Sä'êqs tgōn 5
the against he had met. Then he made a stick. Spruce this
man

dzāpt, g·ē'kᵘ tgōn dzāpt, hô'ak·s tgōnL dzāpt, sEm-ga'n 6
he made, hemlock this he made, balsam this he made, cedar
tree

tgōnL dzāpt, sgunä'e tgōnL dza'pt. Qâ'ôdEt sîl-qas-qâ'ôt'Ent 7
this he made, yellow this he made, It was as large as
cedar finished

aL Lgō'uLkᵘ. NLk·'ēt wī-sE-mē'L lakᵘ. NLk·'ēt ma'qsaanL 8
as the boy. Then greatly he burn a fire. Then he placed
made

qasqē'sgum gan. NLk·'ēt lē-sg·i'L huX qē'sgum gan. 9
slender trees. Then on he laid also a slender tree.

NLk·'ē sE-mē'L lakᵘ aL laXt. NLk·'ēt lē-ia'qL g·at aL 10
Then he burn a fire at under it. Then on he the at
made hung man

lax-ga'n. NLk·'ēt qē'LqanL lakᵘ. NLk·'ē meL Lîpla'nL 11
on the Then he poked the fire. Then hurnt the body of
tree.

g·a'dEm gan. NLk·'ē wī-amhē't aL ayawā'tkᵘt. Nî'g·î 12
the man of wood. Then he shouted and cried. Not

nakᵘL hēt, k·'ē ha'ut. NLk·'ēt sa-ma'gat. NLk·'ēt huX 13
long he spoke, then he stopped. Then off he took Then again
it.

gō'uL k·'ēlt. NLk·'ē huX hwîlt. Nî'g·î nakᵘL ayawā'tkᵘt, 14
he took one. Then also he did so. Not long he cried,

took it down. Then he tied the red cedar to the tree and poked the
fire. There were very many sparks. The figure cried for a long
time, and then stopped. He took it down and hung up the yellow
cedar. It did not stop. Then he took the image of yellow cedar.

He went on, and came to a place where he heard a man splitting
firewood with his wedge and hammer. His name was Gˑixˑsats'ā′ntxˑ.
When he came near, he asked him, "Where is the house?" At the
same time he gave him tobacco. Then Gˑixˑsats'ā′ntxˑ began to swell
when he tasted the tobacco. (The people of olden times called it
"being troubled.") He also gave him red paint and sling-stones.

---

1 kˑ'ē   huX   ha'ut.   NʟK·'ē   huX   sa-maˊgat.   NʟK·'ēt
   then   also   he stopped.   Then   also   off he took   Then
                                                                     it.

2 lē-tsē'êpʟ   sɛm-ga'n.   NʟK·'ēt   huX   qē'ʟqanʟ   lakᵘ.   NʟK·'ē
   on he tied   cedar.   Then   again   he poked   the fire.   Then

3 sɛm-kˑ'a-wī-hē'ʟ   qanā'luk.   NʟK·'ē   nakᵘt   wi-yē'tkᵘt
   very exceed- many   sparks.   Then   long   it cried
         ingly

4 ayawā'tkᵘtgˑê.   NʟK·'ē   huX   ha'ut.   NʟK·'ēt   huX   sa-maˊgat.
   it cried.   Then   again   it stopped.   Then   also   off he took it.

5 NʟK·'ēt   gō'uʟ   sgunä'ê.   NʟK·'ē   nĭ'gˑîdi   qē'sxkᵘtgˑê.   NʟK·'ē
   Then   he took   yellow   Then   not   it stopped.   Then
                        cedar.

6 iä'ɛt;   gu'kdēt   gˑa'dɛm   ga'nɛm   sgunä'ê.
   he went;   he took   the man of   wood of   yellow
                                                    cedar.

7 NʟK·'ēt   nɛxna'ʟ   hwîl   hahä'ʟ   t'an   dzāpʟ   lakᵘ.   Hē-yu'kt
   Then he   heard   where   noise   who   made   fire-   He began
                                                                  wood.

8 guXʟ   lakᵘ   aʟ   lēt   qanʟ   daqʟ.   Gˑîxˑsats'ā′ntxˑ   hwaʟ
   to take   firewood   with   wedge   and   hammer.   Gˑîxˑsats'ā′ntxˑ   was the
                                                                                        name of

9 gˑa'tgˑê.   `NʟK·'ē   hagun-iä'ʟ   gˑa'tgˑê.   NʟK·'ēt   gˑē'dɛxs
   the man.   Then   toward went   the man.   Then   he asked

10 Gˑîxˑsats'ā′ntxˑ: "Ndaʟ   hwîl   hētkᵘʟ   hwîlp?"   NʟK·'ēt   gˑenʟ
    Gˑîxˑsats'ā′ntxˑ: "Where   (verbal   stands   the house?"   Then   he gave
                                    noun)   food

11 gˑa'tgˑê   aʟ   hwîndô'ô.   NʟK·'ē   ā'dˑîkˑskᵘʟ   hwîl   gˑîtkᵘs
    the man   of   tobacco.   Then   came   (verbal   swelled
                                                               noun)

12 Gˑîxˑsats'ā′ntxˑ.   Wî-t'ē'sʟ   hwîl   gˑî'tkᵘtgˑê.   At   hwîl
    Gˑîxˑsats'ā′ntxˑ.   Much was   (verbal   he swelled.   Because
                                       noun)

13 baqʟ   hwîndô'ô   qan   hwîlt   (nʟ   sɛ-wa'deʟ   waʟɛn-gˑigˑa't
    he   the tobacco   therefore   he did so   (they   called it   ˑ the former people
    tasted

14 aʟ   aba'gˑaskᵘ),   t   hwîl   baqʟ   akˑsda'ʟ   hwîndô'ô.   NʟK·'ēt
    he was   because   he tasted   sweetness of   tobacco.   Then
    troubled),

15 huX   gˑînā'ᴜnʟ   mɛs-a'ust   qanʟ   Xts'a.   NʟK·'ēt   māʟs
    also   he gave   red paint   and   sling shot.   Then   told him
             him

Then G·ix·sats'ā′ntx· told him where the child was.   He said, "Wait
in the woods until they are all asleep, then go up to the roof of the
house."   The man went, and when he came nearer, he heard the voice
of his boy, who was crying; but as soon as the boy stopped, the chief
ordered his men to poke the fire until many sparks flew up.   When
all the people were asleep, the man went to the roof of the house
where the child was.   The child recognized his father and cried;
but his father rebuked him, saying, "Don't cry, don't cry!   They
might hear you in the house."   The boy stopped and the man took
him off.   In his place he tied the wooden image to the smoke hole.
Then he went down.   Early in the morning the chief ordered his
people to poke the fire.   Then the wooden image cried while the man

G·îx·sats'ā′ntx·ᴌ	hwîl	lē-hō′kskⁿᴌ	ᴌgō′uᴌkᵘᴌ	g·a′tg·ê.	"Tsᴇ 1
G·îx·sats'ā′ntx·	where	on was with it	the child of	the man.	

k·'ax-d·ā′nēn	aᴌ	g·ilē′lîx·	ᴌā	dᴇm	wâ′wôqdēt	dᴇm	k·'ē 2
"Only stay	in	in the woods	when	(fut.)	they sleep	(fut.)	then

mᴇn-iē′ᴇn,"	dē′yas	G·ix·sats'ā′ntx·.	K·'ē	iä′êᴌ	g·a′tg·ê. 3
up go,"	thus said	G·ix·sats'ā′ntx·.	Then	went	the man.

Nᴌk·'ē	hagun·a′qᴌkⁿt.	Nᴌk·'ēt	nᴇxna′ᴌ	am-hē′ᴌ	ᴌgō′uᴌkᵘtg·ê 4
Then	toward he got.	Then	he heard	the voice of	his child

aᴌ	ayawā′tkᵘt.	Q'ai-lîg·i-qē′sxkᵘᴌ	ᴌgō-tk·'ē′lkᵘ,	k·'ēt	huX 5
at	crying.	But as soon as stopped	the little boy,	then	again

gun-qē′ᴌqanᴌ	sᴇm'â′g·itᴌ	lakᵘ.	K·'ē	huX	ā′d'îk·skᵘᴌ	hwîl 6
ordered to poke	the chief	the fire.	Then	again	came	(verbal noun)

wī-hē′ᴌᴌ	qanā′luk.	ᴌā	wâ′wôqᴌ	hwîlp,	uᴌk·'ē	mᴇn·iä′ᴌ 7
many were	the sparks.	When	slept	the house,	then	up went

g·a′tg·ê.	Nᴌk·'ē	hagun-iä′êt	aᴌ	hwîl	lē-hō′kskᵘᴌ	ᴌgō′uᴌkᵘt. 8
the person.	Then	toward he went	to	where	on was with it	his child.

Nᴌk·'ēt	hwîlā′x·ᴌ	ᴌgō-tk·'ē′lkᵘ	nᴇguâ′ôdᴇt.	Nᴌk·'ē	wī-yē′tkⁿt. 9
Then	knew	the boy	his father.	Then	he cried.

Nᴌk·'ēt	lä′ᴇᴌ	neguâ′ôdᴇt:	"G·îlô′,	g·îlô′!	nᴇxna′yîtg·ê	aᴌ 10
Then	rebuked him	his father:	"Don't,	don't!	they hear it perhaps	in

ts'ᴇm-hwî′lp."	Nᴌk·'ē	ha′uᴌ	ᴌgō-tk·'ē′lkᵘ.	Nᴌk·'ēt	sā-gō′dîᴌ 11
in the house."	Then	stopped	the little boy.	Then	off took

g·at	ᴌgō′uᴌkᵘtg·ê.	Nᴌk·'ēt	ia′gai-lē-tq'al-da′k·ᴌᴇᴌ	g·a′dᴇm 12
the man	his child.	Then	how-ever on against he tied	the person of

gan.	Nᴌk·'ē	d'ᴇp-iä′êt.	Nᴌk·'ē	hē′ᴌuk.	Nᴌk·'ēt	huX 13
wood.	Then	down he went.	Then	morning.	Then	again

gun-sᴇ-mē′ᴌᴇᴌ	sᴇm'â′g·itᴌ	lakᵘ.	Nᴌk·'ē	huX	ayawā′tkⁿᴌ 14
or-dered to burn make	the chief	the fire.	Then	again	cried

and his son were making their escape. But the wooden image did not cry long. Then it stopped. The chief became suspicious, and sent a man to the roof. He went up, and, behold, there was a stick. The boy was lost, and the wooden image was on the roof. The chief said, "Pursue them!" The people did so. The man heard them approaching. When they were close behind him, he threw tobacco, red paint, and sling-stones in their way. The paint was red; the sling-stones were blue.

The chief's people found these and picked them up. Some persons took the sling-stones, and others took the red paint and put it on their faces.[1] While they were doing so, the man and his son continued to

---

1 Lgō-tk·'ē'Lkᵘ,   aL   La   k·'ē'   dē-iä'L   g·a'tg·ê   Lgō'uLkᵘt.
  the boy,   at   when then   with went   the man   his child.
  little

2 Nî'g·î   nakᵘL   ayawā'tkᵘL   g·a'dɛm   ga'ng·ê.   K·'ē   ha'nt.
  Not   long   cried   the person of wood.   Then   he stopped.

3 NLk·'ēt   lîk·s-g·a'd'ɛnL   sɛm'âg·ît   qan   mɛn-hē'tsL   k·'âlL
  Then   took notice   the chief   there-   up he sent   one
                                              fore

4 g·at.   K·'ē   mɛn-iä'L   g·at;   gwinā'dēL   gan.   Gwâtkᵘʟ
  man.   Then   up went   a person;   behold   wood.   He was lost

5 Lgō-tk·'ē'Lkᵘg·ê;   gan   lē-hō'ksgut.   K·'ē   a'lg·îxL   sɛm'â'g·it:
  the boy;   wood   on was with it. Then   said   the chief:
  little

6 "Ām,   mɛsɛm   yôxkᵘt."   NLk·'ē   hwîlL   qal-ts'a'pg·ê.   K·ēt
  "Good, you   pursue   Then   they did it the people.   They
                   them."

7 yô'xdēiL.   K·'ē   nɛxna'L   g·a'tg·ê   hwîl   Lā   ā'd'îk·skᵘL   t'an
  pursued   Then   heard   a person   where   (perf.) came   who
  them.

8 yôxkᵘt.   NLk·'ē   Lā   q'ai'yîm   dēlpkᵘt   aL   qalā'nt,   uLk·'ēt
  pursued   Then   when   close by   near him   at   behind   then
  them.   him,

9 sqa-lā'g·îl   hwîndô'ô   qanL   mɛs-ā'ust   qanL   Xts'a.   Hwîl
  across he   tobacco   and   red paint   and   sling shot. Where
  threw

10 iLä'êL   hwîlL   mɛs-a'ust.   NLk·'ē   gusgwâ'ôskᵘL   Xts'a.
   it was   where   the red paint. Then   was blue   the sling shot.
   red

11 NL   lē-hwa'îL   qal-ts'a'pL   sɛm'â'g·it.   NLk·'ē   dô'qdēiL
   Then on found it the people of the chief.   Then   they took up

12 mɛs-ā'us   qanL   Xts'a.   Lā   qats'ō'oL   g·a'tg·ê   t'an   dôqL
   the red paint and   the   Some   persons   who   took
                        sling shot.

13 mɛs-ā'ust.   NLk·'ē   qats'ō'ot   t'an   dôqL   Xts'a.   D'ä'Ldet   aL
   red paint.   Then   some   who   took   sling   They put it on
                                                        shot.

14 qa-ts'ɛlts'a'ldet.   YukL   gwanɛm   hwî'ldet,   uLk·'ē   nakᵘL
   their faces.   While   they were   this,   then   it was
                                 doing   long

---

[1] This accounts for the colors of the stars.

run. Again the man heard the pursuers approaching. Now he came to G·ix·sats'ā'ntx·, who said, "Run quickly, my dear. They will not catch you." The Star had taken the boy, and therefore the Star's tribe were pursuing them. The man gave G·ix·sats'ā'ntx· tobacco, and then G·ix·sats'ā'ntx· swelled very much, so that he obstructed the trail, and therefore the Star tribe could not reach the man.

Now he came near the hole of the sky. He came to it, and went down the chain of arrows. As soon as he reached the ground, he pulled the arrows down, and they all dropped to the ground. He had saved his boy. Then he went down the mountain and ran home. He got the boy back, and therefore he and his wife were glad.

---

hwîl (verbal noun)	de-ba'xL made run	g·a'tg·ê the man	Lgō'uLk^{u}t. his son.	NLk·'ē Then	huX again	nExna'L he heard	Lā — 1
hwîl where	q'ai'yîm close	ad'ā'd'îk·sk^{u}t they came	aL at	q'ai'yîm close	qalā'nt. behind him.	NLk·'ēt Then	— 2
hwaL he came to	hwîl where	hwîls was	G·îx·sats'ā'ntx·. G·îx·sats'ā'ntx·.	NLk·'ē Then	tgōnL this	hēs said	— 3
G·îx·sats'ā'ntx·: G·îx·sats'ā'ntx·:	"Alō-bā'n, "Quickly run,	nāt! my dear!	nî'g·i not	dEmt (fut.)	g·îdi-gō'udēt they catch		— 4
nē'En." you."	PElî'st The star	t'anL who	gōL took	Lgō-tk·'ē'Lk^{u}g·ê. the little boy.	NîLnê'L They	t'an who	— 5
yôxk^{u}L pursued	g·a'tg·ê the man	qal-ts'a'pL the tribe of	pElî'st. the star.	NLk·'ēt Then	g·ē'nL he gave him food	g·a'tg·ê the person	— 6
G·îx·sats'ā'ntx· G·îx·sats'ā'ntx·	aL of	hwîndô'ô. tobacco.	NLk·'ē Then	g·îtk^{u}s swelled	G·îx·sats'ā'ntx· G·îx·sats'ā'ntx·		— 7
wī-t'ē'sL greatly	hwîl he	g·î'tk^{u}tg·ê. swelled.	Lō-qan On account of	haXha'gwaganL obstructing	qē'nEx. the trail.		— 8
NLqan Therefore	aqL-yô'xk^{u}L not pursued him	qal-ts'a'pL the tribe of	pElî'stg·ê. the star.	Lā When	q'ai'yîm close	dē'lpk^{u}L near	— 9
g·a'tg·ê the man	aL at	hwîl where	nānô'ôL the hole of	lax-ba', the sky,	nLk·'ēt then	hwat. he found it.	NLk·'ē Then	d'Ep- down — 10
iä'êt. he went.	D'Ep-iô'xguL Down he went	hwîl where	lō-ndE-Lôglô'ôdEL in place of joining each other	hawî'l. arrows.	NLk·'ēt Then	La — 11
d'Ep-a'qLk^{u}t. down he reached.	NLk·'et Then	d'Ep-sa'g·îL down he pulled	hawî'l. the arrows.	NLk·'ē Then	mak·L dropped	gul-q'ane't. all of them.	— 12
Dē-mâ'tguL He was saved	Lgō'uLk^{u}tg·ê. his son.	NLk·'ē Then	iaga-iē'êt. down he went.	Wîtk^{u}t He came	aL at	lax- on — 13
sqanē'st. the mountain.	NLk·'ē Then	na-ba'xt out of the woods ran	aL to	qal-ts'a'p. the town.	Mâtk^{u}L He was saved	Lgō'uLk^{u}t; his son;	— 14
gulîk·s-daa'qLgut. back he got him.	NLk·'ē Then	lō-ā'mL in good	qâ'ôtt his heart	qanL and	nak·st. his wife.		— 15

Rotten-feathers

[Told by Moses]

There was a town, and a large prairie on which many children were playing. They were always making a noise. They did so every morning all the year round. Then the Heaven heard it. He was much annoyed, and therefore he sent down feathers. They came down, soaring over the children. One boy saw them. He was almost grown up and was very strong. He took the feathers and put them on his head. Then he ran about.

Logômîx ‘Q’ā′x·

Rotten-feathers

1   Hētk^{u}ɴ   qal-ts’a′p.   Nɴk·’ē   d’āɴ   wī-lax-ha′p’ᴇsk^u,   nêɴne′ɴ
   There stood   a town.   Then   there was   a great   on prairie,   there

2   hwîl   qalā′qɴ   wī-hē′ldᴇm   k’ōpᴇ-tk·’ē′ɴk^u.   Qanē-hwîla   xstamqɴ
   where   played   many   little children.   Always   noise of

3   alēmhē′detg·ê.   Hē′ɴuk,   nɴk·’ē   huX   hwî′ldētg·ê.   Txānē′tk^{u}ɴ
   their voices.   It got morning,   then   again   they did so.   Every

4   saɴ   hwî′ldēt.   Txānē′tk^{u}ɴ   k’ōɴ   hwî′ldēt.   Nɴk·’ē   nᴇxna′ɴ
   day   they did so.   All   year   they did so.   Then   heard it

5   lax-ba′g·ê.   Nɴk·’ēt   lō-hwa′ntk^{u}ɴ   qâ′ôtt.   Wī-t’ē′s   hwîl
   the heaven.   Then   in was annoyed   his heart.   Much   being

6   lō-hwa′ntk^{u}ɴ   qâ′ôtt,   nᴇtqan   d’ᴇp-ma′gaɴ   qaq·ā′x·.   Nɴk·’ē
   in   annoyed   his heart,   therefore   down came   a feather.   Then

7   dē-d’ᴇp-yu′kt   aɴ   lax-ō′ɴ   k’ōpᴇ-tk·’ē′ɴk^u.   Nɴk·’ēt   g·a′aɴ   k·’âɴ
   also down it came   to   on top of   the little children.   Then   saw it   one

8   ɴgō-tk·’ē′ɴk^u,   ɴa   ts’ō′sg·îm   wī-t’ē′st,   ɴa   sᴇm-dax-g·a′tt.   Nɴk·’ēt
   little boy,   (perf.)   a little   large,   (perf.)   very strong.   Then he

9   gō′uɴ   qaq·ā′x·,   nɴk·’ē   lē-hē′t’ᴇnt   aɴ   lax-t`ᴇm-qē′st.   Nɴk·’ē
   took   the feather,   then   on he put it   at   on his head.   Then

10   k’uɴ-ba′xt.
   about he ran.

94

The children had a stick with which they struck a wooden ball. After a little while that boy began to rise, his feet leaving the ground. Then another one rushed up to him and took hold of his feet. His hands stuck to the feet of the first boy, and his feet also left the ground. Then another boy rushed up to him and took hold of his feet, but he also went up. Still another one rushed up to them, taking hold of the feet. He also was lifted upward. Still other ones ran up to them, until all the children were gone. Then a man saw it and rushed up to the children. He also hung onto them. Another one rushed up to them, and took hold of his feet. They all went up to heaven, the whole town, and nobody was left. The Heaven took them all up. He was annoyed on account of the noise of the children.

---

1. Tgōnʟ hwîlʟ k'ōpɛ-tk·'ē'ʟkᵘ; ganʟ dô'qdēt; nʟk·'ē huX
This / did / the little children; / sticks / they held; / then / also

2. ganʟ ia'tsdet. Hō'g·igaʟ ʟēt'ʟ ga'ng·ê. Nʟne'ʟ ia'tsdet aʟ
stick / they struck. / Like / a ball / the stick. / Then / they struck

3. gan. Nʟa ts'ō'sg·îm nakᵘt dē-iax'ia'qʟ k·'âlʟ ʟgō-tk·'ē'ʟkᵘ,
the wood. / Then / a little / long / with hung him / one / little boy,

4. nʟk·'ē lîslē'skᵘʟ asîsā'it ʟa mɛn-dā'uʟt. Nʟk·'ē tq'ē'saaʟ k·'âlʟ
then / hung / his feet / (perf.) / up he went. / Then / rushed / one

5. dɛxdô'gôʟ asîsa'it. Nʟk·'ēt tq'al-hathē't an'ô'nt aʟ asîsa'iʟ
he took / his feet. / Then / against stuck / his hands / to / the feet of

6. ʟgō-tk·'ē'ʟkᵘg·ê. Nʟk·'ē huX dē-lîslē'skᵘʟ asîsa'ît. Nʟk·'ē
the little boy. / Then / also / also hung / his feet. / Then

7. huX tq'ē'saaʟ k·'âlʟ ʟgō-tk·'ē'ʟkᵘ; huX dɛxdô'qʟ asîsa'ît.
also / rushed to him / one / little boy; / also / he took / his feet.

8. Nʟk·'ē huX dē-iax'ia'qt. Nʟk·'ē huX tq'ē'saaʟ k·'âlt. Nʟk·'ē
Then / also / on his part he hung. / Then / again / rushed / one. / Then

9. dɛxdô'qʟ asîsa'ît. Nʟk·'ē huX iax'ia'qt. Nʟk·'ē huX tq'ē'saaʟ
he took hold of / his feet. / Then / also / he hung. / Then / again / rushed to them

10. k·'âlt. ʟā mɛn-qâ'ôdɛʟ k'ōpɛ-tk·'ē'ʟkᵘ, nʟk·'ēt g·a'aʟ t'ē'sɛm
one. / When / up were finished / the little children, / then / saw it / a large

11. g·at. Nʟk·'ē dē-tq'ē'saat. Nʟk·'ē huX dē-iax'ia'qt. Nʟk·'ē
man. / Then / on his part he rushed to them. / Then / also / on his part he hung. / Then

12. huX tq'ē'saaʟ huX k·'âlt. Nʟk·'ē huX dɛxdô'qʟ asɛsa'it
again / rushed / again / one. / Then / also / he took / the feet

13. ʟā wagait-lax-ha' hwîl mɛn-sa'k·skᵘdet. Nʟk·'ē qanē'-hwîla
(perf.) / up to sky / where / up they went. / Then / always

14. hwîlʟ txānē'tkᵘʟ qal-ts'a'p. Nî'g·î ʟgō-q'am-g·îna-d'ā'ʟ k·'âlt.
did / all / town. / Not / little only behind was / one.

15. Sɛm-mɛn-qâ'ôdet aʟ lax-ha'g·ê. Lō-hwa'ntkᵘʟ qâ'ôdɛt aʟ hwîl
Very up they were finished / by / the heaven. / In was annoyed / its heart / because

Therefore the Heaven took them all up. Not even one was left.
The whole town disappeared. Only dogs were there, running about
howling.

　　Now there was a young menstruating girl who had been in a small
house behind the village. She was there with her little grandmother.
When she left her little house and went back to the village, she saw
that the whole great town was empty. Then the woman walked
along the street crying. Now she found an old wedge made of crab-
apple wood, one made of sloe wood, one of spruce wood, and she found
a little grindstone, a little knife, and some snot. She put them into
her belly and went to the rear of the house. She did not put them
aside. Then she lay down for four days and four nights. Then she

---

1　qane-hwîla　　xstamkᵘʟ　　alēmhē′dɛʟ　　txanē′tkᵘʟ　　k'opɛ-tk‧′ē′ʟkᵘ.
　　always　　　　noise　　　　their voices　　　all　　　　　　the　　children.
　　　　　　　　　　　　　　　　　　　　　　　　　　　　　　little

2　Nîʟne′t　qan　　hwîlā′gut,　　lax-ha′g‧ê　　t'an　　mɛn-qâ′ôt'ɛnt.　　Nî′g‧î
　　Therefore　　it was　　the heaven　　who　　up　　finished　　　　Not
　　　　　　　　done,　　　　　　　　　　　　　　　　them.

3　mānʟ　　ʟgō-q'am-k‧‧â′lt.　　Sɛm-qâ′dɛʟ　　qal-ts'a′pg‧ê,　　k‧sax-as'o′sʟ
　　was left　little only one.　　Very　were　　the people,　　　only　　dogs
　　　　　　　　　　　　　　　finished

4　k'uʟ-na-gaq'ē′dɛt.
　　about from all howled.
　　directions

5　Nʟk‧′ē　　q'am-k‧‧â′lʟ　　tk‧′ē′ʟgum　　hana′q　　ia′skᵘ.　　Nʟk‧′ē　　hētkᵘʟ
　　Then　　only one　　　young　　　girl　　menstru-　　Then　　stood
　　　　　　　　　　　　　　　　　　　　ating.

6　ʟgō-hwî′lp　　aʟ　　g‧ilē′lîx‧.　　Nʟhwîl　　lō-d‧â′ʟ　　tk‧′ē′ʟgum　　hana′q
　　a　house　　　at　　inland.　　　There　　in sat　　a young　　　girl
　　little

7　qanʟ　　ʟgō-nts'ē′itst.　　la′skᵘ　　nʟqan　　d‧āt　　aʟ　　g‧îlē′lîx‧.　　Nʟk‧′ē
　　and　　her　little　　　　Menstru-　therefore　she sat　at　　inland.　　　Then
　　　　grandmother.　　　ating

8　k‧saXt　　aʟ　　ʟgō-hwî′lpt.　　Nʟk‧′ē　　na-iē′êt.　　K‧′ēt　　g‧a′at.　　Nî′g‧î
　　she went　at　her　little　　Then　　out of she　Then　she saw it.　Not
　　out　　　　house.　　　　　　woods went.

9　ha′yuksʟ　　wî-txanē′tkᵘʟ　　wî-qal-ts'a′p.　　Nʟk‧′ē　　tgōnʟ　　hwîʟʟ
　　was left　　great　all　　　　the　people.　　Then　　this　　did
　　　　　　　　　　　　　　　great

10　hana′qg‧ê.　　K'uʟ-sag'ap-iä′êt　　aʟ　　k'uʟ-wî-yē′tkᵘt.　　Nʟk‧′ēt　　hwaʟ
　　the woman.　　About along the　she　at　about　she cried.　Then she　found
　　　　　　　　street　　　　went

11　q'am-lē′dɛm　　sgan-mē′lîk‧st　　qanʟ　　lē′dɛm　　sgan-sna′x　　qanʟ
　　an old　wedge of　crab apple　　and　　a wedge of　sloe　　and

12　lē′dɛm　　sä′êqs　　qanʟ　　ʟgō-an-qä′x　　qanʟ　　ʟgō-ha-q'ô′ʟ　　qanʟ
　　a wedge　spruce　and　　a grindstone　and　　a　knife　　and
　　of　　　　　　　　　little　　　　　　　little

13　k‧si-nō′ʟqt.　　Nʟk‧′ēt　　lō-d‧a′ʟt　　aʟ　　ts'ɛm-ba′nt.　　Nʟk‧′ē　　q'aldîx‧-iä′êt.
　　snot.　　　　Then　　in　she　in　　in　her　　Then　　to the rear　she
　　　　　　　　　　　put it　　　　　belly.　　　　　of the house went.

14　Nî′g‧ît　　sä-d‧â′ʟt　　aʟ　　dāg‧ig‧ä′êlt.　　Lā　　txalpXʟ　　saʟ　　hwîlt
　　Not　　away she　at　　when she lay　(Perf.)　four　　days　she did
　　　　put them　　　　down.　　　　　　　　　　　　　so

came to be with child and gave birth to a boy, to another one, and
to still another one, and to two more. They were very strong.
There were three males and one stone and one knife and one snot.
The one was named Little-crab-apple-tree, the next one Little-sloe-
bush, the next one Little-spruce, the following Little-mountain, the
next one Little-knife, and one more was called Snot. The woman
had six children.

The woman and her little grandmother suckled them. Now they
were a little older, and then they were grown up. Now they also
began to play. They took a stick and played ball. (In olden times the
people called this "ball-play.") Then the mother said to her children:
"Stop, children! Your grandfathers were killed on account of this

| qanʟ | yu'ksa. | Nʟk·'ē | ā'd'îk·skᵘʟ | hwîl | ō'bᴇnt. | Nʟk·'ē | aqʟkᵘʟ | 1 |
| and | evenings. | Then | she came | (verbal noun) | pregnant. | Then | she gave birth to | |

| k·'âlʟ | ʟgō'uʟkᵘt. | Nʟk·'ē | huX | k·'âlt. | Nʟk·'ē | huX | k·'âlt. | 2 |
| one | boy. | Then | again | one. | Then | again | one. | |

| Q'ai-baɡadē'lʟ | dax-g·ig·a'dᴇt. | Gulâ'n | ē'uXt | dē-k·'â'lʟ | lô'ôpg·ê | 3 |
| Together | two were strong. | Three | men | with one | stone | |

| dē-k·'â'lʟ | ha-q'ō'ʟ | dē-k·'â'lʟ | nä'êʟq. | ʟgō-dᴇp-sgan-mē'lîk·st | hwaʟ | 4 |
| with one | knife | with one | snot. | Little- crab-apple-tree | was the name of | |

| k·'âlt; | nʟk·'ēt | ʟgō-dᴇp-sgan-sna'x | hwaʟ | k·'âlt; | nʟk·'ē | 5 |
| one; | then | Little- sloe-bush | the name of | one; | then | |

| ʟgō-dᴇp-am-sä'êqs | hwaʟ | k·'âlt; | nʟk·'ē | ʟgō-dᴇp-sqane'st | hwaʟ | 6 |
| Little- spruce | the name of | one: | then | Little- mountain | the name of | |

| k·'âlt; | nʟk·'ē | ʟgō-dᴇp-ha-q'ō'ʟ | hwaʟ | k·'âlt; | nʟk·'ēt | Nä'êʟq | 7 |
| one; | then | Little- knife | the name of | one; | then | Snot | |

| hwaʟ | huX | k·'âlt. | Q'âᴇldâ'lʟ | ʟg·îʟ | hana'qg·ê. | 8 |
| the name of | again | one. | Six were | the children of | the woman. | |

| Nʟk·'ē | qanēt-hwîla | lēmâts'îk's a'ant | aʟ | txanē'tkᵘʟ | sa | qanʟ | 9 |
| Then | always | she suckled them | at | all | days | and | |

| ʟgō-nts'ē'ts. | Nʟk·'ē | ʟa | ā'd'îk·skᵘt | dᴇm | hwîl | k'ōpᴇ-t'êst'ē'st. | 10 |
| the grand- little mother. | Then | (perf.) | came | (fut.) | being | a little large. | |

| Nʟk·'ē | ʟa | t'êst'ē'st. | Nʟk·'ēt | huX | sī-d'ā'dēt | dᴇm | huX | 11 |
| Then | they | were large. | Then | again | newly started they | (fut.) | also | |

| hwîl | qalā'qdēt. | HuX | dô'qdᴇʟ | gan. | Nʟk·'ēt | huX | ia'tsdēʟ | 12 |
| (verbal noun) | they played. | Again | they took | sticks. | Then | again | they struck | |

| ʟet. | Tgōnʟ | sᴇ-hwa'dᴇʟ | waʟᴇn-g·ig·a't. | T'ak· | t | sᴇ-hwa'detgê. | 13 |
| a ball. | This | made name | the ancient people. | T'ak· | | they made its name. | |

| Nʟk·'ē | a'lg·îXʟ | nôxʟ | k'ōpᴇ-tk·'ē'ʟkᵘg·ê: | "G·îlâsᴇm, | ʟgō'uʟkᵘ. | 14 |
| Then | said | the the little mother of | children: | "Stop, | child. | |

game. The Heaven took the whole tribe up. Long ago the children did the same thing that you are doing now. Therefore do not do so." One day the children did so again. Their mother and the little grandmother were unable to stop them. Now they were young men. There were five young men and one girl. They were called Little-crab-apple-tree, Little-sloe-bush, Little-spruce, Little-grindstone, and Snot; but the little girl was called Little-knife. They were playing all the time. They were very strong. The little girl was the sixth one. Now the Heaven heard them again when they started playing.

---

1 Āmᴸ   dᴇm   ha'usᴇm.   Niᴌne'ᴸ qan   lō-nô'ôsdet   niä'en   aᴸ
  Good   (fut.)   yon stop.   Therefore   in were killed   your grandfathers   at

2 g·i-k'ō'ᴸ.   Nᴇ'ᴸqan   mᴇn-qâ'ôdᴇᴸ   qal-ts'a'p   aᴸ   ts'ᴇm-lax-ha'g·ê.
  long ago.   Therefore   np went   the tribe   to   in the sky.

3 Hwîl   hwî'ᴌ   k'ōpᴇ-tk·'ē'ᴌkᵘ   an-hwunsᴇm   aᴸ   g·i-k'ō'ᴸ.   Qan
  They did the same   the little   children   what yon do   at   long ago.   Therefore

4 g·ilô'   dzē   huX   hwî'lsᴇm."
  do not   on your part   do so."

5 Nᴌk·'ē   ʟa   huX   k·'ēlᴸ   sa,   nᴌk·'ē   huX   hwîlᴸ
  Then   when   again   one   day,   then   again   did so

6 k'opᴇ-tk·'ē'ᴌkg·ê,   skwāe't   lä'lêᴸ   nô'xdet   qanᴸ   ʟgō-ntsē'tsdēt.
  the little children,   she gave up them   stopped   their mother   and   little their grandmother.

7 Nᴌk·'ē   ʟa   dax-g·ig·a'det   ʟā   q'ap-q'aima'qsdēit.   Kᵘstᴇnsâ'l
  Then   (perf.)   were strong   (perf.)   they were real young men.   Five

8 k'ōpᴇ-ē'uXt   dē-k·'â'lᴸ   ʟgō-hana'q.   ʟgō-dᴇp-sgan-mē'lîk·sᴸ   hwaᴸ
  little men   with one   little woman.   Little- crab-apple-tree   the name of

9 k·'â'ltg·ê.   Nᴌk·'ē   ʟgō-dᴇp-sgan-sna'x   hwaᴸ   k·'â'ltg·ê.   Nᴌk·'ē
  one.   Then   Little- sloe-bush   the name of   one.   Then

10 ʟgō-dᴇp-am-sä'êqs   hwaᴸ   k·'â'ltg·ê.   Nᴌk·'ē   ʟgō-dᴇp-am-qä'ᴇx
   Little- spruce   the name of   one.   Then   Little- grindstone

11 hwaᴸ   k·'â'ltg·ê.   Nᴌk·'ēt   Nä'ᴇʟq   hwaᴸ   k·'âlt.   Nᴌk·'ē
   the name of   one.   Then   Snot   the name of   one.   Then

12 ʟgō-dᴇp-ha-q'o'ᴸ   hwaᴸ   ʟgō-hana'qg·ê.   Nᴌk·'ē   qane-hwîla
   Little- knife   the name of   the little woman.   Then   always

13 qalā'qdēt   ʟa   t'êst'ē'sdet   ʟā   sᴇm-dᴇx-g·îg·a'tdēt.   Ts'ōq'âldâ'ldêᴸ
   they played   when   they were great   (perf.)   very strong they were.   The sixth one was

14 ʟgō-hana'q.
   a little woman.

15 Nᴌk·'ēt   huX   nᴇxna'ᴸ   lax-ha'g·ê   hwîl   ʟa   huX
   Then   again   heard   the sky   where   (perf.)   again

16 sᴇt'ā'tkᵘstᴸ   hēᴸ   k'opᴇ-tk·'ē'ᴌkᵘg·ê.   Nᴌk·'ē   ha'ts'îk·sᴇm   huX
   started   said   the little children.   Then   again   also

Then he sent the feathers. They came down again, soaring over the children. The eldest boy saw them and took them. He put them on his head and ran about, playing. Then his feet began to rise from the ground. The sky took him up. His younger brother, Little-sloe-bush, ran up to him, but his feet were lifted from the ground. He could not pull his brother down. When he felt that he was getting weak, he said, "Break, my roots!" and his feet left the ground. Then the Little-spruce-tree rushed up to them. He tried to keep his feet to the ground, but when he grew weak, he also said, "Break, my roots!" Then Little-grindstone rushed up to them, and suddenly there was a great mountain. He also tried to keep his feet down while the Heaven was pulling him upward. He did not move because the

---

d'ɛp-ma'gaʟ	qaq'ā'x·.	Nʟk·'ē	huX	dē-d'ɛp-yu'kt	aʟ	lax'-ō'ʟ	1
down he sent	feathers.	Then	again	also down they came	to	on top of	

k'opɛ-tk·'ē'ʟkᵘ.	Nʟk·'ēt	g·a'aʟ	ʟgō-sē'lg·ît.	Nʟk·'ēt	huX	gō'ut. 2
the children little	Then	saw it	the eldest little	Then	again	he took it.

K·'ēt	lē-hē't'ɛnt	aʟ	lax-t'ɛm-qē'st.	Qanē-hwîla	k'uʟ-ba'xt	aʟ 3
Then	on he put it	at	on his head.	Always	about he ran	at

qalā'qtg·ê.	Nʟk·'ē	ā'd'îk·skᵘʟ	hwîl	huX iax'ia'qt	ʟā	ha'ts'îk·sɛm 4
playing.	Then	came	(verbal noun)	again it hung	(perf.)	again

dɛm	huX	mɛn-dô'qʟ	lax-ha'g·ê.	Nʟk·'ē	huX iax'ia'qt.	Nʟk·'ē 5
(fut.)	again	up took him	the heaven.	Then	again he hung.	Then

tq'ē'saaʟ	ʟgō-wa'k·t	ʟgo-dɛp-sgan-sna'x	hwa'tg·ê.	Nʟk·'ēt	huX 6
rushed to him	his brother little	Little- sloe-bush	his name.	Then he	also

dɛxdô'qʟ	asîsa'ît.	Nʟk·'ē	nî'g·ît	huX	daa'qʟkᵘt.	Skwāe't huX 7
he took	his feet.	Then	not	also	he succeeded.	He gave up again

dē-dā'mgantg·ê.	Nʟk·'ē	ʟat	baqʟ	dɛm	hwîl alî'skᵘt,	nʟk·'ē 8
also	pull.	Then	when	he felt	(fut.) being weak,	then

tgōnʟ	a'lg·îxtg·ê:	"ʟā	dɛm	wudɛn-bîsbē'sʟ,	wî'sdeîst," 9
this	he said:	"(Perf.)	(fut.)	along tear,	my roots,"

dē'ya.	Nʟk·'ē	huX	dē-lîslē'skᵘʟ	asîsa'ît.	Nʟk·'ēt tq'ē'saas	ʟgō- 10
thus he said.	Then	also	also hung	his feet.	Then rushed to him	little

dɛp-am-sä'êqs.	Nʟk·'ē	huX	skwa'et	asîsa'ît.	Nʟk·'ē	ʟa huX 11
spruce-tree.	Then	also	he gave up	his feet.	Then	(perf.) also

ā'd'îk·skᵘʟ	dɛm	alî'skᵘt.	Nʟk·'ē	huX	a'lg·îxtg·ê.	Tgōnʟ hēt: 12
he came	(fut.)	weak.	Then	also	he spoke.	This he said:

"La	huX	wudɛn-bîsbē'sʟ,	hwî'sdeîst	hâ'u!"	Nʟk·'ē	tq'ē'saas 13
"(Perf.)	also	along	tear,	my roots!"	Then	rushed to him

ʟgō-dɛp-am-qä'x.	Nʟk·'ē	sä-hē'tkᵘʟ	wî-sqanē'st.	Nʟk·'ē	skwa'et 14
Little- grindstone.	Then	suddenly stood	a mountain great	Then	he gave up

huX	dē-dā'mganʟ	lax-ha'g·ê.	Nî'g·î	huX	ʟantkᵘt	aʟ hwîl 15
again	also pulling	the heaven.	Not	also	it moved	because

mountain was all stone, but after a while the mountain moved. Then
Snot rushed up to them. He also stuck to the ground. The little girl
was running about, rubbing her hands. She was called Little-knife.
When Snot's feet were also lifted from the ground, she rushed up to
them and climbed her brothers' heads until she reached the eldest one.
Then she cut the feathers over her eldest brother's head. She cut them
right in the middle, and the children fell down to the ground. They
did not go up to the sky. The feathers always stayed on the eldest
brother's head, and he was called Rotten-feathers.

Now Rotten-feathers and his younger brother went on all alone.
They came to a town, and there Rotten-feathers married a woman.
Then he returned to his own town, and there he stayed with her.

---

1 lô'op   qan   hwîlt.   Sī-gō'n   k·'ē   huX   ʟantkᵘt.   NʟK·'ē   tq'ē'saas
  stone   there-   it did so. After a while also   it moved.   Then   rushed to
              fore   him

2 Nä'êʟq.   NʟK·'ē   qanē-hwîla   tq'al-sa'k·t.   NʟK·'ē   k'uʟ-ba'xʟ
  Snot.   Then   always   against he   Then   about ran
                                  stuck.

3 ʟgō-hana'qg·ê.   At   qä'êxʟ   an'ô'nt,   ʟgō-dɛp-ha-q'o'ʟ
  the girl.   She   rubbed   her hands,   Little-   knife
  little

4 hwa'tg·ê.   Nîʟ   lā   dē-lîslē'skᵘʟ   asîsa'îs   Nä'êʟq,   k·'ē
  her name.   When   also   hung   the feet   Snot,   then
                                           of

5 dē-tq'ē'saaʟ   ʟgō-hana'qg·ê.   Sɛm-mɛn-yô'xgut   lax-qa-t·em-q'ē'sʟ
  also rushed to the girl.   Very up she went   on the heads of
  them   little

6 g·îmx·dē'tkᵘtg·ê.   K·'ē   wagaît-mɛn-dā'uʟt.   NʟK·'ēt   sa-xtse-q'ō'tsit
  her brothers.   Then   until up she went.   Then   quick-across she
                                                          ly middle cut it

7 wagait-lax-ō'ʟ   Lē   k·s-qâ'gum   t'an   gōʟ   qaq·ā'x·g·ê.
  up to   on top of   the first one who   took   the feather.

8 NʟK·'ē   xtse-q'ō'st.   K·'ē   ha'ts'ik·sɛm   mak·t   aʟ   lax-dz·ä'dz·îk·s.
  Then   across she   Then   again   they fell to   on the ground.
            middle cut it.

9 Nî'g·i   huX   mɛn-sa'k·skᵘt   aʟ   lax-ha'.   NʟK·'ē   qane-hwîla
  Not   also   up they went   to   the sky.   Then   always

10 lē-hē'tkᵘʟ   qaq·ā'x·   aʟ   lax-t'ɛm-qē'st.   NʟK·'ē   ā'd'îk·skᵘʟ   dɛm
   on stood   feather   on   on -his head.   Then   came   (fut.)

11 hwa'dɛs   Lôgômîx·q'ā'x·.
   his name Rotten feathers.

12 NʟK·'ē   tgōnʟ   hwî'ldetg·ê;   sɛmgal   ām   hwîl   hwî'ldetg·ê.
   Then   this   they did;   very   good   they   did.

13 NʟK·'ē   Lô'ôdot   q·am-k·'ä'lʟ   Lôgōmîx·q'ā'x·   qanʟ   k·ûlʟ   wak·t
   Then   they went   only one   Rotten feathers   and   one   his
                                                                         brother

14 stᵉlt.   NʟK·'ēt   hwa'dîʟ   k·ēlʟ   qal-ts·a'p.   NʟK·'ēt   gōuʟ
   accom-   Then   he found   one   town.   Then he   took
   panying.

15 hana'q,   at   nak·skᵘt.   NʟK·'ē   dē-lō-ya'ltkᵘt   aʟ   lɛp-qal-ts·a'pt.
   a woman,   he   married her. Then   also he returned to   his   town.
                                                                  own

They had a boy. When he was grown up, his father, Rotten-feathers, named him. Then he went . . . . .[1]

Nʟk·'ēt	dē-d'ā't	lât.	Nʟk·'ē	ʟā	ā'd'îk·skⁿt	dɛm	ʟgō'uʟkᵘt.	1
Then	with her was he	in it.	Then	(perf.)	came	(fut.)	her child.	

Nʟk·'ē	ʟgō'uʟkᵘt,	tk·'ē'ʟgum	g·at	ʟgō'uʟkᵘtg·ê.	Nʟk·'ē	ʟā	2
Then	his son,	a child	man	his child.	Then	when	

wī-t'ē'st,	nʟk·'ēt	ētkᵘʟ	hwas	nɛguâ'ôdɛt.	Lôĝômix·q'ā'x·ʟ	3
large,	then	he called	his name	his father.	Rotten-feathers	

hwat.	Nʟk·'ē	qâ'ôdɛt	.	.	.	.	4
his name.	Then	he went					

---

[1] For continuation, see page 234.

K·'ēlkᵘ

[Told by Moses]

A number of children played camping every day. Many played this game in one large hollow log. They went into it and played that it was their house. They made a fire in it and ate there. They took a large quantity of provisions into the log. They ate salmon. They did so every day. One day when they were playing camping, the tide rose high and the large tree floated out to sea. The children did not know it. They were playing inside. Now the log had drifted far out to sea. Then one child went out, and he saw that the log had drifted

---

K·'ēlkᵘ

1 Txanē'tkᵘʟ sa hîs-dzô'qsʟ k'opᴇ-tk·'ē'ɪkᵘ. Wī-hē'lt, q'am-k·'ē'lʟ
   Every   day played camping little children.   Many,   only one
   play- ed

2 wī-ga'n. Wī-lō-nô'ôʟ wī-ts'ä'wut. Wī-d'ᴇ'xʟ wī-ga'n. Nʟ
   large log. A large in hole large inside. A large large log. Then

3 hwî̂l g·its'ᴇʟ-qâ'ôdᴇʟ k'opᴇ-tk·'ē'ɪkᵘ. Nîʟne'ʟ hwî̂'lpdētg·ê̂
   where in went the little children. Then their house

4 wī-qalk·si-nô'ôm gan. Nʟk·'ēt lō-sī-me'ɪdēʟ lakᵘ lât. Nʟk·'ē
   large through hole of the tree. Then in they made burn fire in it. Then

5 huX txâ'xkᵘdēt wī-hē'lʟ ts'ele'mdet. Hân ts'ele'mʟ gul-q'anē'tkᵘʟ
   also they ate many traveling provisions. Salmon the traveling provisions of all

6 k'ōpᴇ-tk·'ē'ɪkᵘ. ʟā nakᵘʟ hwî̂'ldet aʟ txanē'tkᵘʟ sa, nʟk·'ē
   the little children. When long they did so in every day, then

7 ʟa huX t'ēsʟ ak·s ʟā huX lō-dzô'qdet aʟ wī-ts'ᴇm-ga'n.
   (perf.) again great the water (perf.) again in they camped in large in the log.

8 Nʟk·'ē huX pta'lîk·s. Nʟk·'ē g·î̂g·â'k·sʟ wī-ga'n. Nʟk·'ē
   Then again the water rose. Then floated the large log. Then

9 uks-o'lîk·skᵘt. Nî̂'g·ît hwîlā'x·ʟ k'opᴇ-tk·'ē'ɪkᵘ. Yukʟ
   from land to sea it drifted. Not knew it the little children. Beginning

10 gwanᴇm-qalā'qdet aʟ lo-ts'ä'wuʟ wī-ga'n ʟā hwagait-uks-dā'uʟ
   they were playing at in the inside of the large log (perf.) away from land it was to sea going

11 aʟ hwagait-g·ī'ks ʟā uks-na'kᵘt. Nʟk·'ē k·si-ʟô'ôtkᵘʟ k·'âɪʟ
   at way off shore when from land to sea far. Then out went one

12 ʟgō-tk·'ē'ɪkᵘ. Nʟk·'ēt g·a'at hwî̂l ʟā hwagait-uks-o'lîk·skᵘt aʟ
   little child. Then he saw where (perf.) away from land to sea it drifted to

102

away. Then all the children went out, and they cried. The log was drifting about in the ocean.

One of the children was wise. He saw gulls flying about, and then he returned into the hollow log and said, "Gulls are always sitting on top of us. What can we do to catch them?" Then one boy said, "Let us hit our noses, and we will rub the blood all over the log, then the feet of the gulls will stick to the log." They did so. They hit their noses until they bled. Then they rubbed the blood on the log. Then they entered the log again. Now many gulls came and sat down on the log. About noon their feet dried to the log. Then one of the boys went out. The gulls tried to fly away, but they could not do

---

hwagait-g·ī′îks.	NᴸK·'ē	k·si-qâ′ôdEL	k'opE-tk·'ē′ʟkᵘ	NᴸK·'ē 1
way off shore.	Then	out went	the little children.	Then

sîg·a′tkᵘdēt;	qanē-hwîla	sîg·a′tkᵘdet.	NᴸK·'ē	k'uʟ-dā′uʟʟ	wī-ga′n 2
they cried;	always	they cried.	Then	about went	the log large

aʟ	hwagait-lax-sē′Elda.	3
on	way out on the ocean.	

NᴸK·'ē	huX	k·si-ʟô′ôtkᵘʟ	ʟgō-hwîl-xô′ôsgum	ʟgo-tk·'ē′ʟkᵘ. 4
Then	again	out was put	a little wise	little child.

NᴸK·'ēt	g·a′aʟ	hwîl	lēba′yukʟ	qē′wun. NᴸK·'ē ha′ts'îk·sEm 5
Then	he saw	where	flew	gulls. Then again

lō-ya′ltkᵘt	aʟ	ts'ä′wuʟ	wī-ga′n.	K·'ēt	maʟʟ: "Qanē-hwîla 6
he returned	to	the inside of	the log. large	Then	he told: "Always

lē-hwa′nʟ	qē′wun	aʟ	lax-ō′Em. Aq-dEp-hwîlā′gut."	NᴸK·'ē tgōn 7
on sit	gulls	on	top of us. What can we do?"	Then this

hēʟ	k·'âlʟ	ʟgo-tk·'ē′ʟkᵘ:	"Ām dEp d'îsd'ē′sʟ	qa-dz'a′gam, 8
said	one	little boy:	"Good we strike	our noses,

nʟ	dEm	k·'ē	iʟä′êʟaat,	dEp dEm k·'ē	mant aʟ	dāx·ʟ 9
then	(fut.)		they bleed,	we will then	rub at	around

wī-ga′n.	Nʟ	dEm	k·'ē	tq'al-hathē′t ts'ōbä′qʟ	qē′wun	lâ′tg·ê." 10
the log. large		(Fut.)	then	against stand the feet of	the gulls	on it."

NᴸK·'ē	hwî′ldētg·ê.	D'îsd'e′sdEʟ	qa-dz'a′qdēt.	K·'ē ā′d'îk·skᵘʟ 11
Then	they did so.	They struck	their noses.	Then came

hwîl	iʟä′êʟaat.	NᴸK·'ēt k·'îlq'al-ma′ndēit	aʟ	wī-ga′n. NᴸK·'ē 12
(verbal noun)	they bled.	Then round they rubbed it	on	the log. large Then

la′mdzîxdēt	aʟ	ts'ä′wuʟ wī-ga′n.	NᴸK·'ē ad'ä′d'îk·skᵘʟ wī-hē′ldEm 13
they entered	at	the inside of the log. large	Then came many

qē′wun.	NᴸK·'ē	lē-hwa′nt	lâ′ôt.	K·'ē tq'al-gulgwa′lukʟ asîsa′it. 14
gulls.	Then	on they sat	on it.	Then against dried their feet.

ʟa	sEm-bagait-d'ä′ʟ ʟôqs,	nʟk·'ē huX k·saXʟ	ʟgō-k·'ä-wī-t'ē′st. 15
When very	middle was the sun,	then again went out	a really large. little

so because their feet were glued to the log. Then the boy took hold of them and twisted off their necks. He killed many gulls and took them into the log. Then the boys were glad. They ate the meat of the gulls and forgot that they were drifting about on the ocean.

The land was far away. They were on the edge of the ocean. One day they heard a great noise. The boys went out and, behold, they were drifting round in a whirlpool. Then they began to cry. The tree almost stood on its end, because the whirlpool was swallowing it.

While it was drifting there on end a man ran out to it. He had only one leg. He harpooned the great log and pulled it ashore. He hauled

---

1 NᴸK·'ē   lēba'yukᴸ   qē'wun.   Nî'g·ît   daa'qᴸk{}^{u}dēL   dᴇm
  Then   flew   the gulls.   Not   they succeeded   (fut.)

2 lēba'yukdētg·ê;   tq'al-gulgwa'lk{}^{u}ᴸ   qa-ts'ōbä'q'dēt   aᴸ   gan.   NᴸK·'ē
  they flew;   against were dried   their feet   on   the log.   Then

3 dôqᴸ   k·'âlᴸ   ʟgo-tk·'ē'ʟk{}^{u}.   NᴸK·'ēt   lō   haʟ-t'uxt'a'qᴸ   t'ᴇm-lā'nîx·t
  took them one   little boy.   Then   in   along he twisted   their necks

4 gul-ganē'ᴸ   wī-hē'ldᴇm   qē'wun.   NᴸK·'ēt   lō-d'ᴇp-dā'ᴸet   aᴸ   hwîl
  all   many   gulls.   Then   in down he put   in   where
                                                                           them

5 nānô'ôᴸ   wī-ga'n.   NᴸK·'ē   lō-am'ā'mᴸ   qagô'ôᴸ   k'opᴇ-tk·'ē'ʟk{}^{u}.
  the hole of   the large log. Then   in good were   the hearts of the little boys.

6 G·ē'îpdeᴸ   sma'x·tg·ê   ʟā   t'a'k·dᴇʟ   hwî'ldetg·ê   ʟā   hwagait-
  They ate   meat   (perf.) they forgot   what they did   when   far

7 k'uɪ-dā'wîʟdēit   aᴸ   hwagait-lax-sē'lda.
  about they went   at   far on the ocean.

8 Nî'g·i   lîg·i-tsagam-dē'lpk{}^{u}dēt   aᴸ   lîg·i-lax-ts'ä'ᴸ   ak·s.   NᴸK·'ē
  Not   any- from sea short   at   some- on the   the   Then
              way to land   where edge of   water.

9 ʟa   huX   k·'ēlᴸ   sa   dē-nᴇxna'dēiʟ   wī-xstō'ntk{}^{u}.   K·'ē   k·si-
  when   again   one   day   also they heard   a great noise.   Then   out

10 ʟô'ôʟ   k'opᴇ-tk·'ē'ʟk{}^{u}.   Gwinā'dēʟ,   an-tgo-lē'lbîk·sk{}^{u}   hwîl   ʟa
   went   the little boys.   Behold,   the whirlpool   (verbal when
                                                                                  noun)

11 lē-lō-d'ᴇp-yu'kdet.   NᴸK·'ē   ā'd'îk·sk{}^{u}ᴸ   hwîl   sīg·a'tk{}^{u}dēit   ʟa
   on in down they went.   Then   came   (verbal they cried   when
                                                            noun)

12 lō-d'ᴇp-hē'tk{}^{u}ᴸ   wī-ga'n   aᴸ   dᴇm   ʟôqk{}^{u}ᴸ   an-tgo-lē'lbîk·sk{}^{u}.
   in down-ward stood   the large log to   (fut.)   swallow them   the whirlpool.

13 NᴸK·'ē   ʟa   lō-d'ᴇp-hē'tk{}^{u}t,   dē-uks-ba'xᴸ   k·'âlᴸ   g·a'tg·ê.
   Then   when   in down-ward stood,   also from land ran one   man.
                                                 to sea

14 Q'am-k·'ē'lᴸ   asa'ēᴸ   g·a'tg·ê.   NᴸK·'ēt   g·aʟk{}^{u}ᴸ   wī-ga'n   aᴸ
   Only   one foot   man.   Then   he harpooned   the large log with

15 qalā'st.   K·'ēt   tsagam-dā'mgantg·ê.   NᴸK·'ē   tsagam-a'qᴸk{}^{u}t.
   his harpoon. Then   from sea to land he pulled it. Then   from sea to land it reached.

it ashore. The boys were not dead. He had saved them. Then the boys went up to the house of the man. There were many boys. One-leg gave them to eat. The beach in front of the house smelled of seal. The man was spearing seals all the time at the edge of the whirlpool. He watched for seals, and therefore he stayed there. There was also another man living there whose name was Hard-instep. He was much troubled, for he was jealous because One-leg had saved the boys. One-leg was spearing seals all the time, and he carried them up for the children. They ate, and they grew up to be young men.

After a while the children remembered those whom they had left behind, and they began to cry. Then One-leg asked the children why they cried, and they told him. Then he said, "The town of your fathers

---

Nî'g·i	daXʟ	k'opɛ-tk·'ē'ʟkᵘ.	De-lē-mâ'tguʟ	g·a'tg·ê.	Nʟk·'ē	1
Not	dead were	the little boys.	He saved them	the man.	Then	
bax-ʟô'ôʟ	k'ôpɛ-tk·'ē'ʟkᵘ	aʟ	ts'ɛm-hwî'lpʟ	g·a'tg·ê.	Wî-hē'ltʟ	2
up went	the little boys	to	in the house of	the man.	Many	
k'opɛ-tk·'ē'ʟkᵘ.	Nʟk·'ē	yuk-txâq'ɛns	Q'am-k·'ē'lɛm	asa'ē.	ʟā	3
little boys.	Then	began fed them	Only- one-	foot.	When	
îskᵘʟ	qa-g·ä'ut	aʟ	ēlx	qanēt-hwîla	g·aʟkᵘʟ	g·a'tg·ê	aʟ	4
stench	in front of the house	of	seals	always	speared them	the man	at	
lax-ts'ä'ʟ	an-tgo-lē'lbîk·skᵘ.	Nîʟ	q'ap-lî'ʟg·ît	qan	dzôqt	lât.	5
on the edge of	the whirlpool.		He watched it	therefore	he stayed	there.	
HuX	k·'âlʟ	g·at	huX	dzôqt	aʟ	awa'at.	Qâ'dɛm	lax-snä'qsʟ	6
Also	one	man	also	stayed	in	his proximity.	Hard-	on- instep	
hwa'tg·ê.	Nʟk·'ē	sɛm-aba'g·askᵘs	Qâ'dɛm	lax-snä'qs.	G·askᵘʟ	7
his name.	Then	much troubled	Hard-	on- instep.	Jealous was	
qâ'ôtt	hwîl	g·a'aʟ	qabē'iʟ	k'opɛ-tk·'ē'ʟkᵘ	dē-lē-mâ'tgus	Q'am-k·'ē'lɛm	8
his heart	when	he saw	how many were	the little boys	saved by	Only- one-	
asa'ē.	Nʟk·'ē	qanet-hwîla	g·aʟkᵘs	Q'am-k·'ē'lɛm	asa'eʟ	ēlx.	9
foot.	Then	always	he speared	Only- one-	foot	seals.	
Nʟk·'ē	qane-hwîlat	bax-hwî'lgaʟ	k'opɛ-tk·'ē'ʟkᵘ.	Nʟk·'ē	10
Then	always	up he carried	the little children.	Then	
qanē-hwîla	txâ'xgut.	ʟa	ā'd'îk·skᵘʟ	dɛm	q'aima'qsit.	11
always	they ate.	(Perf.)	they came	(fut.)	youths.	
Nʟk·'ē	ʟa	sî-gō'n,	nʟk·'ēt	am-qâ'ôʟ	k'ôpɛ-tk·'ē'ʟkᵘ	ʟā	12
Then	when	after a while,	then	they remembered	the little children	(perf.)	
qalā'ndēt.	Nʟk·'ē	sîg·a'tkⁿdēit.	Nʟk·'ēt	g·îda'xs	Q'am-k·'ē'lɛm	asa'ē	13
they left behind.	Then	they cried.	Then	asked	Only- one-	foot	
dza'gan	sîg·a'tkᵘʟ	k'opɛ-tk·'ē'ʟkᵘ.	Nʟk·'ēt	ma'ʟdēit.	Nʟk·'ē	14
why	cried	the little children.	Then	they told.	Then	
a'lg·îxs	Q'am-k·'ē'lɛm	asa'ē:	"Nî'g·î	nakᵘʟ	ʟē	ts'aps	dɛp	15
said	Only- one-	foot:	"Not	far		the town of		

is not far. It is over there. To-morrow morning you shall start. You
may use my canoe, which is at the end of the village." Early the next
morning One-leg sent the boys, saying, "Take the cover off from my
canoe. It is near by yonder." The children went, and grew tired
walking about. They could not find the canoe. Finally they returned.
Then One-leg asked, "Did you find it?" The boys said, "No." He
sent them again, and they went; but again they grew tired walking
about, but they did not find it. Again they returned. Then One-
leg himself went. He went to a rotten tree that was there. It
was covered with small branches. He took off the branches and they
beheld a large canoe. It was made in the shape of a man, with a mouth
at one end. It was the same at the other end. Its name was "Wâ'sE-
at-each-end." It did not allow anything to cross its bow or its stern.

---

1 nEguâ'ôdEn.   Q'ai'yîm   gōst.   DEm   sī-g·â'ôtk°   nē'sEm   adzid'ā'Lak°.
  your fathers.   Close by   those.   (Fut.)   start   you   to-morrow.

2 Qal-g·â'L   mā'lēdō   dEm   hâ'hîsEm   dEm   dā'wuL   nē'sEm
  By is   my canoe   (fut.)   you use it   (fut.)   go   you
  itself

3 adzid'ā'Lak°."   NLk·'ē   ā'd'îk·sk°L   mEsā'x·.   NLk·'ēt   hashē'ts   Q'am-
  to-morrow."   Then   came   daylight.   Then   sent them   Only-

4 k·'ē'lEm   asa'EL   k'ōpE-tk·'ē'Lk°.   "Adô',   sEm-sā-d'ā'Lt   Lē   â'dEl
  one-   foot   the   boys.   "Go on,   very off   put   the   cover of
  little

5 māl.   G·â'ô   aL   q'ai'yîm   dō."   K·'ē   sak·sk°L   k'ōpE-tk·'ē'Lk°.
  the   It is   at   close   yonder."   Then   went   the   children.
  canoe.   little

6 NLk·'ē   skwā'EL   k'uL-Lô'ôdet.   Nîg·ît   hwa'dēt.   NLk·'ē
  Then   they gave   about   going.   Not   they found   Then
       up   it.

7 lō-yîlya'ltk°det.   NLk·'ēt   g·ē'dExs   Q'am-k·'ē'lEm   asa'ē: "Nē
  they returned.   Then   asked   Only-   one-   foot: "Not

8 mEsEm   hwa'da?"   NLk·'ēt   nē'etk°L   k'ōpE-tk·'ē'Lk°.   NLk·'ēt
  did you   find it?"   Then   said no   the   boys.   Then
                                 little

9 ha'tsîk·sEm   huX   hashē'tst.   NLk·'ē   huX   Lô'ôdet.   HuX   skwā'EL
  once more   again   he sent   Then   again   they went.   Again   they gave
            them.   up

10 k'uL-Lô'ôdet.   HuX   nîg·ît   hwa'det.   NLk·'ē   huX   yîlya'ltk°det.
  about   they   Again   not   they   Then   again   they returned.
  went.   found it.

11 NLk·'ē   lEp-iä'ês   Q'am-k·'ē'lEm   asa'ê.   NLk·'ē   hagun-iä'êt   aL   hwîl
  Then   him- went   Only-   one-   foot.   Then   toward   he   to   where
  self   went

12 sg·îl   wī-anksî-sga'n.   Lē-d'ā'L   Lgo-ga'n   lâ'ôt.   NLk·'ēt   sa-d'ā'LL
  lay   a rotten   tree.   On were   little sticks   on it.   Then   off he put
       large

13 Lgō-ga'ng·ê.   NLk·'ē   alō-d'ā'L   wī-mā'l.   G·atL   mā'lg·ê   ts'Em-ā'qL
  the   sticks.   Then   open-   there   a canoe.   A man   canoe   a mouth
  little   ly   was   large

14 an-gō'st.   NLk·'ē   huX   hwîl·   an-gō'st.   Lāx-wâ'sEL   hwaL
  one end.   Then   also   it was   the other end.   At-   Wâ'sE   the
                                       each-end-   name of

When a man crossed it, it ate him. Then One-leg said, "Don't pass in front of the canoe." And they obeyed because they were afraid. Then they put it into the water. It was a fine, large canoe. They put many seals aboard, which were to serve as food for the canoe. Then the boys went aboard. They fed the canoe. Its bow and its stern ate five seals each. Then the canoe went. After it had finished eating the seals it went very fast. Then they gave five seals more to the bow and five to the stern, and it went on again.

Finally the children landed at the town of their fathers. They went ashore. Their fathers and mothers and all their relatives were crying. Then the boys came back. That is the end.

---

mā′lg·ê.　　Nī′g·ît　　mâ′t′ɛnʟ　　dɛm　　sqa-iä′t　　lât.　　Tsɛ　　da　　sqa- 1
the canoe.　　Not　　it let go any-　　(fut.)　　across went　　to it.　　If　　across
　　　　　　　　　　thing　　　　　　the way　　　　　　　　　　the way

yô′xkᵘʟ　　g·at,　　nʟk·′ēt　　g·ē′îpt.　　Nʟk·′ē　　a′lg·îxs　　Q'am-k·′ē′lɛm 2
went　　a man,　　then　　it ate him.　　Then　　said　　Only-　　one-

asa′ē:　　"G·îlô′　　mɛtsɛsɛm　　sqa-yô′xkᵘt,"　　dēya′　　aʟ　　k′ôpɛ-tk·′ē′ʟkᵘ. 3
foot:　　"Don't　　you　　across　　go,"　　thus　　to　　the　　boys.
　　　　　　　　　　　　　　　　　　he said　　　　little

Nʟk·′ē　　hwîlt.　　Laxbēts′ē′Xt.　　Nʟk·′ēt　　iaga-ʟô′ôdet　　ts'ɛm-a′k·s. 4
Then　　they　　They were afraid.　　Then　　down　　they　　in　　the
　　　did so.　　　　　　　　　　　　　　　　put it　　　　　water.

Wī-sɛm-k·′ā-ama　　mā′l　　tgō′stg·ê.　　Nʟk·′ēt　　sīlô′kᵘdēt　　aʟ　　k·′ā- 5
Large very ex-　　good　　canoe　　that.　　Then　　they put in　　　exceedingly　　　　　　　　　　　　　　　　　　　　　　　　ceedingly

wī-hē′ldɛʟ　　ēlx.　　Nʟk·′ē　　lɛp-dô′xʟ　　ts'ēlē′mʟ　　mā′lg·ê.　　Nʟk·′ē 6
many　　seals.　　Then　　its　　was　　food　　the canoe.　　Then
　　　　　　　　　　own

lō-magam-qâ′ôdɛʟ　　k′ôpɛ-tk·′ē′ʟkᵘ.　　Nʟk·′ēt　　g·î′ndetʟ　　mā′lg·ê. 7
in　　they went　　the　　boys.　　Then　　they fed　　the canoe.
　　　　　　　little

Kᵘstēnsʟ　　g·ē′îpʟ　　g·îtsäq　　aʟ　　ēlx.　　Nʟk·′ē　　huX　　kᵘstēnsʟ 8
Five　　ate　　the how　　　seals.　　Then　　also　　five

g·ē′îpʟ　　anō-g·îlā′n.　　Nʟk·′ē　　baxʟ　　mā′lg·ê　　aʟ　　lax-a′k·s　　sɛm- 9
ate　　the stern.　　Then　　went　　the canoe　　on　　on　　the　　really
　　　　　　　　　　　　　　　　　　　　　　　　water

k·′ā-a′le-ba′xtg·ê.　　Q'am-ʟîʟä′êxkᵘʟ　　ēlx.　　Nʟk·′ēt　　huX　　g·ē′ndetg·ê 10
ex-　　fast　　it went.　　Only　　it finished　　seals.　　Then　　again　　they gave him
ceedingly　　　　　　　　　　eating　　　　　　　　　　　　　　to eat

kᵘstēnsʟ　　ēlx　　aʟ　　g·îtsä′ɛq.　　Nʟk·′ē　　huX　　kᵘstēns　　aʟ　　g·îlā′n. 11
five　　seals　　to　　the how.　　Then　　also　　five　　to　　the stern.

Nʟk·′ē　　huX　　ba′xtg·ê. 12
Then　　again　　it went.

Nʟk·′ē　　k·′a′tskᵘtg·ê　　aʟ　　qal-ts'a′ps　　dɛp　　nɛguâ′ôʟ　　k′ôpɛ-tk·′ē′ʟkᵘ. 13
Then　　landed　　at　　the town of　　their　　fathers　　the　　children.
　　　　　　　　　　　　　　　　　　　　　little

Nʟk·′ē　　k·′atskᵘt.　　Nʟk·′ē　　wī-t′ē′sʟ　　hwîl　　sig·a′tkᵘʟ　　qa-nɛguâ′ôtkᵘdet 14
Then　　they landed.　　Then　　much　　(verbal　　cried　　their fathers
　　　　　　　　　　　　　　　　noun)

qanʟ　　qa-nâ′nôxkᵘdet　　qanʟ　　gul-ganē′ʟ　　hwîlhwîlā′îskᵘdet.　　Nʟk·′ē 15
and　　their　　mothers　　and　　all　　their relatives.　　Then

gu′lîk·s-ax'a′qʟkᵘdet.　　Sā′-baxt. 16
back　　they got.　　The end.

The Sealion Hunters

[Told by Moses]

There were four men—one of the Wolf clan, one of the Raven clan, one of the Eagle clan, and one of the Bear clan. They were great hunters. There were four rocks. The men went out in their canoes to these rocks, and when they arrived there they found the rocks full of sealions. The rock of one of the men was not full. He caught only two. The men of the Raven clan, of the Wolf clan, and of the Eagle clan caught a great many. Then the one man was ashamed because he had caught only two. The next time they started he came home

---

The Sealion Hunters

1 K·'âlɴ g·at, ɴʟk·'ē huX k·'âlɴ g·at. Nʟk·'ē huX k·'âlɴ
　 One　　 man,　 then　 again　 one　 man.　　 Then　 again　 one

2 g·at. Nʟk·'ē huX k·'âlɴ g·at. Lax-k·ebō' qanʟ qanha'da qanʟ
　 man.　 Then　 again　 one　 man.　 A wolf clan　 and a　 raven clan　 and a
　　　　　　　　　　　　　　　　　 man　　　　　　　　　 man

3 g·îsbēwuduwE'da qanʟ lax-skī'yêk. Gwīx·-wô'Eʟ k·'âlɴ qanha'da.
　 g·îsbēwuduwE'da　 and an　 eagle clan man.　 A hunter was　 one　 raven clan
　 clan man　　　　　　　　　　　　　　　　　　　　　　　　　　　 man.

4 Nʟk·'ē huX gwīx·-wô'Eʟ k·'âlɴ lax-k·ebō'. HuX hwîlɴ k·'âlɴ
　 Then　 again　 a hunter was　 one　 wolf clan　 Again　 was so　 one
　　　　　　　　　　　　　　　　　 man.

5 lax-skī'yêk. Nʟk·'ē huX hwîlɴ k·'âlɴ g·îsbēwuduwE'da
　 eagle clan man.　 Then　 again　 was so　 one　 g·îsbēwuduwE'da
　　　　　　　　　　　　　　　　　　　　　　 clan man.

6 D'āɴ lô'ôp. Nʟk·'ē huX d'āɴ k·'elt. Nʟk·'ē huX d'āɴ
　 There　 a rock.　 Then　 again　 there　 another.　 Then　 again　 there
　 was　　　　　　　　　　　　 was　　　　　　　　　　　　　　 was

7 k·'elt. Nʟk·'ē huX d'āɴ k·'elt. Nʟk·'ē sī-lâ'tkut. Nʟk·'ēt
　 another.　 Then　 again　 there　 another.　 Then　 they started　 Then
　　　　　　　　　　　　　 was　　　　　　　　　 in their canoes.

8 hwa'det. Nʟk·'ē lē-mEtmē'tkut aɴ t'ē'bEn. Nî'g·idi lē-mē'tkut
　 they　　 Then　 on they were full　 of　 sealions.　 Not　 on　 was full
　 reached them.

9 aɴ k·'âlɴ g·a'tg·ê q'am-t'Epxā'tɴ dēdaa'qʟgutg·ê. K·'ē
　 at　 one　 man　 only　 two　 he got.　 Then

10 mEtmē'tkuɴ mmāl aɴ t'ē'bEn, lax-k·ebō'g·ê qanʟ lax-skī'yêk
　 full were　 the　 of　 sealions,　 the wolf clan　 and　 the eagle clan
　　　　　　 canoes　　　　　　　　　　 man　　　　　　　　 man

11 qanʟ qanha'da. Nʟk·'ē dzâqʟ k·'âlɴ g·a'tg·ê, hwîl q'am-
　 and　 the raven　 Then　 was　 one　 man,　 because　 only
　 clan man.　　　　　　 ashamed

12 t'Epxā'tɴ dēdaa'qʟgut. Nʟk·'ē huX sī-lâ'tkut, huX mîx·mā'x·ɴ
　 two　 he got.　 Then　 again　 they　 again　 they loaded
　　　　　　　　　　　　 started,

108

again almost empty handed. He had caught only one. Then he was sad.

One evening he started and stole the sealions that were on the rock of the man of the Wolf clan. When, the next morning, this man started there were no sealions on his rock. Then he knew that another person had stolen them. Therefore he carved the figure of a sealion out of wood and put it into the water. It was under water a short time and came up again and floated. Then he carved a sea-lion out of another piece of wood. He put it into the water, and again it floated. He tried four kinds of wood, but they did not prove to be good. Then he took a piece of hard wood, red in color like the skin of a sealion. He carved it and threw it into the water. Now it was very good. It did not become weak. He laid it on his own rock.

---

mmāl. the canoes.	Nʟk·'ē Then	huX again	qal-wî'tkᵘʟ empty handed was	g·a'tg·ê. the man.	Q'am-k·'ä'guʟ Only one	1
dēdaa'qʟgut. he got.	NʟK·'ē Then	lō-sī'êpkᵘʟ in was sick	qâ'ôtt. his heart.			2
NʟK·'ē Then	yu'ksa. evening.	NʟK·'ē Then	sî-g·â'ôtk"t. he started.	NʟK·'ēt Then	lē'luksʟ t'ē'bɛn he stole sea-lions	3
lē-hwî'lt on it was	aʟ at	lax-lô'ôpʟ on the rock of	lax-k·ebō'. the wolf clan man.	NʟK·'ē Then	sî-g·â'ôtkᵘʟ g·a'tg·ê. started the man.	4
Nî'g·i Not	lē-dô'xʟ on were	t'ē'bɛn sea lions	aʟ at	lax-lô'ôptg·ê. on his rock.	Hwîlā'yît hwîlt He knew (verbal noun)	5
lē'luksʟ stole them	g·a'tg·ê. a person.	Qan There-fore	hwîlʟ did so	lax-k·ebō'. the man of the wolf clan.	K·'ēt dzāpʟ gan Then made a he stick	6
hō'g·igaʟ like	t'ē'bɛn. a sealion.	K·'ēt Then	lō-mā'k·sît in he put it	aʟ at	ts'ɛm-a'k·s. NʟK·'ē in the Then water.	7
Lô'ôt. it emerged.	Nî'g·i Not	nakᵘʟ long	hwîl (verbal noun)	Lô'ôt, it emerged,	nʟk·'ē k·sāqô'st. then it came up.	NʟK·'ēt Then	8
huX again	dzāpʟ he made	huX again	k·'ē'ɛlʟ one	gan. stick.	NʟK·'ēt huX lō-mā'k·sît Then again in he put it	9
aʟ on	ts'ɛm-a'k·s. in the water.	NʟK·'ē Then	huX again	Lô'ôt. it emerged.	Txalpxʟ gan an-hwî'ntg·ê, Four sticks what he tried,	10
aʟ but	nîg·i not	am'ā'mt. they were good.	NʟK·'ē Then	hēt he said	dzāpʟ ts'ē'pgum gan, hwîl iʟä'ê he made a hard wood, being red	11
hō'g·îgaʟ like	anā'sʟ the skin of	t'ē'bɛn. the sea-lion.	NʟK·'ēt Then	lō-mā'k·sît in he put it	aʟ ts'ɛm-a'k·s. at in the water.	12
NʟK·'ē Then	sɛm·dɛx-g·a'tt. very it was strong.	Nî'g·î Not	huX again	alî'skᵘt. it was weak.	NʟK·'ēt lē-sg·î't Then on he laid it	13
aʟ on	lɛp-lax-lô'ôpt. own on his rock.					14

Now, the other person started again at night, intending to steal the sealions. When he came to the rock, he saw the sealion lying there. He took his harpoon and speared it. Then the sealion dived and swam away. (In former times harpoons were fastened to cedar-bark lines.) The man held the line and paid it out. For a long time the sealion dragged the canoe along, and the line was all paid out. Then the person tried to let it go, but the line stuck to his hands and the sea lion swam away with him.

It was four nights since he had left. For four days the sealion swam through the water. The man and his companions had lost sight of the mountains and they were far out at sea. The man was crying all the time. They went on for a long time—for ten days and ten nights.

---

1 | NʟK·'ē | huX | sî-g·â'ôtkᵘʟ | huX | k·'âlʟ | g·a'tg·ê | aʟ | axkᵘ.
Then | again | started | again | one | person | at | night.

2 | Lē'lukst, | qan | sî-g·â'ôtkᵘt | aʟ | axkᵘ. | NʟK·'ē | lā | huX
He was a thief, | therefore | he started | at | night. | Then | (perf.) | again

3 | hagun-ẏu'kt. | K·'ēt | g·a'at | hwîl | lē-sg·i'ʟ | t'ē'bEn. | NʟK·'ēt
toward he came. | Then | he saw | (verbal noun) | on lay | sealions. | Then he

4 | gōl | dāpxʟ. | NʟK·'ēt | g·aʟkᵘt. | NʟK·'ē | sō'uxskᵘʟ | t'ē'bEng·ê.
took | a harpoon. | Then | he speared it. | Then | dived | the sealion.

5 | NʟK·'ē | laqt. | Tgōnʟ | hwîlʟ | waʟEn-g·ig·a't: | maō'lkᵘ | tsE
Then | it swam. | This | did | the ancient people: | a cedar-bark rope

6 | dä'xdEʟ | dāpxʟ. | NʟK·'ē | laqt. | NʟK·'ē | dîx·-ẏu'kʟ | g·at | maō'lkᵘ.
they fastened to | the harpoon. | Then | it swam. | Then | fast held | the man | the line.

7 | NʟK·'ē | ʟa | lō-qâ'ôdEt. | NʟK·'ē | ʟa | nakᵘʟ | t | hwîl | dE-Lô'ôL
Then | (perf.) | in it was finished. | Then | (perf.) | long | | (verbal noun) | caused it to go.

8 | t'ē'bEn | mā'lg·ê. | NʟK·'ē | ʟā | lō-qâ'ôdEʟ | maō'lkᵘ. | NʟK·'ēt | baqʟ
the sealion | canoe. | Then | (perf.) | was finished | the line. | Then | tried

9 | g·at | dEm | tqalē'ʟ | maō'lkⁿ. | NʟK·'ē | tq'al-hē'tʟ | māō'lkᵘ | aʟ
the person | (fut.) | let go | the line. | Then | against stuck | the line | at

10 | ts'Em-an'ô'nʟ | g·a'tg·ê. | NʟK·'ēt | qane-hwîla | de-la'qʟ | t'ē'bEng·ê.
in the hand of | the man. | Then | always | with swam it | the sealion.

11 | NʟK·'ē | dēdā'uʟ | ʟā | txaḷpxʟ | ẏu'ksa. | NʟK·'ē | ʟā | txaḷpxʟ
Then | they had left | (perf.) | four | evenings. | Then | (perf.) | four

12 sa | lē-hwî'ldet | aʟ | lax-a'k·s. | Nî'g·it | g·a'adEʟ | sqanē'st | ʟā
days | on they were | on | on water. | Not | they saw | the mountains | (perf.)

13 | k'ut-gwâ'tkᵘʟ | sqanē'st; | ʟat | hwa'dEʟ | lax-sē'lda. | Lō-hwa'nt;
around were lost | the mountains, | (perf.) | they found | on the ocean. | in they were;

14 | qane-hwîla | sig·a'tkᵘt. | Hwä'i! | ʟa | nakᵘʟ | hwî'ldet | ʟā | k·'apʟ
always | they cried. | Well! | (perf.) | long | they did so | (perf.) | ten

15 sa. | NʟK·'ē | k·'apʟ | sqä'êxkᵘ. | NʟK·'ē | ʟā | huX | sqä'êxkᵘ | aʟ
days. | Then | ten | nights. | Then | (perf.) | again | dark

The sealion kept on going all the time. Now he went ashore at a distant country and they landed on a sandy beach. They pulled the canoe up and placed it under the trees. Then they sat down. Behold, early in the morning a canoe was coming. One small man was in the canoe, but he was using a large canoe. When he came opposite them, he rose. He held a line. Then he jumped into the water. For a short time he clubbed halibut under water, and then he took his line and strung them up. He caught many halibut, and had a long string. Then he emerged again. He took his canoe and went aboard. He put all the halibut that he had caught under water into the canoe. The men who were sitting under the trees saw what he was doing. He stayed in the canoe for a long time. Then he took his line a second time and dived. Again he clubbed halibut

qanet-hwîla	dE-ʟô′ôʟ	t'ē′bEng·ê.	Nʟk·'ē	tsagam-a′qʟkᵘdet	aʟ 1
always	caused it to go	the sealion.	Then	from sea to land they reached	at

hwagait-hwîl	nakᵘ.	Nʟk·'ē	g·â′ôdet	aʟ	lax-ā′us. Nʟk·'ēt 2
long ways being	far.	Then	they were	at	on the beach. Then

bax-sa′k·dEʟ	māl.	Hwagait-ma′qdēt	aʟ	spagait-ganga′n. Nʟk·'ē 3
up they pulled	the canoe.	Away they put it	at	among trees. Then

hwa′ndēt.	Nʟk·'ē	sEm-hē′ʟuk.	Gwinā′dEʟ,	māl	ʟā	ā′d'îk·skᵘt. 4
they sat down.	Then	really morning.	Behold,	a canoe	(perf.)	came.

G·udā′t	ʟgō-tk·'ē′lkᵘ;	wī-t'ē's	māʟʟ	hâ′ît,	ʟāt hwaʟ	qa-g·ä′Xdēt. 5
One man in canoe	a boy; little	a large	canoe	he used,	(perf.) he came	in front of them.

Nʟk·'ē	lō-hē′tkᵘʟ	g·a′tg·ê.	Yu′kdEʟ	maō′lkᵘ.	Nʟk·'ē	sō′uqst. 6
Then	in stood	a person.	He held	a line.	Then	he dived.

Nʟk·'ē	dā′uʟt	aʟ	ts'Eō′yuX	qanʟ	huX yu′kdet	nî′g·i 7
Then	he went	at	the bottom of the sea	and	again he held	not

wī-na′kᵘt.	Nʟk·'ēt	q'ax·q'aiā′nʟ	txox·	aʟ	ts'Eō′yuX.	Nʟk·'ēt 8
very long.	Then	he clubbed	halibut	at	the bottom of the sea.	Then

gōʟ	maō′lkᵘ.	Nʟk·'ēt	sa-gē′dEt.	Wī-hē′lʟ	txox·	an-hwî′nt. 9
he took	the line.	Then he	made a string of them.	Many	halibut	he made.

Wī-na′kᵘʟ	qē′ttg·ê.	Nʟk·'ē	g·a′bEnt.	Nʟk·'ēt	gōʟ mālt, 10
Very long was	his string.	Then	he emerged.	Then he	took his canoe,

nʟk·'ē	lôgôm-ba′xt.	Nʟk·'ēt	lôgôm-dô′qʟ	txox·	dzāpt aʟ 11
then	into he went.	Then	into he took	the halibut	what he made at

ts'Eō′yuX	ʟa	lôgôm-qâ′ôt'Ent.	G·a′aʟ	g·at	hwant	aʟ 12
the bottom of the sea	(perf.)	into he had taken it all.	They saw	the men	sitting	at

g·ilē′lîx·g·ê.	Nakᵘʟ	lō-d'ā′t	aʟ	ts'Em-mā′l.	Nʟk·'ēt huX gō′uʟ 13
inland.	Long	in he was	at	in the canoe.	Then again he took

maō′lkᵘ.	Nʟk·'ē	hatsEm	huX	sō′uqskᵘt.	Nʟk·'ē huX yukt 14
the line.	Then	once more	again	he dived.	Then again he began

under water.   Then the men who were sitting under the trees
launched their canoe and paddled up to the canoe of the little man.
One of them took two halibut, and they returned to the shore as
quickly as they could.   There they sat down.   They had been sitting
there a long time when the person emerged, holding in his hands a
string of fish, which he had caught.   He put them into his canoe; but
now he missed two halibut.   He put the fish into the canoe, and
pulled up his anchor.   Then he went ashore.   He landed on the
sandy beach, went up and found the four men, then he asked, "Who
of you stole my halibut?" and three of the men said, "This one took
them."   They said so, pointing to their companion.   Then the man took
him by the feet, struck him against a stone, and killed him, because

---

1 q'aiā'nL   txox·   aL   ts'Eō'yuX.   NLk·'ēt   tgōn   hwîLL   g·a'tg·ê
   clubbed   halibut   at   the bottom of   Then   this   did   the persons
                                       the sea.

2 hwant   aL   g·îlē'lîx·.   Iaga-gō'utdeL   māl.   NLk·'ē   uks-hē'tkᵘdet
   sitting   at   inland.   Down they took   the   Then   from land they stood
                                          to the beach   canoe.   to sea

3 lôgôm-dô'qdeL   t'Epxā'tL   txox·.   NLk·'ē   tsagam-lō-ya'ltkᵘdet
   into   they took   two   halibut.   Then   from sea   they returned
                                                                  to land

4 aL   sEm-t'ē'Eldet.   NLk·'ē   hatsîk·sEm   huX   hwa'ndēt   Lā
   at   very   quickly.   Then   once more   also   they sat   (perf.)
                                                                         down

5 nakᵘL   hwa'ndēt,   nLk·'ē   huX   g·a'bEnl   g·a'tg·ê.   HuX   yu'kdēL
   long   they sat,   then   again   emerged   the person.   Again   he held

6 qēt   wî-hē'lL   txox·L   huX   dzāpt.   NLk·'ēt   huX   lôgôm-d·ā'tElL
   a string many   halibut   again   he made.   Then   again   into   he
   of fish   put them

7 aL   ts'Em-mā'l.   Gwât'Est   aL   t'Epxā'tL   txox·.   NLk·'ēt   Lā
   at   in   the   He missed   at   two   halibut.   Then   when
            canoe.

8 lôgôm-qâ'ôdEt,   nLk·'ēt   sa'g·îL   qadä'lEpt,   k·'ē   tsagam-hē'tkᵘt.
   into   he put   then he   pulled up   his anchor,   then   from sea   he stood.
          them all,   to land

9 NLk·'ē   g·â'ôt   aL   lax-ā'us.   NLk·'ē   bax-iä'êt.   Hwa'yit   hwîl
   Then   he was   on   the beach.   Then   up   he   He found   where
                                                                   went.

10 hwanL   g·a'tg·ê   txalpxdâ'l.   NLk·'ēt   g·ē'dExt: "Nē'sEm   t'an
    were   the men   four.   Then   he asked: "You   who

11 dôqL   txox·g·înā'?"   NLk·'ē   hēL   gulâ'nL   g·a'tg·ê: "Tgōn
    took   halibut perhaps?"   Then   said   the three   men: "This one

12 t'an   dôqt."   Dehē'da   aL   k·'âlL   Ldā'tēitg·ê.   NLk·'ēt   gō'uL
    who   took   They said   to   one   with them.   Then he   took
               them."   so

13 g·a'tg·ê.   DExdô'qL   asîsa'ît   qan   ya'dziqLdet   aL   lô'ôp.   NLk·'ē
    the man.   He took   his feet   and   struck him with   at   a stone.   Then
                                                            them

he had stolen the halibut. Now there were only three men left. Their companion was dead.

Then the man returned and landed at his town. He carried his halibut up to the house and said to his friends, "There are people on the other side of the bay. I killed one of them because he stole two halibut." The people said, "Call them." Then they sent a man to call them, and when they came the people gave them to eat.

There were many people. They were all of the same size. They were very small. The three men were by far the largest. They stayed there a long time. Then the people made wooden clubs, and said, "To-morrow we shall be attacked by warriors." The sky darkened, although it was not extraordinarily dark. Now, there was a

nô′ôL	g·a′tg·ê,	t	hwîl	lē′luksL	txox·.	NLk·′ē	q'am-gulâ′nL 1
was dead	the man,	he	being who	stole	halibut.	Then	only three

g·atL	mā′ntg·ê.	Nô′ôL	stîk·'â′ldēit.	2
men	were left.	He was dead	the one who was with them.	

NLk·′ē	lō-ya′ltk^uL	g·a′tg·ê.	NLk·′ē	g·atsk^ut	aL qal-ts'a′p. 3
Then	returned	the man.	Then	he landed	at the town.

NLk·′ē	bax-hwî′lgaL	txox·	aL	ts'Em-hwî′lp.	NLk·′ē	maLt: 4
Then he	up carried	the halibut	to	in the house	Then	he told:

"Huwa′nL	g·at	aL	an-dâ′.	Dza′k^udēEL	k·'âlt	t hwîl lē′luksL 5
"There are	persons	at	the other side.	I killed	one	he being who stole

t'Epxā′tL	txox·.	Nagan	hwîlā′gut."	NLk·′ē	hēL qal-ts'a′p: 6
two	halibut.	Therefore I	did so to him."	Then	said the people:

"Ām	mE	hūwô′ôt."	NLk·′ē	sak·sk^ut	t'an hūwô′ôt. NLk·′ē 7
"Good	you	call them."	Then	left	who called them. Then

ad'ā′d'îk·sk^ut.	NLk·′ē	yukt txâq'Endēt. 8
they came.	Then	they began to feed them.

Wī-hē′lL	qal-ts'a′pg·ê.	NLk·′ē	nî′g·i	t'êst'ē′st.	Adîk·′ē′lēL 9
Many	people.	Then	not	they were large.	The same size

qadEpdē′it.	K·′ē	t'êst'ē′sL	g·at	gulâ′ntg·ê.	Hwä′i! lā 10
how large.	Then	largest were	the persons	three.	Well! (Perf.)

nak^uL	hwî′ldēt.	NLk·′ē	tgōnL	hwîlL	qal-ts'a′pg·ê. Dzā′pdēL 11
long	they did so.	Then	this	did	the people. They worked

gan	aL	sE-ha-qalā′Xdēit.	NLk·′ē	tgōnL	hē′det: "DEm 12
sticks	and	made cluhs.	Then	this	they said: "(Fut.)

ā′d'îk·sk^uL	g·îtwî′ltk^u	adzid'āLa′k^u."	NLk·′ē	ā′d'îk·sk^uL 13
come	warriors	to-morrow."	Then	it came

sqä′êxk^u	aL	lax-ha′.	Nî′g·i	sEm-wa'ts'a-sqä′êxk^u.	NLk·′ē 14
dark	on	the sky.	Not	very extraordinarily dark.	Then

great sandy point below the town. There was an open prairie
there. Then many birds came—swans, cranes, geese, gray cranes,
laughing-geese, ducks, blackbirds of the sea, ducks of Nass river,
gulls, cormorants. They alighted on the prairie. Then the people
rose. They took their wooden clubs and ran down right among the
birds, and began to strike them. The feathers of the birds were
flying about, filling the mouths and the noses of the people. Many
of them died, and only a moderate number returned.

The three men did not join them. They looked at the fight. Then
they said, "It is not difficult to fight with the birds. Let us try
to-morrow." They did so. At daybreak the birds arrived and sat

---

1 uks-hē′tkᵘʟ   wī-lax-ā′us   aʟ   qa-g·ī′ksîʟ   ts'ap   qanʟ   wī-lax-ha′p'eskᵘ.
  from stood   a beach   at   in front of   the town and   a on   grass.
  land to sea   great   great

2 Nʟk·'ē   ā′d'îk·skᵘt   wī-hē′lt   hwîl   lîks-g·ig·a′tʟ   ts'ō′tsg·ê.
  Then   came   many   being unusually many   birds.

3 Qa′q   tgōn,   qada′lq   tgōn,   ha′q   tgōn,   q'asqâ′ôs   tgōn,
  Swans those, sand-hill   those, geese those, cranes   those,
                 cranes

4 Lē′wun   tgōn,   naxnā′x   tgōn,   sᴇm-ts'ō′tsᴇm   lax-mô′ôn   tgōn,
  laughing-   those, ducks   those, real   birds   on the sea those,
  geese

5 amg·ä′g·îm   Lē′sᴇms   tgōn,   qē′wun   tgōn,   hā′uts   tgōn.
  sawbills of Nass river   those, gulls   those, shags   those.

6 Nʟk·'ē   sagait-k·'ē′Eʟʟ   hwant   aʟ   wī-lax-ha′p'ᴇskᵘ.   Nʟk·'ē
  Then   all together   sat down   on   the on   grass.   Then
                                              great

7 haldᴇm-gô′ldᴇʟ   qal-ts'a′p,   yu′kdēʟ   ga′ng·ê   ʟa   dzā′pdēt.
  rose   the people,   they took   the sticks (perf.) they made.

8 Ha-q'alā′Xʟ   hwa′tg·ê.   Nʟk·'ē   wi′d'axdēt.   Nʟk·'ē   ʟwa′ik·ckᵘdēt
  Clubs   their name. Then   they ran.   Then   they were mixed
                                                            with

9 ts'ō′ots.   K·'ē   lîk·s-g·at   qabē′iʟ   qal-ts'a′pg·ê.   Nʟk·'ēt   ia′tsdet.
  the birds. Very   many   several   people.   Then   they struck
                                                                       them.

10 Nʟk·'ē   mētkᵘʟ   Lē   lax·ʟ   ts'ō′otsg·ê.   Nʟk·'ē   lō-me′tkᵘʟ
   Then   were   Lē   down of   birds.   Then   in full
            scattered

11 ts'ᴇm-ā′qt   qanʟ   ts'ᴇm-dz'a′qt   txanē′tkᵘʟ   g·a′tg·ê.   Nʟk·'ē
   the mouths   and   the noses   all   the people. Then

12 daXt;   sᴇm-lîk·s-g·a′dᴇm   qāgâ′t   dᴇp   gō′stg·ê.   Q'am-ā′mʟ
   dead   very different   minds   (plur.)   those.   Only a fair
   they were;

13 qabē′îʟ   helya′ltgut.
   number   returned.

14 Nʟk·'ē   ʟa   hēʟʟ   hwî′ldetg·ê   aʟ   q'am-a′lgaʟʟ   gulâ′nʟ   g·at.
   Then   many they did so at   only looking on   the three   men.

15 Nʟk·'ē   tgōnʟ   hēʟ   g·a′tg·ê: "Nî′g·idi   qaqē′tkᵘʟ   an-hwî′nsᴇmᴇst.
   Then   this   said   the men: "Not   hard   what you do.

16 Dᴇm   dē-ba′gam   adzid'ā′ʟakᵘ."   Nʟk·'ē   hwî′ldet.   ʟa   mᴇsā′x·,
   (Fut.) on our we try   to-morrow."   Then   they did so. When   daylight,
           part

down on the prairie. They called it war. The birds did not come
there to feed. Then the three men ran down. They did not take any
clubs, but they just took the birds and twisted off their necks. They
did so and accomplished a great deal. Not one of the men was dead,
but they killed a great many birds. Then the people were glad. They
are called G·ilg·inā'mgan.[1] The three men had killed almost one-half
of the birds. The birds came there for one month. Then they left.
Now the people resolved to take pity on the three men. They did
so, and sent them back to their own town. They returned, and that
is the end.

| nᴌk·'ē | ʟa | huX | ā'd'î̆k·sku̸ʟ | ts'ōts. | Nʟk·'ē | huX | hwant | aʟ | 1 |
| then | (perf.) | again | came | birds. | Then | again | they sat down | on | |

| wī-lax-hā'p'ᴇsku̸. | G·îtwî̆'ltku̸t | sᴇ-hwa'tdētg·ê, | aʟ | k·'ē | nî̆'g·î̆ | 2 |
| the on great grass. | War | they call it, | | then | not | |

| hwî̆lt | q'ap-txâ'xku̸ʟ | wī-hē'ldᴇm | ts'ōts. | Nʟk·'ē | dē-wi'd'axʟ | 3 |
| did | really eat | many | birds. | Then | on their part ran | |

| q'am-gulâ'nʟ | g·a'tg·ê. | Nî̆'g·î̆di | dô'qdēʟ | ha-q'alā'X. | Q'am-dô'qdēʟ | 4 |
| only the three | men. | Not | they took | the clubs. | Only they took | |

| ts'ōts. | K·'ēt | q'am-lo-haʟ-t'uXt'a'ku̸det; | txanē'tku̸ʟ | an-hwî̆'ndet. | 5 |
| the birds. | Then | only in along they twisted off; | all | what they did. | |

| Sᴇm-xstā | haʟa'ᴇlisî̆ʟ | gulâ'nʟ | g·a'tg·ê. | Nî̆'g·î̆dî̆ | nô'ôʟ | k·'âlt. | 6 |
| Very gain | their work | the three | men. | Not | dead | one. | |

| Qaʟa'bᴇʟ | hwî̆l | lî̆k·s-g·ig·a'ʟ | ts'ō'ts. | Nʟk·'ē | lō-am'ā'mʟ | qagâ'otʟ | 7 |
| As many | | different kinds of | birds. | Then | in good were | the hearts of | |

| qal-ts'a'p. | G·îlg·înā'mgan | hwaʟ | qal-ts'a'pg·ê. | ʟā | wī-hē'lʟ | 8 |
| the people. | G·ilg·inā'mgan | the name of | the people. | (Perf.) | many | |

| hwî̆lʟ | gulâ'nʟ | g·a'tg·ê | ʟa | dᴇm | dōx-sē'luksku̸ʟ | ts'ō'ots · | 9 |
| did | the three | men | (perf.) | (fut.) | almost half | birds | |

| at | ia'tsʟ | q'am-gulâ'nʟ | g·a'tg·ê. | K·'ēlʟ | ʟôqsʟ | hwî̆l | ts'ō'ots. | 10 |
| | they killed | only three | men. | One | moon | where | birds. | |

| Nʟk·'ē | qâ'ôdetg·ê. | Nʟk·'ē | sᴇ-gâ'ôtku̸ʟ | qal-ts'a'p | aʟ | dᴇm | 11 |
| Then | it was finished. | Then | resolved | the people | to | (fut.) | |

| q'am-qâ'ôdî̆t | aʟ | gulâ'nʟ | g·a'tg·ê. | Nʟk·'ē | hwî̆'ldētg·ê. | 12 |
| take pity | on | the three | men. | Then | they did so. | |

| Dē-ya'ltku̸det | aʟ | lᴇp-qal-ts'a'pt. | Nʟk·'ē | gulî̆k·s-ax'a'qʟku̸dēt. | 13 |
| They returned | to | their own town. | Then | back they reached. | |

| Nʟk·'ē | sa-ba'xt. | | | | | 14 |
| Then | the end. | | | | | |

---

[1] The Kwakiutl have the same legend. They call the tribe of dwarfs G·ing·inā'nᴇmis, i. e., children of the sea. The Tsimshian name is evidently a phonetic distortion of the Kwakiutl word, so
that it seems probable that this whole tradition, which is so remarkably alike to the ancient legend
of the pygmies and the cranes, is of Kwakiutl origin (see F. Boas, Indianische Sagen von der
nord-pacifischen Küste Amerikas, pp. 88, 192).

SMOKE-HOLE

[Told by Moses]

There was a man who never slept in his house. He always lay at the edge of his smoke-hole. Therefore he grew exceedingly strong. When he went to gather firewood, he pulled out a whole tree and carried it home on his shoulder. In the evening, when he had eaten, he went up and lay down at the edge of the smoke-hole. He never lay down in his house. Therefore his name was Smoke-hole. Nobody could carry what he was able to carry. He always carried firewood on his shoulders. He carried whole trees on his shoulders.

AM'ALA'

SMOKE-HOLE

1 Yu'ksa. NLk·'ē nîg·idi lō-g·ä'êL g·a'tg·ê aL ts'ɛm-hwî'lp;
  Evening.   Then   not   in   lay   a man   at   in   the house

2 lax-ts'ä'L ala' hwîl dē-g·īg·ä'êl aL txanē'tkʷL yu'ksa. NLqan
  on the edge of   the smoke-hole   where he on his part   always lay   at   all   evening.   Therefore

3 ā'd'îk·skʷL hwîl dax-g·a't. NLk·'ē sa-â'Lkʷt. NLk·'ēt sô'adîL
  he came   being   strong.   Then   he fire-made wood.   Then he   pulled out

4 k·'ēlL gan. NLk·'ēt huX txā-qō'ltsɛgat. NLk·'ē q'am huX
  one   tree.   Then   again   all he carried on shoulder.   Then   only   again

5 Lä'êxkʷt. NLk·'ē huX yu'ksa. NLk·'ē huX mɛn-dā'uLt.
  he finished eating.   Then   again   evening.   Then   again   up   he went.

6 NLk·'ē huX g·ä'êLt aL lax-ts'ä'L ala'. Nî'g·idi g·ä'êLt aL ts'ɛm-
  Then   again   he lay   at   on   the edge of   the smoke-hole.   Not   he lay down   at   in

7 hwî'lp. NLqan hwatas Am'ala'. Nîg·idit gō'uL g·at dē-
  the house.   Therefore   his name was   Smoke-hole.   Not   took   a person   on his part

8 gō'udɛt. Qanēt-hwîla txa-qalqō'tsɛgaL lakʷ Txa-qō'ltsaqdēL gan.
  he took.   Always   all he carried on shoulder   fire-wood.   All he carried on shoulder   trees.

116

Ts'ak·

[Told by Moses]

There was a boy named Ts'ak· and his old grandmother. They had a small house, and a small brook was running near by. There were salmon in the brook. Ts'ak· went down carrying a stick with a bone point, and speared the salmon. He got a great many. Then he made a rope of cedar twigs and strung them up. Then Ts'ak· went up the little river and caught many salmon. Then he returned, but he did not find the string of fish that he had placed in the water. He had lost it. Then he was sorry, because the great Grizzly Bear had eaten all the salmon which he had strung on the cedar twigs. He said, "Big drop-jaw Grizzly Bear has done this." Then the great Grizzly

---

Ts'ak·

K·'âlʟ ʟgo-tk·'ē'ʟkᵘg·ê Ts'ak·ʟ hwa'tg·ê dē-k·'â'lʟ ʟgo-nts'ē'etst. 1
One, little, boy, Ts'ak·, his name with, one, little grandmother.

Nʟk·'ē hētkᵘʟ ʟgo-hwî'lpdetg·ê. Nʟk·'ē baxʟ ʟgo-a'k·s 2
Then, (there) stood, little their house. Then, ran, a water little

aʟ awa'adetg·ê hwîl mē'siʟ hân. Nʟk·'ē iä's Ts'ak·, 3
at, their proximity, where, in river, salmon. Then, went, Ts'ak·,

yu'kdîʟ gan hwîl lē-d'ä'ʟ nā'tstg·ê. Nʟk·'ēt g·aʟkᵘʟ 4
he carried, a stick, where, on was, a bone point. Then, he speared

hân, wī-hē'ldEʟ daa'qʟgutg·ê. Nʟk·'ē t'akᵘʟ q'âqʟ. Nʟk·'ēt 5
salmon, many, he got. Then, he twisted, cedar twigs. Then

k·'ax-sa-qē'detg·ê. Nʟk·'ē hnX gali-iä's Ts'ak· aʟ magâ'nʟ 6
for a while, he made, a string. Then, again, up went river, Ts'ak·, to, up river of

ʟgo-a'k·s. Nʟk·'ēt g·aʟkᵘʟ wī-hē'ldEʟ hân. Hwä'i! Nʟk·'ē 7
the little water. Then, he speared, many, salmon. Well! Then

ʟa lō-ya'ltkᵘt. Nʟk·'ē nî'g·it hwaʟ hwîl g·âk·sʟ qēttg·ê. 8
(perf.), he returned. Then, not, he found, where, lay in water, his string of fish.

Gwâtkᵘʟ qēttg·ê. Nʟk·'ē ā'd'îk·skᵘʟ hwîl lō-si'êpkᵘʟ qâts 9
It was lost, his string of fish. Then, came, being, in sick the, heart of

Ts'ak·, aʟ hwîl iä'êʟ wī-lig·'ē'Enskᵘʟ t'an dzaʟ hân lē 10
Ts'ak·, because, went, the, great grizzly bear, who, ate all, the salmon, (perf.)

k·s-qâ'gnm g·a'ʟkᵘtg·ê, nʟk·'ē lē sa-qē'dEt aʟ q'âqʟ. Nʟk·'ē 11
first, he speared, then, (perf.), he made string, a, of, cedar twigs. Then

a'lg·îxs Ts'ak·: "ʟa huX nēʟ wī-tk·'aä'gat, t'an hwîlä'gut 12
said, Ts'ak·: "(Perf.), again, he, great drop-jaw, who, has done it

117

Bear came down and said to Ts'ak·, "Why do you scold me?" Ts'ak· replied, "Why do you eat all the salmon I catch?" Then they began to scold each other, and the great Grizzly Bear said, "I shall snuff you in if you say 'Go ahead.'" Then Ts'ak· said, "Go ahead." At once the Grizzly Bear snuffed him in, and Ts'ak· was in his stomach. Ts'ak· carried a strike-a-light, pitchwood, and tinder. He was in the stomach of the great Grizzly Bear, but he was not afraid. He struck his firestones and made a fire of pitchwood in the great Grizzly Bear. Now there was a great fire. The great Grizzly Bear ran about, and smoke came out of his mouth. Before long he fell

1 wī-lig·'ē'Ensk͏ᵘ," an-hē'tg·ê.   NʟK·'ē   nā-iä'ʟ   wī-lig·'ē'Ensk͏ᵘ.   NʟK·'ē
   the grizzly bear," what he said.   Then   out of he   the grizzly bear.   Then
   great   woods went   great

2 a'lg·îxt   as   Ts'ak·:   "Ā'go   ma   gan   hak·sif'st?"   NʟK·'ē   a'lg·îxs
   he said   to   Ts'ak·:   "What you   for   scold me?"   Then   said

3 Ts'ak·:   "Ā'go   ma   gan   dzaʟt   hân   ʟē   dzā'bēE?"   NʟK·'ē   yuk
   Ts'ak·:   "What you for   eat all the   (perf.) I made?" Then   begin-
                                salmon   ning

4 mEn-hē'tdetg·ê   qanʟ   wī-lig·'ē'Ensk͏ᵘ.   NeʟL   qan   hēʟ   wī-lig·'ē'Ensk͏ᵘ:
   to each they spoke and   the grizzly bear. Therefore said the grizzly bear:
   other   great   great

5 " Nē'mts'axkuēg·a   nē'En,   'Hwä'i!   gwôm'   mē'yaan,"   dē'yaʟ
   "I snuff in maybe   you,   'Well!   go ahead,' say so,"   thus said

6 wī-lig·'ē'Ensk͏ᵘ   as   Ts'ak·.   NʟK·'ē   hēs   Ts'ak·:   "Hwä'i!   gwôm!"
   the grizzly bear to   Ts'ak·.   Then   said Ts'ak·:   "Well!   go ahead!"
   great

7 dē'yas   Ts'ak·   aʟ   wī-lig·'ē'Ensk͏ᵘ.   NʟK·'ē   nē'mts'axkᵘt.   Tgōnʟ
   said   Ts'ak·   to   the grizzly bear. Then   he snuffed him in. This
                         great

8 hēʟ   wī-lig·'ē'Ensk͏ᵘ.   NʟK·'ē   lō-d'ā's   Ts'ak·   aʟ   ts'Em-qalâ'sʟ
   said the grizzly bear.   Then   in was   Ts'ak·   at   in the stomach
         great   of

9 wī-lig·'ē'Ensk͏ᵘ.   K'uʟ-yu'kdEts   Ts'ak·   ʟgo-qa'mdEm   lô'ôp   qanʟ
   the grizzly bear.   About he carried Ts'ak· little fire   stones and
   great

10 sg·înî'st   qanʟ   x·da'askᵘ.   NʟK·'ē,   ʟa   lō-d'ā's   Ts'ak·   aʟ
   pitchwood   and   tinder.   Then,   when in was   Ts'ak·   at

11 ts'Em-qalâ'sʟ   wī-lig·'ē'Ensk͏ᵘ,   nʟk·'ē   nîg·i   alî'skᵘʟ   qâts   Ts'ak·.
   in the stomach the grizzly bear,   then   not   weak   the   Ts'ak·.
        of   great   heart of

12 NʟK·'ēt   ôx·s   Ts'ak·   ʟgo-qa'mt.   NʟK·'ē   meʟt.   NʟK·'ēt   lō-sE-
   Then   struck Ts'ak·   little fire. Then   it burnt. Then he   in made

13 me'ʟEʟ   sg·înî'st   aʟ   ts'ä'wuʟ   wī-lig·'ē'Ensk͏ᵘ.   NʟK·'ē   wī-t'ē'sʟ
   burn   pitchwood   at   the inside the grizzly bear.   Then   was great
                             of   great

14 hwîl   meʟt.   NʟK·'ē   q'aspē'   k'uʟ-ba'xʟ   wī-lig·'ē'Ensk͏ᵘ.   K·si-yô'xkᵘʟ
   where it burnt. Then   astray   about ran   the grizzly bear.   Out went
                                                  great

15 mēyē'nʟ   ts'Em-ā'qt.   Nîg·i   makᵘʟ   hwîlt,   k·ē   wī-sa-gō'uskᵘt.   Wī-
   smoke of in his   Not   long   he did so, then the fell down.   The
             mouth.   great one   great one

down dead. Then Ts'ak· came out at his anus. He ran about at the
place where lay the great Grizzly Bear whom he had killed.

Then he returned. He strung up his salmon, and went to the little
house of his grandmother. Ts'ak· said, "Grandmother, I killed a great
Grizzly Bear. It is in the woods. Give me your little fish knife." His
grandmother said, "You are a liar, slave! You are fooling me." Ts'ak·
replied, "Grandmother, it is true." Then his grandmother gave him
her little knife, and accompanied him toward the place where the great
Grizzly Bear lay. He cut it, and she carried the meat all day long.
Now they had brought it down and placed it on the drying sticks.
Then Ts'ak· went into the woods to cut fuel. He carried a little
stone ax. Then he cut firewood. He and his grandmother were
very glad.

---

nô'ôt.	NLk·'ē	k·si-yô'xkⁿs	Ts'ak·	aL	ts'ɛm-q'â'ltg·ê.	K·'ē 1
was dead.	Then	out went	Ts'ak·	at	in anus.	Then

k'uL-ba'xs	Ts'ak·	La	sg·iL	wī-lig·'ē'ɛnskⁿ	dza'kⁿdetg·ê. 2
about ran	Ts'ak·	when	lay	the great grizzly bear	killed.

NLk·'ē	lō-ya'ltkⁿL.	Q'ä'qLɛL	hân.	K·'ē	iä't	aL awa'aL 3
Then	he returned.	He strung	the salmon.	Then	he went	to the proximity of

Lgo-hwî'lps	nēts'ē'ɛtst.	NLk·'ē	tgōn	hēs Ts'a'k·g·ê:	"Dzē'ɛts! 4
the little house of	his grandmother.	Then	this	said Ts'ak·:	"Grandmother!

Yuk	nēɛ	dzak't	wī-lig·'ē'ɛnskⁿ.	La sg·ît	aL g·ilē'lîx·.	Ndä'ɛ 5
Just	I	killed	a great grizzly bear.	(Perf.) it lies	in in the woods.	Give me

Lgo-ha-q'ō'Lnîst."	NLk·'ē	a'lg·îxs	nēts'ē'ɛtst:	"Bē'gun,	xa'ɛ, 6
little your fish knife."	Then	said	his grandmother:	"You lie,	slave,

huX	sidô'gang·a	nē'ɛ."	NLk·'ē	a'lg·îxs Ts'ak·:	"Dzē'ɛts, 7
again	you fool mayhe	me."	Then	spoke Ts'ak·:	"Grandmother,

sɛm-hô'!"	NLk·'ēt	g·înä'ms	ndzē'ɛts	Ts'ak·L	Lgo-ha-q'â'L. 8
it is true!"	Then	gave	the grandmother of	Ts'ak·	a little fish knife.

NLk·'ē	iä'êt	stēl-nts'ē'ɛtst	aL	awa'aL	hwîl	sg·îL	wī-lig·'ē'ɛnskⁿ. 9
Then	she went	accompanying his grandmother	to	the proximity of	where	lay	the great grizzly bear.

NLk·'ēt	bāLt,	k·'ēt	nā-hwî'lgaL	Lē	smax·t	aL	wī-sa'.	NLk·'ē 10
Then	she spread it,	then	out of woods she carried	the	meat	at	all day.	Then

nā-qâ'ôdɛt.	NLk·'ēt	lē-lē'skⁿt	aL	lax-wî't.	NLk·'ē	iä'êt aL 11
out of woods finished.	Then	on they hung it	on	on drying sticks.	Then	he went to

g·ilē'lîx·,	lak'L	dzāpt.	Yu'kⁿdɛL	Lgo-dawī'sɛm	lâ'ôp.	NLk·'ēt 12
in woods,	firewood	he made.	He carried	a small ax	stone.	Then

daa'qLk't,	dzāpL	la'k'g·ê.	NLk·'ē	sɛmgal	lō-ä'mL	qâ'ôdɛt qanL 13
he got it,	he made	firewood.	Then	very	in good	his heart and

Lgo-nēts'ē'ɛtst.	14
little his grandmother.	

Now there was a town on the opposite side of the river. In the morning Ts'ak· rose and took some coals. He chewed some tallow and entered the house of the chief. It was full of people who were gambling. Ts'ak· spit into the fireplace. Then his saliva blazed up. One man said to Ts'ak·, "What are you chewing there?" Ts'ak· replied, "The penis of a little dog." The man then said, "Spit into the fire again." Ts'ak· spit into the fireplace, and the fire blazed up. The people took hold of Ts'ak·; they took a rope. There stood a tree to which they tied him. Now he was somewhat troubled. Then many people rushed to the house of his old grandmother and ate all the meat that was in it. Nothing was left. They ate all. They were the Wolves. Now they returned and untied Ts'ak·. They sent him out

---

1 NLk·'ē   hētk^uL   qal-ts'a'p   aL   an-dâ'sda.   NLk·'ē   hē'Luk,
   Then   (there) stood   a town   at   the opposite side.   Then   morning,

2 nLk·'ē   g·în-hē'tk^us   Ts'ak·.   K·'e   dôqL   qam-t'ō'ts.   NLk·'ēt
   then   rose   Ts'ak·.   Then   he took   coals.   Then

3 qē'EnL   hîx·.   NLk·'ē   ts·ent   aL   hwîlpL   sEm·â'g·ît.   Lō-mē'tk^uL
   he chewed   fat.   Then   he entered   in   the house of   the chief.   In   it was full

4 g·at   lât.   Hē'-yukL   xsa'ndet.   NLk·'ē   ts·ēts   Ts'ak·   aL
   people   in it.   Beginning   they played.   Then   spat   Ts'ak·   in

5 ts'Em-an-la'k^u.   NLk·'ē   mELmē'L   ts'ē'dEt   aL   ts'Em-an-la'k^u.   NLk·'ē
   in the fireplace.   Then   burnt   his saliva   at   in the fireplace.   Then

6 a'lg·îxL   k·'âlL   g·at   as   Ts'ak·.   Ētk^uts   Ts'ak·:   ··Agō'L
   spoke   one   person   to   Ts'ak·.   He was called   Ts'ak·:   "What

7 qagä'nEn?"   "Nē,"   dē'yas   Ts'ak·,   "q·âL   Lgo-o's."   ··Hwä'i!
   are you chewing?   "This,"   said   Ts'ak·,   "the penis of   a little   dog."   "Well!

8 Gwôm,   ts'ētL."   NLk·'ēt   lō-ts'ē'tEs   Ts'ak·   ts'Em-an-la'k^u.   Hwä'i!
   Go on,   spit it."   Then he   in spat it   Ts'ak·   in the fireplace.   Well!

9 NLk·'ē   wī-t'ē's   hwîl   mē'LEL   lak^u.   NLk·'ēt   gō'uL   wī-hē'ldEm
   Then   great   where   burnt   fire.   Then   they took   many

10 g·at   Ts'ak·.   K·'ēt   gō'udēL   maō'lk^u.   NLk·'ē   hētk^uL   gan,
   people   Ts'ak·.   Then   they took   a rope.   Then   (there) stood   a tree.

11 neL   hwîlL   tq·al-dEda'k·Ldets   Ts'ak·.   NLk·'ē   k·ō'pE-sEm-hā'xk^ut.
   there   where   against they tied   Ts'ak·.   Then   a little much he was troubled.

12 NLk·'ē   hā'p'aaL   wī-hē'ldEm   g·at.   Ts'ElEm-ha'pdēL   Lgo-hwî'lpL
   Then   they rushed   many   people.   Into they rushed   the house of little

13 nets·ē'Ets   Ts'ak·.   NLk·'ēt   sEm-dza'LdēL   smax·.   Nîg·i
   the grandmother of   Ts'ak·.   Then   very they ate all   the meat.   Not

14 q·am-nā'nt,   sEmgal   txa-dza'Ldet.   K·'ēbō'   dEp   gō'stg·ê.   NLk·'ē
   only was left,   very   all they ate all   Wolves   those.   Then

15 lō-yîlya'ltk^ut.   NLk·'ēt   sa-gō'udEts   Ts'ak·.   NLk·'ēt   k·si-hē'tsdet
   they returned.   Then   off they took   Ts'ak·.   Then   out they sent him

of the house and he returned to his grandmother. When he entered
their little house, all the meat was gone. Then they cried. Ts'ak·
and his grandmother had no food. They were crying all the time.

In the evening Ts'ak·'s grandmother was fast asleep. Then he took
his knife and cut out her vulva. He roasted it. When it was done,
he roused her and said, "Grandmother, awake! Your meal is done.
There was a little of the meat left over, and I roasted it." His grandmother rose and ate it all. Then Ts'ak· ran out and made a song on
his grandmother: "Grandmother ate her own little vulva! Grandmother ate her own little vulva!" Then his grandmother shouted to
Ts'ak·, "Don't enter my house again, slave!"

Now Ts'ak· walked about outside. His grandmother did not let

---

aL	g·alq.	NLk·'ē	lō-ya'ltkᵘts	Ts'ak·	aL	awa'as	nets'ē'Etst.	1
to	outside.	Then	returned	Ts'ak·	to	the prox- imity of	his grand- mother.	

NLk·'ē	ts'ēnt	aL	Lgo-hwî'lpdet.	Nîg·i	haikᵘL	smax·.	K·'ē	2
Then	he entered	at	little their house.	Not	was left	meat.	Then	

sîg·a'tkᵘs	dEp	Ts'ak·	qans	nets'ē'Etst,	aqL-g·ē'îpdEt.	NLk·'ē	3
cried	(plur.)	Ts'ak·	and	his grand- mother,	with- out food they.	Then	

qa'nē-hwîla	sig·a'tkᵘdet.					4
always	they cried.					

NLk·'ē	yu'ksa.	SEm-q'â'tsExt	nets'ē'êts	Ts'ak·	aL	wôqt.	5
Then	evening.	Very motionless	the grand- mother of	Ts'ak·	in	her sleep.	

NLk·'ēt	gō'us	Ts'ak·	ha-q'ō'L.	NLk·'ēt	k·si-q'ō'tsL	mēns	6
Then	took	Ts'ak·	a fish knife.	Then	out he cut	the vulva of	

nets'ē'Etst.	NLk·'ēt	iâ'ôdEt.	NLk·'ē	La	a'nukst.	NLk·'ēt	7
his grand- mother.	Then	he roasted it.	Then	(perf.)	it was done.	Then	

gu'ksaans	Ts'ak·	nets'ē'Etst.	NLk·'ē	hēs	Ts'ak·:	"Dzē'Ets	8
awakened	Ts'ak·	his grandmother.	Then	said	Ts'ak·:	"Grand- mother,	

gū'ksgun!	yukL	La	anu'ksL	iâ'ēE.	Māna'aL	Lgo-sma'x·.	Nîlne'L	9
awake!	it begins	(perf.)	is done	what I roast.	It is left	a little meat.	That	

iâ'dēE."	NLk·'ē	g·în-hē'tkᵘs	nets'ē'Ets.	NLk·'ēt	g·ē'îpt,	nLk·'ēt	10
I roast."	Then	rose	the grand- mother.	Then	she ate it,	then she	

dzaLt.	NLk·'ē	k·si-ba'xs	Ts'ak·.	NLk·'ēt	sE-lē'mx·s	nets'ē'Etst:	11
ate it all.	Then	out ran	Ts'ak·.	Then	he made a song on	his grand- mother:	

"Yä'E,	lEp-g·ē'bEdas	dzē'Edzē	Lgo-lEp-tq'al-mē'nt.	Yä'E,	lEp-	12
'Yä'E,	herself she ate it	my grand- mother	little her against vulva. own	Yä'E,	her- self	

g·ē'bEdas	dzē'edzē	Lgo-lEp-tq'al-mē'nt."	NLk·'ē	wī-amhē't	nets'ē'Ets	13
she ate it	my grand- mother	little her against vulva." own	Then	shouted	the grand- mother of	

Ts'ak·:	"G·îlâ'	dzē	huX	ts'ē'nEn,	xa'E!"		14
Ts'ak·:	"Do not	again	come in,	slave!"			

NLk·'ē	qanē-hwîla	k'uL-iä'Es	Ts'ak·	aL	g·ā'lEq.	Nîg·i	15
Then	always	about went	Ts'ak·	at	outside.	Not	

him in again. She felt ill at ease because her vulva had been cut off.
It grew dark. Then Ts'ak· took a stick and went down to the beach.
It was low water. He walked about on the sand and looked for
cockles, which he wanted to eat. He was crying because he had
nothing to eat.

Behold, he saw a man coming up to him who asked, "Why are
you crying?" Ts'ak· replied, "The Wolves have eaten all the meat
that we had for our food." The man said, "Oh, indeed! Why don't
you take revenge?" Then the man put his hand under his blanket
and pulled out a hollow bone. He said, "Now go across the river;
there you will find a knothole. The daughter of the chief is in the

---

1 ts'ɛlɛm-anâ'ɛls nets'ē'ɛtst. Q'am-ab'abā'gas nets'ē'ɛts Ts'ak· hwîl
  into allowed his grand- Only troubled the grand- Ts'ak· being
    him mother.   was mother of

2 k·si-nē'iL mɛnt. NLk·'ē La ā'd'îk·sk\u{u}L dɛm hwîl yu'ksa,
  out being her vulva. Then (perf.) came (fut.) being evening,

3 nLk·'ēt gō'us Ts'ak·L gan. NLk·'ē iaga-iä'ēt aL g·ä'u La
  then he took Ts'ak· a Then down he to the front (perf.)
      stick.   went   of the house

4 sɛm-sg·î'L ak·s. NLk·'ē k'uL-haL-iä'êt aL lax-ā'us; t
  really lies water. Then about along he at on the he
  (low water)   went   sand;

5 k'uL-g·îg·ē'ɛll qabâ'q dɛm g·ē'îbɛt; aL k'uL-wīyē'tk\u{u}t hwîl
  about looked for cockles (fut.) his food; and about he cried being

6 aqL-g·ē'îbɛt, nēl qan hēt.
  with- food, therefore he said
  out   so.

7 Hwä'i! Gwinā'dɛL, g·at ā'd'îk·sk\u{u}t aL qâqt. NLk·'ē a'lg·îxL
  Well! Behold, a man came to his Then said
          front.

8 g·a'tg·ê: "Agō'L qan hahē'nîst?" NLk·'ē dē'lɛmɛxk\u{u}s Ts'ak·:
  the man: "What for are you talk- Then answered Ts'ak·:
        ing?"

9 "Yuk-dza'L k·'êbō' smax· La dɛm g·ē'îbɛm." NLk·'ē hēl
  "Just ate the the (perf.) (fut.) our food." Then said
   all wolves meat

10 g·a'tg·ê: "Â, net! Hwä'i! tsɛ dē'ltk\u{u}nēn ana'!" NLk·'ē
  the man: "Ah, indeed! Well!   reciprocate do!" Then

11 lō-na'k\u{u}sL g·a'tg·ê aL ts'ɛm-lax-â't. NLk·'ēt sag·îL ts'ēp
  in he the man at in on blan- Then he pulled a bone
  stretched   ket.   out

12 qalk·si-nô'ôL Le ts'ä'wut. "Tgōn tsɛ hwî'lɛn: Tsɛ tsaga-
  through a hole its inside. "This do: Across

13 iä'nēn, mɛ tsɛ k·'ē' g·a'aL hwîl nanô'ôL an-t'ɛm-anē'st. D'āL
  go, you then see where holes knothole. It is

14 Lgō'uLk\u{u}L sɛm'â'g·it aL q'alā'nL hwî'lbɛst. Mɛ tsɛ k·'ē'
  the child of the chief at the rear of the house. You then

15 ts'ɛlɛm-hē't'ɛnt aL an-t'ɛm-anē'st. Tsɛ sɛm-na-hē't'ɛnɛn aL
  into place it in the knothole. Very down place it on

rear of the house. Put this tube through the knothole. Aim right at the heart of the chief's child. Then blow through it." Ts'ak· did so. The bone struck the heart of the chief's child. Then the chief cried, thinking that his child would die quickly. They sent for many shamans (they are the ones who cure disease), but they did not succeed. Then Ts'ak· said to his grandmother, "Go on, Grandmother, and tell them that I will cure her." But Ts'ak· was not a shaman. His grandmother left. She entered the chief's house and said to him, "That slave talks nonsense again. He says he will cure the child of the chief." Then the foolish people rushed up to her and threw her out of the house, because Ts'ak· was not a shaman. That was the reason why they did so. Ts'ak·'s grandmother went to the little house, and as soon as she saw Ts'ak·

---

qâ'ôdeL	Lgō'uLkᵘL	sEm'â'g·it.	ME	tsE	k·'ē'	qalk·si-suwa'nt."	1
the heart of	the child of	the chief.	You	then		through blow."	

NLk·'ē	hwîls	Ts'ak·.	NLk·'ē	hētkᵘL	ts'ēp	aL	qâ'ôdEL	2
Then	did so	Ts'ak·.	Then	stood	the bone	in	the heart of	

Lgō'uLkᵘL	sEm'â'g·it.	NLk·'ē	La	hētkᵘL	ts'ē'pg·ê.	K·'ē	3
the child of	the chief.	Then	(perf.)	stood	the bone.	Then	

ayawā'tkᵘt.	Wī-t'ē's	hwîl	ayawā'tkᵘt.	T'ēlL	dEm	q'â'tsigat.	4
she cried.	Great	being	her crying.	Quickly	(fut.)	she dies.	

NLk·'ē	qaqâ'ôdet	wi-hē'ldEm	halai't.	NeLnē'	t'an	suwa'nt.	5
Then	they went for	many	shamans.	Those	who	cure.	

K·'ē	nî'g·i	daa'qLkᵘdet.	NLk·'ē	a'lg·îxs	Ts'ak·	aL	nets'ē'Etst:	6
Then	not	they succeeded.	Then	said	Ts'ak·	to	his grand-mother:	

"Adô'!	dzē'Ets!	maL	tsen	dEm	suwa'nt."	ALk·'ē'	nî'g·idi	7
"Go!	grand-mother!	tell	I	(fut.)	cure her."	But	not	

halai'ts	Ts'ak·.	NLk·'ē	dā'uLs	nets'ē'Etst.	NLk·'ē	ts'ēnt	aL	8
a shaman	Ts'ak·.	Then	went	his grand-mother.	Then	she entered	at	

bwîlpL	sEm'â'g·it.	"Yukt	huX	dagalā'mgait	xa'E	dEm	9
the house of	the chief.	"Beginning	again	talks nonsense	the slave	(fut.)	

suwa'nt-gaL	Lgō'uLkᵘL	sEm'â'g·ît."	NLk·'ē	ha'p'aL	ax-	10
he cures he says	the child of	the chief."	Then	rushed	with-out	

qagâ'dEm	g·at.	NLk·'ēt	k·si-ô'x·dēt	nets'ē'Ets	Ts'ak·	aL	11
hearts	the men.	Then	out they threw	the grand-mother of	Ts'ak·	to	

g·alq,	aL	hwîl	nî'g·idi	halai'ts	Ts'ak·,	nîLne't qant	12
outside,	because		not	a shaman	Ts'ak·,	therefore	

hwîlā'kᵘdetg·ê.	NLk·'ē	hagun-iä's	nets'ē'Ets	Ts'ak·	aL	13
it was done.	Then	toward went	the grand-mother of	Ts'ak·	to	

awa'aL	Lgo-hwî'lpdetg·ê.	Hwîl k·'ēt	g·a'as	Ts'ak·	nets'ē'Etst,	14
the prox-imity of	little their house.	At once	saw	Ts'ak·	his grand-mother,	

she said, "They turned me out of the house!" But Ts'ak· repeated, "Go on, Grandmother. I really want to cure her." Then she went again and entered. She said again, "He wants to cure the chief's daughter." And two wise men said, "Let him do as he says"; and they agreed that he should cure her. Ts'ak·'s grandmother went out and returned. She told him that they had agreed. Then Ts'ak· rose and called the wren, the x-sk·īek·, the x-sg·a'nt, and all the little birds. Then Ts'ak· dressed himself. He carried one little bird named Rattlebox. They went in, and Ts'ak· sat down at the feet of the chief's daughter, who was very sick, and all the birds sat down. They

1	nɪk·'ē	tgōn	hēs	nets'ē'Ets	Ts'a'k·g·ê:	"Yukt-k·si-ô'x·det	nēE
	then	this	said	the grand- mother of	Ts'ak·:	"Just out was thrown	I

2	aʟ	g·alq."	Nʟk·'ē	ha·ts'Ek·sEm	huX	a'lg·îxs	Ts'ak·:
	to	outside."	Then	once more	again	said	Ts'ak·:

3	"Adô',	dzē'Ets!	DEm	q'ap-suwa'nêîst."	Nʟk·'ē	ha'k·sEm	huX
	"Go,	grand- mother!	(Fut.)	really I cure her."	Then	once more	again

4	iē'êt	nets'ē'Ets	Ts'ak·.	Nʟk·'ē	huX	ts·ēnt.	Nʟk·'ē	ha'k·sEm
	went	the grand- mother of	Ts'ak·.	Then	again	she entered.	Then	again

5	huX	a'lg·îxt:	"Q'ap-hä'q'aʟ	xa'E	aʟ	dEmt	suwa'nʟ
	again	she spoke:	"Really urges	the slave	to	(fut.)	he cures

6	ʟgō'uʟkᵘʟ	sEm'â'g·it."	Nʟk·'ē	a'lg·îxʟ	bagadē'lʟ	hwîl	qaxâ'ôsgut:
	the child of	the chief."	Then	said	two		wise men:

7	"Ām,	mEsEm	hwîl	t'anʟ	hēt."	Nʟk·'ēt	anâ'qdēʟ	dEm
	'Good,	you	do	what	he says."	Then	they agreed	(fut.)

8	suwa'ansks	Ts'ak·.	Nʟk·'ē	k·saXs	nets'ē'Ets	Ts'ak·.	Nʟk·'ē
	he cure	Ts'ak·.	Then	went out	the grand- mother of	Ts'ak·:	Then

9	lō-ya'ltkᵘt.	Anâ'qdētg·ê.	Nʟk·'ē	haldEm-ba'xs	Ts'ak·.	Nʟk·'ēt
	she returned.	They had agreed.	Then	rose	Ts'ak·.	Then

10	wô'ôʟ	ts'Epts'a'p	qanʟ	x-sk·ī'ek·	qanʟ	x-sg·ant	qanʟ
	he invited	the wren	and	(a bird)	and	eat- ing (a bird) gum	and

11	txanē'tkᵘʟ	hwîl	sEsō'sʟ	k'ōpE-ts'ō'ôts.	Nʟk·'ē	nōtks	Ts'ak·.
	all	being	small	little birds.	Then	dressed	Ts'ak·.

12	Nʟk·'ēt	hwa'lîx·t	k·'ä'guʟ	ʟgo-ts'ō'ôts	anda-basä'xs.	Ts'ak·.
	Then	he carried	one	little bird	rattlebox,	Ts'ak·.

13	Nʟk·'ē	ʟô'ôdet.	Nʟk·'ē	la'mdzîxdet.	Nʟk·'ē	d'ās	Ts'ak·	aʟ
	Then	they went.	Then	they entered.	Then	sat down	Ts'ak·	at

14	asEsa'et	hwîl	g·ä'êʟ	ʟgō'uʟkᵘʟ	sEm'â'g·it.	Wī-t'ē'sʟ	sī'êpkᵘt.
	her feet	where	lay	the child of	the chief.	Much	she was sick.

15	Nʟk·'ē	huwa'nʟ	txanē'tkᵘʟ	k'ōpE-ts'ō'ôts.	Dô'qdēʟ	gan,
	Then	they sat down	all	the little birds.	They took	sticks,

carried small sticks. Now the chief's great slave rose in the corner of the house. He was a giant, and his head reached up to the corner of the house. He had a big belly. Then one boy went toward the rear of the house, and stood near by in front of him. The boy took a stick and struck the slave's belly while Ts'ak· was performing his incantations. Therefore the people used to call the slave Drum-belly. Now Ts'ak· pulled out the sickness and saved her. He took all her father's elk-skins in payment. She gave herself to him in marriage, and he took all her grease boxes. Then Ts'ak· became a great chief, because he had saved the chief's child. He married her, and the chief gave with her his giant slave whose name was Drum-belly. Ts'ak· really married the daughter of the chief.

---

sEsō'sEm	gan.	NLk·'ē	lō-mEn-hē'tkᵘl	wī-xa'atkᵘsL	sEm'â'g·it 1
little	sticks.	Then	in up stood	the slave of great	the chief

aL	amō'st.	Wī-g·a'L	hwagait-lō-tq'al-gō'uskᵘL	t'Em-qē'st	aL 2
in	the corner.	He was a great man	up to in against it reached	his head	to

amō'st.	Wī-la'îL	ban.	NLk·'ē	wīts'En-iä'L k·'âlL 3
the corner.	Greatly large was	his belly.	Then	back from went one the fire

Lgo-tk·'ē'Lkᵘ.	NLk·'ē	hagun-hē'tkᵘt	aL	qa-sä'EXt. Yu'kdEL 4
little boy.	Then	toward he stood	at	his front. He held

Lgo-tk·'ē'LkᵘL	gan,	at	dEm	ia'tsL	banL wī-xa'E	La yukL 5
the little boy	a stick,	he	(fut.)	strike	the belly of great the slave	when he began

suwa'anskᵘt.	NLk·'ēt	ia'tsL	Lgo-tk·'ē'Lkᵘ	banL	wī-xa'E. 6
he cured.	Then	struck	the little boy	the belly of	the slave great

NEl	su-hwa'dEL	waLEn-g·ig·a't	as	Anō'LEm	ban.	NLk·'ēt 7
That	made	name of olden times	the people	of	Drum-	belly. Then

sa'g·îs	Ts'ak·	ha-sī'êpkᵘ.	NLk·'ē	mâ'tkᵘtg·ê.	NEl hwîlt, 8
out pulled	Ts'ak·	the sickness.	Then	she was saved.	That he did,

wī-hē'ld	hwîl	hwî'ls	Ts'ak·.	NLk·'ē	Lat qâ'ôt'Ens Ts'ak· 9
much		he did so	Ts'ak·.	Then	(perf.) he finished it Ts'ak·

Lē	Liâ'ns	nEgwâ'ôdEt.	Hana'qstg·ê	.qanL	txanē'tkᵘL hahē'nq. 10
the	elks of	her father.	She gave herself as wife	and	all grease boxes.

NLk·'ē	La	wi-t'ē'sL	hwîl	sEm'â'g·îts	Ts'ak·. NLk·'ē La 11
Then	(perf.)	was great	being	chief	Ts'ak·. Then (perf.)

dE-mâ'tkᵘs	Ts'ak·	Lgō'uLkᵘL	sEm'â'g·it.	NLk·'ēt	nak·skᵘt. 12
he saved	Ts'ak·	the child of	the chief.	Then	he married her.

Na'k·sgus	Ts'ak·	Lgō'uLkᵘL	sEm'â'g·it.	NLk·'ē	tq'al- 13
He married	Ts'ak·	the daughter of	the chief.	Then	against

hō'ksaanL	sEm'â'g·iL	wī-xa'E.	Anō'LEm	banL	hwa'tg·ê. 14
to be with her he caused	the chief	the slave great	Drum-	belly	his name.

NLk·'ē	sEm-hō'm	na'k·skᵘs	Ts'ak·	Lgō'uLkᵘL	sEm'â'g·it. 15
Then	really	married	Ts'ak·	the child of	the chief.

He stayed there a long time, and then he got tired of the woman.
He heard that there was a woman on the other side of the mountain. He said he would go. Ts'ak· left his wife. Only his slave, the wren, and another bird accompanied him. They went a long time and arrived at the foot of the mountain. The trail led to it, but there was no way of going on. Then Ts'ak· caught a robin. He skinned it and put on its skin. He flew upward and nearly reached the top of the mountain. Then he came to a great fire, which was just like lightning. It burnt the robin's wings, and he fell back to the foot of the mountain. Then Ts'ak· took off his skin. He caught a bluejay, skinned it, and put on its skin. Again he flew upward and almost reached the top of the mountain. Again he came to the place where

1 Hwä'i! La nak^uL hwîl hwî'ldet, nLk·'ē La q'âtsk^uL qâ'ôts
Well! When long they did so, then (perf.) was tired the heart of

2 Ts'ak· aL hana'qg·ê. Hwä'i! NLk·'ē naxna's Ts'ak· hwîl
Ts'ak· of the women. Well! Then heard Ts'ak· where

3 d'āL k·'âlL hana'q aL hwagait-an-dâ'ôL sqanē'st. NLk·'ē hēt
was one woman at away the opposite side of the mountain. Then he said

4 dEm iē'êt. NLk·'ē iē'êt; k^usta'qsdEs Ts'ak· na'k·stg·ê.
(fut.) he goes. Then he went; he left Ts'ak· his wife.

5 K·sax-Lgo-ts'Epts'a'p stēlt qanL Lgo-x-sk·'ī'ek·. NLk·'ē Lô'ôdet.
Only little wren accompanied him and little (a bird). Then they went.

6 Nak^uL hwîl Lô'ôdet. NLk·'ē tq'al-la'k·det aL dēpL wī-sqanē'st.
Long where they went. Then against they arrived at the foot of a great mountain.

7 SEm-gō'usk^uL qē'nEx as gō'stg·ê. NLk·'ē aqL-yô'xk^us Ts'ak·.
Really reached the trail to that. Then without- (place) to go out Ts'ak·.

8 NLk·'ēt gō'uL sâ'ôq. NLk·'ēt tsâ'ôdEt. NLk·'ē lō-Lô'ôtk^ut.
Then he took a robin. Then he skinned it. Then in he put himself.

9 NLk·'ē mEn-g·ibā'yukt. La dēlpk^uL dEm mEn-a'qLk^ut, nLk·'ē
Then up he flew. When shortly (fut.) up he reached, then

10 ā'd'îk·sk^ut hwîl me'LEL wī-sqanē'st hō'g·igaL ts'amtx·. NLk·'ē
he came where burnt the mountain great like lightning. Then

11 meLme'LEL qaq'ā'x·L sâ'ôq. NLk·'ē ha'ts'îk·sem t'Egua'ntkt
burnt the wings of the robin. Then once more he fell

12 aL dēpL sqanē'st. NLk·'ēt sa-ma'gas Ts'ak·. NLk·'ēt huX
to the foot of the mountain. Then he off took it Ts'ak·. Then he again

13 gō'uL gusgwâ's. NLk·'ēt huX tsâ'ôdEt. K·ēt huX
took a bluejay. Then he again skinned it. Then again

14 lō-Lô'ôtk^ut. NLk·'ē ha'k·sEm huX mEn-g·ibā'yukt aL
in he put himself. Then once more again up he flew at

15 wī-sqanē'st. NLk·'ē ha'k·sEm huX k·îlgal-me'LEL sqanē'stg·ê.
the mountain great. Then once more again all over burnt the mountain.

it was burning all over.　Then the bluejay fell down.　He dropped down again to the foot of the mountain.　Ts'ak· was very much troubled because there was no way to go on.　He and his great slave, Drum-belly, lay down on the grass, and slept.　It was almost daylight, and Ts'ak· was still asleep.　Then he heard a voice: "My grandmother invites you in."　He did not know who was speaking, and lay down again.　He bit a hole in his blanket and looked through it.　Behold, there was a little Mouse that came out of a bunch of grass and said, "My grandmother invites you in."　Now he saw the little Mouse disappearing under the bunch of grass.　He rose, went to the grass, and pulled it out.　Behold, there was a house under it.　A woman was sitting there.　"Enter, my dear, if it is you who wants

---

K·'ē Then	huX again	iaga-t'Egua'ntk^uL down fell	gusgwâ'ôs. the bluejay.	K·'ē Then	ha'k·sEm once more	huX 1 again
ōk·st he dropped	aL to	mēnL the foot of	sqanē'stg·ê. the mountain.	NLk·'ē Then	aba'g·ask^us was troubled	Ts'a'k·g·ê 2 Ts'ak·
aqL-yô'xk^ut. without (way) to go.		NLk·'ē Then	lā'Ldet they lay down	aL at	lax-hā'p'Esk^u. on grass.	K'uL-stē'lL 3 About accompanied him
wī-xa'Eg·ê, the slave, great	Anō'LEm Drum-	banL belly	hwa'tg·ê. his name.	NLk·'ē Then	wâ'wôqdētg·ê. 4 they slept.	
Hwä'i! Well!	La when	dēlpk^uL shortly	dEm (fut.)	mEsā'x·, daylight,	q'ai-huwô'qs still slept	Ts'ak·; nLk·'ē 5 Ts'ak·; then
hēL saying	naxna'yit: he heard:	"Yukt-wô'ôn "She invites you	dzē'EtsēE." my grand-mother."	NLk·'ē Then	nî'g·it 6 not	
hwîlā'x·s he knew	Ts'ak· Ts'ak·	hē'tg·ê. said.	NLk·'ē Then	ha'k·sEm once more	huX again	g·ä'êLt. 7 he lay down.
NLk·'ē Then	nā-ha'ts'iL entirely he bit	gula'tg·ê. his blanket.	NLk·'ē Then	qalk·si-g·a'ask^ut through he looked	lâ'Et. 8 at it.	
Gwinā'dEL, Behold,	Lgo-qā'k·L a little mouse	k·si-wî'tk^ut out came from	aL from in	ts'Em-an-ha'p'Esk^u. bunch of grass.	NLk·'ē 9 Then	
ha'ts'îk·sEm once more	huX again	hēt it said	as to	Ts'ak·: Ts'ak·:	"Yukt-wô'ôn "She invites you	dzē'EtsēE." 10 my grand-mother."
NLk·ēt Then	q'ai-g·îlā'ls still observed	Ts'ak· Ts'ak·	Lgo-qā'k·L the little mouse	ts'ElEm-dā'uLt into it went	aL 11 to	
ts'Em-an-hā'p'Esk^u. in bunch of grass.	NLk·'ē Then	hētk^us he stood	Ts'ak·. Ts'ak·.	NLk·'ē Then	hagun-iē'êt. 12 toward he went.	
K·'ēt Then	hasba-bē'sL upside down he tore	hā'p'Esk^u the grass.	Gwinā'dEL, Behold,	hwîlp a house	lukL-hē'tgut 13 under stood	
aL at	laXL the underside of	hā'p'Esk^u. the grass.	NLk·'ē Then	a'lg·îxL said	hana'q a woman	lō-d'ā'tg·ê 14 in sitting
lât: in it:	"Ts'ē'nEn "Enter my dear,	nāt, my	tsEda if	nē'En you	dEm (fut.)	t'au qâ'ôL 15 who goes for

to get a wife." Ts'ak· entered and sat down. The woman said to Ts'ak·, "Throw your earrings into the fire." He did so. He threw his earrings into the fire. Then the woman pulled them out of the fire by magic. She was the Mouse. Then she kept Ts'ak· and his great slave in the house, but she sent back the wren and the other bird. Ts'ak· finished eating. He was quite satiated. Then the woman stopped giving food to them. She said, "I myself am the trail leading through the mountain. I am not a shaman, but my sister on the other side is a great shaman. She will give you advice." Then she opened one corner of her house. Ts'ak· and his great slave went through it, under the mountain. The trail led that way. They passed through it; then they found another house and another woman. She was also a Mouse. Then he and the great slave entered, and the

---

1 dEm   nak·st."   NLk·'ē   ts'ēns   Ts'ak·.   NLk·'ē   La   d'āt,
   (fut.)   his wife."   Then   entered   Ts'ak·.   Then   when   he sat
                                                                                              down,

2 nLk·'ē   a'lg·îxl   hana'q   as   Ts'ak·:   "Txē'ldEL   qants'ēmō'En."
   then   spoke   the   to   Ts'ak·:   "Put into the your earrings."
                                 woman   fire

3 NLk·'ē   hwîls   Ts'ak·.   Txē'ldEL   qants'ēmu'Xtg·ê.   NLk·'ēt
   Then   did so   Ts'ak·.   He put into   his earrings.   Then
                                             the fire

4 nā'mtsElL   hana'qg·ê.   K·sEm-qā'k·L   hwaL   hana'qg·ê.   NLk·'ē
   took them out the woman.   Female mouse   the   the woman.   Then
   of fire by magic   name of

5 yukL   wô'ôtkⁿt   as   Ts'ak·   qanL   wī-xa'E.   La   k·'ē
   begin-   he was invited   Ts'ak·   and   the slave.   (Perf.)   then
   ning   great

6 gulîk·s-hashē'tset x-sk·ī'ek·   qanL   ts'Epts'a'p.   Hwä'i!   La   läxkⁿs
   back   she sent   (a bird)   and   the wren.   Well!   When   finished
                                                                               eating

7 Ts'ak·,   sEm-ts'ä'x·ts   Ts'ak·.   NLk·'ē   ha'wuL   hana'q   t'an
   Ts'ak   really satiated   Ts'ak·.   Then   stopped   the   who
                 was   woman

8 yō'ôg'ans   nē'tg·ê.   NLk·'ē   a'lg·îxl   hana'qg·ê: "LEp-nē'EL
   made eat   him.   Then   spoke   the woman: "Self   I

9 qēnEX.   NLk·'ē   nîg·ide   halai'dēE.   Lg·ī'gwēE   aL   an-dâ'
   the trail.   Then   not   I am a   My sister   on   the
                                             shaman.   other side

10 wī-halai'dEt.   NELnē'   dEm   t'an   yō'LEmgan."   NLk·'ēt   ma'dEL
   a   shaman.   She   (fut.)   who   advises you."   Then   opened
   great

11 hana'q   amō'sL   hwîlpt.   Nîlne'L   qalk·si-yô'xkⁿs   Ts'ak·   qanL
   the   the   the house. There   through followed   Ts'ak·   and
   woman   corner of

12 wī-xa'E.   laXL   sqanē'sL   yô'xkⁿdetg·ê.   Nêlne'L   hwîl
   the slave   the under-   the   they followed.   There   where
   great   side of   mountain

13 q'ap-qalk·si-sg·î'L   qē'nEX.   NLk·'ē   La   qalk·si-a'qLk·det,   nLk·'ēt
   really through lay   the trail. Then   when   through   they got,   then

14 huX   hwaL   hwîlpL   k·'ûlr   hana'qg·ê.   HuXt   k·sEm-qā'k·L
   again   they   the house   one   woman.   Also   female mouse
                found   of

woman said, "Throw your earrings into the fire." Ts'ak· did so. He
threw his earrings into the fire, and she pulled them out by magic.
Then the woman said to Ts'ak·, "All the princes from everywhere try
to marry the daughter of the chief. The stone door of his house has
killed a great many. It shuts rapidly. He uses it to kill the princes.
You must count how often it opens. It will open four times. Then
put this across the doorway. Wait a little while before you enter."
Then the woman gave him a little carving of ice, not very long.
Ts'ak· wore a marten robe and a dancing robe. He came near the
house. Then he asked the great slave to sit down. He alone
approached it. Now he came near the door. Then he did as the

hwaɪ	hana′qg·ê.	Nʟk·'ē	huX	ts'ēnt	lât	qanʟ	wī-xa′ᴇ.	1
the name of	the woman.	Then	again	he entered	in it	and	the slave. great	

Nʟk·'ē	huX	a′lg·îxʟ	hana′qg·ê:	"Nāt,	txē′ldᴇʟ	qants'ēmō′ᴇn!"		2
Then	again	spoke	the woman:	"My dear,	throw into the fire	your earrings!"		

Nʟk·'ē	hwîls	Ts'a′k·g·ê.	Txē′ldᴇʟ	qants'ēmu′Xt.	Nʟk·'ē		3
Then	he did so	Ts'ak·.	He threw into the fire	his earrings.	Then		

ha′k·sᴇnɪ	huX	nā′mtsᴇʟʟ	hana′qg·ê.	Nʟk·'ē	a′lg·îxʟ	hana′qg·ê	4
once more	again	took them out of fire by magic	the woman.	Then	spoke	the woman	

as	Ts'ak·:	"ʟa	txanē′tkuʟ	k'ōpᴇ-wī′lk·sîʟkuʟ	hwîl	dzîxdzô′q	5
to	Ts'ak·:	"(Perf.)	all	little princes of		camps	

dᴇm	t'an	nak·sʟ	ʟgō′uʟkuʟ	sᴇm'â′g·it.	ʟa	wī-hē′lʟ	ia′tst.	6
(fut.)	who	marry	the daughter of	the chief.	(Perf.)	many	he killed.	

Lô′ôp	ā′dz'ᴇpʟ	sᴇm'â′g·idᴇst..	Hāha′gwax,	nîʟne′t	hâ′yit	aʟ	7
Stone	the door of	the chief.	It claps together,	that	he uses	against	

txanē′tkuʟ	k'ōpᴇ-wî′lk·sîʟku.	K·'ē	huX	daXʟ	an-hwu′nt.	8
all	little princes.	Then	again	dead	who do so.	

Hwä′i!	dᴇm	lē′tsxan	qapē′iʟ	dᴇm	q'aqt;	txalpx	dᴇm	q'aqt,	9
Well!	(fut.)	count	how often	(fut.)	it opens;	four times	(fut.)	it opens,	

mᴇ	dᴇm	k·'ē′	lō-sqa-hē′t'ᴇns	gōn	sê!"	Nʟk·'ēt	g·înā′mʟ	10
you	(fut.)	then	in sideways	place	this	!"	Then	she gave him	

hana′q	ʟgo-ala′g·îm	dā′wut,	ʟgo-ts'ō′sg·îm	wī-na′ku.	"Tsᴇda	ʟa	11
the woman	a little carving of	ice,	a little	small very long.	"If	(perf.)	

ts'ᴇlᴇm-a′qʟgun	mᴇ	dzᴇ	ksi-gō′ut,"	dēya′.	Gwīs-haʟ	gula′îs	Ts'ak·	12
into	you get	you	take it out,"	thus she said.	Blanket	marten	the blanket of	Ts'ak·	

qanʟ	gwīs-halai′t.	Nʟk·'ē	ʟa	hagun-dē′lpkus	Ts'ak·,	nʟk·'ē	13
and	blanket dancing.	Then	(perf.)	toward	near	Ts'ak·,	then	

d'ā′dᴇʟ	wī-xa′ᴇ.	Nʟk·'ē	k·sax-ne′t	Ts'ak·ʟ	hagun-ie′êt.	K·'ē	14
he sat down	the slave. great	Then	only he	Ts'ak·	toward	he went.	Then	

hagun-a′qʟkut	aʟ	awa′aʟ	ptô′ᴇ.	Nʟk·'ēt	hwîl	t'an	t häʟ	hana′qʟ	15
toward	he reached	at	the proximity of	the door.	Then	he did	what said	the woman	

woman had instructed him.   He counted four, then he placed the carving of crystal across the door so that it was unable to close again. Ts'ak· entered.   He was not killed by the door.   He came in and stepped up to the place where the chief's daughter was lying.   Then Ts'ak· lay down.   The chief's daughter was very glad when she saw the beautiful man.   They were playing all night.   Then the chief heard it.   Very early in the morning he said to his sister's sons, "Light the fire."   His nephews did so.   They started a great fire.   Then the chief told them to take the skin of the great bear, and he ordered them to spread it out in the rear of his house.   Then the chief said, "Let my son-in-law come to the middle of the house."   Ts'ak· rose and stepped down to the middle of the house.   Then he saw that the hair of the bear was very long.   The chief intended to kill Ts'ak· with it.   He was

1 t'an   yō'Lᴇmqtg·ê.   Lē'tsxaL   txālpxt.   NLk·'ē   lō-sqa-hē't'ᴇnL
   who   gave him advice.   He counted   four.   Then   in side he placed
                                                                                        ways

2 ala'g·îm   tgwat.   NLk·'ē   nîg·i   huX   Lagait-a'qLk^ut   hwîl   k·'ē
   the carv-   crystal.   Then   not   again   it could reach   being   then
   ing of

3 qaq'a'kt.   NLk·'ē   ts'ēns   Ts'ak·.   Nîg·i   nô'ôt.   Ts'ᴇlᴇm-a'qLk^ut.
   open.   Then   he   Ts'ak·.   Not   he   Into   he
                          entered   died.   reached.

4 NLk·'ē   mᴇn-iē's   Ts'ak·   aL   hwîl   lē-g·ä'êL   Lgō'uLk^uL
   Then   up went   Ts'ak·   to   where   on lay   the child of

5 sᴇm'â'g·it.   NLk·'ē   g·ä'ᴇls   Ts'ak·.   NLk·'ē   sᴇmgal   lō-ā'mL   qâ'ôL
   the chief.   Then   he lay   Ts'ak·.   Then   very   in good   heart
                           down   was

6 Lgō'uLk^uL   sᴇm'â'g·it   hwîl   ā'd'îk·sk^uL   sᴇ'm-ama   g·at.   NLk·'ē
   the daughter of   the chief   where   came   a very good   man.   Then

7 yukL   qalā'qdet   aL   wī-a'xk^u.   NLk·'ē   naxna'L   sᴇm'â'g·it.   Sᴇm-
   begin-   they played   at   all night.   Then   heard it   the chief.   Very
   ning

8 hē'Luk,   nᴇk·'ē   a'lg·îxL   sᴇm'â'g·it   aL   guslî'sk^ut: "Sᴇm-sᴇ-me'L
   morning,   then   spoke   the chief   to   his sister's   "Very make burn
                                                           sons:

9 la'gust."   NLk·'ē   hwîlL   guslî'sk^ut.   Wī-t'ē'st   hwîl   sᴇ-me'LdeL
   the fire."   Then   did so   his sister's   Great   where   was   to burn
                                     sons.   made

10 lak^u,   nLk·'ēt   gun-gō'udᴇL   sᴇm'â'g·iL   La   ana'sL   wī-o'l.   K·'ēt
   the   then   he them to   the chief   the   skin of   the bear.   Then
   fire,   caused take   great

11 gun-ba'Lt   aL   qalā'nL   hwîlpt.   NLk·'ē   a'lg·îxL   sᴇm'â'g·it:
   he   to   at   his house.   Then   spoke   the chief:
   caused spread out   the rear
                       of

12 "T'ᴇm-iä'tᴇn   La'msᴇᴇst."   NLk·'ē   g·în-hē'tk^us   Ts'ak·.   NLk·'ē
   "To the make   my son-in-law."   Then   arose   Ts'ak·.   Then
   middle   him go

13 t'ᴇm-iē'êt.   NLk·ēt   g·a'as   Ts'ak·   qan   nē'LeguLē   lax·L
   to the he   Then   saw   Ts'ak·   how   long   the
   middle went,   hair of

14 o'lg·ê   aL   dᴇm   dzak^us   Ts'ak·   qan   hwîlt.   "Tsᴇda   Lat
   the   to   (fut.)   kill   Ts'ak·   there-   he did   "If   (perf.)
   bear   fore   so.

to sit down on it, and then the hair would enter his anus, and thus he
was to die. Thus thought the chief. But Ts'ak· placed the carving
of ice under his feet, and he moved it over the skin. A noise was
made by the breaking of the bear's hair. Ts'ak· sat down, and the
hair did not enter his anus. Now the chief was ashamed because
Ts'ak· was not dead. He said, "Walk to the middle of the house."
Thus he spoke to his child. His daughter went down to the middle of
the house and sat down beside Ts'ak·. He married her. Then they ate.

When Ts'ak· had finished eating, the chief said to his nephews,
"Make a large pyre and place stones on it." His nephews did so.
They built a large pyre of wood and placed stones on it. When the
stones were hot, the chief ordered a large box to be taken down to the

---

| lē-d'a'tkᵘs | Ts'ak·, | dɛm | k·'ē | dz'ɛpdz'a'bîk·skᵘt | aʟ | ts'ɛm-q'â'ɛlt, | 1 |
| on he is placed | Ts'ak· | (fut.) | then | they will enter | at | in his anus, | |

| nʟ | dɛm | k·'ē | nô'ôt," | dē'yaʟ | qâtʟ | sɛm'â'g·it. | Nʟk·'ēt | 2 |
| he | (fut.) | then | dies," | thus spoke | the heart of | the chief. | Then | |

| lō-tq'al-hē't'ɛns | Ts'ak·ʟ | ala'g·îm | dā'ut | aʟ | ts'ɛm-asa'it. | 3 |
| in against placed | Ts'ak· | the carving of | ice | at | in his foot. | |

| Nʟk·'ēt | k'uʟ-sa'wut. | Xstamk | hwîl | hēʟā'ʟagaʟ | lax·ʟ | o'lg·ê. | 4 |
| Then | about he shook it. | Noise | where | broke | the hair of | the bear. | |

| Nʟk·'ē | lē-d'ā's | Ts'ak·. | Nʟk·'ē | nî'g·i | dz'ɛpdz'ā'bîsk·skᵘt | aʟ | 5 |
| Then | on he sat | Ts'ak·. | Then | not | they entered | at | |

| ts'ɛm-q'â'ls | Ts'ak·. | Nʟk·'ē | dzâqʟ | sɛm'â'g·it | hwîl | nî'g·i | nô'ôs | 6 |
| in the anus of | Ts'ak·. | Then | was ashamed | the chief | being | not | dead | |

| Ts'ak·. | Nʟk·'ē | a'lg·îxʟ | sɛm'â'g·it: | "T'ɛm-iē'n | dāʟ;" | dē'ya | 7 |
| Ts'ak·. | Then | spoke | the chief: | "To the middle go | my dear;" | thus he said | |

| aʟ | Lgō'uʟkᵘt. | Nʟk·'ē | t'ɛm-iä'ʟ | Lgō'uʟkᵘt. | Nʟk·'ē | d'āt | aʟ | 8 |
| to | his daughter. | Then | to the went middle | his daughter. | Then | she sat down | at | |

| awa'as | Ts'ak·. | Na'k·sgut. | Nʟk·'ē | txâ'xkᵘdet. | | | | 9 |
| the proximity of | Ts'ak· | He married her. | Then | they ate. | | | | |

| La | Läxkᵘs | Ts'ak· | aʟ | yō'ôxkᵘt, | nʟk·'ē | huX | a'lg·îxʟ | 10 |
| When | finished eating | Ts'ak· | at | eating, | then | again | spoke | |

| sɛm'â'g·it | aʟ | guslî'skᵘt: | "Āmʟ | dɛm | dâ'lɛpsɛm!" | Nʟk·'ē | 11 |
| the chief | to | his sister's sons: | "Good | (fut.) | you heat stones in a fire!" | Then | |

| huwî'lʟ | guslî'skᵘt. | Wī-t'ē'sʟ | ha-lē-dâ'lɛpʟ | dza'pdētg·ê. | Lô'ôp | 12 |
| did so | his nephews. | A great | pile of woods and stones | they made it. | Stones | |

| lē-d'ā'ʟdet | lât. | Nʟk·'ē | La | lɛmlā'mk·ʟ | lô'ôpg·ê. | Nʟk·'ēt | 13 |
| on they put | on it. | Then | when | they were hot | the stones. | Then | |

| gun-t'ɛm-gō'udɛʟ | sɛm'â'g·iʟ | wī-qal-hēnq. | Nʟk·'ēt | gun-lō-lô'ôdîk·st. | 14 |
| caused to the middle | to be taken | the chief | the great box. | Then | he in caused | to pour water. |

fire, and water to be poured into it. It was done. Then one man took a pair of tongs; another took another pair of tongs. These two persons took the stones and put them into the box, which was half full of water. Now the water began to boil. When it was boiling over, the chief said to Ts'ak·, "Rise and jump into this hot water." Ts'ak· did so. He jumped into it and sat down. His body was covered by the water. Only a little of his hair was visible. Now the water boiled violently, and Ts'ak·'s wife cried when she saw how he was being cooked. Then a person went down to the box and pulled at Ts'ak·'s hair. It came out, and the person said, "He is well done." Now the chief told them to pour out the water. When they had done so, Ts'ak· rose. Then he went to the rear of the house and said to

---

1 NLk·'ēt   hwîlā'kⁿdet.   NLk·'ēt   gō'uL   k·'âlL   g·at   ha-pts'ä'xkⁿ.
   Then   it was done.   Then   took   one   man   tongs.

2 NLk·'ēt   huX   gō'uL   huX   k·'âlL   k·'ēlt.   NLk·'ēt
   Then   also   took   also   one man   one   Then
                                                        (pair of tongs).

3 ha'kⁿLdeL   lô'ôp   bagadē'lL   g·a'tg·ê.   NLk·'ēt   lō-d'ā'Ldet   aL
   took   stones   two   men.   Then   in they put   in
                                                               them

4 ts'Em-qal-hē'nq   qak·-sē'lukᵘaL   ak·s.   NLk·'ēt   La   haLhâ'LEqLk·ᵘt.
   in   the box   half full of   water.   Then   (perf.)   it was boiling.

5 NLk·'ē   t'ēsL   hwîl   t'uks-iä'êt.   NLk·'ē   a'lg·îxL   sEm'â'g·it
   Then   much   where   out it went   Then   spoke   the chief
            was   (it boiled over).

6 as   Ts'ak·:   "ĀmL   hē'tgun!   ĀmL   dEm   lō-dā'uLEn   aL
   to   Ts'ak·:   "Good   stand up!   Good   (fut.)   in   go   at

7 ts'Em-g·a'mg·îm   ak·s."   NLk·'ē   hwîls   Ts'ak·.   K·'ē   lôgôm-ba'xt.
   in   the hot   water."   Then   did so   Ts'ak·.   Then   into he went.

8 NLk·'ē   lō-d'ā't.   Lō-gwâ'tkᵘL   t'Em-qē'st.   Q'am-ts'ō'sk·   hwîl
   Then   in he sat   In was lost   his head.   Only a little   where
            down.

9 k·si-ma'qskⁿL   qēst.   NLk·'ē   wī-t'ē's   hwîl   haLhâ'LEqLkᵘ,   k·'ē
   out stood   his hair.   Then   much   where   it boiled,   then

10 wiyē'tkᵘL   nak·s   Ts'ak·   hwîl   Lat   g·a'aL   hwîl   a'nuksL   Lē   smax·s
   cried   the   Ts'ak·   being   (perf.)   she saw   where   was done   the flesh
                wife of   (cooked)   of

11 Ts'ak·.   NLk·'ē   hagun-iä'êL   k·'âlL   g·at   t'an   k·si-tsâ'ôdEL   qēs
   Ts'ak·.   Then   toward went   one   man   who   out pulled   the
                                                                                  hair of

12 Ts'ak·.   NLk·'ē   k·si-tsâ'ôt.   NLk·'ē   ma'LEL   g·at   La   gwô'tsîk·s
   Ts'ak·.   Then   out it came.   Then   told   the man   (perf.)   really

13 a'nukst.   NLk·'ēt   gun-sa-qā'tsîL   sEm'â'g·iL   Lē   lō-a'k·sît.   NLk·'ēt
   he was done   Then   caused off pour   the chief   the   inside water.   Then they
   (cooked).   to

14 sā-qā'tsdet,   hwîl   k·'ē'   haldEm-ba'xs   Ts'ak·.   K·'ē   g·îme-iē'êt.
   off poured it,   then   rose   Ts'ak·.   Then   to the he
                                                                  rear   went.

his wife, " Your father will not be able to kill me with all his arts."
Then the woman was glad, but the chief was ashamed.

The next morning the chief said, " Come, Son-in-law. Fetch some
fuel. One of my nephews and two slaves shall accompany you." Ts'ak·
rose. The slaves took stone axes such as the people used in olden
times. Ts'ak· felled a great tree. It fell and he split it. Then one
of the slaves made wedges. They also carried a large stone hammer,
which was fastened with thong to a handle. They put the wedges into
the end of the tree. They struck them with the hammer and the tree
split. Then they pushed Ts'ak· into it and knocked out the wedges.
The tree snapped together, and Ts'ak· was in it. The slaves saw

NLk·'ē	hēt	aL	nak·st:	"Q'ap-nî'g·i	dEm	dē-nō'ôē;	txanē'tk^usL 1
Then	he said	to	his wife:	"Really not	(fut.)	on my part I die;	all

dEm	hwîls	nEgwâ'ôdEn	lâ'ôE.	Q'ap-nî'g·i	dEm	dē-nô'ôē." 2
(fut.)	does	your father	to me.	Really not	(fut.)	on my part I die."

NLk·'ē	lō-ā'mL	qâ'ôL	hana'qg·ê.	La	dzâqL sEm'â'g·it. 3
Then	in good	heart	the woman.	(Perf.)	he was ashamed the chief.

NLk·'ē	huX	k·'ēlL	hē'Luk,	nLk·'ē	huX	a'lg·îxL sEm'â'g·it: 4
Then	again	one	morning,	then	again	spoke the chief:

"ĀmL	dEm	sE-â'Lk^uL,	LamsEî'st.	Bagadē'lL	LiLî'ng·it dEm 5
"Good	(fut.)	make firewood,	my son-in-law.	Two	slaves (fut.)

stēlt	dē-k·'â'lL	guslē'sē."	NLk·'ē	haldEm-ba'xs	Ts'ak·; nLk·'ē 6
accompany him	with one	my nephew."	Then	rose	Ts'ak·; then

dôqL	LiLî'ng·it	dawī'sEm	lô'ôp.	NELnē't	dē-hâ'yîL waLEn- 7
took	the slaves	axes of	stone.	That	on their used part of olden times

g·ig·a't	aL	g·i-k'ō'ôL.	NLk·'ēt	q'ōts	dEp	Ts'ak·L wī-ga'n. 8
the people	at	long ago.	Then	cut	(plur.)	Ts'ak· a tree. great

NLk·'ē	qē'nExt.	NLk·'ē	xtsē-ia'tsdet.	NLk·'ēt	dzîpdza'pL k·'âlL 9
Then	it fell.	Then	in the middle they chopped it.	Then	made one

wī-xa'E	lēt.	K·'ē	ia'gait-yu'kdēL	wī-da'qLEm	lô'ôp.	Tq'al- 10
great slave	wedges.	Then	already they carried	a great	hammer of stone.	Against

da'k·Ldet	aL	ts'aL.	NLk·'ē	lō-ma'qsaandet	aL LExLEpq'a'pL 11
it was fastened	with	skin of the back.	Then	in they put it	at the end of

wī-ga'n.	NLk·'ēt	ô'x·dēt	aL	da'qLEm	lô'ôp. NLk·'ē sagaL 12
the tree. great	Then	they struck with	the hammer of	stone.	Then it split

wī-lō-la'et.	NLk·'ēt	lō-t'ē'sdet	Ts'ak·	lâ'ôt.	NLk·'ēt k·si- 13
great in large.	Then	in they pushed	Ts'ak·	in it.	Then out

ax·'ô'x·dēL	lēt.	NLk·'ē	ha'ts'îk·sEm	huX	hā'k'waxL wī-ga'n 14
they struck	the wedges.	Then	once more	again	clapped together the tree great

lō-sg·i's	Ts'ak·	aL	ts'â'wuL	gan.	NLk·'ēt	g·a'aL LîLî'ng·ît hwîl 15
in lay	Ts'ak·	at	inside of	tree.	Then	saw the slaves where

blood coming out of Ts'ak·'s mouth, and they left nim, saying,
"Now you have been put to shame!" They went home. But Ts'ak·
kicked the great tree, so that one half fell to one side and the other half
to the other. He carried one half on his shoulder and went home.
He threw it into the house, and the whole house front was broken.
Then the chief was ashamed, and he worried because he was unable to
kill Ts'ak·, who was a great supernatural man.

The chief did not know what to use next, but after a while it occurred
to him what to do. One morning he said to Ts'ak· that he should go
and spear a seal that he wanted to eat. His nephew and two slaves
were to go along, so there were four in the canoe. They started,
and found a place where seals were. It was at the edge of a great
whirlpool. They asked Ts'ak· to stand in the bow of the canoe, to

---

1 La ā'd'îk·sk"L iLä'ê aL ts'ɛm-ā'qs Ts'ak·. NLk·'ēt k"sta'qsdēt.
  (perf.) came blood at in mouth Ts'ak·. Then they left him.
                              of

2 NLk·'ē tgōnL hē'det: "Dzâ'gan!" La nā-la'k·det aL ts'ɛm-hwî'lp.
  Then this they said: "Be ashamed!" (Perf.) they went to in the
                                                        home house.

3 NLk·'ēt ank·sksla'qsts Ts'ak· wī-ga'n. NLk·'ē hwagait-sg·i'L Lē
  Then apart kicked Ts'ak· the tree. Then away it lay
                          great

4 stô'ôt aL hwagait-gō'st. NLk·'ēt qō'lts'ɛxs Ts'ak·L wī-stô'ôt.
  the half at away there. Then he carried it Ts·ak· the half.
                                        on his shoulder great

5 NLk·'ē nā-iē'êt. NLk·'ēt ts'ɛlɛm-gu'Xt. NLk·'ē wī-txa gwa'sk"L
  Then out of he Then into he threw Then great all broken
      the woods went.   it.

6 ā'dz'ɛpL hwîlpL sɛm'â'g·it. NLk·'ē dzâqL sɛm'â'g·it, La abū'g·ask"t
  the door of the house the chief. Then was the chief, (perf.) he was
          of   ashamed   troubled

7 aL dɛmt hwîla nō'ôt'ɛns Ts'ak·. Sɛmgal wī·nɛqnô'qL g·at
  to (fut.) being means of Ts'ak·. Very great supernatural man
                  killing

8 gō'stg·ê.
  that one.

9 NLk·'ē aq-huX hâ'yîL sɛm'â'g·it. Sı-gō'n, nLk·'ē huX
  Then with· again using the chief. After then again
      out   a while

10 lo-d'ā'L qâ'ôdɛt. HuX k·ēlL hē'Luk, nLk· et huX hētsL
  ın was it his mind. Again one morning, then again sent

11 sɛm'â'g·ît Ts'ak·. Gun g·a'Lk"dɛt dɛm x-ēlxt. Bagadē'lL
  the chief Ts·ak·. He him to spear (lut.) to seal. Two
              caused   eat

12 Lîlî'ng·it dɛdā'dēt, dē-k·'â'lı guslî'st Ne'L qan lō-txalpxdā'detg·ê.
  slaves were with him with one his Therefore in four were in canoe.
      ın the canoe, nephew

13 NLk·'ē dā'uLdēt. NLk·'ē hwa'dēt hwîl d'āL ēlx, lax-ts·ä'ɛL
  Then they left. Then they found where were seals, on edge of

14 wī-an-tgo-lē'lbîk·sk". NLk·'ēt gun-lē-hē'tk"det Ts'ak· aL
  great around rolling water. Then they on to stand Ts'ak· at
                      caused

hold the harpoon and spear the seal. One of the great slaves stood
near. He intended to push Ts'ak· into the water, that he should die.
While the slave was intending to do so, Ts'ak· threw him into the
water and he died. The whirlpool swallowed him. Then Ts'ak·
began to spear seals and filled his canoe. He returned and landed in
front of the house. The chief had lost one slave, and they told him that
he had been drowned. Then Ts'ak· carried the seals up and they
cooked them. When they were done, he called the whole tribe, and
they ate the seals. Now the chief gave up trying to kill Ts'ak·.

Ts'ak· now thought of returning to his grandmother whom he had
left, and to his first wife. Then he went back, accompanied by his

lax-g·itsä'qL	mäl.	Yu'kdēL	sgan-dä'pxL.		NLk·'ēt	g·aLk^{u}L	1
on how of	canoe.	He held	the shaft the of harpoon.		Then	he speared	
ēlx.	NLk·'ē	q'ai'yîm	hagun-hē'tk^{u}L	wī-xa'E	aL	awa'at	2
a seal.	Then	near	toward stood	the slave great	at	his proximity	
dEm	t'an	t'uks-t'ē'sEs	Ts'ak·	aL	ts'Em-a'k·s.	NeL	dEm	3
(fut.)	who	out pushed	Ts'ak·	at	in water.	He	(fut.)	
k·'ē	nô'ôt.	Q'ai-hē-yu'kL	hēL	qâ'ôdEL	xa'EL	dEm	4
then	dead.	Still began	said	the heart of	the slave	(fut.)	
t'uks-t'ē'sEs	Ts'ak·,	sEm-t'uks-t'ē'sEs	Ts'ak·L	wī-xa'E.	NLk·'ē	5
out push	Ts'ak·,	really out pushed	Ts'ak·	the slave. great	Then	
nô'ôt.	YâpxL	an-tgo-lē'lbîk·sk^u·	NLk·'ē	yukt	g·aLk^{n}s	Ts'ak·	6
he was dead.	It swallowed him	around rolling water.	Then	he began	speared	Ts'ak·	
ēlx.	Sem-mē'tk^{u}L	mäl.	NLk·'ē	lō-ya'ltk^{u}s	Ts'ak·.	K·'ē	7
seals.	Very full	the canoe.	Then	he returned	Ts'ak·.	Then	
k·'atskt	aL	qa-g·ä'uL	hwîlp.	NLk·'ē	gwâ'tEsîL	sEm'â'g·it	8
they landed	at	the front of the houses of	the town.	Then	he lost	the chief	
aL	k·'âlL	wī-xa'E.	NLk·'ēt	ma'Ldet	nô'ôt	aL	ts'Em-a'k·s.	9
at	one	great slave.	Then	they told	he was dead	in	in the water.	
NLk·'ē	bax-hwî'lqdēL	ēlx.	NLk·'ēt	sä'LEpdēt.	NLk·'ē	a'nukst,	10
Then	up they carried	the seals.	Then	they boiled them.	Then	they were done,	
nLk·'ēt	wô'ôdet	txanē'tk^{u}L	ts'ap.	NLk·'ēt	g·ē'îpdeL	ēlx.	11
then	they invited	all the	people.	Then	they ate the	seals.	
NLk·'ē	ha'uL	sEm'â'g·it	aL	dEmt	sîk·'ēL	dzak^{n}s	Ts'ak·.		12
Then	stopped	the chief	to	(fut.)	try	to kill	Ts'ak·.		
Hwä'ı!	Lat	am-gâ'dEs	Ts'ak·	dEm	huX	yaltk^{u}t	aL	awa'as	13
Well!	(Perf.)	he thought	Ts'ak·	(fut.)	again	he returned	to	the proximity of	
nets'ē'Etst,	Lē	k^{u}sta'qsdetg·ê	qanL	Lē	waLEn-na'k·st.	NLk·'ē	14
his grandmother,	(Perf.)	he left them	and		his former	wife.	Then	
lō-ya'ltk^{u}t.	Gulîk·s-stē'lL	sī-na'k·st	qanL	wī-xa'E;	La	15
he returned.	Back accompanied him	his wife new	and	the slave, great	(perf.)	

new wife, and by his great slave Drum-belly, who had stayed alone in
the woods far from the town. They called him, and they returned.
Then they came to the place where the Mouse woman lived. She
said to Ts'ak·, "Did you succeed in your attempt?" Ts'ak· replied,
"I did succeed." Then she gave them to eat until they had enough.
They started again and went through the mountain. When they
had passed through, they entered the house of the other Mouse. The
Mouse women watch both ends of the trail that leads through the mountain. Ts'ak· went on, and reached his own house. That is the end.

---

1 k·'ax·-tq'al-d'ā'adEL   Anō'LEm   ban   aL   g·ilē'lîx·.   NLk·'ē   La
   alone against stayed   Drum-   belly   at   in woods.   Then (perf.)

2 lo-ya'ltkᵘt,   nLk·'ēt   wô'ôt.   NLk·'ē   hēlya'ltkᵘdetg·ê.   NLk·'ē
   he returned,   then   he called Then   they returned.   Then
                                him.

3 ha'ts'îk·sEm   huX   hwa'dēL   hwîl   dzôqL   hana'qt
   once more   again   they found   where   stayed   the woman

4 k·sEm-qā'k·L   hwa'tg·ê.   NLk·'e   a'lg·îxL   k·sEm-qā'k·L
   female mouse   her name.   Then   spoke   female mouse

5 as   Ts'ak·:   "Nē!   Me   daa'qLkᵘL   qan   hwî'lEn?"   NLk·'ē
   to   Ts'ak·:   "Indeed! You   attained   for   you did so?" Then

6 hēs   Ts'ak·:   "Daa'qLguēE,   hâ   net."   NLk·'ē   yukL   wô'ôtkᵘs
   said   Ts'ak·:   "I attained it, yes   indeed." Then   began   he was
                                                                               invited by

7 k·sEm-qā'k·L.   GwātsE's   lets'ä'x·t.   NLk·ē   huX   Lô'ôdet.
   female mouse.   Really   they were   Then   again   they went.
                                   satiated.

8 HuX   ha'ts'îk·sEm   huX   qalk·si-yô'xkᵘdet   laXL   sqanē'stg·ê.
   Again   once more   again   through they went   the under-   the mountain.
                                                            side of

9 NLk·'ē   huX   qalk·si-ax'a'qLkᵘdetg·ê.   NLk·'ē   huX   la'mdzîxdet
   Then   again   through   they reached   Then   again   they entered

10 aL   huX   hwîl   dzôqs   huX   k·'âlL   k·sEm-qā'k·L.   Lāx-lē'Lk·dēL
    at   again   where   stayed   again   one   female mouse.   Both   they watch
                                                                               ends

11 hwîl   qalk·si-sg·i'L   qē'nEx   aL   laXL   sqanē'stg·ê.   NLk·'ē   huX
    where   through   lies   the trail at   the under-   the mountain.   Then   again·
                                                   side of

12 Lô'ôdet.   NLk·'ē   gulîk·s-a'qLkᵘs   Ts'ak·   aL   lEp-hwî'lpt.
    they went.   Then   back   reached   Ts'ak·   at   own his house.

13 NLk·'ē   sā-ba'xt.
    Then   off it runs
               (it is the end).

[Told by Moses]

There was a boy who had lost his father and his mother; only his mother's brother, the chief of the village, remained. One day this chief was purifying himself by drinking a decoction of devil's-clubs. He did so repeatedly because he intended to give a potlatch. One evening he went down to the beach; there he sat down and looked up to the sky. Behold, fire came down from the sky like a shooting star. It came right down. A tree was standing behind the house of the chief, and a branch was standing out from the tree. The fire came right down to it and hung on the end of the branch. The chief

---

Masemstiōntsē′etsk^u

GROWING-UP-LIKE-ONE-WHO-HAS-A-GRANDMOTHER

Lgo-tk·'ē′Lk^u	nô′ôL	nEguâ′ôdEt	qanL	nôxt.	Q'am-k·'â′lL	1
A little boy	was dead	his father	and	his mother.	Only one	
sEm'â′g·it	nEbē′pt.	Hwä′i!	K·'ēlL	sa,	k·'ēt g·ē′ipL sEm'â′g·it	2
chief	his mother's brother.	Well!	One	day,	then ate the chief	
wôō′mst.	HuX	k·'ēlL	sa,	k·'ē	huX hwîlt, huXt g·ē′îpL	3
devil's-club.	Again	one	day,	then	again he did so, again he ate	
wôō′ms.	Hwä′i!	La	yukL	dEm	yukt, nLnēL qan hwîlt.	4
devil's-club.	Well!	He	was about	(fut.)	to give a potlatch, therefore he did so.	
NLk·'ē	yu′ksa,	k·'ē	k·saxt.	K·'ē	iaga-iä′t aL g·ä′u. K·'ē d'ät	5
Then	evening,	then	he went out.	Then	down he went to front of house. Then he sat down	
aL g·ä′u.	K·'ē	g·a′ask^ut	aL	lax-ha′.	Gwinā′dEL, lak^uL ā′d'îk·sk^ut;	6
at front of house.	Then	he looked	to	the sky.	Behold, a fire came;	
wîtk^ut	aL	lax-ha′g·ê	hō′g·igaL	k'watsL	pELî′st. K·'ēt d'Ep-yu′kt.	7
it came	from	the sky	like	excrements of	a star. Then down it came.	
Hwä′i!	Hētk^uL	gan	aL	qa-qalā′nL	hwîlpL sEm'â′g·it. NLk·'ē	8
Well!	It stood	a tree	at	rear of house of	the house of the chief. Then	
sa-hē′tk^uL	anē′sL	gan.	NLnēL	qâ′ôL	qâ′yibêx. NLk·'ē	9
off stood	a branch of	the tree.	Then	it went to it	the light. Then	
lē-ia′qt.	Hwä′i!	G·a′aL	sEm'â′g·it,	d'ät	aL g·ä′u. NLk·'ē	10
on it hung.	Well!	He saw it	the chief,	he sat	at front of house. Then	

137

saw it. He went up to the house and sent for his people. When they entered, he said, "Copper is hanging on the branch of a tree. The young people shall go and knock it down. If one of you young men hit it, he shall marry my daughter."

Early the next morning they went up behind the house of the chief. The old men also went to look. The young men took stones, and threw all day long until their hands were quite sore; then they stopped for a while and ate. Then they went up again and tried to knock the copper down, but they did not succeed. It grew dark. Then the poor little boy went down to the beach in front of the house and sat down near a canoe, where he urinated. Then he saw a man approaching who said, "What are the people talking about?" The boy replied,

---

1 hwîl   k·'ē   bax-iē'êt.   K·'ēt   gun-qâ'ôdEL   qal-ts'a'p.   NLk·'ē
  At   up   he   Then   he   the people.   Then
  once   went.   to go
                                              caused there

2 la'mdzîxL   qal-ts'a'p.   NLk·'ē   maLL   sEm'â'g·itg·ê;   nLk·'ē   a'lg·îxt:
  they entered   the people.   Then   he told   the chief;   then   he said:

3 "Lē-ia'qL   oq   aL   lax-anē'st.   Hwä'i!   DEm   ō'yîL   txanē'tkuL
  "On hangs   a   at   on a branch.   Well!   (Fut.) throw it   all
              copper

4 q'aima'qsit!   AtsEdat   ôx·L   k·'âLL   g·at,   nLnet   dEm   an-na'k·skuL
  youths!   If he   hits   one   man,   then he   (fut.)   who marries

5 Lgō'uLguē."
  my daughter."

6 NLk·'ē   mEsä'x·;   k·'ē   hwîl   k·'ē   bax-Lô'ôdēt   aL   qa-qalä'nL
  Then   daylight;   at once   up they went   to   rear of house

7 hwîlpL   sEm'â'g·it.   NLk·'ē   dē-bax-Lô'ôL   wud'ax-g·ig·a't   aL
  of the   the chief.   Then   also up went   the old men   to
  house of

8 ä'lg·altg·ê.   Lô'ôpL   dôqL   q'aima'qsit.   K·'ē   hwîl   k·'ēt   ô'x·dēt
  look.   Stones   they   the youths.   At once   they threw
                              took   they
                                                                            threw

9 aL   wī-sa'.   Q'ap-sîpsī'êpkuL   qa-an'ô'ndēt.   NLk·'ē   k·'ax-huxhā'odet.
  at   all day.   Really sick were   their hands.   Then   for a   they stopped.
                                                                        while

10 Hwä'i!   Q'am-LaxLä'êxku   txâ'ôxkudēt,   k·'ē   ha'tsEm   huX
   Well!   Only they finished   they ate,   then   once more   again
            eating

11 Lô'ôdet;   k·'ēt   ha'tsEm   huXt   ô'x·det.   Hwä'i!   Nî'g·i
   they   then   once more   again   they   Well!   Not
   went;   threw

12 da-a'qLkudet,   k·'ē   yu'ksa.   NLk·'ē   k·saXL   Lgo-guä'Em
   they reached it,   then   evening.   Then   went out   the   poor
                                                                  little

13 Lgo-tk·'ē'Lku.   NLk·'ē   iaga-iä'êt   aL   qa-g·ä'uL   hwîlp.   G·ô'ôL
   little   boy.   Then   down he   to   front of   the house.   There
                                 went   village of   was

14 mäl   nL   hwîl   d'āt.   Hē-yukL   ē'îst.   K·'ē   hagun-iē'êL   g·at   aL
   a   where he was   sitting. He began   he   Then   toward went   a   to
   canoe   urinated.   man

15 awa'at.   NLk·'ē   a'lg·îxt   as   nē'tg·ê: "Agō'L   La   an-hä'L
   his   Then   he said   to   him: "What   (perf.) what say
   proximity.

"A copper hangs on a tree and the people tried to knock it down, but they did not succeed." "Go on and try to hit it yourself," said the man. Then he took up a stone and gave it to the boy. He took up another one and gave it to him, and still another one and gave it to him. Then he said, "You shall knock it down. Take first this white stone, then this black stone, then this blue stone, and finally this one." The poor little boy took them, and then the man said, "Do not show these stones to the people."

On the following morning the people went again and began to throw. The poor little boy went up with them and said he would throw too.

---

qal-ts'a'p?"   Nᴌkꞏ'ē   hēᴌ   ʟgo-tkꞏ'ē'ʟkᵘgꞏê: "Lē-ia'qʟ   oq   aʟ   1
the people?"   Then   said   the little boy: "On hangs   a   at
copper

lax-ga'n,   nᴌnēᴌ   ō'yîᴌ   qal-ts'a'p.   Nᴌkꞏ'ēt   nîgꞏit   da-a'qʟkᵘdet."   2
on a tree,   that   they throw it   the people.   Then   not   they reach it."

"Hwä'i!   Tsᴇ   ô'yîn,   ana'!"   Nᴌkꞏ'ēt   gō'uᴌ   kꞏ'ēlᴌ   lô'ôpgꞏê.   3
"Well!   Throw it,   go on!"   Then   he took   one   stone.

Nᴌkꞏ'ēt   gꞏînā'mt   aᴌ   ʟgo-tkꞏ'ē'ʟkᵘ.   Nᴌkꞏ'ēt   huX   gō'uᴌ   huX   4
Then   he gave it   to   the little boy.   Then   again   he took   again

kꞏ'ēlt.   Nᴌkꞏ'ēt   gꞏinā'mt.   Hwä'i!   Nᴌkꞏ'ēt   huX   gō'uᴌ   huX   5
one.   Then he   gave it.   Well!   Then   again   he took   again

kꞏ'ēlt;   nᴌkꞏ'ēt   huX   gꞏînā'mt.   Nᴌkꞏ'ē   a'lgꞏîxᴌ   gꞏat   hagun-   6
one;   then   again   he gave it.   Then   he said   the man   toward

hē'tgut   aᴌ   awa'aᴌ   ʟgo-guä'ᴇm   ʟgo-tkꞏ'ē'ʟkᵘ   Nᴌkꞏ'ē   a'lgꞏîxt: 7
standing   at   proximity of   the poor little   little boy.   Then   he said:

"Tsᴇ   ô'yîn,   ana'!   Tgōnᴌ   dᴇm   kꞏs-qā'ôqdᴇn   mā'kꞏsgum   8
"Throw it,   go on!   This   shall   first you   white

lô'ôp.   Nᴌkꞏ'ē   huX   kꞏ'ēlt   t'ō'ôtsgum   lô'ôp.   Hwä'i!   HuX   9
stone.   Then   again   one   black   stone.   Well!   Again

kꞏ'ēlᴌ   lô'ôp   hwîl   gusguä'ôsē.   Hwä'i!   HuX   kꞏ'ēlᴌ   lô'ôp   neᴌ   10
one   stone   being   blue.   Well!   Again   one   stone   that

dᴇm   hwîl   qâ'ôdᴇt."   Dôqᴌ   ʟgo-guä'ᴇm   ʟgo-tkꞏ'ē'ʟkᵘ.   Nᴌkꞏ'ē   11
(fut.)   being   the last."   He took them   the poor little   little boy.   Then

a'lgꞏîxᴌ   gꞏa'tgꞏê   hagun-hē'tgut   aᴌ   awa'at: "Gꞏi'lô   mᴇ   dzē   12
said   the man   toward he stood   at   his proximity: "Do not   you

gun-gꞏa'adᴇt   aᴌ   txanē'tkᵘsᴌ   gꞏa'tgꞏê."   13
cause to see them   at   all   people."

Nᴌkꞏ'ē   huX   mēsā'xꞏ,   nᴌkꞏ'ē   ha'tsᴇkꞏsᴇm   huX   bax-gâ'ôdᴇᴌ   14
Then   again   daylight,   then   once more   again   up   went

txanē'tkᵘᴌ   gꞏa'tgꞏê.   Nᴌkꞏ'ē   hatsᴇm   huX   hē-yukt   ôxꞏdet.   15
all   the people.   Then   once more   again   they began   they threw.

Nᴌkꞏ'ē   dē-bax-iä'ᴌ   ʟgo-guä'ᴇm   ʟgo-tkꞏ'ē'ʟkᵘ.   Nᴌkꞏ'ē   dē-hē'tgꞏê   16
Then   also up went   the poor little   little boy.   Then   also he said

Then the young men rose and pushed him, but the wise men stopped them and said, "Let him throw too." Then the young men sat down. The poor little boy rose and took a stone. He swung it in his hands so that it whistled. It whistled four times, then he let it go. He almost hit the copper. He threw again and almost hit it. He threw the black stone first, then the white one, then the blue one. He almost struck it. Finally he threw the red stone. It hit the copper right on its end. The poor little boy had hit it and it fell down. Then all the young men ran up to it, everyone claiming it. But the poor little boy did not mind. They took it along and ran with it into the house of the chief, intending to marry his daughter, but he who

1 dɛm dēt-ō'x·t. Nʟk·'ē haldɛm-gô'ldēʟ q'aima'qsit. Nʟk·'ēt
(fut.) also he throw. Then they rose the youths. Then

2 k'ut-sa-t'ē'sdeʟ ʟgo-guä'ɛm ʟgo-tk·'ē'ʟkᵘ. Nʟk·'ē al'a'lg·îxʟ
about away they pushed him the poor little little boy. Then they spoke

3 hwîl qaxâ'ôsgut, nʟk·'ēt lä'ɛlt: "ʟa äm dēt-ô'x·t." Nʟk·'ē
the wise men, then they rebuked them: "Good also he throw." Then

4 hwanʟ q'aima'qsit. Nʟk·'ē hētkᵘʟ ʟgo-guä'ɛm ʟgo-tk·'ē'ʟkᵘ.
they sat down the youths. Then he stood the poor little little boy.

5 Nʟk·'ēt gō'uʟ k·'ēlʟ lô'ôpg·ê. Nʟk·'ēt hwîlsā'wuʟ an'ônt.
Then he took one stone. Then he swung his hand.

6 Nʟk·'ēt g·îʟwî'nqt. Txalpxʟ g·îʟwî'nqt. Nʟk·'ēt ôx·t. Nʟk·'ē
Then it whistled. Four times it whistled. Then he threw. Then

7 mâ'dzɛt-ô'x·t. Nʟk·'ē huX k·'ēlt. Nʟk·'ē huX mâ'dzɛt-ôx·t.
almost he hit it. Then again one. Then again almost he hit it.

8 T'ō'tsgum lô'ôp k·s-qâ'oqdɛt, ma'k·sgum lô'ôp k·s-qalā'ndɛt.
The black stone first, the white stone afterward.

9 Hwä'i! Gusgwâ'ôsgum lô'ôp huX k·s-qalā'ndɛt. Nʟk·'ē huX
Well! The blue stone again afterward. Then again

10 mâ'dzɛt-ô'x·t. Nʟk·'ēt lō-k·s-qalā'ndɛt iʟä'êtgum lô'ôpg·ê.
almost he hit it. Then in afterward the red stone.

11 Nʟk·'ēt ôx·t. Hwîl ʟaxʟîp-g·a'ptg·ê, nîʟ ō'îdɛʟ ʟgo-guä'ɛm ʟgo-
Then he hit it. Where its end, there hit it the poor little little

12 tk·'ē'ʟkᵘ. Hwä'i! Ō'îtg·ê. Nʟk·'ē t'ukwa'ntkᵘt. Nʟk·'ē ha'p'aʟ
boy. Well! He hit it. Then it fell down. Then they rushed

13 txanē'tkᵘsʟ wi-hē'ldɛm q'aima'qsit aʟ dɛm t'an nek·st aʟ
all many youths to (fut.) who claimed at it

14 t'an lu'Xdetg·ê. Nʟk·'ē ansegō'ʟ ʟgo-guä'ɛm ʟgo-tk·'ē'ʟkᵘ.
who each tried to get it. Then he paid no attention the poor little little boy.

15 Nʟk·'ē na-dɛ-dä'uʟdet. Nʟk·'ē ts'ɛlɛm-dē-ba'xdet aʟ ts'ɛm-hwî'lpʟ
Then out of woods with they took it Then into with they ran it to in the house of

had hit it was standing behind all these liars. Then the chief said,
"Wait a while."

When it was evening, the growling of a white bear was heard
behind the house of the chief. The chief said, "Whoever kills the
white bear shall marry my daughter." Then all the young men rose
and ran out very suddenly because the chief had said, "Whoever kills
the white bear shall marry my daughter." The young men did not
sleep because they wanted to pursue the white bear. In the evening
the poor little boy again went down to the beach. He sat down there,
and again a person approached him who asked, "What are the people
talking about?" The poor little boy replied, "Last evening a white

sEm'â'g·it	aL	dEm	t'an	nak·sk^uL	Lgo'uLk^utg·ê.	NLk·'ē ia'gai- 1
the chief	to	(fut.)	who	marry	his daughter.	Then, however,
g·ina-he'tgutg·ê	nē	t'an	ôx·t	aL	sa-gabē'k^usdet.	NLk·'ē a'lg·îxL 2
behind stood	he	who	hit it	of	the liars.	Then spoke
sEm'â'g·it:	"G·'ax	hao'n!"				3
the chief:	"Later on!"					
Hwä'i!	La	huX	yu'ksa,	nLk·'ē	ā'd'îk·sk^uL	amhē'L 4
Well!	When	again	evening,	then	came	the voice of
gulîk·s-wô'xgutg·ê	aL	qa-qalā'nL	hwîlpL	sEm'â'g·it.	NLk·'ē 5
at himself barking (white bear)	at	the rear of house of	the house of	the chief.	Then
a'lg·îxL	sEm'â'g·it:	"ĀmL	dEm	guXL	k·'âlL	g·atL 6
spoke	the chief:	"Good	(fut.)	take	one	man
gulîk·s-wô'xgut-hētsē,	nL	dEm	t'an	nak·sk^uL	Lgō'uLguē." 7
at himself barking (the white bear),	then	(fut.)	who	marries	my daughter."
NLk·'ē	huX	haldEm-qô'ldEL	sEm-ala-qô'ldEt.	"DEm	t'an 8
Then	again	they rose	very suddenly they ran.	"(Fut.)	who
g·idi-gō'uL	gulîk·s-wô'xgut-hētsē	nELne't	dEm	an-na'k·sk^uL 9
catches	at himself barking (the white bear),	then he	(fut.)	who marries
Lgō'uLguē."	Hwä'i!	NLk·'ē	nî'g·i	wâ'wôqL	txanē'tk^uL 10
my daughter."	Well!	Then	not	slept	all
q'aima'qsit	aL	dEm	t'an	yôxk^uL	guîk·s-wô'xgut-hētsē.	NLk·'ē 11
the youths	to	(fut.)	who	pursue	at himself barking (the white bear).	Then
yu'ksa,	nLk·'ē	huX	ha'ts'îk·sEm	huX	iaga-iē'EL	Lgo-guä'Em 12
evening,	then	again	once more	again	down went	the poor little
Lgo-tk·'ē'Lk^u.	NLk·'ē	hats'Em	huX	d'āt	aL	g·ä'u.	NLk·'ē 13
little boy.	Then	once more	again	he sat down	at	in front of house.	Then
hak·sEm	huX	hagun-iē'EL	g·atg·ê.	NLk·'ē	huX	g·ē'dExt: 14
once more	again	toward went	a man.	Then	again	he asked:
"Agō an-hē'L	qal-ts'a'p?"	NLk·'ē	ma'L	Lgo-guä'Em	Lgo-tk·'ē'Lk^u: 15
"What say	the people?"	Then	told	the poor little	little boy:

bear appeared behind the town. Whoever catches it shall marry the daughter of the chief." Then the man, who was standing near the poor little boy, said, "Ask for a bow and arrow. You shall shoot it."

Then the poor little boy went up. When it grew dark, all the young men were in the house of the chief. The latter took down to the fire a quiver holding bows and arrows. He gave one bow and two arrows to each man. Then the poor little boy, the chief's own nephew, went down to the fire too. His father and his mother were dead, therefore he was poor. Only his old grandmother took care of him.

---

1 "Mäs-ô'l."   NLk·'ē   huX   yu'ksa,   nLk·'ē   huX   ā'd'îk·sk^ut   aL
   "A bear."   Then   again   evening,   then   again   he came   to
   white

2 qa-qalā'nL   qal-ts'a'p.   NLk·'ē   hux   iaga-iē'êL   Lgo-guä'Em
   the rear of   the town.   Then   again   down went   the   poor
   the houses of   little

3 Lgo-tk·'ē'Lk^u.   NLk·'ē   huX   ā'd'îk·sk^uL   g·at   t'an   huX   g·ē'dExt:
   little boy.   Then   again came   the man   who   again asked:

4 "Q'amēnā   dEm   t'an   guXt,   nLnēt   dEm   t'an   nak·sk^uL
   "Whoever   (fut.) who   catches it, then he (fut.) who   marries

5 Lgō'uLk^uL   sEm'â'g·ît."   NLk·'ē   a'lg·îxL   g·atL   hagun-hē'tgut   aL
   the daughter   the chief."   Then   spoke   the   toward   stood   at
   of   person

6 awa'aL   Lgo-guä'Em   Lgo-tk·'e'Lk^u: "TsE   dē-gunā'yîn   ha-Xda'k^u
   proximity the   poor   little   boy: "Also   demand   a bow
   of   little

7 qanL   hawî'l,   tsE   dē-gō'yîn   ana'!"
   and   arrow,   also shoot it!"

8 NLk·'ē   bax-iä'L   Lgo-guä'Em   Lgo-tk·'ē'Lk^ug·ê.   NLk·'ē   huX
   Then   up went   the   poor   little   boy.   Then   again
                         little

9 ā'd'îk·sk^uL   yu'ksag·ê.   NLk·'ē   huX   ts'ElEm-qâ'ôdEl   txanē'tk^uL
   it came   evening.   Then   again into   they went   all

10 q'aima'qsit   aL   ts'Em-hwî'lpL   sEm'â'g·it.   NLk·'ē   t'Em-gō'uL
    the youths   to   in   the   the chief.   Then   to the   he
                         house of   middle   took

11 sEm'â'g·it   hwîl   lō-dô'xL   ha-Xda'k^u   qanL   hawî'l;   k·'ēlL
    the chief   where   in   were bow   and   arrows;   one

12 ha-Xda'k^u   aL   k·'âlL   g·a'tg·ê,   dē   g·'ē'lbElL   hawî'l   huX   hwîl
    bow   to   one   man,   also two   arrows   again being

13 huX   k·'âlL   g·a'tg·ê.   NLk·'ē   sa-ba'xL   wî-hē'ldEm   g·a'tg·ê.
    again one   man.   Then   from first to many   men.
                                            last

14 NLk·'ē   huX   dē-t'Em-iä'L   Lgo-guä'Em   Lgo-tk·'ē'Lk^u,   lEp-guslē'sL
    Then   also   with to the went the   poor   little   boy,   his   sister's
                     them middle   little   own   son of

15 sEm'â'g·itg·ê.   Q'ap-nô'ôL   nEguâ'ôdEt   qans   nôxt,   nLnet   qan
    the chief.   Really dead   his father   and   his   then he there-
                      was   mother,   fore

16 guä'êtg·ê.   Hwä'i!   LEp-nEbē'pL   sEm'â'g·itg·ê.   K·sax-Lgo-ntsē'ts
    he was poor. Well!   His uncle was the chief.   Only   little   grand-
                           own   mother

He also asked for a bow and two arrows. Then all the young men
made fun of him; but the wise men said to the chief, "Give a bow to
the poor little boy." The chief did so and he took it. It was evening, and a little before daybreak the white bear appeared again behind
the town. All the young men ran out. A long time after they
had left, the poor little boy ran out, too. It was as though a fly were
flying. The wasp pitied him, and therefore the poor little boy was
able to transform himself into a fly. Before the young men could
reach the white bear, the poor little boy had passed them. He hit it and
it lay there. His arrow passed right through it. Then he took the

t'an   habâ'letg·ê.   NʟkꞏʼēLL   huX   det-gu'naʟ   kꞏʼēlʟ   ha-Xda'kᵘ   qanʟ   1
who   took care of him.   Then   also   on his de·   one   bow   and
                                              part he manded

g·ʼē'lbElʟ   hawî'l.   Nʟkꞏʼē   huX   txanē'tkᵘʟ   q'aima'qsiʟ   huX   2
two   arrows.   Then   again   all   the youths   again

ansgwa'tgut   as   nē'tg·ê,   ʟgo-guä'Em   ʟgo-tk·ʼē'ʟkᵘg·ê.   Nʟkꞏʼē   3
made fun   of   him,   the   poor   little   boy.   Then
                                 little

a'lg·îxʟ   hwîl   qaxâ'ôsgut   aʟ   sEm'â'g·it: "Ām   huX   dē-g·înā'mʟ   4
said   the wise men   to   the chief: "Good   also   also   give

ha-Xda'kᵘ   aʟ   ʟgo-guä'Em   ʟgo-tk·ʼē'ʟkᵘ."   Nʟkꞏʼē   hwîlʟ   5
a bow   to   the   poor   little   boy."   Then   he did
                     little   so

sEm'â'g·it.   Nʟkꞏʼēt   k'ō'pE-dē-dô'qtg·ê.   Nʟkꞏʼē   huX   yu'ksa,   6
the chief.   Then he   poorly also took it.   Then   again   evening,

La   dēlpkᵘʟ   dEm   mEsā'xꞏ,   nʟkꞏʼē   huX   ā'd'îk·skᵘʟ   7
when   shortly   (fut.)   daylight,   then   again   came

gulîkꞏs-wô'xgut   aʟ   qa-qalā'nʟ   qal-ts'a'pg·ê.   Nʟkꞏʼē   huX   8
at himself barking   at   the rear of   the town.   Then   again
(the white bear)   the houses of

wē'd'axʟ   txanē'tkᵘʟ   q'aima'qsit.   La   nakᵘʟ   hwîl   sa'k·sdetg·ê,   9
ran   all   the youths.   When   long   where   they were gone,

nʟkꞏʼē   dē-ba'xʟ   ʟgo-guä'Em   ʟgo-tk·ʼē'ʟkᵘ.   Hō'g·igaʟ   hwîl   10
then   also ran   the   poor   little   boy.   Like
                      little

g·ebā'yukʟ   biâ'skᵘ   aʟ   q'ap-q'ä'Em-gâ'ʟ   ap   as   nē'tg·ê,   nîʟnē'ʟ   11
the flying of   a fly   be-   really   took pity   the   of   him,   then he
                         cause   wasp

lō-ʟô'ôtkᵘʟ   ʟgo-guä'Em   ʟgo-tk·ʼē'ʟkᵘ.   Nʟkꞏʼē   hao'ng·ê   hagun-   12
was   trans-   the   poor   little   boy.   Then   before   toward
formed   little

ax'a'qʟkᵘʟ   wī-hē'ldEm   q'aima'qsit;   tk·ʼē   sâ'g·ēwul   ba'xguʟ   ʟgo-   13
he reached it   many   youths;   but   they were   run past   the
                                                     quickly   by   little

guä'Em   ʟgo-tk·ʼē'ʟkᵘ   Nʟkꞏʼē   gu'Xtg·ê.   Nʟkꞏʼē   sg·it.   Hwagait-   14
poor   little   boy.   Then   he shot it.   Then   it lay   Quite
                                                                     there.

qalk·si-dā'uʟ   Xdakᵘʟ   ʟgo-guä'Em   ʟgo-tk·ʼē'ʟkᵘ.   Nʟkꞏʼēt   gō'uʟ   15
through passed   the shot   the   poor   little   boy.   Then he   took
                  of   little

arrow, and fat was seen right across the nock of the arrow. Then the poor little boy returned. Now all the young men reached the bear and took it, though the poor little boy had killed it. Then they rubbed their arrows with blood, intending to say that they had shot it. They lied because they wished to marry the daughter of the chief. Then they carried the white bear into the house of the chief. One young man went down to the fire and said, "Look at my arrow! I shot the white bear." The chief said, "Give me all your bows and arrows that I may examine them and discover who killed the white bear." They gave them to him and he examined them. Then he demanded the arrow of the poor little boy, and, behold, he had shot the white bear. Then they were all very much

---

1 hawî'lg·ê. TgōnL hwîlL hawî'lg·ê: tsâ'gaL hix· La anmā'bwîldetg·ê.
the arrow. This   did   the arrow: across   grease (perf.)   the nock of the arrow.

2 NLk·'ē bwîl k·'ē iä'êL Lgo-guä'Em Lgo-tk·'ē'Lkᵘ aL lō-ya'ltkᵘtg·ê.
At once   he   the   went   poor   little   boy   and   he returned.
          went little

3 NLk·'ē hagun-qâ'ôdEL wi-bē'ldEm q'aima'qsitg·ê t'an gō'uL
Then   toward they went   many   youtbs   who   took
        to it

4 gulîk·s-wô'xgut gō'uiêL Lgo-guä'Em Lgo-tk·'ē'Lkᵘ. NLk·'ēt
at himself barking   shot by the   poor   little   boy.   Then
(the white bear)   little

5 mEnma'ndEL hawî'l aL iLä'ê. At ma'LdEL nē'det t'an gu'Xtg·ê
they rubbed   the   with blood. They told   they   who   shot it
           arrows

6 aL sa-gabē'k'ᵘsdetg·ê aL dEmt hwîl an-na'k·skᵘdEL Lgō'uLkᵘL
at   liars   to   (fut.) being   married   the daughter of

7 sEm'â'g·it. NLk·'ē ts'ElEm-ma'qdeL gulîk·s-wô'xgut aL ts'Em-
the chief.   Then   into   they put   at himself barking in   in
                              (the white bear)

8 hwî'lpL sEm'â'g·it. At ma'LdEL t'Em-ba'xL huX k·'âlL q'aima'sit:
the   the chief. They told   to middle he ran again one   youth:
house of   of house

9 "Nē'E t'an guXt! Ām mE dEm g·a'aL hwîlL hawî'lēE."
"I   who   shot it! Good you see   it did it   my arrow."

10 NLk·'ē a'lg·îxL sEm'â'g·it: "Ndzôl g·ul-ganē'L ha-XdakᵘsE'mEst
Then   spoke   the chief: "Give me   all   your bows

11 dEm lā'galdēE g·ul-ganē'L hawî'lsEm aL dEm t'an ia'gai-gu'XL
(fut.) I examine   all   your arrows to (fut.) who   already shot

12 gulîk·s-wô'xgut." NLk·'ēt g·înamdē'tg·ê. NLk·'ēt laxlā'galL
at himself barking   Then   they gave them.   Then   examined
(the white bear)."   them

13 sEm'â'g·itg·ê. NLk·'ē laxlā'galtg·eL g·ul-ganē'detg·ê. NLk·'ē
the chief   Then   he examined   all   Then

14 dēt-guî'naL hawî'lL Lgo-guä'Em Lgo-tk·'ē'Lkᵘ. Gwinā'dēL, nēt t'an
also he de-   the arrow the   poor   little   boy   Behold,   he   who
manded   of   little

15 guXL gulîk·s-wô'xgutg·ê! NLk·'ē wi t'ē'sL hwîl dzaxdzâ'qdetg·ê.
shot   at himself barking   Then   great   being ashamed tney.
(the white bear)!

ashamed; the chief also was much ashamed. He did not speak, because the poor little boy had first knocked down the copper that was on the tree behind the house of the chief, and then he had also shot the white bear. All the young men, and also the chief, were ashamed, because the poor little boy had accomplished this.

Then the chief made up his mind. He was ashamed, and therefore he sent his slave ordering the people to move away from the village. The great slave ran out, and with a loud voice ordered the people to move. They heard it, and early in the morning they moved. Not a single person stayed behind. They all went by canoe. Only the chief's daughter and the poor little boy were left, and with them his old grandmother. These three stayed behind. The old grandmother

NʟK·'ē	huX	dē-wī-t'ê′sʟ	hwîl-dzâ′qʟ	sɛm'â′g·itgê.	NʟK·'ē	nî′g·i		1
Then	also	also great	being the shame of	the chief.	Then	not		

xsta′ltkg·ê,	aʟ	hwîl	sī′nîʟ	ʟgo-guä'ɛm	ʟgo-tk·'ē′ʟkᵘ	t'an	sa-ō′yîʟ	2
he spoke,	because	before	the little	the poor	little	boy	who off threw	

oq	lē-ia′gat	aʟ	lax-ga′n	aʟ	qa-qalā′nʟ	hwîlpʟ	sɛm'â′g·itg·ê.	3
the copper	on it hung	at	on a tree	at	the rear of the house of	the house of	the chief.	

Hwä′i!	ʟa	huX	hwîlt,	guXʟ	gulîk·s-wô′xgut,	ʟa	huX	neʟ	4
Well!	(Perf.)	again	he did it,	he shot	at himself barking (the white bear),	(perf.)	again	he	

ʟgo-guä'ɛm	ʟgo-tk·'ē′ʟkᵘ	t'an	huX	guXt.	NʟK·'ē	dzaxdzâ′qʟ	5
the poor little	little boy	who	again	shot it.	Then	they were ashamed	

wi-hē′ldɛm	q'aima′qsit.	NʟK·'ē	huX	dē-dzâ′qʟ	sɛm'â′g·ɪt	hwîɪʟ	6
many	youths.	Then	also	also was ashamed	the chief	he did so	

ʟgo-guä'ɛm	ʟgo-tk·'ē′ʟkᵘ.		7
the poor little	little boy.		

NʟK·'ē	sɛ-gâ′ôtkᵘʟ	ts'ɛm-qâ′ôʟ	sɛm'â′g·it.	NʟK·'ē	dzâqt,	8
Then	was made up his mind	in the heart of	the chief.	Then	he was ashamed,	

nʟ	qant	k·si-hē′tsʟ	wī-xa′E	mā′ʟɛl	tsɛn-gun-lu′kʟ	qal-ts'a′p.	9
therefore		out he sent	the. slave great	to tell	desert- caus- ing ing	to move	the people.

NʟK·'ē	k·si-ba′xʟ	wī-xa′E	t'aɴ	gun-lu′kʟ	qal-ts'a′p	aʟ	10
Then	out ran	the slave great	who	caused to move	the people	with	

wī-amhē′tg·ê.	NʟK·'ē	naxna′ʟ	qal-ts'a′p.	Hwä′i!	Hē′ʟuk,	nʟK·'ē	11
loud voi.e.	Then	heard it	the people.	Well!	In the morniog,	then	

lukʟ	qal-ts'a′p,	nîg·i	g·ina-d'ā′ʟ	k·'âlʟ	g·a′tg·ê.	Sɛm-uks-qâ′ôdet.	12
moved	the people,	not	behind was	one	man.	Really out to sea they went	

Sɛm-q'am-k·'â′lʟ	ʟgō′uʟkᵘʟ	sɛm'â′g·ɪt	uks-kᵘsta′qsdɛtg·ê	dē-k·'â′lʟ		13
Really only one	the daughter of	the chief	toward sea she was left	with one		

ʟgo-guä'ɛm	ʟgo-tk·'ē′ʟkᵘ	tq'al	kᵘsta′qsdetg·ê	dē-k·'â′lʟ	ʟgo-	14
the poor little	little boy	against	he was left	with one	little	

nts'ē′ɛtst;	nʟ	qan	gulâ′ôndet	aʟ	g·ina hwa′ndet.	Sɛm-q'am-	15
his grand-mother;	therefore	three	at	behind stayed	Very pieces		

had a few pieces of dried salmon, but the chief's daughter would not eat. She fasted. The poor little boy did the same.

The princess slept in the rear of the house, while the poor little boy slept near the fire. They lay down, and he thought of their poverty. It grew dark, and it grew daylight again. The poor little boy left the house. Near the end of the town there was a great river, and a trail led up the river. The poor little boy went along this trail. He went a long time and came to the shore of a large lake. A grassy opening extended to the water of the lake. There he stood and shouted. The water rose and, behold, the one that had charge of the lake emerged. When it saw the poor little boy standing near the

1 q'aik·'ē'ldEl	hânL	sg·ît	aL	awa'aL	Lgo-nts'ē'Etsdet.	NLk·'ē
sides of dried salmon	salmon	lay	in	the proximity of	their little grandmother.	Then
2 nîg·i	sg·ît	tsE	dEm	g·ē'îpL	Lgō'uLkⁿL	sEm'â'g·it.	NLk·'ē
not	lay	(fut.)		the food of	the daughter of	the chief.	Then
3 naLqL	Lgo-wî'lk·sîLkⁿg·ê.		NLk·'ē	huX	dē-hwî'lL	Lgo-guä'Em
fasted	the little princess.		Then	also	on his part did so	the poor little
4 Lgo-tk·'ē'Lkⁿg·ê.						
little boy.						
5 Hwä'i!	G·itsâ'ôn	hwîl	g·ä'êL	Lgo-wî'lk·sîLkⁿg·ê.	NLk·'ē
Well!	In the rear of the house	where	lay	the little princeess.	Then
6 lax-ts'ä'L	lakⁿ	hwîl	g·ä'êL	Lgo-guä'Em	Lgo-tk·'ē'Lkⁿ.	NLk·'ē
on edge of	fire	where	lay	the poor little	little boy.	Then
7 g·ig·ä'êLt.	NLk·'ē	k'opE-lō-a'lg·îxL	qâ'ôtg·ê.	Hwä'i!	NLk·'ē
they lay down.	Then	poorly in	spoke his heart.	Well!	Then
8 huX	ā'd'îk·sL	yu'ksa.	SEm-hē'Luk	k·'ē	k·saXL	Lgo-guä'Em
again	came	evening.	Very morning	then	went out	the poor little
9 Lgo-tk·'ē'Lkⁿ.	Q'ai'yîm	na-ba'xL	wī-a'k·s	aL	q·'apL	ts'ap.
little boy.	Near	out of woods ran	a water great	at	the end of	the town.
10 NELnē'L	hwîl	lō-gali-sg·ē'L	qē'nExg·ê,	nELnē'tg·ê	lō-yô'xkⁿL
Then that	where	in up river lay	the trail,	then that	in followed
11 Lgo-guä'Em	Lgo-tk·'ē'Lkⁿg·ê.	La	nakⁿL	hwîl	iä't.	nLk·'ē
the poor little	little boy.	When	long	where	he went,	then
12 na-ba'xt	aL	lax-ts'ä'L	wī-t'a'xg·ê.	NLk·'ē	uks-hē'tgut	aL	hwîl
out of woods went	to	on edge of	great lake.	Then	toward the water he stood	at	where
13 uks-d'ä'L	hä'p'Eskg·ê.	NLk·'ē	wī-anhē'tg·ê.	NLk·'ē	g·itkⁿL	ak·s
toward the water was	grass.	Then	he shouted.	Then	it rose	the water
14 aL	hwagait-g·î'îksg·ê.	Gwinä'deL,	g·ä'bEnt	wī-t'an	lō-lē'Lk·L
at	way out offshore.	Behold,	it emerged	great the one who	in watched
15 ts'Em-t'a'xg·ê!	NLk·'ē	g·a'aL	hwîl	lō-uks-hē'tkⁿL	Lgo-guä'Em
in the lake!	Then	it saw	where	in toward water stood	the poor little

water, it came ashore quickly toward the place where the poor little boy was standing. It was a great frog. It had long claws of copper. Its mouth was copper, and so were its eyes and its eyebrows. It came near the poor little boy and almost caught him. Then the boy started to run. It almost caught him, but the boy escaped and the great frog returned. It could not overtake the poor little boy. The poor little boy ran right to the place where a large cedar tree stood. Then he went out of the woods to where the princess and the old grandmother were. Now they had almost nothing to eat. He went about among the empty houses, and there he found a stone ax; after a while he found a handle. Then he tied the ax to the handle. He sharp-

Lgo-tkꞏ'ē'Lkᵘ.	NLkꞏ'ē	sᴇm-t'ᴇm-iē'êt;	at	tsagam-qâ'ôL	hwîl	1
little boy.	Then	very quickly it went;	it	ashore went to	where	

lō-uks-hē'tkᵘL	Lgo-guä'ᴇm	Lgo-tkꞏ'ē'Lkᵘ,	wī-qana'ogꞏê.	Wī-t'ē'sᴇm	2
in toward water stood	the poor little	little hoy,	the frog. great	A large	

qana'o	qan	nē'neguL	La'qstgꞏê	aL	o'qgꞏê.	HnX	hwîlL	3
frog	and	long	its claws	of	copper.	Also	was so	

ā'qtgꞏê.	NLkꞏ'ē	huX	hwîlL	ts'a'ltgꞏê	qanL	lē-gꞏē'êlt.	La	4
its mouth.	Then	also	were so	its eyes	and	its eyebrows.	When	

hagun-dē'lpkᵘt	aL	awa'aL	Lgo-guä'ᴇm	Lgo-tkꞏ'ē'Lkᵘ,	La	5
toward near it	at	the proximity of	the poor little	little hoy,	when	

q'ap-yu'kL	dᴇmt	gō'ut;	La	sᴇwî'ntkᵘt,	kꞏ'ē	hwîl	kꞏ'ē	6
really began	(fut.)	it took him;	when	he gave a start,		at once		

baxL	Lgo-guä'ᴇm	Lgo-tkꞏ'ē'Lkᵘ.	Q'ai'yîm	lō-sq'ô'kꞏsîL	an'ô'n	7
ran	the poor little	little hoy.	Near	in out of reach	hand	

dᴇmt	gꞏidi-gō'ut.	Kꞏ'ē	ha'ts'îkꞏsᴇm	lo-ya'ltkᵘL	wī-qana'o.	8
(fut.) it	caught him.	Then	once more	returned	the frog. great	

Sq'ô'kꞏsîL	Lgo-guä'ᴇm	Lgo-tkꞏ'ē'Lkᵘ.	Hwîl	hē'tkᵘL	wī-sᴇm-ga'n,	9
He was out of reach	the poor little	little boy.	Where	stood	a cedar great	

neLne't	sᴇm-yô'xgut	Lgo-guä'ᴇm	Lgo-tkꞏ'ē'Lkᵘ;	Lē	mēnL	10
there	really went to	the poor little	little hoy;	at	foot of	

wī-gaꞏng·ê,	nLkꞏ'ē	na-ba'xt	aL	hwîl	dē-d'ā'L	Lgo-wî'lkꞏsiLkᵘ	11
a great tree,	then	out of woods he ran	to	where	on her was part	the little princess.	

qanL	Lgo-nts'ē'tstgꞏê.	Wî'tkᵘtgꞏê,	nLkꞏ'ê	agō'L	dᴇm	lîgꞏi-	12
and	little his grandmother.	He arrived,	then	what	(fut.)	or	

gꞏē'bᴇt.	NLkꞏ'ē	hā'ts'îkꞏsᴇm	huX	kꞏsaXt.	NLkꞏ'ē	k'uL-iä't	13
her food.	Then	once more	again	he went out.	Then	about he went	

aL	lax-qal-huwî'lp.	NLkꞏ'ēt	hwaL	dawī'sᴇm	lô'ôpgê.	NLkꞏ'ē	14
at	on empty houses.	Then he	found	an ax of	stone.	Then	

huX	hwaL	La	dᴇm	ha-lē-d'ā'adᴇt.	NLkꞏ'ēt	lē-da'kꞏLtgꞏê.	NLkꞏ'ē	15
also	he found		(fut.)	its handle.	Then he	on tied it.	Then	

ened it on his whetstone, and in the evening he went to cut a tree.
He worked at it the whole day. In the evening it fell. Then he
cut up a small tree, making wedges. When he had finished them,
he took them to the large tree. Then he found a stone hammer. He
tied it to its handle, and split the heart of the large tree. He spread
it out wide enough so that a man could pass through it. Then he
split a small tree. He selected one that was not very tall. Then he
placed these trees across the trail. There were two sticks that he had
cut. These he put across the crack of the large tree.[1] Then he
stopped. He went home and found the princess and the old grand-

1 hē-yu′kt   qäxt   aL   sEl-lô′ôpt.   NLk·′ē   yu′ksa.   NLk·′ē   iē′êt.
   he began   he sharp- at   his whetstone.   Then   evening.   Then   he
              ened it   went.

2 NLk·′ēt   q′âtsL   gan.   K·′ēlL   sa   hwî′ltg·ê.   NLk·′ē   huX
   Then he   cut   a tree.   One   day   he did so.   Then   again

3 k·′ēlL   yu′ksa,   nLk·′ē   qē′nExtg·ê.   NLk·′ē   xtsē-ia′tsL   qē′sgum
   one   evening,   then   it fell.   Then   in mid-   a small
                                                           dle ped
                                                           he chop-

4 gan.   NLk·′ēt   wusEn-yîs′ia′tstg·ê   aL   dEm   sE-lē′ttg·ê.   Hwä′i!
   tree.   Then he   along chopped all   to   (fut.)   make wedges.   Well!
                              over

5 Lîx·Lē′saEnt   sE-lē′ttg·ê.   NLk·′ēt   lō-maqsa′ntg·ê.   NLk·′ēt   huX
   He finished   mak-   his   Then he   in placed them.   Then he   also
                   ing   wedges.

6 hwaL   da′qLEm   lô′ôp.   NLk·′ēt   huX   lē-da′k·Lt   aL   La
   found   a hammer   stone.   Then he   also   on tied it   to
           of

7 ha-lē-d′ā′dEt.   NLk·′ēt   lō-ma′qsanL   lē′tg·ê.   SEm-bagait-gō′og·îtL
   its handle.   Then he   in   placed   the   Right   in the   he split
                                               wedges.   middle

8 Lē   hwîn-ts′ä′wuL   wī-ga′ng·ê.   NLk·′ē   wī-sa′gat.   NLk·′ē   yukt
   the heart of   the   tree.   Then   much it split. Then   he
                   great   began

9 ôx·t.   NLk·′ē   wī-lo-la′it   sEm-qalk·si-ā′tsEgaL   g·a′tg·ê.   NLk·′ēt
   he struck   Then   great in- great   very   through fitted   a man.   Then he
   it.   side

10 huX   xtsē-yîs′ia′tsL   qē′sgum   gan.   Nî′g·it   sE-nē′ElEgut.   NLk·′ē
   again   in mid- chopped   a small   tree.   Not he   made it long.   Then
           dle

11 hwîl   sg·iL   qē′nEx,   nîLnē′   hwîl   sqa-sg·i′L   ga′ng·ê.
   where   lay   the trail,   then it   where   side-   the stick.
                                                      ways
                                                      lay

12 Hwä′i!   K·′ē′lpEl   gan   xtsē-yîs′ia′tsdEt.   NLk·′ē   lo-ma′qsaant
   Well!   Two   sticks   in mid- he chopped   Then   into he put them
                                   dle   them.

13 aL   hwîl   sa′gat   wī-ga′ng·ê   lo-sqa-ax·′ō′yit.   NLk·′ē   hä′ut.
   at   where   he split   the   tree   in side- he ham-   Then   he stop-
                             great   ways mered them.   ped.

14 NLk·′ē   na-iē′êtg·ê.   HuX   wîtk″t   aL   awa′aL   Lgo-wî′lk·siLk″g·ê
   Then   out of he went. Again   he   at   the prox-   the   princess
             woods   arrived   imity of   little

----

[1] He split a large tree and opened the crack, which he spread apart by means of two short sticks,
placing the whole on the trail which led up to the lake.

mother. He did not speak and did not eat. It grew dark, and before
daylight he rose. He went and came to the shore of the great lake.
He stood near the water and shouted four times, looking up to
the sky. The water rose again and, behold, the great frog
emerged. Its claws were copper. Copper was its mouth, its eyes,
and its eyebrows. It went quickly toward the shore, but the poor
little boy did not mind. When it had almost reached him, he ran away.
The frog almost scratched his back. Now he arrived at the place
where he had placed the tree across the trail, and he slipped through.
Then the great frog also struggled to get through, trying to catch
the poor little boy. It tried to squeeze through the crack of the

---

qanʟ ʟgo-nēts'ē'tstg·ê. Nîg·i a'lg·îxt, nʟk·'ē aqʟ-g·ē'bɛt. Nʟk·'ē 1
and his grandmother. Not he spoke, then without food. Then
little

yu'ksa ʟa dēlpkᵘʟ dɛm mɛsā'x·; nʟk·'ē g·în-hē'tkᵘtg·ê 2
it was (perf.) shortly (fut.) daylight; then he rose
evening

haô'ng·ê mɛsā'x·g·ê. K·'ē iē'êt. Nʟk·'ēt huXt hwaʟ 3
before daylight. Then he Then again he
went. reached

lax-ts'ä'ʟ wī-t'a'xg·ê. Nʟk·'ē huX nks-hē'tkᵘtg·ê. Nʟk·'ē txalpxʟ 4
on the the lake. Then again toward he stood. Then four
edge of great water times

wi-amhē't aʟ têʟxkᵘt aʟ lax-ha'g·ê. Nʟk·'ē hā'ts'îk·sɛm 5
loud voice and he at the sky. Then once more
shouted

huX g·itkᵘʟ ak·s. Gwinā'dēʟ, huX g·ā'bɛnʟ wi-qana'og·ê. 6
again rose the water. Behold, again emerged the frog.
great

Oqʟ ʟa ga-ʟa'qstg·ê. Nʟk·'ē oqʟ ā'qtg·ê. Nʟk·'ē huX 7
Copper its claws. Then copper its mouth. Then also

oqʟ ts'a'alt. Nʟk·'ē huX oqʟ lē-g·ē'êlt. Nʟk·'ē sɛm- 8
copper its eyes. Then also copper its eyebrows. Then very

tsagam-t'ɛm-iē'êtg·ê. Nʟk·'ē ansegō'ʟ ʟgo-guä'ɛm ʟgo-tk·'ē'ʟkᵘ. 9
ashore quickly it went. Then paid no the poor little boy.
attention little

ʟa q'ap-q'aiyî'm qa-nā'gut tgōn, nʟk·'ē k·'äxkᵘʟ ʟgo-guä'ɛm 10
When really near as far as this, then escaped the poor
little

ʟgo-tk·'ē'ʟkᵘ. Nʟk·'ē q'aiyî'm qaqā'pxanʟ q'aiyîm hak·'â'ôt. 11
little boy. Then nearly it scratched near his back.

Hwä'i! Hwa'yiʟ hwîl sqa-sg·i'ʟ wī-ga'n, nʟk·'ēt qalk·si-yô'xkᵘʟ 12
Well! He found where side- lay the tree, then through went
ways great

ʟgo-guä'ɛm ʟgo-tk·'ē'ʟkᵘ. Nʟk·'ēt qalk·si-a'qʟkᵘtg·ê. Nʟk·'ē 13
the poor little boy. Then he through got. Then
little

de-qalk·si-ʟô'ôtkᵘʟ wī-qana'o aʟ dɛm tsē'k·'îʟ g·îdi-gō'udɛʟ 14
also through struggled the frog in order to try to catch
great

ʟgo-guä'ɛm ʟgo-tk·'ē'ʟkᵘ. Nʟk·'ēt lō-qalk·si-ha'q'oaxt. Nʟk·'ēt 15
the poor little boy. Then in through it squeezed. Then
little

tree. When the poor little boy saw this, he returned, took his stone
hammer, and struck the sticks with which he had spread the tree out
of the crack. They flew out and the great tree closed, killing the
great frog. It could not get out again. When the poor little
boy saw that it was dead, he put in the wedges and opened the great
tree. Then he took out the dead frog. He laid it on its back and
skinned it. He left the claws on the skin. He finished, took the
skin, and threw away the flesh. Then he took the skin in order to
practice. He put his arms and his legs into it, and laced the chest.
Then he went to the shore of the great lake and dived. He walked

---

1 g·a'aL   Lgo-guä'Em   Lgo-tk·'ē'Lkᵘt   hwîl   qalk·si-ha'q'oaxL
   saw   the   poor   little   boy   being   through   squeezed
                little

2 wī-qana'o.   NLk·'ē   lo-ya'ltkᵘt.   NLk·'ēt   gōL   daqLEm   lô'ôp,
   the   frog.   Then   he returned.   Then   he   the hammer stone,
   great   took   of

3 nLk·'ē   k·si-ax·'ô'x·L   gan   Lē   lo-sqa-ma'qsaant   aL   wī-ga'ng·ê.
   then   out he struck   the   (past) in side- he put them in   the   tree.
                                sticks   ways   great

4 NLk·'ē   k·si-sa'k·skut.   NLk·'ē   hak·sEm   ha'q'oaxL   wī-ga'ng·ê.
   Then   out   they went.   Then   again   closed   the   tree.
                                                                   great

5 NLk·'ē   nô'ôL   wī-qana'o.   Nî'g·i   huX   uks-lō-ya'ltkᵘtg·ê.   Hwä'i!
   Then   it was   the   frog.   Not   again   toward it returned.   Well!
             dead   great   water

6 Lat   g·a'aL   Lgo-guä'Em   Lgo-tk·'ē'Lkᵘ   hwîl   La   nô'ôt,   nLk·'ē
   When   saw   the   poor   little   boy   where   (perf.) it   then
                    little   died

7 ha'k·sEm   huXt   lo-ma'qsaanL   lē'tg·ê.   NLk·'ē   huX   q'aqL
   once more   again   in he put them the   Then   again   opened
                                        wedges.

8 wī-ga'ng·ê.   NLk·'ēt   gōuL   Lgo-guä'Em   Lgo-tk·'ē'Lkᵘ   hwîl   La
   the   tree.   Then   took   the   poor   little   boy   where (perf.)
   great   little

9 nô'ôL   wī-qana'og·ê.   NLk·'ēt   k·si-daa'qLkᵘtg·ê.   NLk·'ēt   hasba-
   was   the   frog.   Then   out he got it.   Then   on its
   dead   great   back

10 sg·î'tg·ê.   NLk·'ēt   ts'â'ôdetg·ê;   txa-lō-ts'â'ôdetg·ê.   Txa-lē-
   he laid it.   Then   he skinned it;   all in he skinned it.   All on

11 hax·hoksaa'nL   La   qa-La'qstg·ê.   Hwä'i!   Lē'saantg·ê.   NLk·'ēt   gō'uL
   he left   its claws.   Well!   He finished.   Then   he took

12 anä'stg·ê.   NLk·'ēt   t'uks-ô'x·L   Lē   smax·t.   NLk·'ēt   gō'uL   anä'st
   its skin.   Then   out   he   its flesh.   Then   he took   its skin
                            threw

13 aL   dEm   sīwî'ltkstg·ê.   NLk·'ēt   lo-Lôô'LaadEL   an'ô'nt   qanL
   to   (fut.) practice.   Then   in he put into it his hands   and

14 qasesa'ēt.   NLk·'ēt   haXha'kᵘL   q'aē'Lktg·ê.   NLk·'ē   uks-iä't
   his feet.   Then   he laced   its chest.   Then   toward he
                                                                    water went

15 aL   lax-ts·ä'L   wī-t'a'x.   NLk·'ē   sō'uqskᵘtg·ê.   NLk·'ē   k'uL-dä'uLt
   to   on edge of   the lake.   Then   he dived.   Then   about   he
                        great   walked

on the bottom of the great lake and caught a trout. Then he returned.
He went ashore carrying a small trout. Then he took the skin off.
He took good care of it. There was a tree that had a long branch.
He hung the skin of the great frog on it. Then he went home.
The princess was still asleep. The poor little boy stepped very softly
and entered the house. He laid down the little trout in front of the
house. Then he entered secretly and lay down. Early in the morning the princess rose. She heard a raven crying on the beach.
When she heard it, she said to the poor little boy, "See why the
raven is crying on the beach." The poor little boy rose and went
out. He went to the front of the house and, behold, a little trout

---

1 aʟ lō-s'iä'nʟ wī-t'a'xg·ê. Nʟk·'ēt g·îdi-gō'uʟ lā'Xg·ê. Nʟk·'ē
on / in the bottom of / the great / lake. / Then he / caught / a trout. / Then

2 lō-ya'ltkᵘt. Nʟk·'ē ts'âk·skᵘt. K'uʟ-yu'kdEʟ lāX, ʟgo-ts'ō'osk·,
he returned. / Then / he went ashore. / About he carried / the trout, / a small, little

3 nîg·i sEm-wī-t'ē'st. Nʟk·'ēt sa-mā'gaʟ lē lō-ʟô'ôtgutg·ê.
not / very large. / Then / off he took / (past) / in was put on.

4 Nʟk·'ēt sa-mā'gat. Nʟk·'ēt sEmt-ama g·a'adEt. Hētkᵘʟ ga'ng·ê.
Then he / off took it. / Then he / very well / he saw it. / There stood / a tree.

5 Nʟk·'ē sa-hē'tkᵘʟ anē'stg·ê. Neʟ hwîlt lē-ia'qʟ anä'sʟ wī-qana'og·ê
Then / off stood / a branch. / There where he / on hung / the skin of / the great / frog

6 aʟ haô'ng·ê mEsā'x·g·ê. Nʟk·'ē na-iä't aʟ ts'Em-hwî'lpdētg·ê.
at / before / daylight. / Then / out of woods went / to / in / their house.

7 Q'ai-huwô'qʟ ʟgo-wî'lk·sîʟkᵘg·ê. SEm-q'a'mts'En k'uʟ-iē'êʟ ʟgo-
Still slept / the little princess. / Very / secretly / about he went / the little

8 guä'Em ʟgo-tk·'ē'ʟkᵘg·ê. Saā'mʟ ts'ēnt aʟ ts'Em-hwî'lpdētg·ê aʟ
poor / little boy. / Slowly / he entered / at / in / their house / and

9 ʟa ʟēskᵘt sg·ît ʟgo-lā'X aʟ qa-g·ä'uʟ hwîlp. Nʟk·'ē q'a'mts'En
he finished / he laid down / the trout little / at / in front of / the house. / Then / secretly

10 ts'ēnt. Nʟk·'ē g·ä'êʟt. Nʟk·'ē hē'ʟuk, nʟk·'ē ʟâ'ôxʟ
he entered. / Then / he lay down. / Then / morning, / then / rose early

11 ʟgo-wî'lk·sîʟkᵘg·ê. Nʟk·'ē naxna'ʟ hwîl a'lg·îxʟ qāq aʟ
the little princess. / Then / she heard / where / spoke / the raven / at

12 g·ä'u. Nʟk·'ē g·în-hē'tkᵘt, naxna'yît hwîl a'lg·îxʟ qāq aʟ
in front of the house. / Then / she rose, / she heard / where / spoke / the raven / at

13 g·ä'u. Nʟk·'ē a'lg·îxt aʟ ʟgo-guä'Em ʟgo-tk·'ē'ʟkᵘ: "G·a'aʟ,
in front of the house. / Then / she said / to / the poor little / little boy: / "See,

14 an-hä'Eʟ qāq aʟ g·ä'u sE!" Nʟk·'ē g·în-hē'tkᵘʟ ʟgo-guä'Em
what says / the raven / at / in front of house / look!" / Then / rose / the little / poor

15 ʟgo-tk·'ē'ʟkᵘ. Nʟk·'ē k·saXt. Nʟk·'ē iaga-iē'êt aʟ qa-g·ä'uʟ
little boy. / Then / he went out. / Then / down he went / to / in front of house

was lying on the sand.   The poor little boy took it and went up with it, and he entered and spoke to the princess, "The raven found a little trout"; but he himself had caught it at the bottom of the lake. The poor little boy had acquired for himself supernatural power, but he did not want the princess to know it, and she did not know it.   It was evening again, and the poor little boy made ready to go.   But the princess did not eat the little trout, only the poor little boy and his grandmother ate what the raven had found in the morning.   Then they lay down.   The princess lay in the rear of the house, and the boy lay near the fire.   In the evening the poor little boy rose and went

---

1 hwî′lpg·ê.   Gwinā′dɛʟ!   ʟgo-lā′X   sîsg·ē′t   aʟ   lax-ā′us.   Nʟk·′ēt
   of house.   Behold!   a   trout   lying   at   on sand.   Then
                                   little

2 gōʟ   ʟgo-guä′ɛm   ʟgo-tk·′ē′ʟkᵘ.   Nʟk·′ē   bax-dē-iä′êt.   Nʟk·′ē
   took   the   poor   little   boy.   Then   up also he   Then
   it   little   went.

3 ts'ēnt   aʟ   ts'ɛm-hwî′lpg·ê.   Nʟk·′ē   a′lg·îxt   aʟ   ʟgo-wî′lk·sîʟkᵘ.
   he   at   in   house.   Then   he spoke   to   the   princess.
   entered   little

4 Ma′ʟdɛt   t   hwaʟ   qāq   ʟgo-lā′X.   Nʟk·′ēʟ   lɛp-g·îdi-gō′udɛʟ
   He told   it   found   the   a   trout.   Then,   self   had caught it
                                   raven   little   however,

5 ʟgo-guä′ɛm   ʟgo-tk·′ē′ʟkᵘ   aʟ   lō-s'iä′nʟ   ts'ɛm-t'a′xg·ê.
   the   poor   little   boy   at   in bottom   in   lake.
   little   of

6 ʟɛp-sɛ-nɛxnâ′gôt   ʟgo-guä′ɛm   ʟgo-tk·′ē′ʟkᵘ.   Nî′g·it   gun-
   Self made   super-   the   poor   little   boy.   Not   he
              natural   little   caused

7 hwîlā′yînt   aʟ   ʟgo-wî′lk·sîʟkᵘ.   Nʟk·′ē   nîg·idet   hwîlā′x·ʟ
   it to be known   by   the   princess.   Then   not she   knew it
                                   little

8 ʟgo-wî′lk·sîʟkᵘg·ê.   Nʟk·′ē   huX   yu′ksa,   nʟk·′ē   sɛm-gua′ldɛm
   the   princess.   Then   again   evening,   then   very   ready
   little

9 qâ′ôdɛt   ʟgo-guä′ɛm   ʟgo-tk·′ē′ʟkᵘ.   Hwä′i!   Nîg·idet   g·ē′îpʟ
   finished   the   poor   ittle   boy.   Well!   Not   ate it
              little

10 ʟgo-wî′lk·sîʟkᵘ   aʟ   ʟgo-lā′Xg·ê.   K·sax-ʟgo-nts'ē′êts   t'an   g·ē′îpt
    the   princess   of   the   trout.   Only   the   grand-   who   ate
    little   little   little mother

11 qanʟ   ʟgo-guä′ɛm   ʟgo-tk·′ē′ʟkᵘ   ʟē   hwa′îʟ   qāq   aʟ   hē′ʟuk
    and   the   poor   little   boy   what   was   the   in   the
             little   found by   raven   morning

12 dä′uʟg·ê.   Hwä′i!   Nʟk·′ē   lä′ʟdetg·ê.   G·îts'ä′n   hwîl   g·ä′êʟʟ
    a little while   Well!   Then   they lay   In the rear   where   lay down
    ago.   down.   of the house

13 ʟgo-wî′lk·sîʟkᵘg·ê,   k·′ē   lax-ts'ä′ʟ   lakᵘ   hwîl   dē-g·ä′êʟʟ   ʟgo-
    the   princess,   then   on edge of   fire   where on his lay down   the
    little   part   little

14 guä′ɛm   ʟgo-tk·′ē′ʟkᵘ.   Haô′ng·ê   nakᵘt   da   yu′ksa,   k·′ē   huX
    poor   little   boy.   Before   long   evening,   then   again

15 g·în-hē′tkᵘʟ   ʟgo-guä′ɛm   ʟgo-tk·′ē′ʟkᵘ.   Nʟk·′ē   huX   iē′êtg·ê.
    rose   the   poor   little   boy.   Then   again   he went.
                   little

out again.   Then he found the great skin of the frog and put it on.
Again he went to the shore of the great lake and dived.   He walked
about on the bottom of the lake and caught a trout, a little larger one.
Then he went ashore again.   Again he put off the skin and hung it on
the branch of the tree.   He went home again and laid it on the sand in
front of the house.   The poor little boy entered secretly and lay down.
When the day broke, a raven was crying on the beach.   The princess
heard it and said to the poor little boy, "Go and hear why the raven
is crying on the beach."   The poor little boy went down again, although
he himself had caught in the lake what the raven found on the beach.
He went down and took it.   Then he returned again and entered.   He

---

NLk·'ēt   huX   hwaL   hwîl   lē-ia'qL   wī-anā'sL   qana'o.   NLk·'ēt   1
Then   again   he found where   on hung   the skin   the frog.   Then
                                                     the   of
                                                     great

huX   gula't.   NLk·'ēt   hā·ts'îk·sEm   huX   uks-iē'êt   aL   lax-ts'ä'L   2
again   he put   Then   once more   again   toward he   at   on edge of
         it on.   water went

wī-t'a'x.   NLk·'ē   huX   sō'uqsk^ut.   NLk·'ē   huX   k'uL-dā'uLt   aL   3
the lake.   Then   again   he dived.   Then   again   about   he   at
great   walked

ts'Em-s'iä'nL   wī-t'a'x.   Hwä'i!   NLk·'ē   huX   g·idi-gō'uL   lāX   4
in the bottom   the lake.   Well!   Then   again   he caught   a trout
        of   great

Lgo-q'ai-ts'ō'sg·îm   wi-t'ē's.   NLk·'ē   huX   ts'âk·sk^ut.   NLk·'ē   huX   5
a   still   small   great.   Then   again   he went   Then   again
little   ashore.

sa-mā'gat.   NLk·'ē   ha·ts'îk·sEm   huXt   lē-ia'qt.   NLk·'ē   huX   6
off he took it.   Then   once more   again   on   he   Then   again
                                                               hung it.

na-iä'êt.   NLk·'ē   ha·ts'îk·sEmt   huX   sg·ît   aL   lax-ā'us   aL   7
out of he   Then   once more   again   he laid   at   on   the   at
woods went.   it   sand

qa-g·ä'uL   hwîlp.   NLk·'ē   ha'k·sEm   huX   q'am-ts'ē'nL   Lgo-   8
in front of   the   Then   once more   again   secretly entered   the
house of   house.   little

guä'Em   Lgo-tk·'ē'Lk^u.   NLk·'ē   huX   q'a'mts'En   g·ē'êLt.   NLk·'ē   9
poor   little   boy.   Then   again   secretly   he lay   Then
                                                                      down.

q'ai-ank·siu'kt   mEsā'x·,   nLk·'ē   huX   a'lg·îxL   qāq   aL   g·ä'u.   10
still   was spread   the   then   again   spoke   the   at   in front of
         out   daylight,   raven   the house.

NLk·'ēt   huX   naxna'L   Lgo-wî'lk·sîLk^u.   NLk·'ē   huX   a'lg·îxt   11
Then   again   heard it   the   princess.   Then   again   she said
                                 little

aL   Lgo-guä'Em   Lgo-tk·'ē'Lk^u: "Hwîlā'x·L   an-hä'êL   qāq   12
to   the   poor   little   boy: "Learn   what says   the
        little   raven

aL   ·g·ä'u   SE!"   NLk·'ē   huX   iaga-dā'uLL   Lgo-guä'Em   13
at   in front of   look!"   Then   again   down   went   the   poor
       house   little

Lgo-tk·'ē'Lk^u.   ALk·'ē   nē   t'an   lEp-g·îdi-gō'ut   aL   ts'Em-t'a'x.   14
little   boy.   Although   he   who   self   caught it   in   in the   lake.

NêLne'L   hwā'îL   qāq.   NLk·'ē   ia'ga iē'êt.   NLk·'ēt   gō'ut.   15
Then   it was   the   Then   down   he   Then   he took
           found by   raven.   went.   it.

laid it before the old grandmother, who split it and roasted it; but the princess did not eat, only the old grandmother and the poor little boy ate of it. He did so every night. Then he finished catching trout in the lake.

One night he went out again and found the skin hanging on the branch. He put it on and went down the river, the outlet of the great lake, at the bottom of the water. He went down to the sea; then he walked about on the bottom of the sea and caught a salmon. Before daylight he laid it down in front of the house. Then he went up the river again under the water. He went ashore out of the great lake and took off the great frog's skin and hung it up. He went home and arrived before daylight. He entered secretly and lay down.

---

1   Nʟk·'ē   ha'k·sᴇm   huX   lō-ya'ltkᵘt.   K·'ē   huX   ts'ent   aʟ
    Then   once more   again he returned.   Then   again   he   at
                                                                   entered

2   ts'ᴇm-hwî'lpt.   Nʟk·'ē   sg·it   aʟ   awa'aʟ   ʟgo-nts'ē'ts.   Nʟk·'ēt
    in   his house.   Then   he laid at   proximity the   Then
                                 it   of   grand-
                                                        little mother.

3   q'âʟʟ   ʟgo-nts'ē'êts.   Nʟk·'ēt   iâ'ôdᴇtg·ê.   Nʟk·'ē   huX   nîg·idet
    split it the   Then   she began to   Then   again not
              grand-   roast it.
              little mother.

4   g·ē'îpʟ   ʟgo-wî'lk·sîʟkᵘg·ê.   K·sax-ʟgo-nts'ē'êts   t'an   g·ē'îpt   qanʟ
    ate it   the princess.   Only   the   who   ate it   and
               little   grand-
                                              little mother

5   ʟgo-guä'ᴇm   ʟgo-tk·'ē'ʟkᵘ.   Txanē'tkᵘʟ   axkᵘ   hwîʟʟ   ʟgo-guä'ᴇm
    the   little boy.   Every   night   he did   the
    poor little   so   poor little

6   ʟgo-tk·'ē'ʟkᵘ.   Nʟk·'ē   ʟat   lō-qâ'ôdᴇnʟ   lāX   aʟ   ts'ᴇm-t'a'x.
    little boy.   Then   (perf.) in finished   the   at   in the lake.
                                 he   trout

7   Nʟk·'ē   huX   iä'êt   aʟ   k·'ēʟʟ   axkᵘ.   Nʟk·'ē   huX   hwaʟ   hwîl
    Then   again   he   at   one   night.   Then   again   he   where
                      went   found

8   lē-ia'qt.   Nʟk·'ē   ha'ts'îk·sᴇm   huX   lō-ʟô'ôtkᵘt.   Nʟk·'ē   g·îsi-yô'xkᵘʟ
    on   it   Then   once more   again   in he was put.   Then   down   he
    hung.   river followed

9   ts'ᴇm-a'k·s   ʟa   anʟla'gaʟ   wī-t'a'xg·ê.   At   na-qâ'ôʟ   lax-mô'ôn.
    in   water   the   outlet of   the   lake.   He   out of went on   the sea.
                        great   woods

10 Nʟk·'ē   huX   k'uʟ-dā'uʟt   aʟ   ts'ᴇō'yuX.   Nʟk·'ē   g·îdi-gō'uʟ   hân.
    Then   again   about   he   at   the bottom.   Then   he caught   a salm-
                     walked   on.

11 Nʟk·'ēt   huX   sg·ît   aʟ   qag·ä'uʟ   hwîlp   aʟ   haô'ng·ê   mᴇsā'x·.
    Then   again   he laid at   in front of the house at   before   daylight.
                       it   the house of

12 Nʟk·'ē   ha'k·sᴇm   huX   gali-yô'xguʟ   ts'ᴇm-a'k·s.   Nʟk·'ē   huX
    Then   once more   again up   he followed in   water.   Then   again
                                 river

13 ts'âk·skᵘt   aʟ   lax-ts'ü'ʟ   wī-t'a'x.   Nʟk·'ēt   huX   sa-mā'gaʟ
    he went   at   on edge of   the lake.   Then   again   off   he put
    ashore   great

14 wī-anä'sʟ   qana'og·ê.   Nʟk·'ē   ha'k·sᴇm   huX   lē-ia'qt.   Nʟk·'ē   huX
    the skin of   the frog.   Then   once more   again on   he   Then   again
    great   hung it.

15 na-iē'êt.   Nʟk·'ē   wîtkᵘt   aʟ   haô'ng·ê   mᴇsā'x·.   Nʟk·'ē   huX
    out of he   Then   he arrived at   before   daylight.   Then   again
    woods went.

When the day broke, the princess rose. Again she heard the raven crying on the beach; there were even two ravens. She called the poor little boy, saying, "See why the ravens are crying on the beach." Again he rose and went down. There was the salmon that he himself had caught in the sea. He took it and went up. He entered, carrying it, and laid it down near the old grandmother. She split it and roasted one-half. When it was done, she addressed the princess, wanting her to eat of it, and she ate with them. The poor little boy and the old grandmother ate one end; the princess ate the other end. He did so every night. Then the princess noticed that the skin of the poor little boy began to be very clean. One night she did not sleep,

---

q'a'mts'ɛn ts'ēnt. Nʟk·'ē huX q'amts'ɛn g·ē'êlt aʟ ʟa dēlpkᵘʟ 1
secretly / he entered. / Then / again / secretly / he lay down / at (perf.) / short time

dɛm hwîl mɛsā'x·. Q'aī-ank·siu'kʟ dɛm mɛsā'x·, nʟk·'ē 2
(fut.) / being / daylight. / Still was spread out / (fut.) / daylight, / then

huX g·în-hē'tkᵘʟ ʟgo-wî'lk·sîʟkᵘ Nʟk·'ēt huX naxna'ʟ hwîl 3
again / rose / the little / princess. / Then / again / she heard / where

a'lg·îxʟ qāq; q'ai-t'ɛpxā'ʟ qā'qg·ê. Nʟk·'ēt huX go'gsaanʟ 4
spoke / the raven; / even / two / ravens. / Then / again / awoke

ʟgo-wî'lk·sîʟkᵘ ʟgo-guä'ɛm ʟgo-tk·'ē'ʟkᵘ. Nʟk·'ē a'lg·îxt: 5
the little princess / the little / poor / little / boy. / Then / she spoke:

"Hwîlā'x·ʟ an-hä'ʟ qāq aʟ g·ä'u!" Nʟk·'ē huX g·în-hē'tkᵘt. 6
"Learn / what says / the raven / at / in front of the house!" / Then / again / he rose.

Nʟk·'ē iaga-iä'êt. Gwinā'dɛʟ, hân ʟē lɛp-g·îdi-gō'udɛt aʟ 7
Then / down he went. / Behold, / the salmon / self / he had caught it / at

lax-mô'ông·ê! Nʟk·'ēt gō'ut. Nʟk·'ē bax-dē-iä'êt; nʟk·'ē dē- 8
on / the sea! / Then / he took it. / Then / up with it he went; / then / with it

ts'ē'nt. Nʟk·'ēt sg·ît aʟ awa'aʟ ʟgo-nts'ē'êtst. Nʟk·'ēt q'âʟt. 9
he entered. / Then / he laid it down / at / the proximity of / his little grandmother. / Then / she split it.

Nʟk·'ēt iâ'ôdɛʟ ʟē stô'ôt. Nʟk·'ē a'nukst. Nʟk·'ē a'lg·îxʟ 10
Then / she roasted / one half. / Then / it was done. / Then / spoke

ʟgo-nts'ē'êtst dēt-gun-g·ē'îpt aʟ ʟgo-wî'lk·sîʟkᵘ. Nʟk·'ēt dē-g·ē'îpt. 11
his little grandmother / also caused to eat it / at / the little princess. / Then / also she ate it.

K·sax ʟa q'apʟ dē-g·ē'îpʟ ʟgo-guä'ɛm ʟgo-tk·'ē'ʟkᵘ qanʟ 12
Only / (perf.) / one end / on their part / ate / the little / poor / little / boy / and

ʟgo-nts'ē'êtst. Hwä'i! K·'ē g·ē'îpʟ ʟgo-wî'lk·sîʟkᵘ ʟa q'ap. 13
his little grandmother. / Well! / Then / ate / the little princess / (perf.) / the end.

Txanē'tkᵘʟ axkᵘʟ hwî'ltg·ê. Nʟk·'ē llîk·s-g·a't'ɛnʟ ʟgo-wî'lk·sîʟkᵘ 14
Every / night / he did so. / Then / took notice / the little princess

hwîl ʟa sak·skᵘʟ anā'sʟ ʟgo-guä'ɛm ʟgo-tk·'ē'ʟkᵘ. Nʟk·'ē 15
being / (perf.) / clean / the skin of / the little / poor / little / boy. / Then

but she watched him until midnight. He was no longer a boy, but a youth. Now she saw that he was very clean. She saw that not long after dark the poor little boy rose. She was still watching when he reentered. She was unable to sleep, and a little before daylight the poor little boy entered the house. He lay down again, but the princess did not sleep. Now it was daylight, and the raven cried on the beach. Then the princess herself rose and went out. She went down to the beach. Behold, a large salmon lay in front of the house on the sand. The princess herself took it, and she entered, carrying it, while the poor little boy was still lying down. She said, "Rise!" Then the poor little boy rose. The princess said to him, "I wish to ques-

1 nîg·i huX wâqt. NLk·'ēt sîx·g·a'adɛt; La k·'êdā'uL axkᵘ, nLk·'ē
   not   again she slept. Then she watched when middle   night then
                                          him;

2 nîg·i wâqL Lgo-wî'lk·sîLkᵘ at sîx·g·a'adɛt hwîl g·ä'ê'LL
   not slept the princess   she watched   where lay
             little

3 Lgo-guä'ɛm Lgo-tk·'ē'Lkᵘ; La nîg·i huX Lgo-tk·'ē'Lkᵘ, La
   the poor   little boy;   (perf.) not more a   boy, (perf.)
   little   little

4 ts'ō'usg·îm wī-t'ē'st. NLk·'ēt g·a'at hwîl La sɛm-sa'k·skᵘt. Haôn
   a little   large.   Then she saw being (perf.) very clean. Before
                             him

5 g·î-na'kᵘt Lda yu'ksa, nLk·'ēt g·a'aL Lgo-wî'lk·sîLkᵘ, hwîl La
   long   when evening, then saw   the princess,   where (perf.)
                                       little

6 huX g·în-hē'tkᵘL Lgo-guä'ɛm Lgo-tk·'ē'Lkᵘ NLk·'ēt q'ai-
   again rose   the poor   little boy.   Then   still
                    little

7 sîx·g·a'adɛL dɛm hwîl huX ts'ent. Hwä'i! K·'ē sä'êqt La
   she watched (fut.) where again he   Well! Then she was (perf.)
   him   entered.   unable to sleep

8 dēlpkᵘL dɛm mɛsā'x·, de-ts'ē'nL Lgo-guä'ɛm Lgo-tk·'ē'Lkᵘ.
   shortly (fut.) daylight, on his entered the poor   little boy.
                            part   little

9 NLk·'ē huX g·ä'êLt, nLk·'ē nîg·i huX wâqL Lgo-wî'lk·sîLkᵘ.
   Then again he lay   then   not again slept the princess.
             down,   little

10 NLk·'ē mɛsā'x·, nLk·'ē huX a'lg·îxL qāq aL gä'u. NLk·'ē
   Then daylight, then again spoke the at in front Then
                                      raven of house.

11 lɛp-g·în-hē'tkᵘL Lgo-wî'lk·sîLkᵘ. NLk·'ē k·saXt. NLk·'ē iaga-iä'êt.
   self rose   the princess.   Then she went Then down she
                    little   out.   went.

12 Gwinā'dɛL, wî-hâ'n sîsg·î't aL qa-g·ä'ut aL lax-ā'us! NLk·'ēt
   Behold,   a salmon lying at in front of at on the Then
             large   the house   sand!

13 lɛp-gō'uL Lgo-wî'lk·sîLkᵘ. NLk·'ē dē-ts'ē'nt aL ts'ɛm-hwî'lp
   self took it the princess. Then with she   at in the
            little   it entered   house

14 aL q'ai-g·ig·ē'êL Lgo-guä'ɛm Lgo-tk·'ē'Lkᵘ. NLk·'ēt a'lg·îxt:
   at still lying   the poor   little boy.   Then she spoke:
                     little

15 "G·în-hē'tgun!" NLk·'ē g·în-hē'tkᵘL Lgo-guä'ɛm Lgo-tk·'ē'Lkᵘ.
   "Rise!"   Then rose   the poor   little boy
                                      little

tion you." The poor little boy sat down near to her, and the princess
said to him, "I know that you found the trout and the small salmon.
The raven did not find them on the beach. Now I have found a large
salmon. I know that you have got many trout. You killed them.
My grandmother dried many salmon, and I have found this large
salmon." Then the poor little boy said, "It is true. My uncle treated
us thus. He deserted you and me and my grandmother. We were
without food, therefore I went into the woods. I came to a large
lake. Then I shouted, and a great frog emerged. It swam ashore
and I killed it. I skinned it, and I put on its skin. Then I caught
trout and salmon and I became very clean. Now I am great. You

---

NₗK·'ē	a'lg·îxɭ	ɭgo-wî'lk·sîɭkᵘ	as	ne'tg·ê:	"DEm	g·ē'daxa	1
Then	spoke	the little princess	to	him:	"(Fut.),	I ask	

nē'En."	NₗK·'ē	d'āɭ	ɭgo-guä'Em	ɭgo-tk·'ē'ɭkᵘ	aɭ awa'at.	2
you."	Then	sat	the poor little	little boy	at her proximity.	

NₗK·'ē	a'lg·îxɭ	ɭgo-wî'lk·sîɭkᵘ	as	ne'tg·ê:	"La	hwîlā'yi	3
Then	spoke	the little princess	to	him:	"(Perf.)	I know	

nē'En	t'an	dEdô'qɭ	lāX	qanɭ	sEsō'sEm	hân,	nētɭ	huwā'iɭ	4
you	who	caught	the trout	and	small	salmon,	not	found by	

qāq	aɭ	g·ä'u.	Hwä'i!	ɭa	huX	hwa'ē	wī-t'ē'sEm	hân	5
the raven	at	in front of the house.	Well!	(Perf.)	again	found by me	a large	salmon	

aɭ	gōn.	Hwä'i!	ɭa	wī-hē'lɭ	lāX	g·îdi-dô'gan.	ɭa	hwîlā'yi	6
at	now.	Well!	(Perf.)	many	trout	you caught.	(Perf.)	I know	

nē'En	t'an	hēya'tst.	ɭa	huX	wī-hē'lɭ	hân	gwa'lkᵘdEɭ	7
you	who	killed them.	(Perf.)	also	many	salmon	dried	

nts'ē'Etsē.	ɭa	huX	hwa'ē	wī-t'ē'sEm	hân."	NₗK·'ē	a'lg·îxɭ	8
my grandmother.	(Perf.)	again	found by me	a large	salmon."	Then	spoke	

ɭgo-guä'Em	ɭgo-tk·'ē'ɭkᵘ:	"Iä'gai-net!	Hwîl	hwî'ls	dEp-bē'Ebē	9
the poor little	little boy:	"However it is true!	Thus	did	my uncles	

as	nē'En	qans	nē'E	qans	ts'ē'edzē.	Sakᵘsta'qsdēt	nē'En	10
to	you	and	me	and	my grandmother.	They deserted	you	

qans	nē'E	qans	ts'ē'Edzē.	NₗK·'ē	aqɭ-g·ē'bEn,	nɭqan	hwî'lēE,	11
and	me	and	my grandmother.	Then	without food you,	therefore	I did so,	

iä'ē	aɭ	g·ilē'lîx·.	Nîk·'ē'	hwaɭ	wī-t'a'x.	NₗK·'ē	qē'ɭxkuē.	12
I went	to	into the woods.	Then I	found	a great lake.	Then	I shouted.	

NₗK·'ē	g·ā'bEnɭ	wi-qana'o.	NₗK·'ē	wîl'am-la'qt.	NₗK·'ē	nē	13
Then	emerged	a great frog.	Then	ashore it swam.	Then	I	

dzakᵘt.	Nîk·'ē'	tsâ'ôdEt,	nEɭnē't	lō-ɭô'ôtguē.	Nîk·'ē'	g·îdi-	14
killed it.	I then	skinned it,	that what	in I was put.	Then I		

dô'qɭ	lāX	qanɭ	hân.	NₗK·'ē	ɭa	sEm-sa'k·skuē.	Hwä'i!	ɭa	15
caught	trout	and	salmon.	Then	(Perf.)	very clean I	Well!	(Perf.)	

have taken notice of me." The princess replied, "You shall marry
me," and he agreed. He married her and he was now a man; he was
no longer the poor little boy.

He caught many salmon, and the house was full. Then he filled
another house. He went into the sea, and caught bullhead. He
dried many. Then he went to catch halibut, and they dried many.
He obtained every kind of fish, and caught a great many. Four
houses were full of provisions. Then he went to catch seals, and he
caught a very great number. He put them into another house. Now
he went to catch porpoises, and placed them in another house. Then
he went to catch sealions, and they obtained a great many large water

1 wī-t'ē'sē   gōn.   La   lîks-g·a't'ɛnɛn   nē'ɛ   gōn."   Nʟk·'ē
  great I   now.   (Perf.) you   of me   now."   Then
                                     have taken
                                     notice

2 dē'lɛmɛxkuʟ   ʟgo-wî'lk·sîʟku: "Hwä'i!   La   ā'm   mɛ   na'k·sguēɛ!"
  replied   the   "Well!   (Perf.)   good   you   marry me!"
              princess:
              little

3 Nʟk·'ē   La   anâ'qt.   Nʟk·'ēt   nak·skut.   Nʟk·'ē   qa'nē-hwîla   hwîl
  Then   (perf.)   he   Then he   married her.   Then   always   being
                        agreed.

4 g·a'tg·ê   La   nî'g·i   huX   ʟgo-tk·'ē'ʟkut.
  a man   (perf.)   not   again   boy.
                        a
                        little

5 Hwä'i!   Nʟk·'ē   wī-hē'ldɛl   hân   dza'ptg·ê,   La   metkuʟ   hwîlp.
  Well!   Then   many   salmon   he made,   (perf.)   full was   the
                                                                                house.

6 Nʟk·'ē   huX   metkut   huX   k·'ēlʟ   hwîlp.   La   qâ'ôʟ   ts'ɛm-a'k·s
  Then   again   full was   again   one   house.   (Perf.)   he went   in   water
                                                                                      to

7 aʟ   lax-mô'ôn.   Nʟk·'ē   g·îdi-gō'uʟ   mas-q'ayā'it.   Nʟk·'ē   huX
  to   on   sea.   Then   he caught   bullhead.   Then   again

8 wī-hē'ldɛt   at   gwa'lgut.   Nʟk·'ē   huX   qâ'ôʟ   txox·.   Nʟk·'ē   huX
  many   he   dried.   Then   again   he went   halibut.   Then   again
                                                      (to catch)

9 wī-hē'ldɛt   at   gwa'lgut.   La   tsadɛba'ant   lo-hwîlɛm   ts'ɛm-a'k·s.
  many   he   dried.   (Perf.)   he obtained every   in   being   in   water.
                                          kind of   (fish)

10 Nʟk·'ē   La   sɛm-wī-hē'ldɛl   dzapt.   La   txalpxʟ   huwî'lp
   Then   (perf.)   very   many   he made.   (Perf.)   four   houses

11 hwîl ,   mɛtme'tkut,   nʟk·'ē   tq'al-qâ'ôʟ   ēlx.   K·'ē   ia'gai-
   being   full,   then   against he   seals.   Then   how-
                                    went   ever

12 sɛm-k·'ā-wī-hē'ldɛl   at   dzapt.   Hwä'i!   La   huX   k·'ēlʟ   hwîlp   hwîl
   very ex-   many   he   made.   Well!   (Perf.) again   one   house   where
   ceedingly

13 lō-dô'xt.   Nʟk·'ēt   huX   tq'al-qâ'ôdɛl   dzīX.   Nʟk·'ē   huX   wi-hē'ld
   in they   Then   again   against he   per-   Then   again   many
   were.   went   poise.

14 t hwîl   dzapt.   Nʟk·'ē   huX   k·'ēlʟ   hwîl   lō-dô'xt.   Hwä'i!
   where   he   Then   again   one   where   in they   Well!
            made.   were.

15 Nʟk·'ē   huX   tq'al-qâ'ôdɛl   t'ē'bɛn.   Hwä'i!   Nēl   hwîl   xstāʟ
   Then   again   against he   sealions.   Well!   That   being   gained
                        went   by

animals. Many houses were full of sealion grease, because the sealions are very large. Then he got whales. He obtained very many.
Now they had two children, and for a long time he caught animals
with his hands. Suddenly he became very tired. He told his wife,
and she began to worry, and rebuked her husband, saying, "Please
stop"; but he caught four large whales and there was a smell of
grease all along the beach in front of their houses. The butts of the
trees where he had carried up the meat and the fat of whales were full
of grease. Bones were lying about in front of his house, and the
grease from the whales covered the water of the sea.

Now, many of the people who, with his uncle, had deserted him

---

dzā′ptg·ê	aL	hwîl	La	dzapL	k·'ā-wī-t'ē′sEm	lō-hwî′lEm	1
he made	at	where	(perf.)	he made	exceedingly large	in being (water)	

ts'Em-a′k·s.	Hwä′i!	Wī-hē′ld	hwîl	lō-dô′xL	hīx·L	t'ē′bEn	2
in water. (animals)	Well!	Many	where	in they were	fat of	sealion	

aL	hwîl	k·'ā-wī-t'ē′st.	Hwä′i!	NLk·'ēt	huX	g·îdi-gō′uL	3
because		exceedingly large.	Well!	Then	again	he caught	

Lpen.	NeL	hwîl	sEm-k·'a-xstā′L	dzāpt.			4
whales.	That	being	very exceedingly	gained he made.			

NLk·'ē	La	bagadē′lL	Lg·i′tg·ê.	Nî′g·i	dēlpk L	hwî′ltg·ê,	5
Then	(perf.)	two	children.	Not	a short while	he did so,	

neL	qan	La	wihē′lL	dzapt	aL	an'o′ntg·ê.	NLk·'ēt	ma′LEL	6
therefore	(perf.)	much	he made	with	his hands.	Then	he told		

La	sā-Lgu′kskutg·ê.	NLk·'ēt	ma′LEt	aL	nak·st.	NLk·'ē	7
(perf.)	suddenly he was overtired.	Then	he told	to	his wife.	Then	

lō-alî′skuL	qâ′ôdEL	na′k·stg·ê.	NLk·'ēt	lä′elL	nak·st:	"ĀmL	La	8
in weak	heart of	his wife.	Then	she rebuked	her husband:	"Good (perf.)		

dEm	ha′un!"	La	txalpxL	wī-Lpe′n	huX	g·îdi-dô′qtg·ê.	La	9
(fut.)	stop!"	(Perf.)	four	large whales	also	he caught.	(Perf.)	

sEm-î′skuL	qa-g·ä′uL	hwî′lpdētg·ê.	Lîg·i-mEtme′tkuL	qa-mē′nL	10
much stench	in front of houses of	their houses.	All over full were	the butts of	

ganga′n	aL	hwîl	bax-hwî′lgaL	hē′ya	Lpen	qanL	txanē′tkuL	11
the trees	at	where	up he carried	fat of	whale	and	all	

qa-sma′x·t.	K·saxL	qa-ts'ē′pt	hwîl	g·î-dô′xt	aL	haL-qa-g·ä′uL	12
meat.	Only	bones	where	lay	at	along the front of the house of	

hwîlpt.	NLk·'ē	metkuL	lax-mâ′ôn	aL	hwîl	iaga-hē′tkuL	t'ēla	13
his house.	Then	full it was	on sea	because		down stood	fat of	

Lpen	aL	lax-mâ′ôn.					14
whale	at	on sea.					

NLk·'ē	La	wi-hē′lt	hwîl	daXL	t'an	ts'Ens-lu′k·at	15
Then	(perf.)	many	where	dead	who	leaving moved behind	

were dead. His uncle was a very great chief. Now his uncle thought
that his daughter, the poor little boy, and the grandmother were
dead, and he spoke to his people. The chief had lost many of his
people, because there was no food. Many of them and all the children
were dead. One day, early in the morning, some people started
to look after the princess, the poor little boy, and the grandmother. They were traveling in four canoes. They were approaching the place. When they were still far from the shore, they saw
grease on the surface of the water. They noticed it. When they
approached the town, they saw several houses full of dried salmon,
trout, halibut, and bullhead, and others in which was the grease of

---

1 hwîl   hōksk^uʟ   wī-nebē′pt.   Sɛm-k·′a-wī-t′ē′s   hwîl   sɛm′â′g·its
   being   they were   great his mother's   Very   ex-   great   being   chief
             with him   brother.   ceedingly

2 nēbē′pt.   Nʟk·′ē   ha-lē-qâ′ts   nēbē′pt   tsɛ   ʟa   nô′ôʟ
   his mother's   Then   he thought   his mother's   if   (perf.)   was
   brother.   brother   dead

3 ʟgō′ʊʟk^ut   qanʟ   ʟgo-guä′ɛm   ʟgo-tk·′ē′ʟk^u   qanʟ   ʟgo-nɛts′ē′ētst.
   his child   and   the   poor   little   boy   and   the   grandmother.
                           little   little

4 Nʟk·′ē   a′lg·îxʟ   sɛm′â′g·itg·ê   aʟ   ʟē   ts′apt.   ʟa   sɛm-gwâ′tk^uʟē
   Then   spoke   the chief   to   his   (Perf.)   much   he lost
                                                people.

5 ts′apt   sɛm′â′g·it   aʟ   nîg·i   sg·iʟ   dɛm   g·ē′ipdetg·ê   neʟqan
   his   the chief   at   not   there   (fut.)   their food,   therefore
   people   was

6 ʟa   wi-hē′ʟʟ   hwîl   daXt   qanʟ   txanē′tk^uʟ   k′opɛ-tk·′ē′ʟk^u.
   (perf.)   many   being   dead   and   all the   little   children.

7 Nʟk·′ē   ā′d′îk·sk^uʟ   hwîl   mɛsā′x·.   K·′ēt   sīg·â′tk^uʟ   qal-ts′a′p
   Then   came   being   daylight.   Then   started   the people

8 dɛm   t′an   g·a′aʟ   ʟgo-wî′lk·sîʟk^u,   qanʟ   ʟgo-guä′ɛm   ʟgo-tk·′ē′ʟk^u
   (fut.)   who   (would)   the   princess   and   the   poor   little   boy
                   see   little   little

9 qanʟ   ʟgō-nēts′ē′etst.   ʟō-txalpxdā′t   ʟē   ts′apʟ   sɛm′â′g·it   aʟ
   and   his grandmother.   In four canoes   the   people   the chief   to
           little   of

10 dɛm   t′an   g·a′at.   Nʟk·′ē   lō-ba′xt   q′ai-hwagai′t-tsɛ-tsagam-
   (fut.)   who   would   Then   they ap-   still   far   toward
                   see it.   proached   shore

11 yu′kdet   aʟ   g·ī′îks.   K·′ē   g·a′adeʟ   t′elx·   aʟ   lax-ō′ʟ   mâ′ôn.
   they went   from   off shore.   Then   they saw   grease   on   on top   the sea.
                                                                        of

12 Nʟk·′ē   lîk·s-g·a′d′ɛndēt   hwî′ltg·ê.   Nʟk·′ū   lō-ba′xdēt   aʟ   ts′ap.
   Then   they took notiec   it was so.   Then   they approached   at   the
                                                                                town.

13 K·′ēt   g·a′adeʟ   qabē′ʟ   huwî′lp   hwîl   mɛtmē′tk^uʟ   gwa′lgwa   hân
   Then   they saw   several   houses   being   full   dry   salmon

14 qanʟ   gwa′lgwa   lāX   qanʟ   gwa′lgwa   txōx·   qanʟ   gwa′lgwa
   and   dry   trout   and   dry   halibut   and   dry

15 mas-q′ayā′it   qanʟ   hwîl   lō-daxdô′xʟ   hē′ya   elx   qanʟ   hwîl
   bullhead   and   where   in   was   fat of   seal   and   where

seals, of porpoises, of sealions, and of whales. He had very much, because he had caught four whales. He had caught very much with his hands. Then his uncle's people landed. They told him that many of the tribe were dead. They entered his house and he fed them. Then they ate dried salmon, fat of the seal, and fat of the porpoise and of the whale. Then he presented them with dried halibut, bullhead, and trout. He gave presents to those whom he had invited in. He gave them fat of the seal, porpoise, sealion, and whale. Then they started and left him. They landed at the place where the chief was living. Then the people came to the beach and told him that the

---

| lō-daxdô′xʟ | hē′ya | dzīX | qanʟ | hwîl | lō-daxdô′xʟ | hē′ya | 1 |
| in was | fat of | por-poise | and | where | in was | fat of | |

| t'ē′bɛng·ê | qanʟ | hwîl | lō-daxdô′xʟ | hē′ya | ʟpen. | NEʟne′t | 2 |
| sealion | and | where | in was | fat of | whale. | Then | |

| sɛm-k·'a-xstā′t | aʟ | hwîl | ʟa | txalpxʟ | t'ē′sɛm | ʟpen | g·îdi-dô′qtg·ê. | 3 |
| very exceed-ingly gained he | at | where (perf.) | | four | large | whales | he caught. | |

| Nʟk·'ē | sɛm-k·'a-xstā′ʟ | dzapt | aʟ | an'ô′ntg·ê. | Nʟk·'ē | k·'ātskⁿʟ | 4 |
| Then | very exceed-ingly gained he | he made | with | his hands. | Then | landed | |

| ts'aps | nēbē′pt. | Nʟk·'ēt | mā′ʟEʟ | k·'ātskᵘt | hwîl | ʟa | lō-nô′ôʟ | 5 |
| the people of | his uncle. | Then | they told | they landed | being | (perf.) | in dead | |

| ʟē | ts'aps | nēbē′ptg·ê. | Nʟk·'ē | la′mdzîxt | aʟ | hwîlpt. | Nʟk·'ēt | 6 |
| the people of | | his uncle. | Then | they entered | in | his house. | Then | |

| g·înā′mʟ | g·ē′iptg·ê. | Nʟk·'ē | txâ′ôxdêtg·ê. | Gwa′lgwa | hânʟ | 7 |
| he gave them | food. | Then | they ate. | Dry | salmon | |

| g·ē′îpdetg·ê; | nʟk·'ē | hē′ya | ēlx | g·ē′îpdet; | nʟk·'ē | hē′ya | dzīX | 8 |
| they ate; | then | fat of | seal | they ate; | then | fat of | por-poise | |

| g·ē′îpdet; | nʟk·'ē | hē′ya | ʟpen | g·ē′îpdet. | Nʟk·'ē | k·saxt-g·inā′mʟ | 9 |
| they ate; | then | fat of | whale | they ate. | Then | only he gave them | |

| gwa′lgwa | txōx· | qanʟ | gwa′lgwa | mas-q'ayā′it, | qanʟ | gwa′lgwa | 10 |
| dry | halibut | and | dry | bullhead, | and | dry | |

| lāX. | Iä′êqdet aʟ | gul-g'anē′ʟ | wô′ôtkᵘtg·ê. | Nʟk·'ēt | k·sax-g·inā′mʟ | 11 |
| trout. | He distrib-uted it to | all | who were invited. | Then | only he gave | |

| txanē′tkⁿʟ | hē′ya | ēlX | qanʟ | hē′ya | dzīX | qanʟ | hē′ya | t'ē′bɛn | 12 |
| all | fat of | seal | and | fat of | porpoise | and | fat of | sealion | |

| qanʟ | hē′ya | ʟpen. | Nʟk·'ē | sig·â′ôtkⁿʟ | wô′ôtkᵘtg·ê. | Nʟk·'ē | 13 |
| and | fat of | whale. | Then | they started | who had been invited. | Then | |

| dā′uʟdetg·ê. | Nʟk·'ē | k·'ā′tskⁿdēt | aʟ | hwîl | dzôqʟ | sɛm'â′g·it. | 14 |
| they left. | Then | they landed | at | where | stayed | the chief. | |

| Nʟk·'ē | ia′ga-laxla′qʟ | qal-ts'a′p. | Nʟk·'ē | maʟa′askᵘdetg·ê | 15 |
| Then | down came | the people. | Then | they were told | |

town of the young man was full of dried trout, salmon, halibut, and
bullhead, and of fat of the seal, porpoise, sealion, and whale, that
the butts of the trees smelled of meat of the whale, sealion, porpoise,
and seal that was lying about, and that four houses were full of dried
trout, halibut, and bullhead.   When the chief heard this, he was very
glad, and he was also glad when he heard that his daughter had two
children.   He said to his people, "Let us move again." The great
slave went out and ordered the people to move back to the place where
the princess and the poor little boy were living.   The old grandmother had died.   Then the people moved, and they stayed at the place

---

1 La mētkᵘL qal-ts'a'p aL gwa'lgwa lāX qanL gwa'lgwa hân
   (perf.) full the town of dry trout and dry salmon

2 qanL gwa'lgwa txōx· qanL gwa'lgwa mas-q'ayā'it qanL
   and dry halibut and dry bullhead and

3 hē'ya ēlX qanL hē'ya dzīX qanL hē'ya t'ē'bEn qanL
   fat of seal and fat of porpoise and fat of sealion and

4 hē'ya Lpen. NLk·'ē La îskᵘL qa-mē'nL ganga'n aL
   fat of whale. Then (perf.) stench the butts of the trees at

5 hwîl k·sax-k'uL-daxdô'xL sma'ye Lpen qanL sma'ye
   where only about lay meat of whale and meat of

6 t'ē'bEn qanL sma'ye dzīX qanL sma'ye ēlx. NLk·'ē txaḷpxL
   sealion and meat of porpoise and meat of seal. Then four

7 huwî'lp hwîl mētme'tkᵘL gwa'lgwa lāX qanL gwa'lgwa
   houses being full of dry trout and dry

8 txōx· qanL gwa'lgwa mas-q'ayā'it. NLk·'ē sEm-lō-ā'mL qâdEL
   halibut and dry bullhead. Then very in good heart

9 wī-sEm'â'g·it hwîl Lat naxna't. NLk·'ē huX lō-ā'mL qâdEL
   the great chief when (perf.) he heard it. Then again in good heart

10 sEm'â'g·itg·ê hwîl Lat naxna't bagadē'lL Lg·iL Lgō'uLkᵘtg·ê.
    the chief where (perf.) he heard two chil-dren his daughter.

11 NLk·'ē huX a'lg·îxt aL qal-ts'a'p: "ĀmL dEm huX lo'gum."
    Then again he spoke to the people: "Good (fut.) again we move."

12 NLk·'ē huX ha'ts'îk·sEm huX k·si-ba'xL wī-xa'atkᵘstg·ê.
    Then again once more again out ran the great slave.

13 At gun-lu'kL qal-ts'a'p aL awa'aL hwîl dzôqL Lgo-wî'lk·sîLkᵘ qanL
    He caused to move the people to the proximity of where stayed the little princess and

14 Lgo-guä'Em Lgo-tk·'ē'Lkᵘ. La k·'ē nô'ôL Lgo-nēts'ē'tsdetg·ê. NLk·'ē
    the poor little little boy. (Perf.) then was dead their little grandmother. Then

15 lukL qal-ts'a'p. NLk·'ē ā'd'îk·skᵘL qal-ts'a'p aL awa'adetg·ê.
    moved the people. Then came the people to their proximity.

16 NLk·'ē ha'ts'îk·sEm huX dzô'qdet aL Le sa-ma'qdetg·ê.
    Then once more again they stayed at (part.) off they had put.

that they had once left. Then the boy gave them much dried trout,
salmon, halibut, and bullhead. He did what was just right. Then
his uncle's people were glad. They were saved, because they now ate
dried trout, salmon, halibut, and bullhead, and he also gave them a
little fat of the seal, porpoise, sealion, and whale; and his uncle's people
were very glad, because they were saved. And all the people said
that the poor little boy, when grown up, should be their chief.

The boy always went out to sea to catch seals for his uncle's people,
and he always told his wife that it was very hard to take off the frog
blanket. Then his wife worried and cried when she lay down. Now

Nʟk·'ēt	k·sax-g·înā′mʟ	āmʟ	qabē′ʟ	gwa′lgwa	lāX	qanʟ		1
Then	only he gave	just	several	dry		trout and		
gwa′lgwa	hân	qanʟ	gwa′lgwa	txōx·	qanʟ	gwa′lgwa		2
dry	salmon	and	dry	halibut	and	dry		
mas-q'ayā′it;	āmʟ	qabē′ʟ	an-hwî′ntg·ê.	Nʟk·'ē	lō-am'ā′mʟ	qagâ′ôʟ		3
bullhead;	just	several	what he did.	Then	in good	hearts		
ts'aps	nēbē′pt.	Nʟk·'ē	lēmâ′tkⁿdetg·ê,	aʟ	hwîl	ʟa	g·ē′îpdet	4
the people of	his mother's brother.	Then	they were saved,	because		(perf.)	they ate	
gwa′lgwa	lāX	qanʟ	gwa′lgwa	hân	qanʟ	gwa′lgwa	txōx·	5
dry	trout	and	dry	salmon	and	dry	halibut	
qanʟ	gwa′lgwa	mas-q'ayā′it.	Nʟk·'ē	huX	k·sax-g·înā′mʟ			6
and	dry	bullhead.	Then	again	only he gave			
ts'ō′osk·ʟ	hē′ya	ēlx	qanʟ	hē′ya	dzīX	qanʟ	hē′ya	t'ē′bɛn	7
a little	fat of	seal	and	fat of	porpoise	and	fat of	sealion
qanʟ	hē′ya	ʟpen.	Nʟk·'ē	wi-t'ē′sʟ	hwîl	lō-am'ā′mʟ	qagâ′ôʟ	8
and	fat of	whale.	Then	much	being	in good	hearts	
ts'aps	nēbē′pt	aʟ	hwîl	ʟa	dē-lemâ′tkⁿtdetg·ê.	Nʟk·'ē		9
the people of	his mother's brother,	because		(perf.)	they were saved.	Then		
a′lg·îxʟ	txanē′tkⁿʟ	qal-ts'a′p	aʟ	dɛm	sɛm'â′g·it	ʟa	hwîl	10
spoke	all	the people	at	(fut.)	chief	(perf.)	being	
wi-t'ē′sʟ	ʟgo-guä′ɛm	ʟgo-tk·'ē′ʟkⁿ.						11
great	the poor little	little boy.						
Nʟk·'ē	qa′nē-hwîla	dā′uʟ	ʟgo-tk·'ē′ʟkⁿ	aʟ	ts'ɛm-mâ′ôn,	aʟ		12
Then	always	he went	the little boy	at	in sea,	and		
g·îdi-dô′qʟ	ēlx	aʟ	g·ē′îpʟ	qal-ts'a′ps	nēbē′pt.	Nʟk·'ēt		13
caught	seal	for	food of	the people of	his uncle.	Then		
qa′nē-hwîla	māʟt	aʟ	nak·st	hwîl	ʟa	wi-t'ē′st	hwîl	14
always	he told	to	his wife	being	(perf.)	much	being	
sa-ʟgu′kskⁿʟ	gwîs-qana′otg·ê.	Nʟk·'ē	sɛm-lō-qē′tkⁿʟ	qâ′ôdɛʟ				15
off difficult to do	his blanket frog.	Then	very in sorry	the heart of				
na′k·stg·ê.	K·'ē	qa′nē-hwîla	wī-yē′tkⁿʟ	nak·st	aʟ	hwîl		16
his wife.	Then	always	she cried	his wife	at	where		

the people brought many elks and slaves. They brought enough elks to fill two houses. And he bought them with trout and dried halibut and salmon and bullhead; he bought many slaves. Then he gave a potlatch. He invited all the people from other places. Then he accomplished what he intended to do. The people went into his house, and he placed the elks and all his other goods and his slaves in the middle of the house. Then he said to his uncle, "You shall distribute them." His uncle agreed, and told him to put on the skin of the white bear. He also wore the great copper that he had thrown down from the tree when he still was the poor little boy. He placed the great copper on his head. Then he walked to the middle of the house and stood near the pile of elk skins; then he sang. When the song was ended, the chief said, "Now I will

---

1 g·ä′ꜱʟt.   Hwä′i!   Tgōnʟ   hwîʟʟ   qal-ts′a′pg·ê.   G·ï′kⁿdîʟ   Liâ′n
   she lay.   Well!   This   did   the people.   They sold   elks

2 qanʟ   Lîʟî′ng·it,   wi-hē′ldɛʟ   Liâ′n.   K·′ē′lb′ɛlʟ   hwîlp   hwîl
   and   slaves,   many   elks.   Two   houses   being

3 mêtmē′tkⁿʟ   Liâ′n   sqa′lsît   aʟ   lāX   qanʟ   gwa′lgwa   txōx·   qanʟ
   full of   elks   he bought   for   trout   and   dry   halibut   and
              them

4 gwa′lgwa   hân   qanʟ   gwa′lgwa   mas-q′ayā′it   qanʟ   wī-hē′ldɛm
   dry   salmon   and   dry   bullhead   and   many

5 Liʟî′ng·itg·ê.   Nʟk·′ē   yukt.   Txa-wô′ôdɛʟ   hwîl   dzaxdzô′q.
   slaves.   Then   he gave a   All   he invited   the camps.
                      potlatch.

6 Nʟk·′ē   daa′qʟkⁿʟ   hwî′ltg·ê.   Nʟk·′ē   ʟa   ts′ɛlɛm-qâ′ôdɛʟ   g·at
   Then   he succeeded   what he   Then   (perf.)   into   went   the
                         did.   people

7 aʟ   ts′ɛm-hwî′lpt.   Nʟk·′ē   t′ɛm-d′ā′ʟʟ   Liâ′n   qanʟ   txanē′tkⁿʟ
   at   in   his   Then   into the   he put   the   and   all
         house.   middle   elk

8 lîg·i-hwî′ltg·ê   qanʟ   txanē′tkⁿʟ   Liʟî′ng·it.   Nʟk·′ē   a′lg·îxs
   his goods   and   all   his slaves.   Then   he said

9 nēbē′pt: "Āmʟ   dɛm   ō′yigan   gōn!"   Nʟk·′ē   anâ′qt.   Nʟk·′ē
   his uncle: "Good   (fut.)   it is thrown   now!"   Then   he   Then
                           away by you   agreed.

10 a′lg·îxs   nēbē′pt: "Dɛm   gulai′ɛnʟ   anā′sʟ   gulîk·s-wô′xgutg·ê.
    said   his uncle: "(Fut.)   you put   the   at himself   barking
                              on   skin of   (the white bear).

11 Nʟk·′ēt   huX   hâx·ʟ   wī-o′q   ʟē   sa-ô′x·dɛʟ   ʟgo-guä′ɛm
    Then   also   he   the cop-   (perf.)   off thrown by   the   poor
                    used   great per   the   little

12 ʟgo-tk·′ē′ʟkⁿ.   Tgōnʟ   hwîlt: ʟē-sg·ī′ît   wī-o′q   aʟ   lax-t′ɛm-qē′st.
    little   boy.   This   he did: on he laid   the cop-   on   on   his head.
                                                    great per

13 Nʟk·′ē   t′ɛm-iä′tg·ê,   nʟk·′ē   hētkⁿt   aʟ   hwîl   mɛn-dô′xʟ   Liâ′ng·ê.
    Then   into the he went,   then   he stood   at   where   up   were   elks.
            middle   laid

14 Nʟk·′ēt   sɛ-lē′mîx·detg·ê.   ʟa   sa-ba′xʟ   lē′mîx·,   nʟk·′ē   a′lg·îxʟ
    Then   he   a song.   (Perf.)   off   ran   the song,   then   spoke
            made   (ended)

call your name"; and he named him Growing-up-like-one-who-has-a-grandmother.   When he had finished, he put off the great copper that he had used, and he put off the skin of the white bear, and he gave away the slaves to all his guests, and he gave them elk skins.   When he had finished, they started away.

After he had finished, he again put on his frog blanket, intending to catch seals for food for the people.   He found it very difficult to take off his frog blanket.   Then he went to bed and told his wife, and she began to cry.   He said, "When I put it on again, I shall not be able to take it off, and if I do so, I may not return; I shall only bring seals and halibut and place them in front of the town.   I shall not

---

1 sEm'â′g·it: "ĀmL dEm ētk^{u}st dEm hwat." NLk·′ē ē′tk^{u}detg·ê
the chief: "Good (fut.) is (fut.) his Then he was
named name." named

2 MasEmsts'ē′tsk^{u}L dEm hwat. Hwä′i! Lēsk^{u}t, nLk·′ēt sa-mā′gaL
Growing-up-like-one- (fut.) his Well! He then off he put
who-has-a-grandmother name. finished,

3 wī-o′qL hâ′yîtg·ê. NLk·′ēt sa-mā′gaL La anā′sL gulîk·s-wô′xgut
the cop- used. Then off he put the skin at himself harking
great per of (the white bear)

4 Lē gulā′yîtg·ê. NLk·′ē k·sax-g·înā′mL LîLî′ng·it aL txanē′tk^{u}L
that he had Then only he gave slaves to all
worn.

5 hwîl dzaxdzô′q Lē wô′ôtg·ê. NLk·′ē k·sax-g·înā′mL Liâ′n
the camps he invited. Then only he gave elks
had

6 aL txanē′tk^{n}L hwîl dzaxdzô′q Lē wô′ôtg·ê. NLk·′ē La
to all the camps he invited. Then (perf.)
had

7 Lēsk^{n}t. NLk·′ē sē-lô′ôtk^{u}t. NLk·′ē sa′k·sk^{u}detg·ê.
he Then they started. Then they went.
finished.

8 Hwä′i! La Lēsk^{n}L hwîlt, nLk·′ē huXt gulā′L
Well! When he he did, then again he put
finished on

9 gwīs-qanā′ot aL dEmt huX g·îdi-dô′qL txanē′tk^{u}L ēlx
his frog to (fut.) again catch all seals
blanket

10 dEm g·ē′îpL qal-ts'a′p. NLk·′ē La sa-Lgu′ksk^{u}L gwīs-qanā′ot
(fut.) food of the people. Then (perf.) off difficult his frog
to do blanket

11 hwîl hwî′lt. NLk·′ē lā′Ldetg·ê. NLk·′ē māLt aL nak·st.
what he did. Then they lay Then he told to his wife.
down.

12 K·′ē ā′d'îk·sk^{u}L hwîl wī-yē′tk^{n}L nak·st. "TsEda huX
Then came crying his wife. "If again

13 hwî′lēE, nLk·′ē nîg·′în dEm huX sā-daa′qLgut. NLk·′ē
I do so, then not I (fut.) again off get it. Then

14 tsEda hwî′lēE, k·′ē nî′g·i dEm huX ā′d'îk·sguēg·ê.
if I do so, then not (fut.) again I come perhaps.

15 Dem q'am-hwîl'am-dâ′ēE ēlx aL qa-g·ä′uL ts'ap qanL
(Fut.) only ashore I lay seals at in front of the and
house of town

come ashore again, and I shall stay in the sea. All the year round I shall secretly put ashore seals, halibut, salmon, porpoises, sealions, and whales as food for my children." He said so every day.

One morning his wife went down to the beach in front of the town, and he was lost. He did not come ashore again. He stayed at the bottom of the sea. Therefore the woman, every morning when she rose, went down to the beach and cried, accompanied by her two children. They saw two halibut, and they took them up to the house. One morning she went out again, crying, and she looked seaward, crying, because her husband was lost in the sea. Then she

---

1   txōx'.   Nʟk·'ē   nî'g·i   dᴇm   huX   ts'â'k·skuēᴇ,   dᴇm   lō-
    halibut.   Then   not   (fut.)   again   I come ashore,   (fut.)   in

2   tq'al-gwâ'tkⁿēᴇ   aʟ   ts'ᴇm-mâ'ôn.   Txanē'tkⁿʟ   k'ōʟ   dᴇm   hwî'lēᴇ
    against   I am lost   at   in   sea.   All   year   (fut.)   I do so

3   aʟ   dᴇm   q'a'mts'ᴇn   tsagam-d'ā'ʟdēᴇ   txanē'tkⁿʟ   ēlx,   txanē'tkⁿʟ
    at   (fut.)   secretly   ashore   I put   all   seals,   all

4   txōx·,   txanē'tkⁿʟ   hân,   txanē'tkⁿʟ   dzīX,   txanē'tkⁿʟ   t'ē'bᴇn,
    halibut,   all   salmon,   all   porpoises,   all   sealions,

5   txanē'tkⁿʟ   ʟpen   dᴇm   g·ē'îpʟ   ʟg·i'ᴇ.   Txanē'tkⁿʟ   k'ōʟ   dᴇm
    all   whales   (fut.)   food of   my   All   years   (fut.)
                                         children.

6   hwîl   hwî'lēᴇ."   Txanē'tkⁿʟ   sa   hwîl   hwî'ltg·ê.
    I do so."   All   days   he did so.

7   Hwä'i!   ʟa   k·'ēʟ   hē'ʟuk,   nʟk·'ē   iaga-iä'ʟ   na'k·stg·ê   aʟ
    Well!   When   one   morning,   then   down went   his wife   to

8   qa-g·ä'uʟ   ts'ap   aʟ   ʟa   gwâ'ôtkⁿt.   Nîg·i   huX   ts'âk·sk ⁿt,   ʟa
    the front of   the   and (perf.)   he was lost.   Not   again   he came   when
    the houses of   town   ashore,

9   hwîl   k·'ē   lō-g·a'dᴇʟ   s'iä'nʟ   mâ'ôn   as   nē'tg·ê.   Nîʟ   qan   hwîʟʟ
    at once   he belonged to   the bot-   the sea   to   him.   Therefore   she did
                            tom of   so

10 hana'q,   na'k·stg·ê.   Txanē'tkⁿʟ   hē'ʟuk   hwîl   g·în-hē'tkⁿt.   k·'ē
    the   his wife.   Every   morning   rising,   then
    woman,

11 huX   k·saxt   aʟ   hwîlp,   k·'ē   huX   iaga-iä't   aʟ   qa-g·ä'uʟ   ts'ap.
    again   she went   of   the house,   then   again   down she   to   the front of   the
          out   went   the houses of   town.

12 NʟK·'ē   aʟ   qa'nē-hwîla   wī-yē'tkⁿt   aʟ   k'uʟ-sᴇl-stē'l   bagadē'ʟʟ
    Then   always   she cried   and   about   accom-   two
                                                         panying

13 ʟg·it.   NʟK·'ēt   g·aadē'ʟ   hwîl   ʟa   g·îna-dô'xʟ   t'ᴇpxā'tʟ   txox'.
    children.   Then   she saw   where   (perf.)   right   were   two   halibut.
                                                         there

14 NʟK·'ēt   bax-dô'qt.   HuX   k·'ēʟ   hē'ʟuk   hwîl   huX   k·saXʟ
    Then   up she took   Again   one   morning   (when)   again   went out
             them.

15 hana'q   aʟ   huX   wī-yē'tkⁿt   aʟ   qa-g·ä'uʟ   ts'ap   aʟ   t'uks-g·a'aʟ
    the   at   again   crying   at   in front of the   the   and   out to   she
    woman   houses of   town   sea   looked

saw two seals. Growing-up-like-one-who-has-a-grandmother had
given them as food to his children. Another morning she went
down. She went down, crying, every morning. She saw a porpoise.
She carried it up. Another morning she went down with her two
children, and she saw a sealion. She went down and carried it up.
Thus her children had always enough. Another morning she went
down, and when she ceased crying she saw a great whale. Then she
did not go down again, because she could not carry the whale. She
said to her father's people "Fasten this whale to the house. The
father of these children sent it here. He also sent the sealions, the

---

lax-mâ'ôn.	NeL	La	hwîl	lō-tq'al-gwâ'tkᵘL	na'k·stg·ê.	NLk·'ē	1
on sea.	He	(perf.)	being	in against lost	her husband.	Then	

huXt	g·a'aL	hwîl	La	huX	g·îna-dô'xL	t'Epxā'tL	ēlx.	2
again she	saw	where	(perf.)	again	right there lay	two	seals.	

At	tsagam-g·î'ns	MasEmsts'ē'tskᵘL	Lg·i'tg·ê.	NLk·'ē huX k·'ēlL	3
He ashore	gave food	Growing-up-like-one-who-has-a-grandmother	his children.	Then again one	

hē'Luk	k·'ē	huX	hwîlL	hana'qg·ê,	aL	qa'nē-hwîla	wī-yē'tkᵘt	4
morning	then	again	did so	the woman,	at	always	she cried	

aL	txanē'tkᵘL	hē'Lukg·ê.	NLk·'ē	huXt	g·a'aL	hwîl	g·îna-dô'xL	5
at	every	morning.	Then	again	she saw	where	right there lay	

dzīX.	NLk·'ē	huX	bax-dô'qdetg·ê.	HuX	k·'ēlL	hē'Luk,	k·'ē	6
porpoise.	Then	again	up she took them.	Again	one	morning,	then	

ha'k·sEm	huX	hwîlL	hana'qg·ê	qanL	bagadē'lL	Lg·ît.	NLk·'ēt	7
once more	again	did so	the woman	and	two	her children.	Then	

huX	g·a'at	hwîl	g·îna-sg·ī'L	t'ē'bEn.	NLk·'ē	huX	iaga-iä't.	8
again	she saw	where	right there lay	a sealion.	Then	again	down she went.	

K·'ēt	huX	bax-gō'ut.	NLk·'ē	qa'nē-hwîla	lts'ä'eL	Lg·it.	HuX	9
Then	again	up she went.	Then	always	were satiated	her children.	Again	

k·'ē'lL	hē'Luk	nLk·'ē	huX	k·saXL	hana'qg·ê.	NLk·'ē	LēskᵘL	10
one	morning	then	again	went out	the woman.	Then	she finished	

huX	wī-yē'tkᵘt.	NLk·'ēt	g·a'aL	hwîl	g·îna-sg·i'L	wī-Lpe'n.	11
again	she cried.	Then	she saw	where	right there lay	a great whale.	

NLk·'ē	nîg·i	huX	iaga-iä'êt	aL	hwîl	wī-t'ē'sL	Lpen	12
Then	not	again	down she went	because		was large	the whale	

q'ap-Lgu'ksaantg·ê.	NeL	qan	a'lg·îxt	aL	ts'aps	nEguâ'ôtg·ê:	"ĀmL	13
really she could not carry it.	Therefore		she spoke	to	the people of	her father:	"Good	

nē'sEm	t'an	tsagam-sî-dä'xL	wī-Lpe'n.	NEguâ'ôdEL	k'ōpE-Lg·î'E,	14
you	who	ashore make fast	the great whale.	The father of	my little children,	

nēLnē'	t'an	tsagam-mā'gat	qanL	txanē'tkᵘL	t'ē'bEn,	qanL	15
he	who	ashore put it	and	all	sealions,	and	

porpoises, the seals, and the halibut.   He told me what he was going to do, because he could not get off his frog blanket, and now he really lives in the sea."

---

1 txanē′tkᵘʟ   dzīX,   qanʟ   txanē′tkᵘʟ   ēlx,   qanʟ   txanē′tkᵘʟ   txōx·.
  all   porpoises, and   all   seals,   and   all   halibut.

2 Iagait-ma′ʟdɛtg·ê   dɛm   hwîlt   as   nē′ɛ;   aʟ   hwîl   ʟa
  Already   he told   (fut.)   he does   to   me;   because   (perf.)

3 sa-ʟgu′kskᵘʟ   wī-gwīs-qana′ot   ʟa   g'ap-lŏ-hwî′lɛm   ts'ɛm-mâ′ôns
  off   it could not   his blanket   frog   (perf.)   really in   being   in   the sea
         come   great

4 nē′tg·ê."
  he."

LITTLE-EAGLE

A Legend of the Eagle Clan

[Told by Moses]

There was a large town. A chief was its master. He was the commander of all the men. His child was a noble prince. The child did not eat, but made bows and arrows all the time. Now the salmon arrived. Then the chief said to his people, "Catch salmon and dry them." The people did so. They dried many salmon. Then the prince took one salmon. He put it on the sand, and gave it to an eagle to eat. One eagle came, and then another one, and they ate

---

LGWA-XSKĪ'YÊK

LITTLE-EAGLE

Hētkᵘʟ	wī-qal-ts'a'p.	K·'âlʟ	sɛm'â'g·iʟ	mē'ndēt.	Nʟnet 1
There stood	a large town.	One	chief	its master.	That one
an-a'lg·igaʟ	txanē'tkᵘʟ	g·a'tg·ê.	Nʟk·'ē	k·'âlʟ	ʟgō'uʟkᵘtg·ê 2
the commander of	all	men.	Then	one	his child
sɛmgal	ʟgo-wî'lk·sîʟkᵘ.	Nîg·îdē	yō'ôxkᵘt,	k·sax-ha-Xda'qʟ 3	
a very high	little prince.	Not	he ate,	only bows	
dē-dza'pt	qanʟ	hawî'l.	Nʟk·'ē	ʟā ā'd'îk·skᵘʟ	hân, nʟk·'ē 4
on his part made	and	arrows.	Then	when came	the salmon, then
a'lg·îxʟ	sɛm-â'g·it	aʟ	ʟē ts'apt:	"Ām mɛ dɛm sɛm	sɛ-hē'ltʟ 5
said	the chief	to	his people:	"Good you	make many
hân	aʟ	mɛ dɛm sɛm gwa'lgut."	Nʟk·'ē	hwîlʟ	qal-ts'a'p. 6
salmon		(fut.) you dry them."	Then	did so	the people.
Nʟk·'ē	wī-hē'lʟ	hân at	gwa'lkᵘdēit.	Nʟk·'ē	tgōnʟ hwîlʟ 7
Then	many	salmon they	dried them.	Then	this did
ʟgō-wî'lk·sîʟkᵘ.	Gō'udɛʟ	k·'ä'guʟ	hân.	Nʟk·'ēt	sg·ît aʟ 8
the little	prince. He took	one	salmon.	Then	it lay on
lax-a'us	at g·înʟ	xsk·a'ak·	lât.	Nʟk·'ē	ā'd'îk·skᵘʟ xsk·āk·. 9
the sand	he gave it to eat to	an eagle	to him.	Then	came the eagle.
Nʟk·'ē huX	ā'd'îk·skᵘʟ	huX	k·'ä'gut.	Nʟk·'ē	g·ē'îpdeʟ hân. 10
Then again	came	again	one.	Then	they ate the salmon.

169

the salmon. Many eagles did so. They ate all the salmon, and then they flew away again. The prince pulled out their feathers and gathered them. Then he was glad, and the eagles also were glad. The prince made arrows; he made many boxes full of them. He used the feathers of the eagles for making his arrows, fastening them to the shaft, and therefore his arrows were very swift. He gave salmon to many eagles. When the salmon were at an end, he stopped.

The prince did not eat. He only made arrows. Now it came to be winter. For about three months the Indians ate only dried salmon and berries mixed with grease and elderberries and currants. They

1 Wī-hē′lʟ xsk·āk·ʟ hwî′ltg·ê. Nʟk·′ē dza′ʟdēʟ hân. Nʟk·′ē
  Many   eagles   did so.   Then   they ate all the   Then
                                                             salmon.

2 lēba′yukt. Nʟk·′ē dzaXʟ hwîl ts′â′ôts′aʟ txanē′tkᵘʟ qaq′ā′x·.
  they flew.   Then   much   where he pulled   all   feathers.
                                     out

3 Nîlne′ʟ saxdâ′iʟ ʟgō-wî′lk·sîʟkᵘ. Nʟk·′ē lō-ā′mʟ qâ′ôtt.
  That is picked up the   prince.   Then   he good heart.
  what   little   was in

4 Nʟk·′ē ia′gai huX dē-lō-am′ā′mʟ qaqâ′ôtʟ. xsk·āk·. Hwä′i! Tgōn
  Then   how- again on in   good   hearts   the eagles. Well!   This
         ever   their part

5 hwîlʟ ʟgō-wî′lk·sîʟkᵘ. Hawî′lg·ê, nîlne′ʟ q′ap-dē-dzā′pt, ʟgō′uʟkᵘʟ
  did   the   prince.   Arrows,   those   really on   made   the son of
         ittle   his part

6 sɛm-â′g·it. K·sax-hawî′lʟ dē-dzā′pt sɛm-wī-hē′lt. Txanē′tkᵘʟ
  the chief.   Only   arrows   on he made very   many.   All
                                  his part

7 qa-xbē′ist hwîl mɛtme′tkᵘt. Hwä′i! Q′ap-k·′ē′lʟ qaq′ā′îx·ʟ
  boxes   being full.   Well! Really one   feather of

8 xsk·ā′k·g·ê, neʟ hâ′yît aʟ hawî′l. Tq′al-dîx·da′k·ʟdît lât·
  an eagle,   that he used for an   Against   he fastened it   to it.
                                  arrow.

9 Nēʟne′ʟ qan sɛm-alē-iä′ēdet. Wī-hē′lʟ xsk·ak· t hwîl g·inā′mʟ
  Therefore very quick- they   Many   eagles   he   gave
             ly   went.

10 hâ′ng·ê. Q′ap-ndaʟ hwîl qâ′ôdɛʟ hân. Nʟk·′ē hawî′tg·ê.
   salmon.   Really where being finished the   Then   he stopped.
                                            salmon.

11 Nîg·idē yō′ôXkᵘʟ ʟgō-wî′lk·sîʟkᵘg·ê. K·sax-hawî′lʟ dē-dzā′pt.
   Not   ate   the   prince.   Only   arrows   on he made.
                   little   his part

12 Nʟk·′ē ā′d′îk·skᵘʟ dɛm hwîl mā′adɛm. ʟā nakᵘʟ hwîl
   Then   came   (fut.) being snow.   When long   being

13 mā′adɛm ʟā lîg·î-gulaɛldɛma ʟôqs, ʟā tgōnʟ hwîlʟ alō-g·ig·a′t,
   snow   when about three maybe months, when this   did   the Indians,

14 k·sax-hâ′nʟ dē-g·ē′îpdet qanʟ ʟa′ix qanʟ mā′ɛ qanʟ lâts
   only salmon on   they ate and berries mixed and berries and elder-
               their part   with grease   berries

15 qanʟ hwē′k·îl. Txanē′tkᵘʟ lē-hwa′nt aʟ lax-qaq′û′qst, neʟ
   and   wild black   All   on   were at   on little bushes, then
         currants.

ate all kinds of berries. Now the salmon was all used up. They did not give any salmon to the prince. When the salmon was almost all used up, the great chief felt sad. He said to his great slave, "Go out and order the people to move." The great slave ran out, crying, "Move, great tribe!" The people did so. They moved in the morning. They left the chief's son and his little grandmother, and one little slave, who was still quite small. He was weak. There was no salmon. They only left him his boxes filled with arrows. But his mother buried a clam shell in which she had placed some fire and one-half of a large spring salmon. Then she told the little grandmother where she had hidden the fire and the salmon.

Now the people went aboard and moved away. Only the prince and his little grandmother and the little slave were left. They had no

---

dē-g·ē'îpdēt.	NLk·'ē	Lā	qâ'ôdEL	hân,	nLk·'ē	nî'g·îdēt	g·ē'ndEL	1
on their part they ate.	Then	when	it was finished	the salmon,	then	not	they gave food	

Lgō-wî'lk·sîLkᵘ	aL	hân.	Lā	nakᵘL	lax-ha',	Lā	ts'ōsk·L	dEm	2
to the little prince	to	the salmon.	When	long	the weather,	when	nearly	(fut.)	

hwîl	qâ'dîL	hân,	nLk·'ē	sī'êpkᵘI,	qâ'ôL	wī-sEm'â'g·it.	NLk·'ē	3
being	gone	the salmon,	then	sick was	the heart of	the great chief.	Then	

a'lg·îxtg·ê:	"Adô',	k·sa'wun.	ĀmL	yukL	gun-lu'kL	qal-ts'a'p;	4
he said:	"Adô,	go out.	Good	begin	to order to move	the town;	

mēya'an!"	Dē'ya	aL	wī-xa'E.	NLk·'ē	k·si-ba'xL	wī-xa'E:	5
say so!"	Thus he said	to	the slave. great	Then	out ran	the slave: great	

"Dzē	lâ'g·în	wī-ts'â'ôp."[1]	NLk·'ē	hwîLL	qal-ts'a'p	luk	aL	6
"Move	great	village."	Then	did so	the people	they moved	in	

hē'Luk.	Uks-ksta'qstEL	sEm'â'g·iL	Lgō'uLkⁿtg·ê	dē-k·'â'lL	Lgō-	7
the morning.	From land to sea left	the chief	his son	also one	little	

ntsē'êts	dē-k·'â'lL	Lgo-xa'E;	sEm-q'ai-tsetsō'osk·L	Lgo-xa'E	8
grandmother	also one	little slave;	very quite small was	the slave little	

hao'ng·it	dax-g·a'tt.	Nîg·i	sg·îL	hân	aL	awa'aL	Lgō-wî'lk·sîLkᵘ.	9
not yet	strong.	Not	was	salmon	at	proximity of	the little prince.	

K·sax-hwîl	lō-daxdô'xL	hawî'l.	Wī-hē'lL	xpē'ist	hwîl	10
Only	where in were the	arrows.	Many	boxes	being	

metme'tkⁿt.	NLk·'ēt	wôqs	nôxt	q'am-xts'a'q;	lō-me'LL	lakᵘ	11
full.	Then	dug	his mother	clam shells;	in burnt	fire	

lâ'ôt	dē-stô'ô	wī-ya'E.	NLk·'ēt	ma'LEL	aL	Lgō-ntsē'tstg·ê.	12
in them	also one half	large spring salmon.	Then she	told	to	the little grandmother.	

NLk·'ē	uks-qâ'ôdEL	luk.	NLk·'ē	qam-k·'â'lL	Lgō-wî'lk·sîLkᵘ	13
Then	from land to sea they were gone	they moved.	Then	only one	little prince	

g·ina-d'ā't	qans	ntsē'tst	qanL	Lgo-xa'E.	Nîg·i	sg·îL	dEm	14
behind was	and	his grandmother	and the	little slave.	Not	was	(fut.)	

---

[1] This sentence is in Tsimshian dialect.

food. Then the little old woman took the coal and made a fire. They
did not eat for a whole day, and for a long time they had no food.
Then the prince went out. Early in the morning he sat outside. It
was low water. Then an eagle was screeching on the beach. The prince
called his little slave: "See why the eagle is screeching on the beach."
The slave ran down and came to the place where the eagle was sitting.
When he was near by, the eagle flew away and, behold, a little trout
was lying on the sand. Then the little slave shouted, telling the
prince, "A little trout, my dear, lies on the beach." Thus spoke the
little slave. Then the prince said, "Take it." The little slave carried
it up, and the prince ordered him to roast it. The slave roasted it,

1 g·ē'îpdētg·ê. Nьk·'ēt gō'uь ьgō-wud'ax-g·a't lak". Nьk·'ēt
   their food.   Then   took   the old person   the   Then
   little   fire.

2 sе-mē'ьt. Nьk·'ē txanē'tk" sa nîg·î txâ'xk"dētg·ê. Nьk·'ē ьā
   she fire.   Then   all   day   not   they ate.   Then when
   made

3 nak"ь hwî'ldēt, aqь-g·ī'pdēt. Nьk·'ē k·saxь ьgō-wî'lk·sîьk".
   long   they did so,   without their   Then   went out   the   prince.
                 food.   little

4 Nьk·'ē d'āt aь g·a'ьеq, aь hē'ьuk. sеm-sg·îь ak·s.
   Then   he sat   at   outside,   at   morning.   Very low   the
                                       was   water.

5 Nьk·'ē a'lg·îxь xsk·ā'ak· aь g·ī'îk·s. Nьk·'ēt wô'ôь
   Then   spoke   an eagle.   at   offshore.   Then   called

6 ьgō-wî'lk·sîьk" ьgo-xa'е: "Adô', g·a'aь an-hä'еь xsk·āk· aь
   the   prince   the slave: "Adô,   see   what says   the eagle   at
   little   little

7 g·ī'îk·s." Nьk·'ē uks-ba'xь ьgo-xa'е. Nьk·'ē hagun-a'qьk"t
   offshore."   Then   from ran   the slave.   Then   toward   he
             land to sea   little   reached

8 aь hwîl dеd'ā'ь xsk·āk·. ьā q'ai'yîm dēlpk"ь ьgo-xa'е,
   at   where   sat   the eagle.   When   close by   near was   the slave,
                                            little

9 nьk·'ē g·iba'yuk"ь xsk·āk·. Gwinā'dēь, ьgo-lā'x sîsg·ît aь lax-ā'us.
   then   flew   the eagle.   Behold,   a trout   lying   on the beach
                                 little

10 Nьk·'ē wî-am-hē'ь ьgo-xa'е, at ma'ьеь aь ьgō-wî'lk·sîьk":
   Then   shouted   the slave,   he   told   to   the   prince:
                    little   little

11 "ьgo-lā'x, nāt, hwîl am-sg·î't aь g·ä'u." Dē'yaь ьgo-xa'е
   "A trout,   my   being on the lies   on   the beach   Thus said   the slave
   little   dear,   beach   of house."   little

12 aь ma'ьеt. Nьk·'ē a'lg·îxь ьgō-wî'lk·sîьk": "Gōьē." Nьk·'ēt
   and   he told it.   Then   said   the   prince: "Take it."   Then
                            little

13 gōь ьgo-xa'е. Nьk·'ē tsagam-iä'êt. Nьk·'ēt gun-iâ'ôdеь
   took it   the slave.   Then   from sea   he   Then   ordered roast it
       little   to land went.   him to

14 ьgō-wî'lk·sîьk" aь ьgo-xa'е. Nьk·'ēt iâ'ôdеь ьgo-xa'е.
   the   prince   to   the slave.   Then   roasted it   the slave.
   little   little   little

and when it was done, he and the little old person ate it. The prince did not eat anything. Only the old person and the slave ate it.

Night came and morning came; then the prince went out again. Again he heard the eagles screeching on the beach. He sent down his little slave, who found a bullhead (sculpin). Then he told the prince, who ordered him to take it up. The little slave took it, and they roasted it. They did so for many days, and the eagles gave them trout and sculpin. Then they had enough to eat.

One morning the prince went out again, and he saw two eagles sitting on the beach screeching. He sent his little slave, who went

---

1 NʟK·'ē a'nukst. NʟK·'ē g·î'pdēt qanʟ ʟgō-wud'ax-g·a't.
Then / it was done. / Then / they ate it / and / the little old person.

2 Nî'g·idēt g·îpʟ ʟgō-wî'lk·sîʟkᵘ. K·sax ʟgō-wud'ax-g·a't t'an
Not / ate it / the little prince. / Only / the little old person / who

3 g·ēîpt qanʟ ʟgo-xa'ᴇ.
ate it / and / the little slave.

4 NʟK·'ē huX yu'ksa. NʟK·'ē huX hē'ᴇluk. NʟK·'ē huX
Then / again / it was evening. / Then / again / it was morning. / Then / again

5 k·saXʟ ʟgō-wî'lk·sîʟkᵘ. NʟK·'ēt huX nᴇxna'ʟ hwîl a'lg·îxʟ xsk·āk·
went out / the little prince. / Then / again / he heard / where / spoke / an eagle

6 aʟ g·î'îk·s. NʟK·'ēt huX uks-hē'tsʟ ʟgo-xa'ᴇ. NʟK·'ēt hwaʟ
at / off shore. / Then / again / from land he to sea sent / the little slave. / Then / he found

7 hwîl sg·îʟ mas-q'ayā'it. K··ēt ma'Lᴇl aʟ ʟgō-wî'lk·sîʟkᵘ.
where / lay / a bullhead. / Then / he told / to / the little prince.

8 NʟK·'ēt huX gun-gō'udeʟ ʟgō-wî'lk·sîʟkᵘ. NʟK·'ē huX
Then / again / caused to take him it / the little prince. / Then / again

9 gō'uʟ ʟgo-xa'ᴇ. NʟK·'ēt huX iâ'ôdēt qans ntsē'etst. ʟā
took it / the little slave. / Then / again / they roasted it / and / his grandmother. / When

10 wî-hē'lʟ saʟ hwî'ldēt, ʟa wîhē'lʟ lāX qanʟ mas-q'ayā'it.
many / days / they did so, / when / many / trout / and / bullhead.

11 T g·ēnʟ xsk·āk·ʟ ʟgō-wî'lk·sîʟkᵘ, nʟk·'ē ʟa lîtsä'x·det.
They gave food / the eagles / the little prince, / then / (perf.) / they were satiated.

12 HuX k·'ē'ᴇlʟ hē'ʟuk, nʟk·'ē huX k·saXʟ ʟgō-wî'lk·sîʟkᵘ aʟ
Again / one / morning, / then / again / went out / the little prince / to

13 g·a'lᴇq. NʟK·'ē g·a'aʟ hwîl hwanʟ xsk·ā'ak· q'ai-t'ᴇpxā't.
outside. / Then / he saw / where / sat / eagles / just two.

14 NʟK·'ē al'a'lg·îxt aʟ alayūwā'tdet. NʟK·'ēt huX hētsʟ
Then / they spoke / and / they made noise. / Then / again / he sent

15 ʟgo-xa'ᴇ. NʟK·'ē huX uks-iē'êʟ ʟgo-xa'ᴇ. NʟK·'ēt huX g·a'at.
the little slave. / Then / again / from land to sea went / the little slave. / Then / again / he looked.

down. He looked, and, behold, there was a salmon. Then he shouted and said, "There is a large salmon, my dear!" And the prince said, "Take it." The little slave said twice, "I can not take it." The prince went down himself and carried it up. They did so several days, finding salmon on the beach. They dried them.

Another morning the prince went out again, and, behold, there were three eagles. They made much noise. The little slave went down, and, behold, there was a large spring salmon. Again the little slave said he could not carry it, and the prince went down himself. He took it up, and the little old person, his little grandmother, split it. They did so many days. They dried spring salmon. They had very many now.

---

1 Gwinā'dēL,   hân!   NLk·'ē   hwîl   k·'ē   wī-am-hē'L,   at   ma'LEL:
   Behold,   a   At once   he shouted,   he   said:
                salmon!

2 " Wī-hâ'n, SE,   nāt!"   NLk·'ē   a'lg·îxL   Lgō-wî'lk·sîLkᵘ: " Gōlāᴇ!"
   "A salmon, look, my   Then   said   the   prince: "Take it!"
   great   dear!"   little

3 NLk·'ē   dē'lᴇmᴇxkᵘL   Lgo-xa'ᴇ: " Lgu'ksaᴇnē,"   g·ē'lp'ᴇlL   hē'tg·ê,
   Then   answered   the slave: "I cannot do it," twice   he said,
                          little

4 aL   wī-am-hē't.   NLk·'ē   uks-iä'êL   Lgō-wî'lk·sîLkᵘ.   NLk·'ē   nē
        shouting.   Then   from went   the   prince.   Then   he
                               land to sea little

5 t'an   gō'ut.   Hwäi!   La   huX   wī-hē'lL   saL   hwî'ldēt   aL   hân,
   who   took it. Well!   When again many   days they did   to   salmon
                                                       so

6 Lā   wī-hē'lt   hwîl   gwa'lukdētg·ê.
   when many   (verbal they dried them.
                   noun)

7 Hwäi!   NLk·'ē   La   huX   k·'ēlL   hē'Luk.   NLk·'ē   huX
   Well!   Then   again   one   morning.   Then   again

8 k·saXL   Lgō-wî'lk·sîLkᵘ.   Gwinā'dēL,   xsk·āk·,   gu'lān.   NLk·'ē
   went out the   prince.   Behold,   eagles,   three.   Then
            little

9 hwud'ax-alēm-hē'det   aL   alayuwā'adᴇt.   NLk·'ē   huX   uks-iä'êL
   they shouted   making noise.   Then   again from went
                                                              land to sea

10 Lgo-xa'ᴇ.   Gwinā'dēL,   wī-ya'ᴇ.   NLk·'ēt   ma'LEL   Lgo-xa'ᴇ   huX
    the slave. Behold,   a spring   Then   he told the slave again
    little   large salmon.   little

11 Lgu'ksaant.   NLk·'ē   huX   lᴇp-uks-iä'L   Lgō-wî'lk·sîLkᵘ.   NLk·'ēt
    he could not Then   again self from went the   prince.   Then
    do it.   land to sea   little

12 lᴇp-gō'ut.   NLk·'ē   tsagam-iä'êt.   NLk·'ēt   q'ōL   Lgo-wud'ax-g·a't,
    self   he   Then   from sea   he   Then   split   the   old   person,
    took it.   to land went.   it   little

13 Lgo-ntsē'tstg·ê.   Hwäi!   La   wī-hē'lL   saL   hwî'ldētg·ê   aL
    the grandmother. Well!   When many   days they did so
    little

14 gwa'lukdēL   ya'ᴇ   Lā   daā'qLkᵘdet   wī-hē'lt.
    they dried   spring when they obtained many.
                 salmon

Another morning the prince went out again. The eagles had given them all kinds of fish, and their houses were full of dried salmon. The. slave was quite large when all the salmon was gone.

One morning the prince went out again, and, behold, he saw an eagle far out on the water. He sent his slave down. The little slave had grown to be a little stronger. Behold, there was a large halibut. The little slave shouted, "There is a large halibut, my dear!" The prince said, "Take it"; but the little slave replied, "I can not carry it." The prince went down himself and dragged it up. The little grandmother split it, and they were satisfied. They did so for many

Nʟk·'ē	huX	k·'ē'ɛlʟ	hē'ʟuk,	nʟk·'ē	huX	k·saXʟ	1
Then	again	one	morning,	then	again	went out	

Lgō-wî'lk·sîʟkᵘ. Lā txanē'tkᵘʟ hwîl lîk·s-g·ig·a't hân an-hwî'nʟ 2
the little prince. When all kinds of salmon what they did

xsk·āk· at tsagam-g·ē'ndēʟ Lgō-wî'lk·sîʟkᵘ, Lā lîg·î-mɛtme'tkᵘʟ 3
the eagles they from sea to land gave food the little prince, when about full

txanē'tkⁿʟ huwî'lp aʟ gwa'lgwa hân. Lā wît'ē'sʟ Lgo-xa'ɛ Lā 4
all the houses of dry salmon. (Perf.) great the slave when little

hwîl am-qâ'ôdɛʟ hân. 5
all was finished the salmon.

NʟK·'ē Lā huX ā'd'îk·skᵘʟ hē'ʟuk. NʟK·'ē huX k·saXʟ Lgo- 6
Then again came morning. Then again went out the little

wî'lk·sîʟkᵘ. Gwinā'dēʟ, xsk·āk· huX g·a'at aʟ g·ī'îk·s uks-nakᵘ 7
prince. Behold, an eagle again he saw it at off shore from land far to sea

tgō'stg·ê. NʟK·'ē huXt uks-hē'tsʟ Lgo-xa'ɛ. la ts'ō'sg·îm 8
that one. Then again down he sent to water the slave little. (Perf.) a little

masʟ Lgo-xa'g·ê Lā Lgō-wī-t'ē's. Lā Lgo-dax-g·a'tt. NʟK·'ē 9
he grew the little slave (perf.) a little large. (Pert.) a little strong. Then

huX uks-iä'êt. Gwinā'dēʟ, wī-txo'x·. NʟK·'ē huX wī-am-hē'ʟ 10
again from land to sea he went. Behold, a halibut large. Then again shouted

Lgo-xa'ɛ at ma'ʟɛtg·ê: "Wī-txox·, sɛ, nāt!" NʟK·'ē ā'lg·îxʟ 11
the little slave he told: "A halibut great, look, my dear!" Then said

Lgō-wîlk·sîʟkᵘ: "Gōʟä', gōʟä'." NʟK·'ēt ma'ʟɛʟ Lgo-xa'ɛ: 12
the little prince: "Take it, take it." Then he told the little slave:

"Lgu'ksaaneɛ." NʟK·'ē lɛp-uks-iä'êʟ Lgō-wî'lk·sîʟkᵘ. NʟK·'ēt lɛp- 13
"I can not do it." Then self from land to sea he went the little prince. Then he himself

tsagam-q'ä'êxqʟt. NʟK·'ēt q'ōʟ Lgo-ntsē'tst. NʟK·'ē sɛm-lîtsä'îʟ 14
from sea to land dragged it. Then split it the little grandmother. Then very were satisfied

qagâ'odētg·ê. Hwä'i! Lā huX wī-hē'lʟ saʟ hwî'ldēt, nʟk·'ē 15
their hearts. Well! (Perf.) again many days they did so, then

days, and dried many halibut.　Another house was full of dried halibut.　Now they had caught all the salmon and all the halibut.

One morning the little prince went out again, and looked out. Behold, there were quite a number of eagles.　He sent his little slave down.　The slave went down, and when he came there, behold, there was a large seal.　Then the little slave shouted twice, "There is a seal on the beach!"　Again the prince went down.　He took the seal and dragged it up to the house.　He split it.　Then they put the fat into a box and dried the meat.　They did not take the bones.　They did so many days, and filled another house.

Another morning the prince went out again and looked down. Behold, there were many eagles.　Then the little slave went down

---

1　Lā　huX　wī-hē′lʟ　txox·ʟ　gwa′lkᵘdēt,　Lā　huX　k·′ēlʟ　hwîlp
　　(perf.)　again　many　halibut　they dried,　(perf.)　again　one　house

2　hwîl　mētkᵘʟ　gwa′lgwa　txox·.　Hwä′i!　ʟa　qâ′ôdEʟ　txanē′tkᵘʟ
　　where　full　dry　halibut.　Well!　(Perf.)　it was　all the
　　　　　　　　　　　　　　　　　　finished

3　hân　qanʟ　txox·.
　　salmon　and　halibut.
　　　　the

4　Nʟk·′ē　huX　ā′d′îk·skᵘʟ　hē′ʟuk.　NʟK·′ē　huX　k·saXʟ　ʟgō-
　　Then　again　came　the　Then　again　went out　the
　　　　　　　　morning.　　　　　　　　　little

5　wî′lk·sîʟkᵘ.　NʟK·′ē　huX　uks-g·a′askᵘt.　Gwinā′dEʟ,　xsk·āk·　q′ai-hē′lt.
　　prince.　Then　again from land　he　Behold,　eagles　quite many.
　　　　　　　　　　to sea　looked.

6　NʟK·′ēt　huX　uks-hē′tsʟ　ʟgo-xa′E.　NʟK·′ē　huX　uks-dā′uʟt.　NʟK·′ēt
　　Then he　again from land　sent　the slave.　Then　again from land　he　Then he
　　　　　　to sea　little　　　　　　to sea　went.

7　huX　huwa′t.　Gwinā′dEʟ,　wī-ē′lx.　NʟK·′ē　g·ē′lp′Eʟ　wī-am-hē′ʟ
　　again　reached　Behold,　a seal.　Then　twice　shouted
　　　　them.　　　　　large

8　ʟgo-xa′E,　at　ma′ʟEʟ:　"Ēlx　g·îna-sg·î′t."　NʟK·′ē　huX　uks-iē′êʟ
　　the slave,　he　told:　"A seal　left　lies."　Then　again　from　went
　　little　　　　　　behind　　　　　　land to sea

9　ʟgō-wî′lk·sîʟkᵘ.　NʟK·′ēt　gō′uʟ　ēlx.　NʟK·′ēt　tsagam-q′ä′êxqʟt.
　　the　prince.　Then he　took　the　Then he　from sea　he dragged
　　little　　　　　　seal.　　　　to land　it.

10　NʟK·′ēt　ba′ʟdētg·ê.　NʟK·′ēt　lō-daxdô′xdēʟ　hix·　aʟ　ts′Em-qal-hē′nq.
　　Then he　split it open.　Then they　in　put　fat　to　in　box.

11　NʟK·′ēt　gwa′lkᵘdēiʟ　smax·t;　ʟā　nî′g·i　an-gō′deʟ　tsits′ē′pt.　ʟā　huX
　　Then　they dried　the meat;　not　he took　the bones.　When again

12　wī-hē′lʟ　saʟ　hwî′ldetg·ê,　ʟā　huX　k·′ēlʟ　hwîlp　hwîl　lō-dô′xt.
　　many　days　they did so,　(perf.)　again　one　house　where　in it was.

13　NʟK·′ē　ʟa　huX　ā′d′îk·skᵘʟ　hē′ʟuk,　nʟk·′ē　huX　k·saXʟ
　　Then　(perf.)　again　came　morning,　then　again　went out

14　ʟgō-wî′lk·sîʟkᵘ.　NʟK·′ē　huX　uks-g·a′askᵘt.　Gwinā′dEʟ,　xsk·āk·
　　the　prince.　Then　again　from　he looked.　Behold,　eagles
　　little　　　　　　land to sea

15　wi-hē′lt.　NʟK·′ēt　huX　uks-hē′tsʟ　ʟgo-xa′E　ʟā　sEm-ʟgo-dax-g·a′tʟ
　　many.　Then　again　from　he sent　the slave,　really a　strong
　　　　　　　land to sea　little　　　　little

again. He was now quite strong, because he had much to eat. When he got there, behold, there was a large porpoise. The little slave shouted twice. Then the prince went down and dragged it up to the house. They cut it and put the meat away. They filled another house.

Thus the eagles returned the food that the prince had given to them in the summer. The eagles reciprocated. They pitied the prince because he had pitied them in summer. The eagles were glad, and therefore they fed the prince.

One morning the prince went out, and, behold, there were many eagles. He sent the little slave down, and when he went down and reached there, behold, there was a large sealion. Again the little slave

---

Lgo-xa′E,   aL   Lā   hwîl   wī-hē′lL   g·ē′îpt,   neLne′L   qan   hwîlt.   **1**
the slave, little   because   much   he ate,   therefore   he was so.

NLk·′ēt   huX   hwat.   Gwinā′dēL,   wī-dzī′X.   NLk·′ē   wī-am-hē′L   **2**
Then   again   he reached them.   Behold,   a porpoise. large   Then   shouted

Lgo-xa′E.   G·ē′lp′ElL   wī-am-hē′t.   NLk·′ē   uks-iä′êL   Lgō-wî′lk·sîLk^u.   **3**
the slave. little   Twice   he shouted.   Then   from land to sea went   the prince. little

NLk·′ēt   huX   tsagam-qä′êqLt.   NLk·′ēt   huX   ba′Ldētg·ê.   **4**
Then   again   from sea to land he dragged it.   Then   again   they spread them.

Wī-hē′lL   hwîl   lō-dô′xt.   NLk·′ē   La   huX   metk^{u}L   k·′ēlL   hwîlp.   **5**
Many   where   in they put.   Then   (perf.)   again   full   one   house.

Hwä′i!   Dēltk^{u}L   xsk·ā′ak·g·ê   aL   Let   hwîl   g·î′ndeL   Lgō-   **6**
Well!   Reciprocated   the eagles   to   him   who   gave the food   the little

wî′lk·sîLk^{u}g·ê   aL   hân   aL   g·î-sē′nt.   NeLne′L   qan   La   dē-dē′ltk^{u}L   **7**
prince   of   salmon   in   the last summer.   Therefore   (perf.)   on their part   reciprocated

xsk·āk·   Lat   sîtyä′wuL   La   q′äEm-qâ′ôL   Lgō-wî′lk·sîLk^u as   **8**
the eagles   (perf.)   exchanged   (perf.)   they took pity on   the little   prince   from

nē′dētg·ê.   NLk·′ē   sEm-lō-am′ā′mL   qagâ′ôL   xsk·ā′ak·g·ê,   nîLne′t   qan   **9**
them.   Then   very in good   hearts   the eagles,   therefore

La   dēt-g·î′ndeL   Lgō-wî′lk·sîLk^u.   **10**
(perf.)   on their part they gave food to   the little prince.

NLk·′ē   Lā   huX   ā′d′îksk^{u}L   hē′ELuk.   NLk·′ē   huX   k·saXL   **11**
Then   again   came   morning.   Then   again   went out

Lgō-wî′lk·sîLk^u.   Gwinā′dēL,   xsk·āk·L   wī-hē′ldEt.   NLk·′ēt   huX   **12**
the little prince.   Behold,   eagles   many.   Then   again

uks-hē′tsL   Lgō-wî′lk·sîLk^{u}L   Lgo-xa′E.   NLk·′ē   huX   uks-iä′êL   **13**
from land to sea sent   the little prince   the little slave.   Then   again   from land to sea went

Lgo-xa′E.   NLk·′ēt   huX   hwat.   Gwinā′dēL,   wī-t′ē′bEn.   NLk·′ēt   **14**
the little slave.   Then he   again   reached there.   Behold,   a large sealion.   Then

huX   ma′LEL   Lgo-xa′E.   G·ē′lb′ElL   wī-am-hē′t,   at   ma′LEL.   **15**
again   told it   the little slave.   Twice   he shouted,   he   told.

told him. He shouted twice and told him. The prince heard it and went down, and, behold, there was a large sealion. Then he returned. He twisted cedar twigs and tied the sealions to the shore. When the tide rose, they drifted ashore, and when the water fell, they lay on the beach. Then they cut them. The sealions were very large and had much fat and much meat. They did this for many days. Then they had a great plenty.

Now the people of his father, who had left him, were dying. One morning the prince went out again, and there were very many eagles; not merely a few. There were a great many eagles on the water. They were flying ashore with a great whale. It lay there. Two nights and two days passed, and there lay another great whale. Then they cut it. (In olden times the Indians chopped the blubber of

1 NLk·'ē   naxna'L   Lgō-wî'lk·sîLkᵘ.   NLk·'ē   huX   uks-iä'êt.
  Then   heard it   the prince.   Then   again   from land he
                           little   to sea went.

2 Gwinā'deL,   wī-t'ē'bEn.   NLk·'ē   lō-ya'ltkᵘt.   NLk·'ē   d'akᵘt   q'ôqL.
  Behold,   a sealion.   Then   he returned.   Then   he   cedar
                  large   twisted   twigs.

3 NLk·'ē   na-gapgā'bEt.   NLk·'ēt   q'am-tsagam-sîdä'Ext.   NLk·'ē   Lā
  Then   they fastened it. Then   only from sea   Then   when
                                              to land he fastened
                                              it.

4 pta'lîk·s,   nLk·'ē   tsE   tsagam-o'lîk·skᵘt.   NLk·'ē   Lā   Lô'ôL   ak·s,
  the water   then   from   it drifted.   Then   when   went out   water,
  rose,   sea   the
                              to land

5 nLk·'ē   g·înā-sg·î't.   NLk·'ēt   ba'Ldetg·ê.   Wī-hē'lL   Lē   hîx·t
  then   left it lay.   Then they   spread it.   Much   the fat
              behind

6 qanL   Lē   smax·t,   aL   hwîl   wī-t'ē'sL   t'ē'bEn.   Hwä'i!   Lā   huX
  and   the meat,   because a large   sealion.   Well!   (Perf.)   again

7 wī-hē'lL   saL   hwî'ldetg·ê.   NLk·'ē   La   sEm-wī-hē'lL   dzā'pdetg·ê.
  many   days   they did so.   Then   very   much   they made.

8 K·'ē   La   daXL   t'an   sakᵘsta'qsdetg·ê.   Txanē'tkᵘL   qal-ts'a'ps
  Then   they   died   who   had left him.   All the   people of

9 nEguâ'ôdEt.   NLk·'ē   Lā   huX   ā'd'îk·skᵘL   hē'Luk.   NLk·'ē   huX
  his father.   Then   again   came   morning.   Then   again

10 k·saxt.   Gwinā'deL,   xsk·āk·   sEm-k·'a-wī-hē'lt.   Nî'g·î   huX   q'am-
   he went   Behold,   eagles   really very many.   Not   again   only
   out.

11 aLebō't.   Lîk·s-g·a'tL,   qabē'L   xsk·āk·,   lax-a'k·s   hwîl   hwî'ldet.
   few.   A great number,   that many   eagles,   on water   they were.

12 Nda   aL   k·'ē   wī-Lpe'n   tsagam-dē-g·ēba'ɣukdetg·ê.   NLk·'ē
   And it was then   a whale   from sea with   they flew.   Then
                           great   to land it

13 g·înā'-sg·ît   k·'ē'lp'ELl   axkᵘ.   NLk·'ē   huX   k·'ē'lp'ELl   sa.   NLk·'ē
   left it lay   two   nights.   Then   again   two   days.   Then
   behind

14 g·ina'-sg·îL   wī-Lpe'n.   NLk·'ēt   q'ô'tsdetg·ê.   (T   hwîlā'guL   waLEn-
   left lay   a whale.   Then   they cut it.   (That what   the
   behind   great   they did   former

whales with stone axes in the same way that we chop wood.) Then
they chopped the blubber of the whale. Then the blubber came out
where they hit it with the ax. Hohoho! They had a great deal,
because the whale was very large. The eagles gave the prince and
the little grandmother and the slave four whales.

Now the people of his father, who had left him, were dying. The
eagles had finished giving food to the prince, and his houses were all
full. The grease covered the sea in front of his house. Then the
prince shot a gull. He skinned it and put on its skin. He took a
piece of seal, not a large piece, and flew away. He went up above to
see his father's tribe who had left him. He flew a long time, and,

---

g·ig·a't	Lpen.	Lô'ôbɛm	dawī'sʟ·	hâ'x·det	at	ia'tsdēʟ hîx·t,	1
people	the whale.	Stone	axes	they used		to chop the fat,	

bō'g·îxdēiʟ	hwîl	t	ia'tsʟ	g·at lakᵘ.	NɛLnē't	hwîla'kᵘdētg·ê.)	2
like	does		ehop	a man firewood.	That is what	they did to it.)	

Hwîl	k·'ē't ia'tsdet.	Nʟk·'ē	k·si-ba'xʟ	t'ēlx·	aʟ hwîl iä'ʟ	3
Then	they chopped it.	Then	out ran	grease	at where went	

dawī's t	ha-yā'tsdētg·ê.	NʟLk·'ē	ā'd'îk·skᵘʟ	t'ēlx·.	Hōhōhō! Sɛmgal	4
the ax	they used for chopping.	Then	came	grease.	Hōhōhō! Very	

wī-t'ē'sʟ	dza'pdētg·ê,	aʟ hwîl	q'ap-wī-t'ē'sʟ Lpe'ng·ê.	NɛLne'ʟ	5
much	they made,	because	very large was the whale.	Therefore	

qan	sɛm-ts'aXʟ	dza'pdētg·ê.	Hwä'i!	Txalpxʟ Lpe'ng·ê	g·înā'mʟ	6
very	plenty	they made.	Well!	Four whales	gave	

xsk·āk·	aʟ Lgo-wî'lk·sîʟkᵘ	qanʟ	Lgo-ntsē'êtst	qanʟ	xa'ɛ.	7
the eagles	to the little prince	and	his little grandmother	and	the slave.	

NʟLk·'ē	La	ā'd'îk·skᵘʟ	dɛm	hwîl	daXʟ	qal-ts'a'ps	8
Then	(perf.)	came	(fut.)	being	dying	the people of	

nɛguâ'ôdet	Lɛ t'an	ts'ɛns-lu'kdētg·ê.	Hwä'i!	Lā qâ'ôdɛʟ	g·înt	9
his father	who	left him moving.	Well!	When it was finished	giving food	

xsk·āk·	Lgo-wî'lk·sîʟkᵘ.	Nîg·î	huX	hwîlt	La qâ'ôdɛt.	10
the eagles	the little prince.	Not	again	they did so	when it was finished.	

Q'ap	Lā	metkᵘʟ	qal-ts'a'p.	NʟLk·'ē	lē-La'pʟ t'ēlx·	aʟ	11
Really	(perf.)	was full	the town.	Then	on was thick grease	at	

lax-a'k·s.	NʟLk·'ēt	guxʟ	Lgō-wî'lk·sîʟkᵘʟ	qē'wun.	NʟLk·'ēt	12
on water.	Then	shot	the little prince	a gull.	Then he	

tsa'adɛt.	NʟLk·'ēt	lō-Lô'ôtkᵘt.	NʟLk·'ē	dôqʟ ēlx	nîg·i t'êst'ē'st.	13
skinned it.	Then he	put it on.	Then	he took seal	not large.	

NʟLk·'ē	hwîl k·'ē	g·eba'yukʟ	Lgō-wî'lk·sîʟkᵘ.	NʟLk·'ē	dā'uʟt;	14
At once		flew	the little prince.	Then	he left,	

lax-â'ʟ	yôxkᵘt	dɛm	g·a'aʟ	Lē ts'aps	nɛguâ'ôdɛt	La t'an	15
above	he followed	(fut.)	to see	the tribe of	his father	(perf.) who	

behold, he saw a canoe coming. The gull flew over the canoe, in which there were a number of men. Then the gull dropped the slice of seal into the canoe, and one of the hunters took it. It was very strange that a gull should drop a piece of dried seal into the canoe. They returned and landed. Then they told what had happened. The chief said to the man and to the slaves, "Go and look for my son." They left after he had told them. In the morning the man and some slaves started in a canoe. They paddled, and arrived at a point of land in front of the old village. Behold, the water ahead of them was covered with grease. It came from the place where they had left the prince. The man and the slaves paddled on. They went ashore at the place where the prince was staying. Behold, they had done a great deal. The houses were full of salmon and spring salmon

1 ts'ɛns-lu'kt. ʟa nakut hwîl g·eba'yukt, gwinā'dɛʟ, malʟ
   leaving had When long (verbal he flew, behold, a
   him moved.   noun)   canoe

2 ā'd'îk·skut. Nʟk·'ē sɛm-lē-g·ibā'yukʟ qē'wun lax-ō'ʟ māl hwîl
   came. Then very over flew the gull on top the where
                          of canoe

3 lō-hwa'nʟ g·at. Nʟk·'ēt ksa-galē'ʟ dâ'sgum ēlx aʟ lax-ō'ʟ
   in were men. Then he dropped a slice of seal on on top
                              of

4 māl. Nʟk·'ēt gō'uʟ gwîx·-wô'ôtg·ê. Nʟk·'ē sɛm-lîk·s-g·a't'ɛnt
   canoe. Then he took it a hunter. Then very strange

5 hwîl gwa'lgwa ēlxʟ galē'deʟ qē'wun aʟ ts'ɛm-māl. Nʟk·'ē lō-
   being dry seal dropped the gull at in the Then
                          canoe.

6 ya'ltkudetg·ê. Nʟk·'ē k·'a'tskudeitg·ê. Nʟk·'ēt ma'ʟdēt. Nʟ qan
   they returned. Then they landed. Then he told. Therefore

7 hēʟ sɛm'â'g·ît aʟ g·at qanʟ ʟîʟî'ng·it: "Adô', sɛm-g·a'aʟ
   said the chief to a and the slaves: "Adô', look for
             man

8 ʟgō'uʟguēg·ê!" Alē sakusta'qsdɛt an-hē'tg·ê, nʟk··ē hē'ʟuk.
   my son!" When they had left what he said, then it was
                            morning.

9 Nʟk·'ē sī-g·â'ôtkuʟ g·at qanʟ ʟîʟî'ng·it nʟnēʟ dɛdā'dēt. Nʟk·'ē
   Then started in a the and the slaves those with him in Then
        canoe man   the canoe.

10 hwā'x·dētg·ê. Nʟk·'ēt hwa'dēl hwîl uks-hē'tkuʟ ts'ɛwî'nqʟ.
   they paddled. Then they where from stood a point of
                reached   land to sea land.

11 Gwinā'dɛʟ, t'ɛlx· ā'd'îk·skut aʟ qâ'qdet aʟ lax-a'k·s. Hwä'i! T
   Behold, grease came at their on on water. Well! It
                  front   the

12 wîtkuʟ t'ɛlx· aʟ qa-g·ä'u hwîl ʟgo-wî'lk·sîʟku Nʟk·'ē hwāx·ʟ
   came grease at in front of the prince. Then paddled
   from   the house of little

13 g·a'tg·ê qanʟ ʟîʟî'ng·it. Nʟk·'ē lō-ba'xdet hwîl dzôqʟ ʟgō-
   the man and the slaves. Then in they ran where stayed the
                           little

14 wî'lk·sîʟku. Gwinā'deʟ, wî-t'ê'sʟ hwîl hwî'ldet. Metkuʟ qal-ts'a'p
   prince. Behold, large what they had Full was the town
                  done.

and halibut and seals and porpoises and sealions and whales. Then
they were much astonished. The slaves stretched out their hands
and dipped up the grease from the surface of the water. Then they
ate it.

The prince did not tell them to land, but after a while they landed.
Then they ate salmon, and they ate spring salmon and halibut and
seal and porpoise and whale. Now the prince said, "Don't take
anything home." Thus he spoke to the man and to the slaves.
"Eat as much as you want, and then leave. Don't tell at home what
you have seen." But one slave hid two pieces under his skin shirt.
He dropped two pieces of seal in there because he thought of his
child. The prince did not give the man and the slaves food. Then

aʟ	hân	qanʟ	ya'ᴇ	qanʟ	txox·	qanʟ	ēlx	qanʟ	dzīX	qanʟ		1
of	salmon	and	spring salmon	and	halibut	and	seal	and	por-poise	and		

t'ē'bᴇn	qanʟ	ʟpen.	Nʟk·'ēt	sᴇm-lō-sanā'ʟkᵘdetg·ê.	Nʟk·'ē	tgōn	2
sealion	and	whale.	Then	very they were astonished.	Then	this	

hwîlʟ	ʟîʟî'ng·it:	t'uks-ʟô'ôdᴇʟ	qa-an'ôndēt,	at	g·a'pdēʟ	t'ēlx·	3
did	the slaves:	out they stretched	their hands,	they	dipped up	the grease	

aʟ	lax-a'k·s.	Nʟk·'ēt	g·ē'îpdet.	4
on	on the water.	Then	they ate it.	

Nʟk·'ē	nî'g·i	hēʟ	ʟgō-wî'lk·sîʟkᵘʟ	dᴇm	k·'a'tskᵘdētg·ê.	Nʟk·'ē	5
Then	not	said	the prince little	(fut.)	they land.	Then	

ʟa	sī-gō'n,	nʟk·'ē	k·'a'tskᵘdet.	Nʟk·'ē	x-hâ'ndētg·ê.	Nʟk·'ē	6
afterward,		then	they landed.	Then	they ate salmon.	Then	

txanē'tkᵘʟ	x-hâ'ndet,	hân	qanʟ	txox·	qanʟ	ēlx	qanʟ	dzīX	7
all	they ate salmon,	salmon	and	halibut	and	seal	and	por-poise	

qanʟ	ʟpen	g·ē'îpdet.	Nʟk·'ē	tgōn	hēʟ	ʟgō-wî'lk·sîʟkᵘ:	8
and	whale	they ate.	Then	this	said	the prince: little	

"G·îlô'	tsᴇ	sô'ôsᴇm,	ana'!"	Dē'ya	aʟ	g·a'tg·ê	qanʟ	ʟîʟî'ng·it.	9
"Don't	take the rest out,		heh!"	Thus he said	to	the man	and	the slaves.	

"Dᴇm	q'am-lîtsē'ᴇx·t	nē'sᴇm,	dᴇm	k·'ē	dā'uʟsᴇm!	G·îlô'	10
"(Fut.)	only satiated	you,	(fut.)	then	leave!	Do not	

mᴇ	dzᴇ	sᴇm	ma'ʟᴇl	atsᴇda	ʟā	k·'a'tsksᴇm."	G·ē'lp'ᴇlʟ	dâsk	11
	you		tell	when	(perf.)	you land."	Two	slices	

tgōnʟ	hwîlʟ	xa'ᴇg·ê	lō-d'ᴇp-nô'ôʟ	k·s-lawusgum	txa't.	Nʟnēt	12
this	did	a slave	in down-ward hole	the shirt of	skin.	That is	

hwîl	lō-d'ᴇp-galē'ʟ	g·ē'lp'ᴇlʟ	dâ'sgum	ē'lîx.	At	am-qâ'ôʟ	13
where	in down he dropped	two	slices of	seal.	He	remembered	

ʟgō'uʟkᵘt.	Nʟk·'ē	nî'g·î	t	g·ᴈnʟ	ʟgō-wî'lk·sîʟkᵘ	g·a'tg·ê	qanʟ	14
his child.	Then	not	he	gave food	the prince little	to the man	and	

he sent them back. Then they reached the town from which they had started.

The prince had said to them, "Tell them that I am dead, and do not say that I have plenty to eat." The man and the slaves landed a little before dark. They went up to the houses and entered the chief's house. The chief asked, "Is my son still alive?" And the man replied, "I think he has been dead for a long time." The slaves and their families were living in one corner of the chief's house. Now they lay down. Then the slave took out a slice of seal meat and gave it to his wife, and he gave another one to his young child. The child ate it, but it did not chew it, and swallowed it at one gulp. The piece of seal choked the child. It almost died, because the seal meat was choking

---

1 Lîlî′ng·it.   NLk·′ēt uks-hē′tst.   NLk·′ē Lā k·′a′tsk^udēit aL qal-
  the slaves.   Then he from sent   Then (perf.) they landed at
               land to sea them.

2 ts'a′p Lē hwîl wî′tk^udētg·ê·
  the where they had come
  town from.

3 TgōnL hēL Lgō-wî′lk·sîLk^ug·ê: "TsE mā′LdEsEm tsE La nô′ôē.
  This said the prince: "Tell you that I am
       little   dead.

4 NLk·′ē g·elô mE dzE sEm ma′LEL dzēdzaX tsE hwî′lēE." Hwäi!
  Don't you tell plenty I do." Well!

5 G·a′tg·ê qanL Lîlî′ng·it k·a′tsk^udēL Lā ts′ōsk·L dEm yu′ksa.
  The man and the slaves landed when a little (fut.) evening.

6 NLk·′ē bax-Lô′ôdet.   NLk·′ē la′mdzîxdet aL hwîlpL sEm′â′g·it.
  Then they went up.   Then they entered at the house the chief.
                                          of

7 NLk·′ēt g·ē′bExL sEm′â′g·ît: "NēL q'ai-dEdē′lsL Lgō′uLguēia?"
  Then asked the chief: "He still alive my son?"

8 NLk·′ē tgōnL hēL g·a′tg·ê: "La nak^uL da nô′ôt-maE." Amō′sL
  Then this said the man: "Long he is I think." The
                                 dead   corner of

9 hwîlpL sEm′â′g·ît hwîl dzôqL Lîlî′ng·it qanL nak·st qanL
  the house the chief where lived the slaves and his wife and
  of

10 Lgo-Lgō′uLk^ut.   NLk·′ē Lā lalā′Ldetg·ê.   NLk·′ēt gō′uL xa′E
  his child.   Then they lay down.   Then he took the
  little   slave

11 k·′ēlL dâ′sgum ē′lix.   NLk·′ēt g·înā′mt aL nak·st.   NLk·′ēt huX
  one slice of seal.   Then gave it to his wife.   Then again
                       he

12 g·înā′mL k·′ē′Elt aL Lgō′uLk^ut, Lgo-q'ai-ts'ets'ō′osk·L Lgo-tk·′ē′Lk^ug·ê.
  he gave one to his child, a still small was the child.
                          little

13 Hwä′i! G·ē′bEL Lgo-tk·′ē′Lk^uL ē′lix.   NLk·′ē nîg·ît qEnt, txä-
  Well! It ate it the child the seal.   Then not it chewed all
              little   it,

14 p′axLô′qgut.   NLk·′ē t'a′g·aqstg·ê.   NLk·′ē ā′d·îk·sk^uL dEm
  at one gulp it swal-   Then it was choking.   Then it came (fut.)
  lowed it.

15 hwîl nô′ôL Lgo-tk·′ē′Lk^u aL hwîl sqa-d′ā′L ē′lix aL
  where dead the child because across was the at
              little   the way   seal

it. The child's mother put her hand into its mouth, trying to pull out the piece of seal, but she could not reach it. Her hand was too short. Then she cried. Now the chief's wife rose and went to the crying woman. She asked her, "Why do you cry?" The slave's wife replied, "My child is choking. We do not know what is obstructing its breath." Then the chieftainess put her hand into the mouth of the child. Her fingers were long. Her hand reached down, and she felt the slice of seal. Then she took it out. Then she knew what it was. Behold, it was seal meat. Then she told the chief, and he asked, "Where did that come from?" He saw that it was boiled seal meat, therefore he asked. Then they told him that the old town was full of the meat of trout and salmon and spring salmon and halibut and seals

g·îme-yô'xk^{u}L   Lē   nāLqt.   Tgōn   hwîls   nôxL   Lgo-tk·'ē'Lk^u.   Lō-   1
through   went   the breath.   This   did   the mother of   the little   child.   In

d'Ep-Lô'ôdEL   an'ô'nt   aL   ts'Em-ā'qL   Lgo-tk·'ē'Lk^u.   NLk·'ē   lō-d'Ep-   2
down she stretched   her hand   to   in the mouth of   the little   child.   Then   in down

sqô'k·sk^{u}t.   DEldē'lpk^{u}L   an'ô'nL   hana'qg·ê.   NLk·'ē   wī-t'ē'sL   3
it was beyond reach.   Short were   the hands of   the woman.   Then   much

hwîl   sīg·a'tk^{u}dētg·ê.   NL   qan   g·in-hē'tk^{u}L   ṅak·sL   sEm'â'g·ît.   4
(verbal noun)   they cried.   Therefore   rose   the wife of   the chief.

NLk·'ē   iä'êt   aL   awa'aL   hwîl   hahä'Et.   NLk·'ē   a'lg·îxt: "Agō'L   5
Then   she went   to   the proximity of   where   they were crying.   Then   she said: "Why

qan   hahä'sEm?"   NLk·'ē   dē'lemExk^{u}L   ṅak·sL   xa'Eg·ê: "Nîg·î   6
do you cry?"   Then   answered   the wife of   the slave: "Not

dEp   hwîlā'x·t   sqa-d'ā't   aL   k·si-yô'xk^{u}L   nāLqL   Lgo-tk·'ē'Lk^u."   7
we   know   across is the way   at   out goes   the breath of   the little   child."

NLk·'ē   lō-d'Ep-Lô'ôdEL   sîg·idEmna'q   an'ô'nt   aL   ts'Em-ā'qL   8
Then   in down put   the chieftainess   her hand   at   in the mouth of

Lgo-tk·'ē'lk^u.   Nē'lEk   qa-tsēwê'nttg·ê.   NLk·'ē   lō-d'Ep-a'qLk^{u}L   9
the little child.   Long were   her fingers.   Then   in down reached

an'ô'nL   sîg·idEmna'q.   NLk·'ē   baqL   hwîl   sqa-d'ā'L   dâ'sgum   ēlx.   10
the hand of   the chieftainess.   Then   she felt   where   across was the way   a slice of   seal.

NLk·'ē   k·si-dô'qt.   NLk·'ē   k·si-daa'qLk^{u}t.   NLk·'ēt   hwîlā'x·t.   11
Then   out she took it.   Then   out she made it reach.   Then she   knew it.

Gwinā'dēl,   ēlx!   NLk·'ēt   ma'LEL   sîg·idEmna'q   aL   sEm'â'g·ît.   12
Behold,   seal!   Then   told   the chieftainess   to   the chief.

NLk·'ē   g·î'daxL   sEm'â'g·it   tsE   hwîl   wîtk^{u}t.   Hwîlā'yît   hwîl   13
Then   asked   the chief   where   it came from.   He knew it   being

a'nuksEm   ēlxt.   NiLne't   qan   g·îda'xt.   NLk·'ēt   ma'Ldētg·ê   Lā   14
done (cooked)   seal.   Therefore   he asked.   Then   they told him   (perf.)

metk^{u}L   qal-ts'a'p   aL   lāX   qanL   hân   qanL   ya'E   qanL   txox·   15
full was   the town   of   trout   and   salmon   and   spring salmon   and   halibut

and porpoises and sealions and whales; that there were four whales, and that the water was covered with grease. They said that the town was full of provisions. Then the chief and the chieftainess and all the princes' uncles could not sleep. One of his uncles had two daughters who were exceedingly pretty.

Early in the morning the chief said, "Order the people to return to the place where we left the prince." He did so on account of the information he had received. Then they arrived, and behold, they saw grease covering the water. Then one of the prince's uncles dressed up his two daughters. Then boards were put across the middle of the canoe, and the children were placed on them. He thought, "My nephew shall marry my daughters." Many canoes were approaching

---

1 qanʟ ēlx qanʟ dzīX qanʟ t'ē′bɛn qanʟ ʟpen, txalpxʟ ʟpen.
  and seal and porpoise and sealion and whale, four whales.

2 Nʟk‧′ē metkᵘʟ lax-a′k‧s aʟ t'ēlx‧. Nʟk‧′ē sɛm-k‧′a-wi-t'ē′sʟ
  Then full it was on the water of grease. Then really very much

3 hwîl metkᵘʟ qal-ts'a′pg‧ê. Nʟk‧′ē nî′g‧î wâqʟ sɛm'â′g‧it qanʟ
  (verbal noun) full the town. Then not slept the chief and

4 sîg‧idɛmna′q qanʟ txanē′tkᵘʟ qa-nɛbē′pkᵘʟ ʟgo-wî′lk‧sîʟkᵘg‧ê.
  the chieftainess and all the mother's brothers of the little prince.

5 K‧′âlʟ nɛbē′ptg‧ê bagadē′lʟ ʟg‧ît max-hāna′q, sɛm-k‧′a-lîk‧s-g‧a′t
  One his mother's brother had two children all women, very exceedingly

6 ama lē′mqsît.
  good pretty.

7   Nʟk‧′ē sɛm-hē′ʟuk, nʟk‧′ē a′lg‧îxʟ sɛm'â′g‧ît. At gun-lu′kʟ ts'ap
  Then very in morning, then said the chief. He ordered to move the town

8 aʟ dɛm lō-hēlya′ltkᵘt aʟ awa′aʟ ʟgō-wî′lk‧sîʟkᵘ, aʟ hwîl
  to (fut.) return to the proximity of the little prince, because

9 ʟāt naxna′ʟ, wî-t'ē′s hwî′ltg‧ê. Nʟk‧′ē daa′qʟkᵘdet ya′ltkᵘdēt
  (perf.) he heard, great he did so. Then they arrived they returned

10 aʟ awa′aʟ ʟgō-wîlk‧sîʟkᵘ. Nʟk‧′ē ʟa ad′â′d′îk‧sdēt, gwinā′dēʟ,
  to the proximity of the little prince. Then when they came, behold,

11 t'ē′lix‧ ʟā g‧a′adet aʟ lax-a′k‧s. Nʟk‧′ēt nō′t'ɛnʟ k‧′âlʟ nɛbē′pʟ
  grease (perf.) they saw it at on the water. Then dressed one uncle

12 ʟgō′uʟkᵘtg‧ê qanʟ huX k‧′âl, bagadē′ltg‧ê. Nʟk‧′ēt lē-sqa-
  his child and also one, two. Then on sideways

13 sg‧î′ʟ d′ū-gan aʟ lō-sē′lukʟ māl. Neʟ t hwîl lē-hwa′ndēʟ
  they put sitting sit-sticks at in the middle of the canoe. That where on they sit

14 ʟg‧î′tg‧ê. Tgōnʟ hēʟ qâ′ôtʟ nɛbē′pʟ ʟgo-wî′lk‧sîʟkᵘg‧ê:
  the children. This said the heart of the uncle of the little prince:

15 "Dɛm na′k‧sguʟ guslē′sᵉE ʟgō′nʟguᵉE qanʟ huX k‧′âlt."
  "(Fut.) marry my nephew my child and again one."

the land. Then the prince went out. He did not allow them to land.
He took one box out and opened it. He took a bow and arrows out
of it and shot at the canoes. He did not desire them to come, because
they had deserted him. Therefore he was very angry. But finally
the people landed and went up. They made little sheds, and he gave
food to his father and mother. He pitied them, therefore he did so.
When they were approaching the shore one woman stretched out
her hands to eat the grease that she saw on the water. Therefore the
prince, the chief's son, was ashamed. He did not marry her, but
he married only the younger one.

The people went ashore. Then the prince invited them into his

---

1 NʟK·'ē ad'ā'd'îk·sdeitg·ê wī-hē'lʟ māl. NʟK·'ē k·saXʟ
Then came many canoes. Then went out

2 ʟgo-wî'lk·sîʟkᵘ. Nî'g·it anâ'qʟ dɛm k·'ēsk·'a'tskdēt. NʟK·'ēt
the prince. Not he agreed (fut.) they land. Then he
little

3 k·si-gō'uʟ k·'ēlʟ xpē'is. NʟK·'ē k·si-gō'ut aʟ g·alq. NʟK·'ēt
out took one box. Then out he took to outside. Then he
it

4 q'ā'gat. NʟK·'ēt lō-gō'uʟ ha-Xda'kᵘ qanʟ hawî'l. NʟK·'ēt
opened it. Then he in took a bow and arrows. Then he

5 guXʟ txanē'tkᵘʟ mmāl. Nî'g·î hasa'qt aʟ dɛm ad'ā'd'îk·skᵘt
shot all the canoes. Not he wanted to (fut.) they come

6 aʟ t hwîl sīsākᵘsta'qsdeit nē'tg·ê. NêʟNē'ʟ qan wī-t'ē'sʟ hwîl
[because they had left behind him. Therefore he was much (verbal
noun)

7 lō-sī'êpkᵘʟ qâ'ôtt. NʟK·'ē k·'ēsk·'a'tskt wi-hē'ldɛm g·at. NʟK·'ē
in sick heart. Then landed many people. Then

8 bax-ʟô'ôdet. NʟK·'ē dzîpdzā'pdēʟ k'ōpɛ-hwî'lp haq'ô'ʟ. NʟK·'ē
up they went. Then they made little houses tents. Then

9 yukʟ t g·înʟ ʟgo-wî'lk·sîʟkᵘ nɛguâ'ôdɛt qans nôxt.
began he to give the prince his father and his
food little mother.

10 Q'äʟ-qâ'ôdɛt lât qan hwîlt. Tgōnʟ hwîlʟ k·'âlʟ hana'qg·ê. Q'ai
He took pity on there- he did This did one woman. First
them fore so.

11 tsɛ tsaganı-yu'kʟ māl aʟ lax-a'k·s, k·'ēt t'uks-ʟô'ôdɛʟ an'ô'nt
when from reached the at on the then she out put her hand
sea to land canoe water,

12 at g·ē'îpʟ t'elx· aʟ g·a'at aʟ lax-a'k·s. NɛʟNē'ʟ qan
she ate grease at seeing on on the Therefore
it water.

13 dzâqʟ ʟgo-wî'lk·sîʟkᵘ, ʟgō'uʟkᵘʟ sɛmı'â'g·it. NʟK·'ē nî'g·ît
was the prince, the child of the chief. Then not he
ashamed little

14 nak·skᵘt; q'am-k·'â'l ʟgo-ts'ɛwî'ng·it, nîʟne'ʟ na'k·sgutg·ê.
married her; only one the youngest, her he married.
little

15 NʟK·'ē ʟā tsagam-qâ'ôdɛʟ qal-ts'a'p, nʟk·'ēt wô'ôʟ
Then when from sea were gone the people, then he invited
to land them

house. The people went in and he gave them meat of trout and salmon and spring salmon and halibut and seals and porpoises and sealions and whales. He gave them to eat. Then his father's people were very glad, and the people gave the prince elk skins and all kinds of goods, canoes, and slaves.

Now the prince came to be a great chief. He had four houses full of elk skins, many slaves, and many canoes. He was a great chief. When his father died, he gave a potlatch. He invited all the people in, and gave away many elk skins and slaves, because his father had been a great chief. After he had given this potlatch his mother died. Then he gave another potlatch. Again he invited all the peo-

1 Lgo-wî′lk·sîʟkᵘ   Nʟk·′ē   ʟa   ts'ɛlɛm-qâ′dɛʟ   qal-ts'a′p,   nʟk·′ē
  the   prince.   Then   when   into   went   the people,   then
  little

2 txâ′g'ant.   ʟaXʟ   g·î′pdetg·ê   qanʟ   hân   qanʟ   ya′ɛ   qanʟ
  he made   Trout   they ate it   and   salmon   and   spring   and
  them eat.   salmon

3 txox·   qanʟ   ēlx   qanʟ   dzīX   qanʟ   t'ē′ben   qanʟ   ʟpen.   Nʟk·′ē
  halibut   and   seal   and   porpoise   and   sealion   and   whale.   Then

4 k·sax-g·inā′mʟ   ʟa   qa-ts'ō'ot.   Nʟk·′ē   sɛm-lō-am'ā′mʟ   qagô′ʟ
  out   he gave   some.   Then   very in   good   hearts

5 qal-ts'a′ps   nɛguâ′ôdɛt.   Nʟk·′ēt   g·ēkʟ   qal-ts'a′p   aʟ
  the people of   his father.   Then   hought   the people   of

6 Lgo-wî′lk·sîʟkᵘ   aʟ   ʟiâ′n   qanʟ   txanē′tkᵘʟ   lîg·î-hwî′l   qanʟ
  the   for   elk   and   all   goods   and
  prince
  little

7 mmāl   qanʟ   sîsō′sɛm   ʟîʟî′ng·it.
  canoes   and   little   slaves.

8 Nʟk·′ē   wī-t'ē′sʟ   hwîl   sɛm'â′g·iʟ   Lgo-wî′lk·sîʟkᵘ.   TxalpxʟL
  Then   he was great   being   a chief   the   prince.   Four
                                                      little

9 huwî′lp   hwîl   mɛtme′tkᵘʟ   ʟiâ′n.   Nʟk·′ē   sɛm-k·a-wi-hē′lʟ
  houses   being   full of   elk.   Then   very   many

10 ʟîʟî′ng·it   qanʟ   mmāl.   Nʟk·′ē   wī-t'ē′sʟ   hwîl   sɛm'â′g·it.
   slaves   and   canoes.   Then   he was great   being   a chief.

11 Nʟk·′ē   nô′ôs   nɛguâ′ôdɛt.   Nʟk·′ē   yukt,   wô′ôʟ   txanē′tkᵘʟ
   Then   died   his father.   Then   he gave a   he   all
                                                   potlatch,   invited

12 hwîl   dzɛxdzô′q.   Nʟk·′ē   wi-hē′lʟ   ʟiâ′n   g·înā′mt   qanʟ   ʟîʟî′ng·it
   the camps.   Then   a   many   elks   he gave   and   slaves
                             great

13 aʟ   hwîl   wi-t'ē′sʟ   sɛm'â′g·its   nɛguâ′ôdɛt.   Hwäi!   ʟā   ʟēskᵘʟ
   because   great was   a chief   his father.   Well!   When   he
                                                                                  finished

14 yu′ktg·ê,   nîʟ   k·′ē   huX   nô′ôs   nôxt.   Nʟk·′ē   ha′ts'ɛk·sɛm   huX
   the potlatch,   then   also   died   his   Then   again   once
                                        mother.   more

15 yukt.   Hux   txa-wô′ôdēʟ   hwîl   dzɛxdzô′q.   Nʟk·′ēt   huX
   he gave a   Again   all he invited   the camps.   Then he   again
   potlatch.

ple, and gave them elk skins and slaves and canoes.   He became a great chief, because he fed the eagles, and the eagles had pitied him. Therefore he became a great chief.   His name was Little-eagle.

---

g·înā′mL	Liâ′n	qanL	Lîlî′ng·it	qanL	mmāl.	Hwäi!	Lā	wī-t’ē′sL	1
gave	elks	and	slaves	and	canoes.	Well!	(Perf.)	he was great	

hwîl	sɛm’â′g·it,	Lɛt	hwîl	g·ēnL	xsk·ā′k·g·ê.	NLk·’ēt	sîtyä′wuL	2
being	a chief,		because	he gave food to	the eagles.	Then	returned it	

xsk·āk·	Lē	qäêm-qâ′ôdɛt.	NLnēL	qan	wi-t’ē′sL	sɛm’â′g·it.	3
the eagles	the	pity.		Therefore	he was a great	chief.	

Lgwa-xskī′yêkL	hwa′tg·ê.	4
Little- eagle	was his name.	

SHE-WHO-HAS-A-LABRET-ON-ONE-SIDE

[Told by Moses]

There was a town. There was a chief and a chieftainess. They had a son. He was almost grown up. He had four friends, who were always near him. They were playing all the time. Once upon a time one of them went out of the house. He saw a little slave girl coming along the street. She entered the last house of the town. There she sat down near the fire. Then the wife of the owner rose, took the back of a salmon, and gave it to the little slave girl, but she did not accept it. The little slave girl rose and left the house. She

---

K·'AL-HÄ'TGUM Q'Ē'SEMKᵘ

ON-ONE-SIDE-STANDING-LABRET

1 Hētkᵘʟ   qal-ts'a'p.   Nʟk·'ē   k·'âlʟ   sɛm'â'g·it,   nʟk·'ē   huX
  There stood   a town.   Then   one   chief,   then   also

2 k·'âlʟ   sîg·idɛmna'q.   Hwäi!   K·'âlʟ   Lgō'uʟkᵘt   tk·'ē'ʟgum   g·at.   ʟa
  one   chieftainess.   Well!   It was   his child   a boy.   When
                                      one

3 ts'ō'osk·ʟ   dɛm   wît'ē'st,   txalpxdâ'l   an-sɛpsī'ebɛnskᵘt.   Nʟk·'ē
  he was a little (fut.) large,   four   his friends.   Then

4 qa'ne-hwila   lō-hwa'ndet   aʟ   awa'aʟ   Lgō'uʟkᵘʟ   sɛm'â'g·it.
  always   in   they sat   at   the prox-   the son of   the chief.
                                        imity of

5 Txanē'tkᵘʟ   saʟ   hwî'ldet.   ʟa   nakᵘʟ   hwî'ldet   aʟ   qa'nē-hwîla
  Every   day   they did so. (Perf.)   long   they did so   and   always

6 qalā'qdet.   Nʟk·'ē   si-gō'n.   nʟk·'ē   k·saXʟ   k·'âlt.   Nʟk·'ēt   g·a'aʟ
  they played. Then   after a   then   went out   one.   Then   he saw
                          while

7 hwîl   sīsa'g·ap-yukʟ   Lgo-wa'tkᵘ.   Sɛm-qasqa'm   hētkᵘʟ   hwîlp   aʟ
  where   on the street   a   slave   Very last of row stood   a house at
           came   little girl.

8 q'apʟ   ts'ap.   Neʟ   hwîl   ts'ēnʟ   Lgo-wa'tkᵘ.   Nʟk·'ē   d·āt   aʟ
  the   the   That   where   entered   the   slave   Then   she sat at
  end of   town.   little girl.   down

9 q'apʟ   lakᵘ.   Nʟk·'ē   hētkᵘʟ   nak·sʟ   g·a'tg·ê.   Nʟk·'ēt
  the end   the fire. Then   stood   the wife   a man.   Then
  of   of

10 gōuʟ   ʟē   k·'ôɛʟ   hân.   Nʟk·'ēt   g·ēnʟ   Lgo-wa'tkᵘ.
   she   the   the back a   Then   she gave   the   slave girl.
   took   of   salmon,   to eat   little

11 Nʟk·'ē   nî'g·it   gō'ut.   Nʟk·'ē   hētkᵘt.   Nʟk·'ē   ha'ts'îk·sɛm
   Then   not   she took   Then   she   Then   once more
                        it.   stood.

12 huX   k·saXt.   Nʟk·'ō   huX   ts'ēnt   aʟ   huX   k·'ēlʟ   hwîlp.
   again   she went   Then   again   she   in   again   one   house.
           out.   entered

entered another house, and again sat down near the fire. The wife of the owner rose and gave her the backs of salmon to eat, but she did not accept them. She left the house. She did so in every house.

The friend of the chief's son who had gone out re-entered and said to the prince, "A little slave girl is coming along the street." Then his friends spoke: "Why don't you marry her when she comes in here?" When she came near the chief's house, they took a mat and spread it in the rear of the house. The prince sat down on it. Then the little slave girl entered. Her head was very large. She was not at all clean. One of the prince's friends said, "Sit down over here." Then the little slave girl walked to the rear of the house and sat down by the side of the prince. His friends started a large fire. Her hands,

---

NLk·'ē huX d'āt aL q'apL lakᵘ. NLk·'ē huX hētkᵘL nak·sL   1
Then again she sat at the end the Then again stood the wife
              down of fire.   of

g·at. NLk·'ēt huX g·ēnt aL k·'ôE. NLk·'ē nî'g·it g·ē'îpt.   2
the Then again she gave of back. Then not she ate it.
man.   her to eat

NLk·'ē ha'ts'îk·sEm k·saXt. Txanē'tkᵘL huwî'lp hwîl hwî'lt.   3
Then once more she went All houses she did so.
             out.

    NLk·'ē k·saXL k·'âlL g·at, an-siEp'ē'nskᵘL Lgō'uLkᵘL   4
    Then he went out one man, a friend of the son of

sEm'â'g·it. NLk·'ē ha'ts'îk·sEm huX ts'ēnt. NLk·'ē a'lg·îxt   5
the chief. Then once more again he entered. Then he spoke

aL Lgo-wî'lk·sîLkᵘ: "Sîsîsag'ap-yukL Lgo-wa'tkᵘ." NLk·'ē   6
to the prince: "On the street is a slave girl." Then
    little   coming little

al'a'lg·îxL an-sEpsī'ep'Enskᵘ Lgo-wî'lk·sîLkᵘ. TgōnL hē'det: 7
spoke the friends of the prince. This they said:
                 little

"Ha'o! Ām mE dEm na'k·sg·ê, atse La dē-ts'ē'nt." NLk·'ēt   8
"Ah! Good you (fut.) marry her, when (perf.) also she enters." Then

gō'udeL sqa'naa. K·'ēt ba'Ldet aL q'alā'n. NLk·'ē lē-d'ā'L Lgo-   9
they took a mat. Then they spread at rear of Then on sat the
                  it house.   little

wî'lk·sîLkᵘ lâ'Et. NLk·'ē ā'd'îk·skᵘL Lgo-wa'tkᵘ. NLk·'ē ts'ēnt. 10
prince on it. Then came the slave girl. Then she
                       little   entered

Qa-la'îL Lgo-t'Em-q'ē'st; nî'g·i sak·skᵘt. NLk·'ē a'lg·îxL k·'âlL 11
As large her head; not clean. Then spoke one
as that little

an-sī'Ep'EnskᵘL Lgo-wî'lk·sîLkᵘ: "Hwagait-g·ē'ê dEm hwîl d'ān." 12
friend of the little prince: "Over there is (fut.) where you sit
                                         down."

NLk·'ē g·îmē-iä'L Lgo-wa'tkᵘ. NLk·'ē d'āt aL stô'ôk·sL Lgo- 13
Then to rear went the slave Then she sat at the side of the
     of house little girl.   down   little

wî'lk·sîLkᵘ. NLk·'ē yukt sE-me'Lt an-sîpsī'ep'Enskᵘt lakᵘ. NLk·'ē 14
prince. Then began to burn the friends fire. Then
               to make

wī-me'LL lakᵘ Txanē'tkᵘL an'o'nt qanL qasîsa'it qanL LîpLa'nt 15
much burnt the All her hands and her feet and her body
       fire.

her feet, and her whole body were covered with scabs. The prince's
friends saw it. Then the chieftainess rose. She took some dry
salmon, roasted it at the fire, and when it was done she broke it to
pieces and put it into a dish, which she placed before the boy and the
little slave girl. Then they ate. When the dish was empty, one of
the friends stepped up to them, intending to take the dish. Then the
little slave girl took one large scab from her body and put it into the
dish. She said, "Place it in front of the chief." One of the men
did so. The great chief looked at it. Behold, it was a large abalone
shell. Then the chief was very glad.

The chieftainess took another dish, and she put into it crab apples
mixed with grease. Another man placed it in front of the prince and

---

1   hwîl   tq'al-hwa′nʟ   ama′lkᵘ   at   g·ā′aʟ   an-sᴇpsī′ep'ᴇnskᵘʟ
   where   against   were   scabs   they   saw it   the friends of

2   ʟgo-wî′lk·sîʟkᵘ.   Nʟk·′ē   bētkᵘʟ   sîg·idᴇmna′q.   Nʟk·′ēt   gōuʟ
   the   prince.   Then   stood   the chieftainess.   Then she   took
   little

3   gwa′lgwa   hân.   Nʟk·′ēt   meʟt   aʟ   lax-ts′ä′ʟ   lakᵘ.   Nʟk·′ē   a′nukst.
   dry   salmon.   Then she   roasted   at   on edge of   fire.   Then   it was done
                         it

4   Nʟk·′ēt   xtsē′ᴇlt.   Nʟk·′ēt   lō-dô′xt   aʟ   ts'ᴇm-ts'a′k·.   Nʟk·′ē
   Then   she broke it   Then   in she put   at   in   dish.   Then
        to pieces.   it

5   sg·it   aʟ   qa-sä′Xʟ   ʟgō′uʟkᵘt   qanʟ   ʟgo-wa′tkᵘ.   Nʟk·′ē
   she laid   at   front of   her son   and   the   slave girl.   Then
   it   little

6   txâ′xkᵘdetg·ê.   Nʟk·′ēt   lō-dza′ʟdeʟ   ts'ak·.   Nʟk·′ē   hagun-iä′ʟ
   they ate.   Then   in they ate all   dish.   Then   toward went

7   k·′âlʟ   an-sī′ep'ᴇnskᵘt   dᴇm   t'an   gō′uʟ   ts'ak·.   Nʟk·′ēt
   one   his friend   (fut.)   who   took   a dish.   Then

8   g·îdi-gō′uʟ   ʟgo-wa′tkᵘ.   Nʟk·′ē   sä-gō′udᴇl   k·′ᴇlʟ   wī-ama′lkᵘ.
   right   she took   the   slave girl.   Then   off   she took   one   big   scab.
   there   it   little

9   Tgōn   hwîl   tq'al-d′ā′t.   Nʟk·′ēt   lō-sg·i′t   aʟ   ts'ᴇm-ts'a′k·.   Nʟk·′ē
   This   where   against it was.   Then   in she laid   at   in   the dish.   Then
                             it

10   a′lg·îxʟ   ʟgo-wa′tkᵘ: "Qa-sä′Xʟ   sᴇm'â′g·it   mᴇ   hwîl   sg·it."   Nʟk·′ē
   said   the   slave girl: "In front of   the chief   you   where   lay it."   Then
        little

11   hwîlʟ   k·′âlʟ   g·at.   Nʟk·′ēt   g·a′aʟ   wī-sᴇm'â′g·it.   Gwinā′dᴇʟ,
   did so   one   person.   Then   saw it   the   chief.   Behold,
                                 great

12   wī-bᴇlā′.   Nʟk·′ē   sᴇm-lō-ā′mʟ   qâ′ôʟ   sᴇm'â′g·it.
   a   haliotis   Then   very   in   good   heart   the chief.
   great shell.

13   Nʟk·′ēt   huX   gō′uʟ   sîg·idᴇmna′q   ts'ak·.   Nʟk·′ēt   lō-g·a′nʟ
   Then   again   took   the chieftainess   a dish.   Then   in she put

14   ʟa′ix   lâ′ôt.   Nʟk·′ēt   huX   sg·iʟ   k·′âlʟ   g·at   aʟ   qa-sä′Xʟ
   crab apple   in it.   Then   again   laid it   one   person   at   front of
   and grease

the little slave girl. (In olden times the people used to call this "slave wife.") When they had eaten, she took off another scab, and, behold, there was a large abalone shell. That is what was on her body. She placed it in the dish, and then she said, "Place it before the chieftainess." A man did so. Then the chief and the chieftainess and the prince were very glad when they knew that she was not a slave, as the prince's friend had said.

Now they finished eating. In the evening a woman came to the house and pushed aside the door. She stood in the doorway and said, "Did not She-who-has-a-labret-on-one-side enter this house?" One of the prince's friends said, "Come in, come in! She has married the chief's son." The woman replied, "Indeed, my dear, then take good

---

Lgo-wî'lk·sîLkᵘ	qanʟ	Lgo-wa'tkᵘ.	(Nʟ	su-hwa'tEʟ	waʟEn-g·ig·a't	1
the little prince	and	the little slave girl.	(That	made	name	the former people	

aʟ	na'k·sEm	watkᵘ.)	Nʟk·'ē	huXt	lō-dza'ʟdēʟ	ts'ak·	qanʟ	2
at	wife	slave.)	Then	again	in they ate all	the dish	and	

Lgo-wî'lk·sîʟkᵘ.	Nʟk·'ēt	huX	sā-gō'udEʟ	k·'ēlʟ	wî-bElā'.	3
the little prince.	Then	also	off she put	one	great haliotis shell.	

Nʟne'ʟ	tq'al-hwa'nt	aʟ	ʟEpʟa'nt.	Nʟk·'ēt	huX	lō-sg·i't	aʟ	4
That	against were	on	her body.	Then	again	in she laid it	in	

ts'Em-ts'a'k·.	Nʟk·'ē	tgōn	hēʟ	Lgo-wa'tkᵘ:	"Qa-sä'Xʟ	5
in dish.	Then	this	said	the little slave girl:	"Front of	

sîg·idEmna'q	neʟne'	mE	hwîl	sg·it."	Nʟk·'ē	hwîʟʟ	k·'âlʟ	6
the chieftainess	there	you	where	lay it."	Then	did so	one	

g·a'tg·ê.	Nʟk·'ē	sEm-lō-ā'mʟ	qâ'ôʟ	sEm'â'g·it	qanʟ	sîg·idEmna'q	7
person.	Then	very in good	heart	the chief	and	the chieftainess	

qanʟ	Lgo-wî'lk·sîʟkᵘ	ʟa	nîg·it	hwîlā'x·det	nî'g·idi	wa'tkᵘʟ	8
and	the little prince	when	not	they knew	not	a slave girl	

sgōst	dē-hē'de	an-sîpsī'ep'Enskᵘʟ	Lgo-wî'lk·sîʟkᵘ.	9
that on their part	said	the friends of	the little prince.	

Nʟk·'ē	ʟa	qâ'ôdeʟ	txâ'xkᵘdetg·ê;	nʟk·'ē	ʟa	yu'ksa,	nʟk·'ē	10
Then	when	it was finished	they ate;	then	when	it was evening,	then	

ā'd'îk·skᵘʟ	hana'q	aʟ	g·a'lEq.	Nî'g·i	ts'ent,	q'am-k·'āʟ-Lô'ôdEʟ	11
came	a woman	to	outside.	Not	she entered,	only aside she pushed	

ā'dz'Ep.	Nʟk·'ē	ts'ElEm-hē'tkᵘt.	Nʟk·'ē	a'lg·îxt:	"Nē'êʟ	ts'ēns	12
the door.	Then	into she stood.	Then	she spoke:	"Not	entered	

K·'āʟ-hä'tgum	q'ē'sEmq	aʟ	ts'Em-hwîlbā'?"	Nʟk·'ē	a'lg·îxʟ	13
On-one-side-	standing-	labret	at	in house?"	Then	spoke	

k·'âlʟ	an-sī'ep'Enskᵘʟ	Lgo-wî'lk·sîʟkᵘ:	"Ts'ēn	sE!	Ts'ēn	sE!	14
one	friend of	the little prince:	"Come in!		Come in!		

Nak·skᵘʟ	Lgō'uʟkᵘʟ	sEm'â'g·it."	"Â,	net,	anxa'E;	tse	15
She married	the son of	the chief."	"Oh,	yes,	my dear;		

care of her." Thus said the woman who was standing in the doorway. She continued, "My people will come to visit the chief's son to give food to him. They will bring much food—boxes of grease, boxes of crab apples mixed with grease, boxes of cranberries, soapberries, and dried meat, and much fat."

It grew dark. Early the next morning there was a fog on the river. Then many canoes that were full of boxes approached. One canoe was full of boxes of crab apples, one was full of berries, another one full of soapberries, another one full of meat, still another one full of fat, and two canoes were full of elk skins, marten skins, and copper plates. They put them into the house of the chief,

---

1 k'ṓpɛ-ama-g·a'adɛsɛm." Nʟk·'ē a'lg·îxʟ hana'q tsʽɛlɛm-hē'tkⁿtg·ê.
   a little well look out for her." Then said the into she stood.
                                            woman

2 Tgōnʟ hē'tg·ê: "Dɛm ā'd'îk·skⁿʟ ʟē ts'ā'bē, dɛm t'an
   This she said: "(Fut.) come my (fut.) who
                                   people,

3 g·ēnʟ ʟgō'uʟkⁿʟ sɛm'â'g·it aʟ wī-hē'ldɛm wunē'x·; ande-t'ē'lx·
   give the son of the chief at much food; box of grease
   food

4 qanʟ ande-ʟa'îx qanʟ ande-t'emē'et qanʟ hwîl lō-dô'xʟ
   and box crab apple and box (a red and where in are
        of and grease; of berry)

5 ma'ɛ qanʟ hwîl lō-dô'xʟ îs qanʟ gwa'lgwa smax·. Nʟk·'ē
   berries and where in are soap- and dry meat. Then
                              berries

6 sɛm-wī-hē'lʟ hîx·."
   very much fat."

7 Nʟk·'ē yu'ksa, nʟk·'ē sɛm-hē'ʟuk. Nʟk·'ē sg·iʟ iē'n.
   Then evening, then very morning. Then there was fog.

8 Nʟk·'ē ā'd'îk·skⁿʟ wī-hē'ldɛl mmāl. Metkⁿʟ q'amä'êdɛl
   Then came many canoes. It was full one canoe

9 māl aʟ heē'nɛq. Nʟk·'ē huX q'amä'êdɛl māl; metkⁿt
   canoe of boxes. Then again one canoe canoe; it was full

10 aʟ ande-ʟa'îx. Nʟk·'ē huX q'amä'êdɛl māl; metkⁿt aʟ
    of box crab apples Then again one canoe canoe; it was full of
       of and grease.

11 hwîl lō-dô'xʟ ma'ɛ. HuX hwîlʟ huX k·'ēlʟ māl. HuX
    where in were berries. Also was so more one canoe. Also

12 metkⁿt aʟ hwîl lō-dô'xʟ îs. Nʟk·'ē huX hwîlʟ huX
    it was full of where in were soap- Then also was so more
                              berries.

13 k·'ēlʟ, metkⁿt aʟ smax· Nʟk·'ē huX metkⁿʟ huX k·'ēlt
    one, it was full of meat. Then also full also one

14 aʟ hîx·. Nʟk·'ē qalbä'êlkⁿsʟ mmāl hwîl mîtme'tkⁿʟ ʟiâ'n
    of fat. Then two canoes canoes where full elks

15 qanʟ txanē'tkⁿʟ hat' qanʟ haya'tskⁿ. Nʟk·'ē metkⁿʟ hwîlpʟ
    and all marten and copper. Then was full the house
                                                              of

which was entirely filled by the goods.   Then the chief and the chieftainess were very glad.

Now the prince was a great chief.   The name of She-who-has-a-
labret-on-one-side's mother was Evening Sky.   She was a supernatural being.   Nobody could see her.   Her people lived far away
from all other people on the other side.   They were not Indians;
therefore, they had much wealth and much food.   Now the prince
invited the people in.   Then they came, and his father's house was
filled with them.   Crab apples and grease were given them to eat, and
various berries and meat and fat.   When they finished eating, they
brought out soapberries.   After the feast, on the next day, the people were again invited in.   Then the prince put into the middle of the

---

sɛm'â'g·it	aL	ʟa	ts'ɛlɛm-d'ā'ʟdet.	Nʟk·'ē	sɛm-lō-ā'mʟ	qâ'ôtʟ	1
the chief	at		into	they put it.	Then	very in good	heart
sɛm'â'g·it	qanʟ	sîg·idɛmna'q.					2
the chief	and	the chieftainess.					
Nʟk·'ē	ʟa	wī-t'ē'sʟ	hwîl	sɛm'â'g·itʟ	ʟgo-wî'lk·sîʟk^u.		3
Then	(perf.)	great	being	chief	the prince.		
					little		
HuXdza'n	hwaʟ	nôxs	K·'aʟ-hä'tgum	q'ē'sɛmq.	Naxnô'qg·ê;		4
Evening sky	was the	the	On-one- standing-	labret.	She was a super-		
	name of	mother of	side-		natural being;		
nîg·idet	g·a'aʟ	g·at.	Qal-dâ'ʟ	dē-ts'a'pt;	nî'g·idi	alō-g·ig·a't;	5
not	sees her	a person.	Alone on	on their her	not	real men;	
			other side	part people;		(Indians)	
neʟ	qan	wī-hē'ldɛʟ	lîg·i-hwî'ltg·ê	qanʟ	wī-hē'ldɛʟ	wunē'x·.	6
therefore		many	her goods	and	much	food.	
Nʟk·'ēt	wô'ôʟ	ʟgo-wî'lk·sîʟk^u	hwîl	dzaxdzô'q.		Nʟk·'ē	7
Then	invited	the prince		the people.		Then	
		little					
ad'ā'd'îk·sk^ut.	Nʟk·'ē	metk^uʟ	hwîlps	nɛguā'ôdet	aʟ	wi-hē'ldɛm	8
they came.	Then	was full	the house	his father	of	many	
			of				
g·at.	Nʟk·'ēt	txâ'q'andetg·ê	ʟā'ixʟ	g·a'tk^utg·ê	qanʟ	ma'ɛ	9
people.	Then	they fed them	crab apples	their food in	and	berries	
			and grease	the feast			
ʟwa'ik·sk^utg·ê	qanʟ	smax·ʟ	g·a'tk^utg·ê	qanʟ	hîx·.	Nʟk·'ē	10
mixed	and	meat	their food in the	and	fat.	Then	
			feast				
ʟa	qâ'ôdɛʟ	ʟā'îx	qanʟ	ma'ɛ	qanʟ	smax· qanʟ hîx·, nʟk·'ē	11
when	they	crab apple	and	berries	and	meat and fat, then	
	finished	and grease					
dē-da-ā'd'îk·sk^uʟ	îs.	Nʟk·'ē	ʟa	qâ'ôdɛʟ	wunä'x·,	nʟk·'ē	12
also	they brought	soap-	Then	when	they finished	the food,	then
		berries.					
huX	ā'd'îk·sk^uʟ	mɛsā'x·	Nʟk·'ēt	huX	wô'ôʟ	g·at.	Nʟk·'ē	13
again	came	daylight.	Then	again	he	the	Then
					invited	people.	
huX	ts'ɛlɛm-qâ'ôdɛʟ	g·at.	Nʟk·'ē	t'ɛm-d'ā'ʟʟ	Liâ'n	qanʟ	14
again	into	had gone	the	Then	to the he	elks	and
			people.		middle put		

house elk skins, copper plates, slaves, and canoes, which he was going to use in the potlatch. He distributed them among the people. After he had finished, the people went back and returned to their own towns. He did so for many days. He gave many potlatches. Then he came to be a great chief. Then he married again. He had two wives. (In former times they called this "one wife on each side.")

Then the prince started in his canoe to visit the town Chilkat.[1] The elks come from this place. The inlanders kill them. The prince intended to buy elk skins for copper plates and seal meat. Now he arrived at Chilkat. Then he bought elk skins, and he took another wife.

Now She-who-has-a-labret-on-one-side was left behind. The prince had a brother who was very awkward. The prince went to Chilkat

1	haya'tsk^u	qanL	LiLî'ng·it	am-yu'kt	qan	hwî̂lt	qanL	mmāl.
	copper	and	slaves	used in potlatch		therefore	and	canoes.

2	NLk·'ē	k·saX-g·inā'mt	aL	txanē'tk^uL		g·at.	NLk·'ē
	Then	out he gave them	to	all		the people.	Then

3	Lēsk^ut.	NLk·'ē	sak·sk^uL	hwî̂l-dzaxdzô'q.	Hē'lyaltk^u	aL
	he finished.	Then	left	the people.	They returned	to

4	lEp-qal-ts'î̂pts'a'pdetg·ê.	NLk·'ē	La	wī-hē'lL	saL	hwî̂'ldetg·ê.
	own their towns.	Then	(perf.)	many	days	they did so.

5	NLk·'ē	La	wī-hē'lL	yukL	Lgo-wî̂'lk·sîLk^u.	NLk·'ē	La	wī-t'ē'sL
	Then	(perf.)	many	potlatches made	the prince. little	Then	(perf.)	he was a great

6	sEm'â̂'g·it.	NLk·'ē	si-gō'n,	nLk·'ē	huX	nak·st.	La	bagadē'lL
	chief.	Then	after a while,	then	again	he married.	(Perf.)	two

7	nak·st.	NL	su-hwa'dEL	g·ī-k'ō'L	aL	lāx-hwa'nEmLk^u.
	his wives.	That	made name	long ago	of	on each side sitting.

8	NLk·'ē	sī-g·â̂'tk^uL	Lgo-wî̂'lk·sîLk^u	at	qâ'ôL	k·'ēlL	qal-ts'a'p.
	Then	started by canoe	the prince little	to	go to	one	town.

9	Tsî̂Lqā't	hwaL	qal-ts'a'pg·ê.	K·sax	nē'det	hwî̂l	ba'k^uL
	Chilkat the name of	the	the town.	Only	they	where	come from

10	Liâ̂'ng·ê.	TsEtsā'utk^udet	t'an	ia'tsL	Liâ̂'ng·ê.	NLne'L	dEm
	elks.	The inlanders are	who	kill	elks.	That is	(fut.)

11	g·ē'k^uL	Lgo-wî̂'lk·sîLk^u	Liâ̂'n	aL	haya'tsk^u	qanL	ē'lîx.	NLk·'ēt
	buys	the prince	elks	for	copper	and	seals.	Then he

12	hwaL	Tsî̂Lqā't.	NLk·'ēt	g·ē'Ek^uL	Liâ̂'n.	Sī-na'k·sL	ma'gant.
	found	Chilkat.	Then	he bought	elks.	A wife new	he took.

13	K·'ē	g·ina-d'ā'L	K·'āL-hä'tgum	q'ē'sEmq.	NLk·'ē	d'āL
	Then	behind remained	On-one-side- standing-	labret.	Then	there was

14	wak·L	Lgo-wî̂'lk·sîLk^u	wī-ē'yît,	wī-dōla-g·a'tk^u,	La	hēlL
	the brother of	the prince little	awkward,	a im- great proper man,	when	much

_____

[1] The narrator maintained that this was a place inland near the headwaters of Nass river.

very often. Then She-who-has-a-labret-on-one-side said to the awkward man, "You shall go to Chilkat too." The awkward man answered, "I have nothing to sell." Then She-who-has-a-labret-on-one-side said, "I will give you something that you may sell there. Take red paint along." Thus spoke She-who-has-a-labret-on-one-side to the awkward man. "You shall buy weasel skins for the little box full of red paint, but don't let your brother see it when you arrive there. When you arrive at Chilkat, walk about, and when you see the young women, then put your finger into the red paint and put it on their faces." He did so. When all the young men and the young women saw it, they were anxious to buy it, and they asked him, "Is it expensive?" And they asked the great awkward man, "What do

hwîlL	Lgō-wî′lk·sîLkᵘ,	at	qâ′ôL	TsîLqā′t.	NLk·′ē	a′lg·îxs	1
did	the little prince,	he	went to	Chilkat.	Then	spoke	

K·′āL-hä′tgum	q′ē′sEmq	aL	wī-dōla-g·a′tgum	g·at:	"Āmɪ	2
On-one-side-standing-	labret	to	the im-great proper	person man:	"Good	

dEm dē-ma′xgunîst." NLk·′ē dē′lEmExkᵘL wī-dōla-g·a′tgum g·at: 3
(fut.) on your part you go in canoe." Then replied the im-great proper person man:

"A′qLdē an-wâ′t′ēdîst." NLk·′ē a′lg·îxs K·′āL-hä′tgum q′ē′sEmq: 4
"Without I my trade." Then said On-one-side- standing- labret:

"DEm g·înā′mēEL dEm an-wâ′t′enîst. MEs-ā′ust, nLneɪ dEm an- 5
"(Fut.) I give (fut.) your trade. Red paint, that (fut.)

wâ′t′enîst;" dē′yas K·′āL-hä′tgum q′ē′sEmq aL wī-dōla-g·a′tgum 6
your trade;" thus said On-one-side- standing- labret to the im-great proper person

g·at. "Lgo-xbē′îst hwîl lō-la′k·t metkᵘ aL mEs-a′ust. Mî′k·sîL 7
man. "A little box where in is full of red paint. Weasel

tsE dē-g·ē′egun. G·îlô′ mE tsE gun-g·a′adEt aL wa′g·în. TsE 8
on your part you buy. Do not you make see it (show it) to your brother.

da Lā k·′a′tsgun aL TsîLqā′t, me tsE k·′ē k′uL-iē′ên dEm 9
When you land at Chilkat, you then about go (fut.)

g·a′an hwîl k′uL-Lô′ôL q′aima′qsEm hā′naq mE tsE k·′ē′ 10
you see where about go young women you then

mE lō′-k·′ē′tsElt. NLk·′ē tgōn ts′a′ElL q′aima′sEm hana′q, nēL 11
you in put finger. Then this the face of young woman, then

mE dEm hwîl tq′al-d′ā′tElt." NLk·′ē hwîlt. NLk·′ēt g·a′aL 12
you will being against put it." Then he did so. Then saw it

txanē′tkᵘL sîl-q′aima′qsît qanL txanē′tkᵘL hā′naq. NLk·′ē 13
all the fellow youths and all the women. Then

sEm-abaxba′g·askᵘdetg·ê. NLk·′ēt g·ē′dExdēiL wī-g·a′tg·ê: "Nē′îL 14
much they were troubled. Then they asked the great man: "Is it

wī-t′ē′sda?" NLk·′ē a′lg·îxL wī-g·a′tg·ê: "Wī-t′ē′s." "Agō′L 15
great?" Then said the great man: "Great." "What

you want in exchange?" He replied, "I want weasels." Then the men and the women brought weasel skins, and the awkward man bought them. He had a whole box full of weasel skins. Then he had sold all his red paint.

When the prince saw him, he made fun of his own brother. Then they returned, and arrived at their own town. In the evening She-who-has-a-labret-on-one-side questioned the awkward man, her brother-in-law, and he showed her what he had purchased. Early the next morning She-who-has-a-labret-on-one-side said to the awkward man, "Go to the place where the water runs down. I shall go to meet you there." She intended to leave her husband, because he did not take her along when he went to Chilkat. Therefore she was

---

1. dɛm   dē-g·ē'gunîst?"   NʟK·'ē   huX   a'lg·îxʟ   wī-g·a't: "Mî'k·sîʟ
do you   on   to buy?"   Then   again   said   the man: "Weasels
want your part   great

2. dē-hasa'gaē."   NʟK·'ē   dôqʟ   hana'q   ʟa   ga-mî'k·sîʟ   ē'uxt.   NʟK·'ēt
on my   I want."   Then   took   the   the weasels   the   Then
part   woman   of   men.

3. g·īkᵘʟ   wī-g·a'tg·ê,   wī-la'îʟ   ʟgo-xbē'îst,   hwîl   metkᵘʟ   mîk·sî'ʟ.
bought   the man,   a   thus   little   box,   being   full of   weasels.
great   great large

4. NʟK·'ē   qâ'ôdɛʟ   mɛs-ā'ust.
Then   it was   the   paint.
finished   red

5. NʟK·'ēt   g·a'aʟ   ʟgō-wî'lk·sîʟkᵘ.   NʟK·'ē   ansgwa'tkᵘt   lâ'ôt
Then   saw it   the   prince.   Then   he made fun of   him
little

6. lɛp-wa'k·ʟ   ʟgō-wî'lk·sîʟkᵘ   aʟ   wī-lɛp-wa'k·tg·ê.   NʟK·'ē   ʟā
the   brother   the   prince   of   great   his   brother.   Then   (perf.)
own   of   little   own

7. lō-ya'ltkᵘdet.   NʟK·'ē   k·'a'tskᵘdēt   aʟ   ʟɛpʟ-ts'a'pdet.   NʟK·'ē   ʟā
they returned.   Then   they landed   at   own   their town.   Then   (perf.)

8. yu'ksa,   nʟk·'ē   g·ē'dɛxs   K·'aʟ-hä'tgum   q'ē'sɛmq   wī-g·a'tg·ê,
evening,   then   asked   On-one-   standing-   labret   the   man.
side-   great

9. wak·ʟ   na'k·stg·ê.   NʟK·'ēt   gun-g·a'adɛʟ   wī-g·a't   qabē'îʟ
the   her husband.   Then   showed   the man   how
brother of   great   much

10. sqa'lsîtg·ê.   NʟK·'ē   sɛm-hē'ʟuk,   nʟk·'ē   a'lg·îxs   K·'āʟ-hä'tgum
what he   Then   very   early,   then   said   On-one-   standing-
had bought.   side-

11. q'ē'sɛmq   aʟ   wī-dōlā-g·a'tgum   g·at: "Adô',   iē'ên   aʟ   hwîl
labret   to   the im-   person   man: "Go,   go   to   where
great proper

12. iaga-ba'xʟ   ak·s;   dɛm   iä'nēɛ   aʟ   awa'an."   ʟā   lō-hē'ʟ   qâ'ôts
down   runs   water;   (fut.)   I go   to   your   (Perf.)   in said   the
proximity."   heart of

13. K·'āʟ-hä'tgum   q'ē'sɛmq,   dɛmt   kᵘsta'qsîʟ   nak·st   aʟ   hwîl
On-one-   standing-   labret,   (fut.)   wanted to   her   because
side-   she   leave   husband

14. nî'gidēt   k·'uʟ-ma'g·ant   at   hwîl   qaqâ'ôʟ   Tsîʟqā't.   Nîʟne'ʟ   qan
not   about   he took her   to   where   he went to   Chilkat.   Therefore
in canoe

ashamed. She took the awkward man and washed him in order to
purify him. Then she intended to marry him. She was going to
leave the prince who had first married her. Then the awkward man
went out, as She-who-has-a-labret-on-one-side had told him. He
went to the place where the water was running down, and he stayed
in the water for a long time. Then She-who-has-a-labret-on-one-
side came. There were four deep water holes in the creek. She
washed him in the first hole, then in the second one, in the third one,
and in the fourth one. Then his skin was very clean, and he became a
beautiful man. After he was purified, he married She-who-has-a-
labret-on-one-side. Then her mother, the Evening Sky, came again,

---

dzâqs	K·'aʟ-hä'tgum	q'ē'sEmq;	nt qan	gōʟ	wī-dōla-g·a'tgum	1
was ashamed	On-one- side- standing-	labret;	therefore	she took	the im- great proper person	
g·at	aʟ	dEmt	iô'ôk·st.	Nʟā	dEm saˑk·sku̯tg·ê,	nʟ dEm k·'ēt	2
man	to	(fut.)	wash him.	Where	(fut.) he was clean,	(fut.) then	
nak·sku̯t.	DEm	ha'ut'Ens	K·'aʟ-hä'tgum	q'ē'sEmq	ʟgō-wî'lk·sîʟku̯,		3
she marries him.	(Fut.)	she leaves	On-one- side- standing-	labret	the prince, little		
ʟa	t'an	k·s-qâ'gam	nak·sku̯t.	Nʟk·'ē	ʟa iä'ʟ	wi-dōla-g·a'tgum	4
(perf.)	who	first	he married her.	Then	(perf.) went	the im- great proper person	
g·at.	Hwîlt	an-hē's	K·'aʟ-hä'tgum	q'ē'sEmq.	Nʟk·'ē	iä'êt	5
man.	He did	what said	On-one- side- standing-	labret.	Then	he went	
aʟ	hwîl	g·îsi·ba'xʟ	ak·s.	Nʟk·'ē	lôgôm-d'ā't.	ʟā nak̯ku̯ʟ	6
to	where	down ran river	water.	Then	into he sat.	When long	
d'āt,	nʟk·'ē	ā'd'îk·sku̯s	K·'aʟ-hä'tgum	q'ē'sEmq.	Nʟk·'ē		7
he sat,	then	came	On-one- side- standing-	labret.	Then		
txalpxʟ	hwîlt	g·îsi-lō-wâ'wôq'Eʟ	ak·s	lō-ʟîpʟa'p.	Nʟk·'ē		8
four	where	down in he dug	water	in deep.	Then		
iô'ôk·sʟ	anā'sʟ	wī-g·a't	aʟ	k·'ēlʟ	ts'Em-a'k·s.	Nʟk·'ēt	9
she washed	the skin of	the man great	in	one	in water.	Then	
huX	lôgôm-qâ'ôʟ	huX	k·'ēlt.	Nʟk·'ē	huXt	lō-la'qsku̯t.	10
again	into he went	again	one.	Then	again	in she washed him.	
Nʟk·'ēt	huX	qâ'ôʟ	huX	k·'ē'lt.	Nʟk·'ēt	huX	lō-la'qsku̯t	11
Then	again	he went	again	one.	Then	again	in she washed him	
ʟā	gulā'alt.	Nʟk·'ēt	huX	lō-qâ'ôʟ	k·'ēlt.	Nʟk·'ēt	huX	12
	a third time.	Then	again	in he went	one.	Then	again	
lō-la'qsku̯t.	Txa'lpxg·ê.	Nʟk·'ē	sEm-saˑk·sku̯ʟ	ʟa	anā'st.		13
in she washed him.	Four.	Then	really clean was	his	skin.		
Nʟk·'ē	ā'd'îk·sku̯ʟ	hwîl	sEm-k·'ä-ā'mʟ	wī-g·a'tg·ê.	Nʟk·'ēt		14
Then	came	(verbal noun)	very ex- ceedingly good	the man. great	Then		
nak·sku̯s	K·'aʟ-hä'tgum	q'ē'sEmq	aʟ	ʟā sEm-saˑk·sku̯t.	Nʟk·'ē		15
he married	On-one- side- standing-	labret	when	very he was clean.	Then		

bringing many elks, copper plates, canoes, slaves, and much food. Then the great awkward man invited all the tribes, intending to give a potlatch. Then he did so. Then the former husband of She-who-has-a-labret-on-one-side was ashamed because the awkward man was going to give a potlatch. He was no longer awkward, because he had been purified, because She-who-has-a-labret-on-one-side had washed him.

Now the tribes came. Then they ate all the food. The day after they finished eating, all the tribes went into his house. They put the elks, the copper plates, slaves, and canoes in the middle of the house. Then the great awkward man, the husband of She-who-has-a-labret-on-one-side, came. He wore a blanket made of weasel skins

---

1 hā′ts′îk·sᴇm   huX   ā′d′îk·skᵘs   K·sᴇm-huXdza′n,   nôxs
   once more   again   eame   woman   evening sky,   the
                                                                        mother of

2 K·′aʟ-hä′tgum   q′ē′sᴇmq.   HuX   dᴇ-ā′d′îk·skᵘʟ   wi-hē′ldᴇl   liâ′n
   On-one-   labret.   Also   she   to come   many   elks
   standing-   caused
   side-

3 qanʟ   haya′tskᵘ   qanʟ   māl   qanʟ   ʟîʟî′ng·it   qanʟ   wī-hē′ldᴇm
   and   copper   and   canoes   and   slaves   and   much

4 wunä′x·.   Nʟk·′ē   wô′ôʟ   wī-dōla-g·a′tgum   g·at,   txanē′tkᵘʟ
   food.   Then   he in-   the im- person   man,   all
                             vited   great proper

5 hwîl   dzaxdzô′q   dᴇm   yuk.   Nʟk·′ē   hwîlt.   Nʟk·′ē   dzâqʟ
   tribes   for   a pot-   Then   he did   Then   was
                            latch.   so.   ashamed

6 ʟē   nak·s   K·aʟ-hä′tgum   q′ē′sᴇmq,   aʟ   hwîl   ʟa   dᴇm   yukʟ
   the   husband of On-one-   labret,   because (perf.) (fut.)   gave a
   past   standing-   potlatch
                       side-

7 wī-dōla-g·a′tgum   g·at.   ʟā   nîg·i   huX   dē-dōla-g·a′tkᵘt   aʟ   hwîl
   the im- person   man.   (Perf.) not   more   also   man   because
   great proper   proper

8 ʟā   sᴇm-sa′k·skᵘt   at   hwîl   la′qsaans   K·′aʟ-hä′tgum   q′ē′sᴇmq.
   (perf.) very he was clean,   because washed him   On-one-   labret.
                                                              standing-
                                                              side-

9 Nʟk·′ē   ā′d′îk·skᵘʟ   hwîl   dzaxdzô′q.   Nʟk·′ē   wī-hē′lʟ   g·ē′îpdet
   Then   came   the tribes.   Then   many   they ate it

10 txanē′tkᵘʟ   wunä′x·.   Nʟk·′ē   ʟa   ʟēskᵘʟ   txâ′xkᵘdētg·ê.   Nʟk·′ē
    all   the food.   Then   they   eating.   Then
                                                     finished

11 huX   k·′ēlʟ   sa,   nʟk·′ē   ts′ᴇlᴇm-qâ′dîʟ   txanē′tkᵘʟ   hwîl
    again   one   day,   then   into   went   all

12 dzaxdzô′q   aʟ   ts′ᴇm-hwî′lp.   Nʟk·′ēt   t′ᴇm-d′ā′ldeʟ   liâ′n   qanʟ
    the tribes   into   in the house.   Then   toward they put   elks   and
                                                          middle

13 haya′tskᵘ   qanʟ   ʟîʟî′ng·it   qanʟ   mmāl.   Nʟk·′ē   ʟa   t′ᴇm-qâ′ôdᴇt,
    copper   and   slaves   and   canoes.   Then   when   to the they were
                                                                                       middle gone,

14 nʟk·′ē   ā′d′îk·skᵘs   wī-dōla-g·a′tgum   g·at,   nak·s   K·′aʟ-hä′tgum
    then   came   the im-   person   man,   the hus- On-one-
                                great proper   band of   standing-
                                                                              side-

15 q′ē′sᴇmq.   Gwis-mî′k·sîʟ.   gulā′ît.   ʟē-hwa′nʟ   bᴇlā′   lâ′ᴇt.
    labret.   Blanket   weasel   he had   On   were   haliotis on it.
                                         on.   shells

set with abalone shells.　He used a weasel hat.　Then he entered and
stood in front of the elk skins.　Then they sang.　After they had
finished singing, they stopped, and he gave away abalone shells, copper plates, elks, slaves, and canoes.　Then the tribes were glad, and
the awkward man had become a great chief.

NʟK·'ēt　hâx·ʟ　qaidɛm　mí'k·sîʟ.　NʟK·'ē　ts'ēnt.　NʟK·'ē　hētkᵘt　1
Then　he　a hat of　weasels.　Then　he　Then　he stood
　　　used　　　　　　　　　　　entered.

aʟ　qa-g·i'k·sîʟ　hwîl　dôxʟ　ʟiâ'n.　NʟK·'ē　lē'mix·dēt.　ʟa　ʟēskᵘʟ　2
at　in front of　where　were　the　Then　they sang.　When　they
　　　　　　　　　elks.　　　　　　　　　　　finished

lē'mix·det,　nʟK·'ē　ha'widētg·ê.　NʟK·'ē　tsā'eqdēt　bɛlā'　qanʟ　3
singing,　then　they stopped.　Then　he gave　haliotis　and
　　　　　　　　　　　　　　　away　shells

hāya'tskᵘ　qanʟ　ʟiâ'n　qanʟ　ʟîʟî'ng·it　qanʟ　mmāl.　NʟK·'ē　4
copper　and　elks　and　slaves　and　canoes.　Then

lō-am'ā'mʟ　qaqâ'ôdɛʟ　hwîl　dzaxdzô'q　hwîl　wī-t'ē'sʟ　sɛm'â'g·iʟ　5
in　good　hearts were　the　tribes　being　a great　chief

wī-dōla-g·a'tgum　g·at.　6
the im-　person　man.
great proper

The Grizzly Bear

[Told by Moses]

There were four brothers, the sons of a great chief. Their mother was a great chieftainess. They lived in a large town. In midwinter the people had eaten all the winter provisions, and were starving. The brothers were great hunters. Now, the two eldest ones remembered what they used to do, because they were starving. They were hunters, and they went out together. The wife of the eldest one did not accompany him. They went a long distance, and came to a house where they stayed over night. In the morning the younger brother.

The Grizzly Bear

1   Txālpxdâ′lʟ   g·a′tg·ê,   k·’âlʟ   sē′lg·ît,   nʟk·’ē   k·’âlʟ   lō-an-iē′êt.
    Four   men,   one   the eldest,   then   one   the next.

2   Nʟk·’ē   huX   k·’âlʟ   tsuwî′ng·it.   Nʟk·’ē   k·’âlʟ   wī-sɛm’â′g·it
    Then   also   one   the youngest.   Then   one   great   chief

3   nɛguâ′ôdetg·ê.   Nʟk·’ē   k·’âlʟ   nô′xdetg·ê,   wī-na′k·sʟ   sɛm’â′g·it.
    their father.   Then   one   their mother,   the   wife of   the chief.
                                                         great

4   Wī-t’ē′sʟ   qal-ts’a′pdetg·ê.   Hwä′i!   ʟa   sē′lukʟ   mā′dɛm,   nʟk·’ē
    Large was   their town.   Well!   When   the mid-   the winter,   then
                                             dle of

5   qatqâ′ôdɛt   g·ē′ipʟ   txane′tk"ʟ   qal-ts’a′pg·ê.   Nʟk·’ē   ago’   tse
    was finished   the food   the whole   people.   Then   what   (dubi
               of   tative)

6   g·ē′îpdet.   Guîx·-dzagu′sk"ʟ   k·’â′ltg·ê.   Nʟk·’ē   huX   hwîʟʟ
    they eat.   A hunter was   one.   Then   again   he was
                                                     so

7   tsuwî′ng·it.   Nʟk·’ēt   am-qâ′ôdɛtʟ   ʟē   hwîl   huwî′ldetg·ê,   nʟa
    the youngest one.   Then   they remembered   what they used to do,   be-
                                                     cause

8   aqʟ-g·ē′îpdet.   K·’ē   ʟô′ôdetʟ   bagadē′lʟ   guîx·-qa-ia′tsgut.   Nʟk·’ē   ʟā
    no   food.   Then   they went   the two   hunters.   Then   (perf.)

9   wī-t’ē′sʟ   sē′lg·ît.   Nʟneʟ   stō′ldet.   Nî′g·îdi   stɛlʟ   sē′lg·îtʟ
    great   the eldest.   Then   they went   Not   went   the eldest
                         in company.   with him   one’s

10   nak·st,   q’am-k·’â′lʟ   hōksk"ʟ   aʟ   wak·k"t.   K·’ē   ʟô′ôdet.   Nak"ʟ
    wife,   only   one   was with   of   his   Then   they went.   Long
                          him   brothers.

11   hwîl   ʟô′ôdet,   k·’ēt   hwa′dēʟ   hwîlp.   Nʟk·’ē   lō-dzô′qdet   lât.
    where   they went,   then   they found   a house.   Then   in   they stayed   in it.

rose. He had two powerful dogs. He started, carrying his lance.
He put on his snowshoes and went. He came to the foot of a mountain. He climbed it, and when he was halfway up the mountain he
heard the voice of his dog up above. He could not climb any higher
because there was a glacier. Then he took his little stone ax and
chopped steps in the glacier. Thus he came to the foot of a ridge
on which a tree was standing. There his dogs were barking. When
he came near, he saw a large Grizzly Bear and two large cubs in a hole
under the tree. As soon as he went near, the Grizzly Bear stretched
out her arms and pulled the man into her den. She killed him. Then
his brothers had lost him.

Hē′Lᴜk	nʟk·’ē	haldᴇm-ba′xʟ	tsuwî′ng·ît.	T’ᴇpxā′ʟ	as’o′st,	1
In the morning	then	rose	the younger.	Two were	his dogs,	
sᴇmg̣al	hagulâ′q̣ʟ	as’o′s.	Nʟk·’ē	iē′êʟ	g·a′tg·ê.	Yu′kdᴇl g̣an.	2
very	powerful	dogs.	Then	went	the man.	He carried a stick.	
Lē-d’ā′ʟ	t’ō′otskᵘ	lât.	Nʟk·’ēt	hax·hâ′x·ʟ	nax.	Nʟk·’ē iē′êt.	3
On was	knife	on it.	Then he	put on	snow-shoes.	Then he went.	
Nʟk·’ēt	hwaʟ	depʟ	sqane′st.	Nʟk·’ē	bax-iē′êʟ.	ʟat hwaʟ	4
Then he	reached the	foot of	a mountain.	Then	up he went.	When he reached	
ʟē	sē′lukt,	nʟk·’ē	naxna′ʟ	am-hē′ʟ	os aʟ lax-ha′.	K·’ē	5
the middle,		then	he heard	the voice of	the dog at above.	Then	
aq̣ʟ-hagun-yô′xkᵘt.	Dā′uʟ	sqanē′stg·ê.	Nʟk·’ēt	gō′uʟ	ʟgo-	6
not toward he could get.	Ice was	the mountain.	Then he	took	a little	
daxwᴇ′nsᴇm	lô′ôp.	Nʟk·’ēt	tsaga-hîs’ia′tsʟ	dā′uʟ	sqanē′stg·ê.	7
ax	stone.	Then	across he chopped	the ice of	the mountain.	
Nʟk·’ēt	hwaʟ	k’ō′ukᵘt	hwîl	d’ᴇp-hē′tkᵘʟ	g̣an.	Neʟne′ʟ hwîl	8
Then	he reached (foot of a ridge)	its tail	where	down stood	a tree.	That where	
hahä′ʟ	os.	Nʟk·’ē	hagun-a′q̣ʟkᵘt.	Gwina′dēʟ,	ts’ᴇm-dz’ä′dz’îk·s	9
the noise of	the dog.	Then	toward he reached.	Behold,	in the ground	
hwîl	lō-d’ā′ʟ	wî-lig·’ē′Enskᵘ,	t’ᴇpxā′tʟ	ʟî′k·ʟg·ît	ʟa	10
where	in was	a great grizzly bear,	two	cubs	(perf.)	
sᴇm-t’êst’ē′st.	Nʟk·’ē	hagun-iä′êʟ	g·at	aʟ hwîl	ts’ᴇlᴇm-nô′ôt.	11
very large.	Then	toward went	the man	to where	into hole.	
Nʟk·’ē	k·si-na′kᵘst	sᴇm-ts’ᴇlᴇm-gō′dᴇl	g·at.	Nʟk·’ēt	gōʟ	12
Then	out she stretched	very into she took	the man.	Then	took him	
ʟî′k·ʟg·ît.	Nʟk·’ēt	dza′kᵘdet.	Nô′ôʟ	g·a′tg·ê.	Nʟk·’ē	gwâ′disiʟ	13
the cubs.	Then	they killed him.	Dead	the man.	Then	lost him	
wak·kᵘt.						14
his brothers.						

After two days, when he did not return, the next brother rose. He also had two dogs. He started, carrying his lance. He came to the same place where his brother had been. The dogs ran up the mountain, and he came to the steps that his brother had chopped in the glacier. He climbed up, and he also came to the Grizzly Bear. She took him into her den, and the cubs killed him. He and his two dogs were dead. In this way another brother was lost.

Only one remained. He was a very awkward man. He also rose and started early in the morning. He carried his lance, and his two dogs accompanied him. He put on his snowshoes and went up the mountain on the same trail that his brothers had taken. Now he

---

1   La   g·ē′lp’ɛlL   sa   qa-nā′guʟ   gwâtkᵘt,   nʟk·’ē   huX   haldɛm-ba′xʟ
    When   two   days   how long   he was lost,   then   again   rose

2   huX   k·’âlʟ   wak·t.   HuX   t’ɛpxā′tʟ   as’o′st.   Hē′ʟuk,   nʟk·’ē
    again   one   brother.   Also   two   dogs.   In the morning,   then

3   huX   iē′êt.   HuX   t’ɛpxā′tʟ   as’o′st.   HuX   yu′kdɛL   gan   hwîl
    also   he went.   Also   two   dogs.   Also   he carried   a stick   being

4   lē-d’ā′ʟ   t’ōtskᵘ.   Nʟk·’ē   huX   iē′êt.   Lat   huX   hwaʟ   Lē
    on was it   a knife.   Then   also   he went.   When   also   he found   what

5   hwa′yiʟ   wak·t,   k·’ē   huX   bax-sa′k·skᵘʟ   as’o′s.   Ha·ts’ɛk·sɛm
    had found   his brother,   then   also   up   ran   the dogs.   Once more

6   huX   hwa′dēʟ   Le   hwîl   hwî′lʟ   wa′k·tg·ê.   G·a′at   hwîl
    also   he found   what had   done   his brother.   He saw   where

7   tsaga-hîs’ia′tskᵘt   Lē   dā′uʟ   sqanē′stg·ê.   Nʟk·’ē   huX
    across   was chopped   the   ice of   the mountain.   Then   again

8   hagun-a′qʟkᵘt.   Nîg·î   nakᵘ   hwîlt,   k·’ēt   huX   ts’ɛlɛm-gō′ut.
    toward   he got.   Not   long   he did so,   then   also   into   she took him.

9   Nʟk·’ē   huX   dzakᵘʟ   Lîk·ʟg·î′t.   K·’ē   huX   nô′ôt   qanʟ
    Then   again   killed him   the cubs.   Then   again   he was dead   and

10   t’ɛpxā′tʟ   as’o′st.   K·’ē   huX   gwâ′disiʟ   k·’âlʟ   wak·t.
    two   dogs.   Then   again   was lost   one   younger brother.

11   La   q’am-k·’â′lʟ   mānt   sɛm-wī-dula-g·a′tkᵘt,   nʟk·’ē
    When   only one   left over   a great im-very proper   man,   then

12   dē-haldɛm-ba′xt.   Nʟk·’ē   de-iä′êt   aʟ   hē′ʟuk   huX   de-t’ɛpxā′tʟ
    also   he rose.   Then   also he went   in   the morning   also   with two

13   as’o′st   huX   de-yu′kdɛL   gan.   Lē-d’ā′ʟ   ts’ōtskᵘt   lâ′ôt.   Nʟk·’ēt
    dogs   also   on his part he carried   a stick.   On was   a knife   on it.   Then he

14   hax·hâ′x·ʟ   nax.   Nʟk·’ē   huX   dē-bax-iä′êt   aʟ   lax-sqanē′st.
    put on   snowshoes.   Then   again   on his part on up he went   to on   the mountain.

15   Hasp’a-lō-yô′xkᵘt   Lē   yôxkᵘʟ   wak·kᵘt.   Nʟk·’ē   nɛxna′ʟ   hwîl
    The same in road   he went   that   had gone   his brothers.   Then   he heard   where

heard the dogs barking. He went near, and had just placed himself
in position when the great Grizzly Bear stretched out her arms, and the
great man fell into the den headlong. Then he struck the Grizzly Bear
and his hand got into her vulva. Then she said to her cubs, "My dear
ones, make the fire burn brightly, for your father is cold." She felt
much ashamed because the man had struck her vulva, therefore she felt
kindly toward him, and did not kill him. She liked him. She said,
"I will marry you." And the big man agreed. Then the great
Grizzly Bear was very glad because the Indian had married her.

When he had stayed there many years and was lost to his people,
he said one day that he longed for his father and his mother, his
wife, his little boy, and his little sister, and that he wished to go

---

tqa-wô'xʟ as'o's.　Nʟk·'ē dē-hagun-a'qʟkᵘt.　Nʟk·'ē q'ai-he-yu'kʟ 1
barked　the　Then　also toward　he　Then　just he began
　　dogs.　　　　reached.

ama hē'tkᵘtst.　Tk·'ē sā-k·si-na'kᵘs wī-lig·'ē'ᴇnskᵘ.　G·itsʟ-k·s-qâ'qʟ 2
well　he placed　Then　sud- out stretched　the　grizzly bear.　Into　first
himself.　denly (her paws)　great

t'ᴇm-qē'sʟ wī-g·a'tg·ê.　Nʟk·'ē hwîla t'a'askᵘt tgōn.　Sᴇm- 3
the head of　the　man.　Then　this　he slapped this.　Right
　　great　　　　way

lō-g·īē'tguʟ an'ô'nʟ wī-mē'nʟ wī-lig·'ē'ᴇnskᵘg·ê.　Nʟk·'ē a'lg·îxʟ 4
in　he got　his hand　the vulva　the　grizzly bear.　Then　said
　　　　great of　great

wī-lig·'ē'ᴇnskᵘ aʟ ʟî'k·ʟg·ît·　"Nāt! Sᴇm-se-me'ʟʟ la'gust, yukʟ 5
the　grizzly bear　to　her cubs:　"My　Very make burn　the fire,　he
great　　　　　dear!　　　　begins

xs-gunä'qs nᴇguâ'ôtsᴇnı."　Sᴇm-dzâ'qʟ qâtʟ wī-lig·'ē'ᴇnskᵘ t hwîl 6
feels cold　your father."　Much was　the heart the grizzly bear　because
　　　　ashamed　of　great

lō-ba'qʟ wī-g·a't mēnt.　Neʟne'ʟ qan wī-ama g·at nîg·ît huX 7
in　felt　the man　her　Therefore　much good　the　not　also
　　great　vulva.　　　　man

dzakᵘt at hwîl lō-bā'ᴇlt.　Niʟnē't qan sī'b'ᴇnt.　Nʟk·'ē a'lg·îxʟ 8
she killed　because　in he felt.　Therefore　she liked　Then　said
him　　　　him.

wī-lig·'ē'ᴇnskᵘ: "Dᴇm na'kskuē nē'ᴇn."　Nʟk·'ēt anâ'qʟ wī-g·a'tg·ê. 9
the　grizzly bear:　"(Fut.) I marry you."　Then　agreed the　man.
great　　　　　　great

Sᴇm-lō-â'mʟ qâʟ wī-hana'gam lig·'ē'ᴇnskᵘ at hwîl nak·skᵘʟ 10
Very in good　heart　the　woman　grizzly bear　because　he married
　　　　great　　　　her

wī-alō-g·ig·a't.　Nʟk·'ē qanē-hwîla lā'ʟdet. 11
the　Indian.　Then　always　they lay
great　　　　down.

ʟa hē'lʟ k'ōʟ hwîlʟ gwâtkᵘʟ wī-g·a'tg·ê.　Nʟk·'ē a'lg·îxʟ 12
When　many　years　he did so　he was lost　the　man.　Then　said
　　　　　　great

wī-g·a'tg·ê, wai-g·a'tkᵘ as nᴇguâ'ôdet qans nôxt qanʟ nak·st 13
the　man,　lonesome　for　his father　and　his　and　his wife
great　　　　　　mother

qanʟ ʟgō-ʟgō'uʟkᵘt qanʟ ʟgō-g·î'mx·dit.　Nʟk·'ē hēt dᴇm 14
and　his　boy　and　his　sister.　Then　he　he
　　little　　　little　　　said　would

home. The great Grizzly Bear agreed, and she said, "I will accompany you." On the next morning they went down the mountain and approached the town. Now the great man entered. The great chief, his father, his mother, and his wife were crying. The man entered and sat down. Then he said that his wife was standing outside. His little sister went to call her. She looked about for her outside the village, and found the great Grizzly Bear. She ran into the house crying, because she was much afraid. "A great ugly monster is standing outside." Then the man, the great Grizzly Bear's husband, went out himself. He called her into the house, and she entered. Then she sat down on a mat that they had spread for her. Her paws were very large, and the chief and his wife were scared.

---

1 na-iē′êt. NᴌK·′ēt anâ′qᴌ wī-lig·′ē′Ensk^u: "DEm ste′lē nē′En,"
  out of go.   Then   agreed the grizzly bear: "Shall accom- you,"
  woods   great   pany I

2 dē′ya aᴌ wī-g·a′tg·ê. NᴌK·′ē ᴌa ḥuX hē′ᴌuk, nᴌk·′ē
  thus she to the man.   Then when again morning, then
  said   great

3 na-ᴌ ô′ôdet. NᴌK·′ē ba′k^udēt aᴌ qal-ts'a′p. NᴌK·′ē ts'ēnᴌ
  out of they went. Then they came from to the town. Then entered
  woods   there

4 wī-g·a′t. NᴌK·′ē wī-yē′tk^uᴌ wī-sEm'â′g·it, wī-nEguâ′ôdEt qanᴌ
  the man. Then cried   the chief, great his father and
  great   great

5 nôxt qanᴌ nak·st. NᴌK·′ē ts'ēnt, k·′ē d′āt. NᴌK·′ēt maᴌEᴌ,
  his and his   Then he entered, then he sat Then he told,
  mother   wife.   down.

6 heē′tk^uᴌ nak·st aᴌ g·a′ᴌEq. K·′ē k·saXᴌ ᴌgō-g·î′mx·dit, dEm
  standing his wife at outside. Then went out his sister, (fut.)
                                          little

7 t'an ts'EIEm-wô′ôᴌ nak·st. NᴌK·′ē k'uᴌ-g·îg·ē′êlt aᴌ g·a′ᴌEq.
  who into called his wife. Then about she looked at outside.
                                      for her

8 SEm-hwa′îᴌ ᴌgo-tk·′ē′lk^u hwîl heē′tk^uᴌ wī-lig·′ē′Ensk^u
  Indeed she the child where stood the grizzly bear
  found   little   great

9 sEm-ts'EIEm-ba′xt aᴌ wī-amhē′t aᴌ ayawā′tk^ut aᴌ wi-yē′tk^ut,
  very into she ran shouting and crying and crying,

10 aᴌ qasqâ′ᴌ xbētsa′Xt: "Wī-t'ē′sᴌ hwîl sē′lukt, hŏhŏhŏhŏ!
   at much afraid: "Great being ugly, hohoho!

11 wī-sӑa′k· lō-wē′ltk^u." NᴌK·′ē lEp-k·sa′Xᴌ g·a′tg·ê, lEp-na′k·sᴌ
   great monster." Then himself went the man, her husband
                           out   own

12 wī-lig·′ē′Ensk^u. NᴌK·′ē hēt ts'EIEm-wô′ôt. NᴌK·′ē lEp-ts'ē′nt.
   the grizzly bear. Then he into he invited Then self she
   great   said   her.   entered.

13 NᴌK·′ē d′āᴌ wī-lig·′ē′Ensk^u aᴌ hwîl ba′ᴌEᴌ sqa′na. Qa-lā′iᴌ
   Then she sat the grizzly bear at where was spread a mat. That large
         down   great

14 wud'ax-k·′ēla'at. Hā sEmgal xpēts'ē′Xᴌ sEm'â′gît qanᴌ nak·st.
   her paws. Much was scared the chief and his wife.
   large

Then they ate salmon, and she also ate; and they gave her a dish filled with crab apple mixed with grease, and she ate it. The people were much astonished.

After a while the great Grizzly Bear said to her husband, "Give me your child; I wish to see it." Then the man took the child, because the great Grizzly Bear wanted to have it. He gave it to her, and the child did not cry.

Another day the Bear said, "Call your wife." Then the woman came, the first wife of the man. She entered and sat down next to the man, her own husband. Later he had married the Grizzly Bear. His one wife was the Bear, the other was a woman of his own tribe. The woman only had a child. The Grizzly Bear had no children. But

---

Nʟkꞏ'ēt	x-hâ'ndit.	Nʟkꞏ'ēt	gꞏēpʟ	wī-ligꞏ'ē'Ensk^u	Nʟkꞏꞏꞏ'ēt 1
Then they	ate salmon.	Then	ate it	the grizzly bear. great	Then

lō-dꞏ'ā'ʟ	La'ix	aʟ	ts'ᴇm-ts'a'kꞏ.	Kꞏ'ēt huX sgꞏēt.	Nʟkꞏ'ēt huX 2
in put	crab apple and grease	in	inside of dish.	Then again it lay in it there.	Then again

gꞏepʟ	wī-ligꞏ'ē'Ensk^u.	SEmgal	lō-sanā'ʟguʟ	qaɭ-ts'a'p	hwî'ltgꞏê. 3
ate	the grizzly bear. great	Very	astonished was	the town	what he did.

Nʟkꞏ'ē	La	sī-gō'n,	nʟkꞏ'ē a'lgꞏîxʟ	wī-ligꞏ'ē'Ensk^u aʟ	nakꞏst: 4
Then	when	later on,	then said	the grizzly bear great	to her husband:

"Adô,	gō'uʟ	ʟgō'uʟgun,"	dē'ya aʟ	nakꞏst:	"Dᴇm gꞏa'aē." 5
"Adô,	take	your child,"	thus she said	to her husband:	"Will I see it."

Nʟkꞏ'ē	dā'uʟʟ	k ꞏ'âlʟ	gꞏat	t'an gōʟ ʟgo-tkꞏ'ē'ʟk^u.	Nʟkꞏ'ē da- 6
Then	went	one	man	who took the little child.	Then he caused

ā'dꞏîkꞏsk^{u}t,	nʟkꞏ'ēt	gunaʟ	wī-ligꞏ'ē'Ensk^u.	Nʟkꞏ'ēt	gꞏînā'mdētgꞏê. 7
it to come,	then	wanted it	the grizzly bear. great	Then they	gave it.

Nʟkꞏ'ē	nîgꞏî	ayawā'tk^{n}ʟ	tkꞏ'ēʟk^u.	8
Then	not	cried	the child.	

Nʟkꞏ'ē	huX	a'lgꞏîxʟ	wī-ligꞏ'ē'Ensk^u	aʟ huX	kꞏ'ē'lʟ	sa: 9
Then	again	said	the grizzly bear great	at again	one	day:

"Āmʟē	wô'ôʟ	na'kꞏsîn."	Nʟkꞏ'ē	ā'dꞏîkꞏsk^{u}ʟ hana'q	ʟē 10
"Good	invite	your wife."	Then	came the woman	

waʟᴇn-na'kꞏsʟ	gꞏa'tgꞏê.	Kꞏ'ē	ts'ēnt.	Kꞏ'ē d'āt	aʟ awa'aʟ 11
formerly the wife of	the man.	Then	she entered.	Then she sat down	at the proximity of

gꞏa'tgꞏê,	lᴇp-na'kꞏstgꞏê.	Kꞏ'ē	sē-na'kꞏsguʟ wī-ligꞏ'ē'Ensk^u.	Kꞏ'âlʟ 12
the man,	her own husband.	Then	he newly married the grizzly bear. great	One

ligꞏ'ē'Ensk^u	nakꞏsʟ	gꞏa'tgꞏê;	dē-kꞏ'â'lʟ	lᴇp-hana'q	aʟ lᴇp- 13
grizzly bear	the wife of	the man;	also one	own woman	of his own

ts'a'pt.	Kꞏ'âlʟ	ʟgō'uʟk^{u}t	hana'qgꞏê.	Nʟkꞏ'ē	nîgꞏîdi 14
town.	One	child	the woman.	Then	no

her own children were in her house on the mountain. They had not accompanied her when she came out of the woods. Thus they lived for many months.

When it came to be summer, just before the berries were ripe, the great Grizzly Bear said to the woman, "I think the berries are ripe on my mountain," and asked her to accompany her. They went up the mountain, and found that the berries were ripening, and they picked them. The woman picked her berries into a bag, but the great Grizzly Bear had no bag. Her stomach was her bag. She just ate the berries she picked. Then they returned. They approached their husband's house and entered. The Grizzly Bear said, "Now call the people." Then one man went out to invite the people in. The woman

---

1 Lgō'uLkᵘL   wī-lig·'ē'Enskⁿg·ê.   Hwîl   k·'ē   hwanL   dē-Lg·ît   aL
  child   the   grizzly bear.   Then   were   on her   her   in
                 great   part   children

2 ts'Em-dē-hwî'lpt   aL   lax-sqanē'st,   nig·îdēt   na-sEl-stē'lt.   Hwä'il
  in   also   her   at   on   the   not   out of   they accom-   Well!
       house   mountain,   woods   panied her.

3 Wī-na'kᵘL   hwî'ldētg·ê   wī-hē'lL   Lôqs.
  Long   they did so   many   moons.

4 NLk·'ē   La   ā'd'îk·skᵘL   dEm   hwîl   sē'nt;   nLk·'ē   La   sē'nt,
  Then   when   it came   to be   being   summer;   then   when summer,

5 nLk·'ē   La   qâ'ôqt   dEm   mukL   mā'E.   NLk·'ē   a'lg·îxL
  then   (perf.)   before   (fut.)   ripe   berries.   Then   said

6 wī-lig·'ē'Enskᵘ   aL   hana'qg·ê: "La   mu'kdE-maL   Lē   hwîl
  the   grizzly bear   to   the woman: "(Perf.)   ripe   perhaps   where
  great

7 hwî'lēE."   NLk·'ēt   sä'lîx·t,   nLk·'ē   Lô'ôdēt.   NLk·'ēt   hwa'dēt.
  I was."   Then she   asked her to go   then   they went.   Then   they reached
              along,   there.

8 NLk·'ē   La   ts'ôsk·t   dEm   hwîl   mukt.   NLk·'ēt   g·ē'Eldēt.
  Then   a little   (fut.)   being   ripe.   Then   they picked
                                                          them.

9 NLk·'ē   lō-dô'xL   g·ē'Ell   hana'q   aL   ts'Em-dē'Lkᵘ.   NLk·'ē   dē-
  Then   in it was   what she   the woman   at   in   her bag.   Then   on her
            picked   part

10 nî'g·îdi   dēLkᵘL   wī-lig·'ē'Enskᵘ;   ts'Em-qalâ'st   de-dē'Lkᵘt.
   not   bag   the   grizzly bear;   in   her   on her   her bag.
                        great   stomach   part

11 Q'am-g·ē'îpL   dē-g·ē'Elt.   NLk·'ē   lō-yîlya'ltkᵘdēitg·ê.   NLk·'ē
   Only   she ate   on her   what she   Then   they returned.   Then
                      part   picked.

12 ba'kᵘdet   aL   ts'Em-hwî'lpL   na'k·sdet.   NLk·'ē   la'mdzîxdēt.   NLk·'ē
   they came   to   in   house   their husband.   Then   they entered.   Then
   from there

13 a'lg·îxL   wī-lig·'ē'Enskᵘ: "Ām,   mE   dEm   wô'ôL   qal-ts·'a'p."   NLk·'ē
   said   the   grizzly bear: "Good,   you   (fut.)   invite   the people."   Then
              great

14 a'lg·îxL   aL   g·a'tg·ê.   NLk·'ē   dā'ulL   k·'älL   g·at   t·an   huwô'ôL
   she said   to   a man.   Then   left   one   man   who   invited

15 wī-hē'ldEm   g·at.   NLk·'ē   t'Em-gō'uL   hana'q   dēLkᵘt.   NLk·'ē
   many   men.   Then   toward   took   the woman   her bag.   Then
                                the middle

took her bag to the middle of the house. The great Grizzly Bear was
also in the house. The great Grizzly Bear said to her husband,
"Take some dishes to the rear of the house." Her husband did so.
Then she defecated into a dish, and the berries she had eaten fell
into it. Now the dish was full of berries that she had picked. The
Indians saw her defecating into the dishes. Then the Grizzly Bear told
the man to take the dishes that were full of what had come out of her
anus and place them before the people; but they were afraid to eat it
because they had seen that they had come out of her anus. They only
ate the berries that the Indian woman had picked. They took home
the food that the great Grizzly Bear had given them, and the wives of
the people ate it at their own houses. Then the great Grizzly Bear
was glad.

---

ts'ɛm-g·îtsâ'ôn,	nLnɛL	hwîl	dē-lō-d'ā'L	wī-lig·''ē'ɛnsk".	NLk·'ē	1
in in the house,	that is where	being	also in was	the great grizzly bear.	Then	

a'lg·îxt	aL	nak·st:	"Hūts'ɛn-d'a'Lt	qa-ts'ō'oL	ts'ak·."	NLk·'ēt 2
she said	to	her husband:	"Back from fire put	some	dishes."	Then

gun-hūts'ɛn-d'a'Lt	nak·st.	NLk·'ē hwîlt.	NLk·'ē wī-ts'ɛm-g·â'ôlt 3
made back from put them fire	her husband.	Then he did so.	Then large in her anus

dē-k·si-yô'xk"L	mā'ɛ	Le	g·ē'îptg·ê	ma'Ldēt	dēt-g·ē'ɛlt. 4
on out went her part	berries	what	she ate	she said	on she picked her part them

NLnēL	Le	g·ē'îpt	lō-d'ā'Lɛt.	NLk·'ē	ts'ɛm-g·â'ôlt	dē- 5
What	she	ate	in she put.	Then	in her anus	also

k·si-yô'xk"t.	NLk·'ē	mɛtme'tk"L	ts'ak·	aL	dē-sɛ-mā'it.	Tk·'ē 6
out went.	Then	full was	the dish	of	on her she berries. part made	Then

g·a'aL	alō-g·ig·a't	hwîl	gwa'tstg·ê	lâ't.	Hwä'i!	NLk·'ēt 7
saw it	the Indians	where	excre- per- ments haps	in it.	Well!	Then she

gun-dô'gôt	La	mɛtme'tk"L	ts'ak·	aL	ma'ɛ t'an	k·si-yô'xk"L 8
or- to take dered		full	dish	of	berries that	out came

ts'ɛm-g·â'ôlt.	NLk·'ē	dôxt	aL qa-ga-sä'XL	qaL-ts'a'p.	NLk·'ē 9
in her anus.	Then	she laid it	at before the	people.	Then

laxbēts'ē'x·dēt	aL	dɛmt g·ē'pdēît,	aL hwîl	gwa'tstg·ê	lâ'ôt, 10
they were afraid	to	(fut.) eat it,	because	excre- per- ments haps	in it,

aL hwîlt	g·a'adet	hwîl k·si-yô'xk"L	ts'ɛm-g·â'ôlt.	K·sax-sɛ-mā'iL 11
because	they saw it	where out of it came	in her anus.	Only made berries

k·sɛm-alō-g·ig·a't,	nēLne'L	g·ē'îpdet.	NLk·'ē	sô'ôdēt	aL 12
woman Indian,	that	they ate.	Then	they took the rest home	of

dē-g·înā'mL	wī-lig·''ē'ɛnsk"g·ê.	NLk·'ē	g·ē'îpL	ga-nē'nik·sk"dētg·ê 13
also she had given them great	the grizzly bear.	Then	ate it	their wives

aL	lɛp-ts'ɛm-huwî'lpL	qal ts'a'pg·ê.	Hwä'i!	NLk·'ē	lō-ā'mL 14
at	own in the houses of	the people.	Well!	Then	in good

qâ'ôdɛL	wī-lig·''ē'ɛnsk".	15
heart	the grizzly bear. great	

Now, salmon were in the river in front of the town. The chief made a weir, and placed a fish trap in it. He finished it. In the evening the people went to sleep, and before daybreak the great Grizzly Bear rose and went down to the weir. She saw that the trap was full of salmon, and she emptied it. She took the salmon into the house. Then she ordered the chief, her father-in-law, to distribute them among the people. He did so. The next night she did the same, but the people did not know it. She did so many days. Then she and the woman dried many salmon, and the house was full of fish that she and the other woman had dried.

One morning a young man went down to the weir. When he saw that there were no salmon in the trap, because the great Grizzly Bear had

1 Hwäi! NLk·'ē La mē'sîL hân aL ak·s qa-g·ä'wuL qal-ts'a'p.
   Well!   Then   when swam   salmon in the   in front of   the town.
                        the   water

2 NLk·'ē tgōn dzāpL sɛm'â'g·it su-hwa'tdēt aL t'ēn. NLk·'ē
   Then   this   made   the chief   made   name   of   weir.   Then

3 d'āL hwô'ô; nLk·'ē d'āL Lamga'ng·ê. NLk·'ē Lēskᵘt.
   there a trap; then   there (another kind Then   it was
   was   there   was   of trap).   finished :

4 Lē'saandēt. NLk·'ē yu'ksa. NLk·'ē lāLL qal-ts'a'p. Q'ai-tsô'osk·L
   They finished it Then   it was   Then   lay   the people.   Only   a little
                        evening.   down

5 dɛm hwîl mɛsā'x; nLk·'ē g·in-hē'tkᵘL wī-lig·'ē'ɛnskᵘ. NLk·'e
   (fut.) when daylight; then   rose   the grizzly bear.   Then
                                              great

6 iaga-iä'êt aL awa'aL hwîl hētkᵘL t'ēn. NLk·'ē g·a'aL hwîl
   down she to the prox- where stood a weir.   Then   she saw where
   went   imity of

7 metkᵘL Lā'mgan aL hân. NLk·'ē sɛmt-lō-qâ'ôdɛnt. NLk·'ēt
   full the trap   of   salmon. Then   very in she emptied it. Then she

8 bax-dô'qt aL ts'ɛm-hwî'lp. NLk·'ēt gun-iä'gɛt aL sɛm'â'g·it
   up took to   inside of house. Then she ordered to dis- to   the chief
   them   tribute

9 wī-La'msg·ê aL qal-ts'a'p. NLk·'ēt iä'qdēt. NLk·'ē huX
   the father-in- to   the town. Then they distributed Then   again
   great law   them.

10 yu'ksa. NLk·'ē huX hwîlt. Nî'g·idet hwîlā'x·L qal-ts'a'p.
    it was   Then   again she did Not   knew it   the people.
    evening.   so.

11 Lā wī-hē'lL saL hwî'ltg·ê, nLk·'ē La wī-hē'lL gwa'lkᵘdēt
    When many   days she did so, then   when many   she dried

12 qanL sîl-hana'qt Lā metkᵘL hwîlp, at hwîl gwa'lguL
    and   her woman   when was full house, she what dried
          fellow   the

13 wī-lig·'ē'ɛnskᵘ qanL sîl-hana'qt.
    the grizzly bear and   her woman.
    great   fellow

14 NLk·'ē hē'Luk, nLk·'ē iaga-iē'êL k·âlL q'aima'sɛm g·at.
    Then   it was   then   down went   one   young   man.
           morning,

15 ALa lā-hē'tkᵘL qâ'ôdɛt aL hwîl nî'g·îdēt hwa'dēL hân.
    When stood   his heart because not he   found   salmon.

taken them up to her husband's house, he felt badly. He grew angry, and scolded the great Grizzly Bear. He felt badly because he did not get anything. The young man said, "You rise too early, great Drop-jaw." Thus he said to the great Grizzly Bear, and he scolded again, "You feed us with your excrements." Then the great Grizzly Bear took notice of it. She became angry, ran out, and rushed up to the man who was scolding her. She rushed into the house, took him, and killed him. She tore his flesh to pieces and broke his bones. Then she went. Now she remembered her own people and her two children. She was very angry, and she went home. Her husband followed her, but the great Grizzly Bear said, "Return home, or I

NLk·'ē	nî'g·ît	g·a'aL	hân	aL	ts'ɛm-Lā'mgan	Lāt	huX	1
Then	not he	saw	salmon	at	in the trap	after	again	

bax-qâ'ôd'ɛnt	wī-lig·'ē'ɛnsk^u	aL	hwîlpL	nak·st,	nîLnē'L	qan	2
up she had finished them	the grizzly bear great	to	the house of	her husband,		therefore	

lō-sī'êpk^uL	qâ'ôdɛt.	NLk·'ēt	hak·st.	Ha'k·sîL	q'aima'sɛm	g·aL	3
in sick was	his heart.	Then he scolded.		He scolded	the young	man	

wī lig·'ē'ɛnsk^u.	Lō-sī'êpk^uL	qâ'ôdet	aL	hwîl	qal-wî'tk^ut.	TgōnL	4
the grizzly bear great.	In sick was	his heart	because	he did not get anything.		This	

hēL	q'aima'sɛm	g·at:	"Ax-dē-ha'wuL	Lô'ôqL	wī-tg·aā'q,"	5
said	the young	man:	"Not on your part quit	early rising	great drop-jaw,"	

aL	wī-lig·'ē'ɛnsk^u,	an-hē't.	Ha'k·sît	qan	hēt.	G·ē'lp'ɛlL	6
to	great grizzly bear,	that he is what said.	He scolded	there-fore	he said so.	Twice	

hwîl	ha'k·st.	"Wī-ang·a'tgum	gwats,"	dē'ya	t hwîl	huX	7
(verbal noun)	he scolded.	"Great giving for food	excrements,"	thus he said	when	again	

hak·st.	NLk·'ēt	ā'd'îx·L	wī-lig·'ē'ɛnsk^ug·ê.	NLk·'ē	ā'd'îk·sk^uL	8
he scolded.	Then she	noticed it	the grizzly bear. great	Then	she came	

hwîl	lō-sī'êpk^uL	qâ'ôdɛt.	NLk·'ē	wī-k·si-ba'xt	aL	wī-Lî'ntx·t.	9
being	in sick	heart.	Then	much out she ran	at	great-ly angry.	

NLk·'ēt	qâ'ôL	hwîl	lō-d'ā'L	g·atL	t'an	hak·st.	NLk·'ē	10
Then she	went to	where	in was	man	who	scolded.	Then	

ts'ɛlɛm-hē'tk^ut.	NLk·'ēt	gō'uL	g·a'tg·ê.	NLk·'ēt	k^uLē-dza'k^ut.	11
into she stood.	Then	she took	the man.	Then	all over she killed him.	

Nô'ôL	g·a'tg·ê.	K^uLē-qâ'ôdɛL	smax·t.	NLk·'ē	hēLā'LagaL	txanē'tk^uL	12
It was dead	the man.	All over was finished	his flesh.	Then	were broken	all	

Le	dzēdz'ē'pt.	NLk·'ē	hwîl	k·'ē	iä'ēt.	Am-qâ'ôdɛL	Lē	ts'apt	13
	his bones.	At once		she went.	She remembered	her people		

hwîl	hwanL	t'ɛpxā'tL	Lg·î'tg·ê.	K·'ē	iä'ɛL	wī-lig·'ē'ɛnsk^u.	Ā'lɛq	14
where	were	two	her cubs.	Then	went	the grizzly bear. great	Angry	

lō-sī'êpk^uL	qâ'ôdt.	NLk·'ēt	yôxk^uL	nak·st.	NLk·'ē	tgōn	hēL	15
in was sick	her heart.	Then	followed her	her husband.	Then	this	said	

210   BUREAU OF AMERICAN ETHNOLOGY   [BULL. 27]

shall kill you." But the man refused, because he loved his great wife. The Grizzly Bear spoke to him twice, wanting him to go back, but he refused. Then she rushed upon him and killed him, and her own husband was dead. Then the great Grizzly Bear left.

1 wī-lig·''ē'ᴇnskᵘ: "Adô', ya'ltgun! Dza'kᵘdē-g·a nē'ᴇn." Nʟk·'ē
the great grizzly bear: "Adô', turn back! Kill I maybe you." Then

2 hä'q'aʟ g·a'tg·ê at hwîl sī'êp'ᴇnʟ wī-na'k·sᴇm lig·''ē'ᴇnskᵘ. G·ē'lp'ᴇl
refused the man because he loved the wife great grizzly bear. Twice

3 hēʟ wī-lig·''ē'ᴇnskᵘ, at gulîk·s-hē'tsʟ nak·st. Nʟk·'ē hä'q'aʟ
said the grizzly bear, great she back sent her husband. Then refused

4 g·a'tg·ê, qan hwîlʟ wī-lig·''ē'ᴇnskᵘ gulîk·s-hē'tkᵘt. Nʟk·'ēt dzakᵘt.
the man, there-fore she did so the grizzly bear great back rushed. Then she killed him.

5 Nʟk·'ēt nô'ôʟ g·a'tg·ê ʟᴇp-na'k·stg·ê. Nʟk·'ē dā'uʟʟ wī-lig·''ē'ᴇnskᵘ.
Then was dead the man her own husband. Then left the grizzly bear. great

6 Nô'ôʟ g·at.
It was dead the man.

[Told by Moses]

There were four children who were always shooting squirrels. They killed them all the time. Then they dried their skins and put away their meat. They did so at the foot of a large spruce tree— they did so for a long time all the year round. Then they had killed all the squirrels. Only the chief of the squirrels and his daughter were left. She was very white. Now, a boy went out and came to the foot of the great spruce tree. He looked upward, and saw a little white squirrel running round the tree. When it had gotten to the other side of the tree, behold, he saw that she

---

SQUIRREL

Txalpxdâ'l	k'opᴇ-tk·'ē'ʟkᵘ	qanē-hwîlat	gu'Xdēit	ts'ᴇnʟî'k·.	1
Four	little children	always	shot	squirrels.	

Nʟk·'ēt qanē-hwîla tsô'ôtdētg·ê.	Gwa'lkᵘdēt ʟa annā'st.	Nʟk·'ēt	2
Then always they killed them.	They dried the skins.	Then	

k·si-d'ā'ʟdēʟ	ʟā	qa-sma'x·t.	Q'am-k·'ē'lʟ	mēnʟ	wī-sä'êqs	hwî̂l	3
out they put		their meat.	Only one	foot of	big spruce tree	(verbal noun)	

huwî̂'ldētg·ê.	Wī-na'kᵘʟ	huwî̂'ldētg·ê.	Txanē'tkᵘʟ	k'ōʟ	4
they did so.	Very long	they did so.	Every	year	

hwî̂'ldētg·ê.	Nʟk·'ē	ʟā	qâ'ôdᴇʟ	ts'ᴇnʟî'k·,	q'am-k·'â'lʟ	5
they did so.	Then	(perf.)	they were finished	squirrels,	only one	

sᴇm'â'g·idᴇm	ts'ᴇnʟî'k·	mā'ntg·ê,	dē-k·'â'lʟ	ʟgō'uʟkᵘt,	ʟgo-	6
chief of	squirrels	left,	with one	his child,	a little	

hana'qʟ	ʟgō'uʟkᵘtg·ê	hwî̂l	mākᵘsʟ	ʟîpʟa'nt.	Nʟk·'ē	huX	7
woman	little his child	(verbal noun)	white	its body.	Then	again	

iä'êʟ	k·'âlʟ	ʟgo-tk·'ē'lkᵘ.	K·'ēt huX hwaʟ mēnʟ wī-sä'êqs.	8
went	one	child.	Then again he found foot of big spruce tree.	

K·'ē	huX	mᴇn-g·a'askᵘt.	Sā-k'utgo-dā'uʟʟ,	ʟgō-mas-ts'ᴇnʟî'k·	9
Then	again	up he looked.	Sud- around went denly	little white squirrel	

aʟ qa-dâ'ʟ	wī-ga'n.	Nʟk·'ē	k'utgo-ba'xt.	Gwinā'dᴇʟ,	q'aima'sᴇm	10
on other side of	big tree.	Then	around it ran.	Behold,	a young	

was a young woman. The boy saw her. The woman called him.
Then the boy placed his bow at the foot of the great tree.

The woman entered the house of her father, who was the chief of
the squirrels. He was much troubled, as all his people were dead.
Therefore he had sent his child to call the boy. The chief questioned
his daughter, and she replied, "The boy is standing outside." Then
the chief said, "Come in, my dear, if it is you who killed my people."
The prince entered and sat down. They gave him to eat. After he
had finished, the chief said, "Why did you kill all my people?" The
prince replied, "I did not know that they were your people, therefore I did so." "Take pity on me," said the chief to the prince.
"When you return home, burn the meat and the skins of all the squir-

---

1 hana'q   hēhē'tgut.   K·'ēt   g·a'aL   Lgo-tk·'ē'Lkⁿ.   NLk·'ēt   wô'ôL
   woman   standing.   Then   he saw   the   Then   she called
                                        her   little boy.   him

2 hana'q   Lgo-tk·'ē'Lkⁿ.   NLk·'ē   Lô'ôdet.   Hē't'EnL   Lgo-tk·'ē'LkⁿL
   the   the   boy.   Then   they went.   He placed   the   boy
   woman   little   upon it

3 ha-Xda'kⁿt   aL   mēnL   wī-ga'n.
   his bow   at   foot of   his tree.

4 NLk·'ē   dEp-ts'ē'nL   hana'q   aL   hwîlps   nEguâ'ôtt;   mēnL
   Then   they entered   the   to   the   her father;   master
                              woman   house of   of

5 ts'EnLî'k·   gō'stg·ê.   Lā   aba'g·askⁿL   sEm'â'g·it   aL   hwîl   Lā
   squirrels   that one.   (Perf.)   troubled   the chief   because   (perf.)

6 lō-nô'ôL   ts'apt.   Nt   qan   hētsL   Lgō'uLkⁿt.   NLk·'ēt   wô'ôL
   all dead   his people. Therefore   he sent   his child.   Then she   invited
                                                                                      in

7 Lgō'uLkⁿL   Lgo-tk·'ē'Lkⁿ.   NLk·'ēt   g·ē'dExL   sEm'â'g·it   Lgō'uLkⁿtg·ê.
   his child   the   boy.   Then   he asked   the chief   his child.
                little

8 NLk·'ē   a'lg·îxL   Lgō'uLkⁿL   sEm'â'g·it: "La   hētkⁿt   aL   g·ā'lEq."
   Then   said   the child of   the chief: "He   stands   at   outside."

9 NLk·'ē   a'lg·îxL   sEm'â'g·it.   TgōnL   hēt: "Ts'ē'nEn,   nāt,   atsEda
   Then   said   the chief.   This   he said: "Come in,   my   if it is
                                                                          dear,

10 nē'En   an   La   lō-nô'ôt'EnL   ts'ā'bEE."   K·'ē   ts'EnL   Lgo-
    you   who   all   killed   my people."   Then   entered   the
                                                                             little

11 wī'lk·sîLk·g·ê.   NLk·'ē   d'āt.   NLk·'ē   wô'ôtkⁿt.   NLk·'ē   Läxkⁿt.
    prince.   Then   he sat   Then   he was   Then   he finished
                                 down.   invited.   eating.

12 NLk·'ē   a'lg·îxL   sEm'â'g·it: "Ago   ma   ga'n   La   lō-nô'ôt'EnL
    Then   said   the chief: "Why did you   all   kill

13 ts'a'bEE?"   NLk·'ē   a'lg·îxL   Lgo-wî'lk·sîLkⁿ: "Nî'g·în   hwîlā'x·t
    my people?"   Then   said   the   prince: "I did not   know it
                                        little

14 nîLnê'L   qan   hwî'lEE."   "TgōnL   dEm   hwî'lEn;   āmL   qam-gâ'dEn
    therefore I did so."   "This   (fut.)   you do;   good   you take pity

15 lâ'ē,"   dē'yaL   sEm'â'g·it   aL   Lgo-wî'lk·sîLkⁿ.   "TsEda   Lā
    on me,"   thus said   the chief   to   the   prince.   "When   (perf.)
                                               little

rels. I will make you a shaman." The chief did so; he made the prince a shaman. Now he was a great shaman. "Your name as a shaman shall be Squirrel," said the chief.

The prince lay down. Then the chief rose and put on his dancing apron. He painted his body red, and put on a crown of bear claws. From his neck hung the skins of squirrels. He held a rattle in his hand and sang, "Ia haä, iâ nigua iahaē! I become accustomed to this side, I become accustomed to the other side." Then the prince became a great shaman. The chief of the squirrels did so a whole year. Then he sent the prince home.

The chief, who had lost his son, had almost forgotten him. Then one of his other sons went to shoot squirrels, and came to the place

lō-ya′ltgun, nʟ dᴇm k‵′ē me-txē′ldîʟ ʟa ga-sma′x‵ʟ wī-hē′ldᴇm 1
you have returned, then (fut.) burn (part.) the meat of (plural) many

ts’ᴇnʟi′k‵ qanʟ ʟa ga-anā′st. Dᴇm sa-hālai′dē nē′ᴇn. Nʟk‵′ē 2
squirrels and (perf.) the skins. (Fut.) make shaman I you. Then

hwîlʟ sᴇm’â′g‵it. Nʟk‵′ēt sa-hālai′ʟ ʟgo-wî′lk‵sîʟkᵘ. Nʟk‵′ē 3
he did so the chief. Then he made him a shaman the little prince. Then

halai′tg‵ê. "Ts’ᴇnlä′k‵ʟ dᴇm hwam halai′dᴇn." Nʟk‵′ē hwîlʟ 4
he was a shaman "Squirrel (fut.) name of shaman you." Then he did so

ʟgō-wî′lk‵sîʟkᵘg‵ê. 5
the little prince.

Nʟk‵′ē sg‵ēl ʟgo-wî′lk‵sîʟkᵘ. Nʟk‵′ē hētkᵘʟ sᴇm’â′g‵it. 6
Then he lay down the little prince. Then he stood the chief.

Hâ′yîʟ an-bᴇlā′n. Nʟk‵′ēt ma′sîʟ ʟᴇpʟa′nt aʟ mᴇs-a′ust. 7
He put on the dancing apron. Then he painted red his body with red paint.

Nʟk‵′ēt hâx‵ʟ ʟaqs. Nʟk‵′ēt iē′tkᵘʟ ʟa anā′sʟ ts’ᴇnʟî′k‵. 8
Then he put on him to wear crown of bear claws. Then hung around from his neck (perf.) the skins of squirrels.

K‵′ēt yō′guʟ ha-sä′x; nʟk‵′ē lē′mîx‵t: "Ia haä′, iâ nigua 9
Then he held a rattle; then he sang: "Ia haä′, iâ nigua

iahaē. Dᴇm qai-k‵ax-māwiʟ an-g‵ī′ᴇ. Dᴇm qai-k‵ax-māwiʟ 10
iahaē. (Fut.) get used to this side. (Fut.) get used to

an-dâ′sdaᴇ." Nʟk‵′ē wī-t’ē′sʟ hālai′ʟ ʟgo-wî′lk‵sîʟkᵘg‵ê. 11
the other side." Then a great shaman the little prince.

ʟā k‵′ē′ᴇlʟ k’ōʟ hwîlt, nʟk‵′ē ʟā wī-t’ē′sʟ hwîl wī-halai′tt. 12
When one year he did so, then (perf.) great (verbal noun) great shaman he.

Nʟk‵′ēt na-hē′tst. 13
Then out of woods he sent him.

ʟā t’ak‵ʟ sᴇm’â′g‵it hwîl gwâtkᵘʟ ʟgō′uʟkᵘtg‵ê. Nʟk‵′ē 14
(Perf.) he had forgotten the chief (verbal noun) was lost his son. Then

huX iä′ᴇʟ k‵′âlt dᴇm huX gō′yîʟ ts’ᴇnʟî′k‵; nʟk‵′ēt huX 15
again went another one (fut.) also shoot squirrels; then again

where his brother had been.   He came to the great spruce tree.   He
looked up, and, behold, the skeleton of a man was hanging in the
branches.   The bones were held together by skin only.   His flesh was
all gone.

The boy returned.   He entered the house and told his father about
it.   The father sent the young men, who saw where the body
was hanging.   Then one young man climbed the tree, took the body
down, and they carried it home.   They entered the house.   Now the
chief's wife took a mat.   She spread it out and laid the body down on
it.   She laid it down very nicely.   The young men placed his hands,
his feet, and his head in the way they belonged, and laid the head
down face upward.   There were only bones.   Then they covered the
mat with another mat.   They painted it red and covered it with bird
down.   Then they sacrificed.   For four nights and days his father and

---

1 hwaL   Lē   hwîl   hwî'lL   wa'k·tg·ê   hwîl   hē'tkuL   wī-sä'qs.
   he   (perf.)   where   he had   his brother   (verbal   stood   big spruce
   found   been   noun)   tree.

2 NLk·'ē   mEn-g·a'asku t.   Gwinā'dēL,   g·at   lē-ia'qt   aL   lax-anē's.
   Then   up   he looked.   Behold,   a man   on hung   on   on branch.

3 K·sax-ts'ē'p   q'am-nē-daxdä'ExL   ts'ēp,   nî'g·î   smax·t.
   Only   bones   only to-   fastened   bones,   no   flesh.
                   gether

4 NLk·'ē   lō-ya'ltkuL   Lgo-tk·'ē'Lku.   NLk·'ē   ts'ēnt.   K·'ēt   ma'Lît
   Then   he returned   the   boy.   Then   he   Then   he told
                                             entered.

5 as   nEguâ'ôdEt.   NLk·'ē   a'lg·îxs   nEguâ'ôdEt   aL   q'aima'qsit.
   to   his father.   Then   said   his father   to   youths.

6 NLk·'ē   q'a'ldîx-qâ'ôdet.   NLk·'ēt   g·a'adet   hwîl   lē-ia'qt.   NLk·'ēt
   Then   to the rear   they went.   Then   they saw   (verbal   on   he   Then
         of the houses   noun)   hung.

7 mEn-qâ'ôL   k·'âlL   q'aima'sEt.   NLk·'ēt   gō'ut.   NLk·'ēt   d'Ep-ie'êt.
   up   went   one   youth.   Then he   took him.   Then   down   he
       for it   went.

8 NLk·'ēt   na-dē-iä'det.   NLk·'ēt   dē-ts·ē'ndēt   aL   ts·Em-hwî'lp.
   Then   out of with   he   Then   with   they   in   in   house.
        the woods   it   went.   it   entered

9 NLk·'ēt   gōL   nak·sL   sEm'â'g·it   sqa'naa.   K·'ēt   baLt.   NLk·'ēt
   Then she   took   the wife   the chief   a mat.   Then   she   Then
                    of   opened it.

10 lē-sg·ē'det   lâ'ôt.   SEm-ama   sg·ē'tdēt.   NLk·'ēt   sEm-ama   dô'xdēL
    on   they   on it.   Very   well   they laid   Then   very well   they laid
        laid it   it.

11 an'ô'nt   qanL   asesa'ēt   qanL   t·Em-qē'st.   SEm-hasba-sg·ē'det
    his hands   and   his feet   and   his head.   Very   face up   they laid
                                                                    it

12 k·sax-ts'ē'p.   NLk·'ēt   huX   lē-sg·ē'deL   k·'ä'guL   sqa'naa   aL
    only   bones.   Then   also   on   they laid   another   mat   on

13 lax-ō't.   Txa-ma'sdēit   aL   mEs-a'ust   qanL   mîx·q·ā'x·   NLk·'ē
    on top   All   they made   with   red paint   and   down.   Then
    of him.   red

14 qa'nē-hwîla   mElgwû'ôksdēt.   La   txalpxL   yu'ksa   qanL   mEsā'x·
    always   they sacrificed.   When   four   nights   and   days

mother did not stay in the house. They had gone to another place, to another house. Only four men, his most intimate friends, watched him. Then they sang "Äe!" accompanying their song with batons. Then they spoke, singing. Then the body came to life again. The bones were covered with flesh. Then he sang. He invited the tribe of his father in and the people came. Then the prince said, "Burn the meat of all the squirrels that I shot during the past years, and burn their bones and the skins, which I am keeping in many boxes." The people did so. They burnt it all.

Then the great master of the squirrels was glad, because his tribe had come to life again. Then the prince sang, "Iā hēiaha ä, hēia haä' ayâ nēgwâ' iahâ! I become accustomed to this side; I become accus-

---

1　nîg·î lō-d'ā'L nEguâ'ôdEt qanL nôxt. G·id'an-d'ā'tk^u aL k·'ēlL
　　not　in　were　his father　and　his mother.　They were in other place　in　other

2　hwîlp. K·sax-txalpxdâ'l lEp-an-sEpsī'Ep'Ensk^u t'an lē'Lk·tg·ê.
　　house.　Only four men　his own　friends　who　watched him.

3　NLk·'ē ā'd'îk·sk^ut dEm hwîl lē'mîx· aL dzä'ēg·îxt: "Äe!"
　　Then　came　(fut.)　when　they sang　and　started beating with sticks:　"Äe!"

4　TgōnL hē'tg·ê. NLk·'ē lē'mîx·tg·ê. NLk·'ē dax-g·a'tt.
　　This　he said.　Then　he sang.　Then　he got strong.

5　Ha'ts'îk·sEm a'd'îk·sk^ut dEm hwîl smax·t. NLk·'ē lē'mîx·t.
　　Once more　came　(fut.)　where　flesh.　Then　he sang.

6　NLk·'ēt wô'ôs nEguâ'dEL qal-ts'a'p aL dEm hētk^ut.
　　Then　he invited　his father　the people　to　stand.

7　NLk·'ē ts'ElEm-qâ'ôdEL qal-ts'a'p. NLk·'ē a'lg·îxL Lgo-wî'lk·sîLkⁿ.
　　Then　into　were gone　the people.　Then　said　the little　prince.

8　TgōnL hēt: "ĀmL dEm txēltk^u La ga-sma'x·L wî-hē'ldEm
　　This　he said:　"Good　(fut.)　burn　the meat of　many

9　ts'EnLî'k· Lē guXgō'yē aL txanē'tk^uL k'ōL. TsE k·sax La
　　squirrels　what　shot by me　in　all the　years.　Only

10　ga-ts'ē'pt dEm txē'ldEsEmEst," dē'yaL Lgo-wî'lk·sîLk^u, "qanL
　　bones　(fut.)　you will burn,"　thus he said　the little prince,　"and

11　La ga-anā'st wî-hē'lL qal-hē'nEq hwîl lō-daxdô'xL ga-anā'st."
　　the skins　many　boxes　where　in are　the skins."

12　NLk·'ē hwîlt lEgEm-qâ't'Endet.
　　Then　they did so　into they put it all.

13　NLk·'ē lō-ā'mL qâ'ôdEL wî-mē'nL ts'EnLî'k·. Ha'ts'Ek·sEm huX
　　Then　in was good　heart of　the master great of　the squirrels.　Once more　again

14　wî-hē'lL ts'a'pdētg·ê. NLk·'ē lēmîx·'L Lgo-wî'lk·sîLk^u: "Iā hēiaha
　　many　his people.　Then　sang　the little prince:　"Iā hēiaha

15　ä, hēia haä' ayâ nēgwâ' iahâ. DEm qai-k·ax-māwiL an-g·ī'E,
　　ä,　hēia　haä'　ayâ　nēgwâ'　iahâ.　(Fut.)　get used to　this side,

tomed to the other side." He stood there, and was a great shaman. Then he stopped. His name as a shaman was Squirrel. That is the end.

---

1 dɛm qai-k·ax-māwiʟ an-dâ'sdaɛ." Nʟk·'ē hētkᵘʟ halai'tg·ê. Nʟk·'ē
  (fut.)   get used to   the other side."   Then   stood   the shaman.   Then

2 ʟā ha'ut. Nʟk·'ē ē'tkᵘdēʟ hwam halai'tt Ts'ɛnʟä'k·ʟ hwa'tg·ê.
  he   stopped.   Then   they named   his   shaman   Squirrel   his name.
                                              name

3 Hwä'i! Qâ'ôdɛt.
  Well!   It is
         finished.

[Told by Moody]

When a sorcerer wants to kill a fellow-man, he takes some of the man's perspiration, or an old shirt, and takes it to the place where he keeps his witch-box. Then he opens his box, takes a string, and fastens a piece of the old shirt to it. He ties it across the box. When he wants the man to die quickly, he takes a piece of the old shirt, and cuts the string in the box so that the piece of shirt falls on the corpse that is in the box. As soon as this is done, and the string breaks, he pretends to cry for his victim; then the man from whom he has taken the piece of shirt must die. When he knows that the person is dead, he

---

WITCHCRAFT

TsEda	hasa'qʟ	haldā'ug·ît	dEmt	dzakᵘʟ	sEl-g·a'tt,	k·'ēt	gōʟ	1
When	wants	a sorcerer	to	kill	a fellow person,	then	he takes	

ts'ā'Edz'îqst;	lîg·i-q'am-k·s-la'wîskᵘʟ	g·at	gō'dEt.	Nʟk·'ē	hwîl	2
dirt (of man);	or old shirt of	a man	he takes it.	At once		

k·'ēt	dôgâ'ôdEt	alaʟ	hwîl	sg·iʟ	qaldEm-haldā'ug·ît,	wô'aʟk·'ēt	3
	he takes it	to	where	lies	box of witch,	and then	

q'ā'gaʟ	qaldEm-haldā'ug·ît.	K·'ēt	gō'uʟ	wôhā'st,	k·'ēt	tq'al-ts'ē'bEʟ	4
he opens	box of witch.	Then	he takes	string,	then against	he fastens it	

ʟgo-q'am-k·s-la'wîskᵘ	lâ'ôt.	K·'ēt	tsaga-hō'ksaant	aʟ	ts'Em-qaldEm-	5
little old shirt	to it.	Then	across he fastens it	at	in box of	

haldā'ug·ît.	Woaʟk·'ē	ʟā	nakᵘʟ	dāt	hwîlā'gut,	hwîl	k·'ē	tsEdā	6
witch.	After	(perf.)	a long time	when he	did this,	then	when		

hasa'qt	tsE	dEmt	t'ēl	nô'ôdEnʟ	g·aʟ,	t	hwîlt	gō'oʟ	q'am-k·s-la'wîskᵘ.	7
he wants	when	(fut.)	quickly	to kill	a man	he then	takes	old	shirt.	

Wôaʟk·'ēt	lō-d'Ep-t'Eklā'aʟsaanʟ	wôhā'st	aʟ	ts'Em-qa'ldEm-	8
Then	in down he breaks it	the string	in	in box of	

haldā'ug·îtg·ê	spagai't-lôga	lō'ʟEq.	Hwîl	k·'ē	ʟēskᵘt	lō-d'Ep-	9
witch	among rotten	corpse.	Then		it is finished	in down	

t'Eklā'aʟsaanʟ	wôhā'st.	K·'ē	hwîl	k·'ē	hîs-wiyē'tkᵘst	at	ā'wuʟ	10
he breaks the	string.	At once			he pretends to cry		for this	

g·aʟ	ʟa	an-hwî'ntg·ê.	Nʟk·'ē	ʟa	ʟēskᵘʟ	hwî'ltg·ê,	k·'ē	hwîl	11
man	(perf.)	he did.	Then	(perf.)	he finishes	doing this,	at once		

k·'ē	t'ēlʟ	nô'ôʟ	g·at	ʟa	an-hwî'ntg·ê.	K·'ē	da	ʟat	hwîlā'x·ʟ	12
quick	dies	the man	(perf.)	when he did it (took it from).	Then	when	(perf.)	he knows		

goes around the house in which the bewitched dead person is lying. After he has finished going around the house, he stops for a while; and when the dead one is buried, he goes to his grave and walks around it. Then he sits down in the grave and rubs his body, pretending to cry all the time. Then he returns, and his work is finished.

It is said that there was a son of a chief who had a friend who was also a prince. The chief was jealous of this prince, and he made up his mind to bewitch him. The chief told his son to invite his friend and to ask him to sleep in his house.

One day the chief's son invited his friend in, and they lay down. The

1 nô'ôL   g·at,   k·'ē   hwîl   k·'ēt   k'utgō-ie'etkuL,   aL   dāx·L   hwîlp
  dead   the   at once   around   he goes   around   house
           man,

2 hwî'l   lō-sg·î'L   nô'ôm   g·at   Lā   haldā'utg·ê.   Hwîl   k·'ē   Lēskut
  where   in lies   the dead   man   (perf.)   the bewitched   Then   he
                                                      one.   finishes

3 daa'qLkuL   k'utgō-ie'êtg·ê,   k·'ē   hwîl   k·'ē   k·'ax-hā'ôt.   Hwä'i!   Da   La
  he gets   around   going,   at once   a   he   Well!   Then when
                                                                while stops.

4 wôqsL   g·a'tg·ê   LE   nô'ôtg·ê,   hwîl   k·'ēt   huX   qâ'ôL   hwîl   sg·ît
  he is   the man   (perf.)   he is dead   then   again   he   where   he lie
  buried   (the dead one),   goes to

5 aL   g·ile'lix·.   K·'ē   hwîl   k·'ē   k'utgo-ie'êt   aL   dax·L   an-sg·î'tg·ê.
  at   back in   At once   around   he   at   around where   he lies.
        woods.   goes

6 LēskuL   hwî'ltg·ê.   K·'ē   hwîl   k·'ēt   lē-qâ'ôL   lax-an-sg·î'st,   k·'ē
  He   doing this.   At once   on   he   on   the grave,   then
  finishes   goes

7 k'uL-lē-Lô'ôtkut   lâ'ôt   aL   k'uL-hîs-wiyē'tkustg·ê.   LēskuL   hwî'ltg·ê.
  about on   he puts   on it   at   about   he pretends to cry.   He finishes   doing this.

8 K·'ē   hwîl   k·'ē   lō-ya'ltkut.   K·'ē   hā'ôt.   Lā   Lēskut.
  At once   he returns.   Then   he stops.   (Perf.)   he has
                                                          finished.

9 K·'âlL   Lgō'uLkuL   sEm'â'g·it,   k·'ē   k·'âlL   an-sē'ip'Ensku   q'aima'sEm
  One   son of   a chief,   then   one   friend   a young

10 g·a'tg·ê   sEm-hu'Xdē   Lgo-wî'lk·sîLkugat.   Wôalk·'ē'   lo-tsagum   gâ'ôL
   man   very   also   a   prince   it is   Then   in   sick   heart
                         little   said.

11 sEm'â'g·it   a'laL   Lgo-wî'lk·sîLkug·ê.   Wôalk·'ē'   hēL   gâ'ôtt   dEm
   the chief   against   the   prince.   Then   said   his   (fut.)
                         little   heart

12 haldā'uXtg·ê.   Wôalk·'ē'   hēL   sEm'â'g·itg·ê   aL   Lgō'uLkut   tgōn
   he bewitch him.   Then   said   the chief   to   his son   that

13 ts'EnEm-stē'ldEt.   K·'ēt   gun-dā'mgaL   Lgo-wî'lk·sîLkug·ê   aL   Lgō'uLkut.
   into   he accom-   Then   he   to stay   the   prince   to   his son.
           pany him.   caused   with him   little

14 Nē   La   k·'ēlL   sa,   k·'ēt   ts'EnEm-stē'lL   Lgō'uLkuL   sEm'â'g·itgê
   Then when   one   day,   then   into   accom-   the son of   the chief
                                          panied him

15 an-sī'ep'Enskug·ê   Lgo-wî'lk·sîLkug·ê.   K·'ē   hwîl   k·'ē   lā'Ldet.
   his friend   the   prince.   At once   they lay
              little   down.

prince lay on the outside and the chief's son on the inside of the bed.
The chief's son fell asleep, but the prince could not sleep, because he
was afraid the chief might bewitch him.　He rose and changed
places with the chief's son.　He lay down on the inside and put the
chief's son on the outside.　When the chief heard that they were
asleep, he rose and slowly walked to the bed on which the prince and
his son were sleeping.　The prince was much afraid when he heard
the chief coming, but he pretended to sleep.　The chief felt about
with his hands until he found the place where the prince had lain
down in the evening.　Then he wiped out the mouth of his own son
(thinking him to be the prince).　Then the chief lay down again.

In the morning the prince rose and went out.　After a short time

---

Lō-k·s-g·ī′êkst　Lgo-wî′lk·sîLk^ug·ê,　k·'ē　lō-k·s-g·its'â′ônL　Lgō′uLk^uL　1
At outside　the　prince,　and　at inside　the son of
little

sEm'â′g·itg·ê.　Hwä′i!　La　wâqL　Lgō′uLk^uL　sEm'â′g·itg·ê,　k·'ē　nî′g·ide　2
the chief.　Well!　When　slept　the son of　the chief,　then　not

wâqL　Lgo-wî′lk·sîLk^ug·ê.　Lō-xb'Etsa′XL　gâôtt　aL　sEm'â′g·itg·ê　dEmt　3
slept　the　prince.　In　afraid　his　of　the chief　(fut.)
little　heart

haldā′uXt　La　sī-gō′ng·ê.　K·'ē　ia′gai-g·in-hē′tk^uL　Lgo-wî′lk·sîLk^ug·ê.　4
he would　(perf.)　just then.　Then　how-　he got up　the　prince.
bewitch him　ever　little

K·'ē　ia′gai-sa-g·ä′êLt　aL　an-g·its'â′ng·ê.　K·'ē　ia′gai-sa-lō-sg·ī′eksL　5
Then　how-　quick-　he lay　at　inside.　Then　how-　quick-　in　was on
ever　ly　down　ever　ly　outside

Lgō′uLk^uL　sEm'â′g·itg·ê.　Hwä′i!　Lat　nExnā′L　sEm'â′g·itg·ê　La　6
the son of　the chief.　Well!　When　he heard　the chief　(perf.)

hwîl　wâ′wôqdēt,　hwîl　k·'ē′　g·in-hē′tk^ut.　K·'ē　hagun-iē′êt　aL　awa′aL　7
that　slept,　then　he got up.　Then　toward　he　into　proxim-
they　　went　ity of

hwîl　lā′LL　Lgo-wî′lk·sîLk^ug·ê　qanL　Lgō′uLk^ut.　Hwîl　k·'ēt　sEm-　8
where　they lay　the　prince　and　his son.　Then　much
down　little

xb'Etsa′XL　Lgo-wî′lk·sîLk^u　Lat　nexna′L　hwîl　ā′d'îk·sL　sEm'â′g·itg·ê　9
afraid　the　prince　when　he　coming　the chief
little　heard

aL　awa′aL　hwîl　lā′Ldet.　Hwîl　k·'ē　hîs-hūwâ′qsL　Lgo-wî′lk·sîLk^ug·ê.　10
to　proxim-　where　they lay.　Then　he　pretended　the　prince.
ity of　　to sleep　little

Hwîl　k·'ēt　lē-ba′qL　sEm'â′g·itg·ê　La　hwîl　g·ä′êL　Lgo-wî′lk·sîLk^ug·ê.　11
Then　on　he felt　the chief　(perf.)　where　he lay　the　prince.
little

K·'ēt　k·si-g·î′mk·L　ts'Em-ā′qL　lEp-Lgō′uLk^utg·ê.　Lēsk^ut　hwîlā′gut.　12
Then　out　he wiped　his mouth　own　his son.　He fin-　what he did.
ished

K·'ē　hwîl　k·'ē′　hatsEm　huX　g·ä′êL　sEm'â′g·itg·ê.　13
At once　once more　again　lay　the chief.
down

Hwä′i!　La　hē′Luk,　k·'ē　g·in-hē′tk^uL　Lgo-wî′lk·sîLk^ug·ê.　K·'ē　14
Well!　When　morning,　then　rose　the　prince.　Then
little

k·saXt.　Hwä′i!　Nî′g·i　nak^ut,　k·'ē　sī′êpk^uL　Lgō′uLk^uL　15
he went　Well!　Not　long,　then　got sick　the son of
out.

the chief's son got sick.   Then the chief knew at once that he had
made a mistake.   For four days the boy was sick.   Then he died.
Now the chief was much troubled.   He cried because his son was dead,
saying, "I have destroyed him myself! I have destroyed him myself!"

---

1 sɛm'â′g·itg·ê.   K·'ē   hwîl   k·'ēt   q'āmgai′t-hwîlā′x·ʟ   sɛm'â′g·it,
      the chief.   At once   already   knew   the chief,

2 hwîl   lɛp-an-hîsiē′êlt   aʟ   ʟgō′uʟgum   g·a′tstg·ê.   Q'am-txa′lpxʟ
   being   him-   mistake   of   his child   male.   Only   four
            self

3 sa   sg·ēʟ   ʟgō′uʟgum   g·a′tg·ê,   k·'ē   nô′ôt.   K·'ē   hwîl   k·'ē′
   days   lay   his child   male,   then   he died.   At once

4 aba′g'askᵘʟ   sɛm'â′g·itg·ê.   Wiyē′tkᵘtg·ê   ʟa   nô′ôʟ   ʟgō′uʟkᵘtg·ê.
   was troubled   the chief.   He was crying   when   was   his son.
                                                               dead

5 Aʟ   an-b'ɛl-hē′t   aʟ   wiyē′tkᵘt: "Lɛp-gu′lik·s-hanwulā′kᵘs   nä′ê,
   In   crying he   cried: "Self   destroyed him   I,
           said

6 lɛp-gu′lik·s-hanwulā′kᵘs   nä′ê."
   self   destroyed him   I."

SUPPLEMENTARY STORIES

The Origin of the G·ispawaduwe'da

[Told by Chief Mountain]

There were two towns in the canyon of Nass river. The one was inhabited by the G·ispawaduwe'da, the other by the G·itg·iniŏ'x. In the first of these towns there were four brothers who were beaver hunters. They went to a lake that was full of beaver dams. They began to open one of the dams in order to allow the water of the lake to run off. When the eldest brother climbed down under the dam, it gave way and buried him, a large tree piercing his heart. When the water had run off, the brothers took out his body. They said to one another, "Why was our brother unfortunate to-day? Certainly his wife was not true to him." The three brothers went home and hid behind the house. They cut pitch wood and made a torch. When it was dark and the people had gone to bed, they went up to the house in which the wife of the eldest brother was living. They went to the place where they knew her bed stood, and listened. They heard her talking with a man who was lying down with her. They waited until they heard them snoring. Then the youngest brother lighted his torch and entered. He stepped up to his mother and asked, "Did any one come to our house while we were away?" His mother replied, "Yes; the chief's son, from the village opposite, came here, and he is here now." Then the young man told his mother of the death of her eldest son, and added that he had certainly died on account of his wife's faithlessness. Then he took his torch and stepped up to the bed of his sister-in-law. He saw that she was lying with one arm stretched out, and that a young man with earrings of abalone shell was lying on her arm. Then he put his torch down, pulled out his knife, and cut off the head of the young man and took it along with him. The woman awoke and found the blood streaming over her bed. She was frightened. She dug a hole under her bed and buried the body. Then she spread her bed again and lay down.

On the following morning the G·itg·iniŏ'x missed their young chief. They inquired where he had gone, and finally learned that he had crossed the river. Then they suspected that he might have been killed by the G·ispawaduwe'da. The three brothers had taken the body of their eldest brother home, and they had hung the head of their enemy over the doorway. The G·itg·iniŏ'x, under the pretext that their fire had gone out, sent a girl slave to the G·ispawaduwɛ'da to ask permission to

221

light a torch.   They told the girl to ascertain if there were any signs of the whereabouts of the young chief.   The young woman obeyed. The river was frozen and she went across, but she did not see anything.   Still the suspicions of the G·itg·iniō′x were not allayed, and every morning they sent the young slave to ask for fire.   Finally one morning when she crossed the threshold, a drop of blood dripped on her foot.   She desired to see where it came from, and pretended to stumble.   She put her torch into the snow and extinguished the flame. Then she returned into the house and lighted her torch again; and when she went out she looked up and saw the head of her young chief, with its large ear ornaments, hanging over the door.   She went out, and when she came to the river she threw her torch away and ran home as fast as she could.   When she approached the village, she wailed and cried, "I saw my master's head!"   Then the G·itg·iniō′x put on their armors and went out to make war upon the G·ispawaduwE′da.

Wa′g·îxs, the wife of the eldest brother, knew all the time what was coming.   She made one hole under her bed to hide herself when the G·itg·iniō′x should come to attack the village, another one for her daughter, whose name was Sqawô.   When she saw the enemy coming, she called her daughter, and they hid in the holes.   The G·itg·iniō′x killed all the G·ispawaduwE′da and set fire to their town.   The mother and her daughter heard the houses falling.   Finally everything was quiet, and the mother put her hand out of the hole in order to feel if the town were still burning.   When she felt that the ashes were cool, she opened the hole and she and her daughter came out. The mother went about the town, but there was not a soul left except herself and her daughter.   She went to the end of the town and sat down (therefore this place is called Hwîl uks-g·i-d′ā′ Sqawô′, Where-Sqawô′-sat-down-near-the-water); and she sang:

Nâ   LEm - t′an nak·skᵘL Lgō - Lkwe Sqa - wô.

That is, "Who will marry my daughter Sqawô?"   When she had finished singing, a grouse came.   He sat down and said, "I will marry your daughter."   The mother asked, "What can you do?"[1]   The grouse replied, "(When we fight) we raise our feathers and frighten man."[2]   The mother replied, "That is not enough," and the grouse left.

The mother sang again, "Who will marry my daughter Sqawô?" Then the squirrel came and said, "I will marry your daughter."   The mother replied, "What can you do?"   Then the squirrel said, "We only throw down acorns and frighten man."[3]   "That is not enough; go away!" said the mother.

[1] Ago′ si-gwîx·-hwî′lEn?
[2] Q′am-hō′saldEm la′yîm, nLk·′c hō′tsiL g·a′dEm.
[3] Q′am-ma′g iidEm mäq, nLk·′c hōtL g·at.

She sang again. The rabbit came and said, "I will marry your daughter." The mother asked, "What can you do?" The rabbit replied, "We open our eyes and move our ears and frighten man." "That is not enough; go away!"

Again she sang, and the owl came and said, "Hm, hm, hm, hm! I will marry your daughter." "What can you do?" "When we talk we frighten man." "That is not enough; go away!"

The owl went, and the mother sang again. All the animals came and wanted to marry her daughter. Finally the bear came and said, "I will marry your daughter." "What can you do?" Then the bear ran away. He threw trees down, tore the ground, and showed that he was very strong; but she was not satisfied, and sent him away.

Again she sang. The grizzly bear came and said, "I will marry your daughter." She asked, "What can you do?"· Then the grizzly bear ran away and howled. He ran to a swamp, and tore out two roots of bullrushes (?), which looked like a man's head. He tore off some alder bark, chewed it, and spit the red juice on the roots so that they looked like bloody heads. These he carried to the woman. She was almost ready to accept him, but finally she sent him away.

She sang again. Then there came a clap of thunder, and she fainted; when she came to, she saw a man standing near by. He said, "I will marry your daughter." "What can you do?" He replied, "I take this club from under my blanket, and as I turn it the ground turns and trees grow up." The woman asked him to show his powers, and he turned the club. At once the woman and the girl were buried underground, and trees grew over them. Then he turned the club again, and they came up again. He said, "I saw how your friends were killed, and your village destroyed. Therefore I have come to marry your daughter."

He took the women under his arms and said to them, "We will go up to heaven now. Don't open your eyes while we are flying, though you hear much noise, else we can not reach heaven." He put the mother under one arm, and the daughter under the other, and flew upward. While he was passing through the clouds there was a great noise, which induced the mother to open her eyes. They fell back at once, and he said, "I will try once more; but if you open your eyes again, I must leave you." He rose a second time; but when they were passing through the clouds they heard the same noise, and the mother could not withstand the temptation to look. As soon as she opened her eyes they fell back. Then the man said, "I can not take you up. I must leave you down here." He tore off a branch of a tree, put the mother into the hole which he had thus made, and put the branch back in its place. He said, "You shall cry whenever the wind moves the tree." That is the reason why the trees moan when they are moved by the wind.

Then he flew up with his wife and arrived in heaven. He went to his house. They entered. After they had eaten he showed the girl where to lie down. He did not lie down with her, but stayed in a room by himself. His name in heaven was Hîslēgiyō'ôntk". Every morning the rays of the sun fell through a chink upon her, and soon she found that she was with child. After a short time she gave birth to a boy, whom she called after the chief in heaven, Hîslēgiyō'ôntk". After some time, when the rays of the sun struck her body, she conceived another son. She called him Ax-t'ɛm-hwîlhwî'lg·it (Headless). Then a third son was born, whom she called Lē-g·a'amɛxsk" (Lying-on). Finally she gave birth to two daughters, whom she called Ksɛm-mamä'm and Ksɛm-gwadzîq-t'ē'lîx· (Woman-excrements-grease).

The chief made bows and arrows for the boys, and ordered them to fight among themselves. They shot at one another and aimed at their eyes. When an arrow had struck one of them, the girl stepped up to him, took it out, and sucked the wound, which closed at once. When they were grown up, the chief made houses for the boys. The front of the house of the eldest had three doors. It was called Lax-ô'ɛm. The doorways were ornamented with skulls. It was dark in the entrances. Therefore the doors were called Qalx·si-sqä'ɛxk". Painted planks were laid in front of the house. The eldest brother had a head ornament of abalone shells. Another one had a head ornament of skins. Still another had a bow inlaid with abalone shells. They had blankets made of ermine skins. They also had the carved club by means of which they were able to overturn houses.

Then the chief in heaven sent the children and their houses down to the place where the village of the G·ispawaduwɛ'da used to stand. Their mother stayed in heaven. Late in the evening the G·itg·iniō'x heard a noise: "Bɛ, bɛ, bɛ!" When they went out to see what caused the noise, they saw that it was foggy. A man went down to the river and heard people singing on the other side. They sang:

"Q'am-uks	Tōdū't	ʟa	qal-ts'aps	dep	alä'lɛx."
"Just out from the shore	Tōdū't		the town of	the	fearless ones."

He ran back to the house and said, "I hear people singing on the other side." The others made fun of him, and said, "Those are the ghosts of the G·ispawaduwɛ'da."

On the following morning they saw four beautiful houses on the site of the former town of the G·ispawaduwɛ'da. The chief of the G·itg·iniō'x ordered his people to cross the ice, and to make war on the occupants of the houses. They began to shoot with arrows. An arrow struck the eye of one of the brothers. Their sister sucked it out, and the wound closed again. After some time the eldest brother shouted, "Stop fighting, else I shall turn over my club, and your town will be buried. Trees will grow up in its place." When they continued the fight, he turned his club, and the whole town disappeared under ground. Trees grew in its place. Then he turned his club again and the town reappeared, but the Gʻitgʻiniō′x continued to fight. Then he turned his club once more. The town was buried again and all the people died.

The brothers traveled all over the world, and made war on all the tribes, and destroyed them by means of their club. The chief in heaven became angry because they abused his gift, and wished that they might forget the club on one of their expeditions. So it happened that they forgot the club when they went out to attack the town Gulgʻē′u. Therefore the place has been called ever since that time Hwîl dʻakʻs-tsʻaX, or Where-the-club-was-forgotten. Then they went to Dᴇmlaxā′m on Skeena river, where they settled, as they were unable to continue fighting on account of the loss of the supernatural club. Their descendants became the Gʻisqʻahā′st.

On account of the gifts received in heaven, this clan have the privilege of using head ornaments of abalone shell, such as they received from Hîslēgiyō′ôntkᵘ.

Asɪ-ʜwî′ʟ

[Told by Chief Mountain]

A long time ago the people of Lax-qʻal-tsa′p and those of Gʻitwᴜnksi′ʟk were starving. There were two sisters living in these towns. When the provisions were almost exhausted, the sister living in Lax-qʻal-tsa′p thought that she would try to reach her sister who lived in Gʻitwᴜnksi′ʟk. She started and went up the valley. After some time she saw a woman approaching. When she came near, she recognized her sister. She knew at once that the people of Gʻitwᴜnksi′ʟk were starving also. The sisters met and sat down and cried. Since that time this place has been called Hwîl-lē-nᴇ-hwa′da (Where-they-met-each-other). The sister who had gone up the river had only a few haw berries, and the other had only a small piece of spawn about as long as her finger. They divided and ate.

In the evening they made a small hut of branches and lighted a fire. The sister who had come from Gʻitwᴜnksi′ʟk had a daughter whom she had taken along. They lay down to sleep. About midnight all of a sudden a man appeared and lay down next the younger sister, who was unmarried. He asked her, "Is it true that all your friends are starving?" She said, "There were no provisions in our village, and so I went to see my sister." The man continued, "Stay here. I will make a fish weir for you." His name was Hō′uX (Good-luck). He was a supernatural being. Early in the morning he rose and made a weir of small sticks and twigs, and soon it was full of trout. He took them out of the weir and the women roasted them. Then he went hunting, and in the afternoon he came back, bringing five porcupines. Then the sisters were glad. On the following day he went hunting again, and brought back a mountain goat. The sisters had made a basket of spruce roots in which they boiled the meat. On the next day he went hunting again and caught a large bear, the fat of which was about as thick as a man's hand is wide. On the fourth day he returned early in the morning, bringing a bighorn sheep. He told the sisters that he had killed ten sheep, and asked them to carry the meat home. The house was now full of meat and fish, because the trap was full every morning.

Soon the woman was with child, and she gave birth to a boy. When the boy was able to walk, his father made snowshoes for him and sent him up the mountains to look for bears. The boy came back in the evening, but he had not killed anything. His father asked him, "Did you not see a bear?" The boy had not seen any. Then his father demanded to see his snowshoes. He examined them and found that he had made a mistake in making them. He made a new pair and sent the boy off again. Soon he returned, bringing a piece of bear meat. He told his father that a bear which he had killed was lying on the mountains. Then his father put on his snowshoes and brought the bear home. On the following day the father went out hunting. Soon he returned, bringing two mountain goats, and told his son that there was a flock of goats on the other side of the mountains. The father sent him after them. Then his mother said, "Now we have a name for our son. We will call him Asi-hwî'l. That means Going-across-the-mountains."

Before the boy left, the father made a new pair of snowshoes for him, and said to him, "With these snowshoes you can climb mountains, however steep they may be. Whenever you come to a difficult place, put on these snowshoes." Then he took a bag made of cedar bark from under his arm. He opened it and took out two tiny dogs, one of which was spotted, the other one red. He put them on the snow and struck them, saying at the same time, "Red, red, red," to one, and, "Spotted, spotted, spotted," to the other. At once they became large dogs. Then he struck them again, and they became small again. He told the boy to take the dogs out of the bag whenever he should see any goats, to make them large, and to command the one to go up the mountains on the right-hand side, and the other to go up on the left-hand side. Then they would run up, barking, and frighten the goats so that they would fall down. Furthermore, he cut a pole for his son, with a goat horn attached to one end, which he was to use in climbing the mountains. He said, "If you strike the rock with the horn, there will be a hole." The other end of the pole was provided with a sharp black bone point. The boy, after having received these gifts, left his parents.

Once upon a time the young man fell in with a powerful man whose name was Wud'ax-mɛxmä'ɛx (Large-ears). This man asked him, "What weapons do you use for killing game?" The boy replied, "I do not use any weapon. I run after them, and they fall down. What kind of weapon do you use for killing game?" "I do not use any weapon. I have supernatural powers." Asi-hwî'l was desirous to know how Large-ears killed his game. They went a short distance together, and came to a place where there were many goats. The youth said, "Let me see how you kill goats." Large-ears took a pair of long mittens from under his blanket. He put them on and clapped his hands. At once all the goats fell down the steep sides of the mountains. They went to another mountain where they saw a number of goats. Then Large-ears said, "Now, let me see how you kill mountain goats." Asi-hwî'l pulled his bag from under his blanket, took the dogs out, and said, "Red, red, red! Spotted, spotted, spotted!" Then the dogs grew large—one went to the right, and the other to the left—and they began to bark. The goats fell down at once. Then Asi-hwî'l put on his snowshoes, and walked right up a vertical cliff. When Large-ears saw this, he was surprised. They parted, and each went home. When Asi-hwî'l came to his father, he told him what had happened, and his father praised him.

After some time Hō'uX said to his wife and to her sister, "Your brothers are coming to look for you. Therefore I must hide in the woods." A short time after he had left, the brothers came. When they saw the house full of meat, they were surprised. Then the women gave them to eat. On the following morning the brothers left, carrying along some meat which the sisters had given them. As soon as they left, Hō'uX returned. The sisters told him that their brothers had asked them to return home. Then Hō'uX said, "Let us part. You may return to your home; I will return to mine." On the following morning many people came to fetch the women and the boy. They took them to Gˑitxadē'n. The boy's uncles gave a feast, and his mother told them the boy's name, Asi-hwî'l. The people bought meat of them, and paid for it with elk skins, which Asi-hwî'l used in giving a potlatch.

A supernatural being who lives in heaven saw that Asi-hwî'l was a great hunter. He covered one of his slaves with ashes, so that he looked like a white bear, and sent him to Nass river. The hunters set out to kill the bear, but they were unable to reach it. When the bear came to Gˑitxadē'n, Asi-hwî'l put on his snowshoes, took his bag and his pole and pursued it. The bear reached Leading point. There a

vertical cliff rises, and the tracks of Asi-hwî'l's snowshoes where he
climbed the cliff are still visible. Beyond the cliff he saw the bear
entering a large house. He stayed at the door and heard the people
singing:

That is, "Asi-hwî'l is picking the bones of my neck." Asi-hwî'l was
unable to enter, and returned. He had lost the bear.

He went to the country of the Tsimshian, and married a girl of that
tribe. The girl's brothers were sealion hunters. Once upon a time,
during winter, gales were raging, and the brothers were unable to
kill any sealions. One day Asi-hwî'l accompanied them. When they
came to the sealions' rock, they found that there was a high swell,
and they were unable to land. But Asi-hwî'l put on his snowshoes,
took his staff, and jumped ashore. Then he ran up the rock and killed
all the sealions. The brothers became jealous of him, and deserted
him. When Asi-hwî'l had killed all the sealions and made ready to
jump back into the canoe, he saw that the brothers had left. The tide
began to rise. When it had almost covered the rock, he put his staff
into a fissure and sat down on top of it. When the flood tide rose
still higher, he tied his bow to the end of his staff and climbed on top
of the bow. There he sat, and whistled the call which his father
had taught him:

Then the tide ceased to rise, and soon the water began to fall.
The rock became dry again. Then he lay down to sleep. While he
was sleeping, somebody nudged him and whispered, "Grandmother
invites you in." He looked down, but he did not see anyone. He pulled
his blanket over his head and tore a hole in it with his teeth. Then
he peeped through the hole. After a little while he saw a mouse

coming out of a place where a bunch of grass was growing. She whispered in his ear, "Grandmother invites you in." Then he pulled off his blanket, and saw the mouse disappearing under the bunch of grass. He pulled it out, and saw a house underneath. The mouse had taken the shape of a woman, and spoke to him, "Enter, if you are Asi-hwî'l, who has been deserted here." He entered, and the woman gave him to eat. The old woman who had invited him in said, "You know that this rock is the house of the sealions. Their chief is very sick. The shamans are unable to cure him. Please try if you can heal him." He promised to do so, and she led him to the chief, who was sick in bed. Asi-hwî'l saw a bone harpoon in his side. He sat down. Then the mouse said to the chief, "He will heal you if you will give him this canoe in payment." So saying, she pointed to the largest canoe. It was made of the intestines of sealions. The chief gave it to him. Then he stepped up to him, and, taking hold of the harpoon, pushed it first slightly into the flesh and then he pulled it out. The chief opened his eyes, and said at once that he felt better. Then they moistened the intestines, placed him inside, tied them up, and put them into the sea. Then they invoked the west wind, which drifted the intestines to the mainland. In the evening he heard the surf, and felt that the sealion's intestines were being knocked about on the beach. Then he opened them, and went out.

He resolved to take revenge. Therefore he carved two killer-whales out of red cedar. He put them into the water. They swam a short distance, but then they became logs, turned over, and drifted about. He called them back, and carved two new ones of yellow cedar. They swam a little longer than the first ones, but then they also became logs, turned over, and drifted about. He called them back and burnt them. Then he carved two new ones of yew wood. They became real killer-whales, who swam, blowing and snorting. They did not turn into wood again. Then he called them back and said to them, "The men who have deserted me will go out sealion hunting to-morrow. As soon as they go out I shall put you into the water. Go and break their canoes." On the following morning, when he saw his enemies coming, he put the whales into the water, and they broke the canoes. Asi-hwî'l went back to his wife and stayed with her.

THE GROUSES

A LEGEND OF THE G·ISPAWADUWE'DA

[Told by Chief Mountain]

A chief had a beautiful daughter. Many young men came to marry her, but he refused her to all of them. Then the chief of the Grouses flew down and alighted on the roof of the old chief's house. He assumed the shape of a man who wore a blanket made of fox skins.

When it was dark, he entered the house without the knowledge of the chief, and lay down with the girl, who accepted him. The Grouse persuaded her to elope with him. At midnight they rose and left the house. They crossed the river and came to a large town which was inhabited by the Grouses. The young Grouse's father gave a feast when he arrived with his wife. They stayed there all winter, and in summer she gave birth to four children.

The old chief searched all over the country for his daughter, but he was unable to find her. When the children began to grow up, their mother said to them, "Don't you want to see your grandfather? He is a chief, and lives on the other side of the river. He has a large house with many steps, and a pole in front of it." The young Grouses wished to see him, and crossed the river on the ice. While going across they said, "Ps, ps, ps, ps!" The children in the chief's village heard the noise, and saw four young Grouses coming. They threw stones at them. Then the Grouses flew back. On the following day the young Grouses tried again, but were driven back by the children. They tried every day. Then the people said to one another, "Next time when the Grouses come, we will not disturb them." On the following day they came again, and went right to the old chief's house. The chief opened the door, and they entered. He spread a mat for them and they sat down. All the people came to see the birds. Finally an old man spoke to the chief, "Don't you remember that you lost your daughter some years ago? The birds must be her children, because they know your house." Then the old chief said to the birds, "Tell your father that I invite him and all his people to a feast to-morrow, and ask your mother also to come." Then the birds rose and left the house. They returned over the ice.

On the following morning innumerable Grouses came across. The ice was black with birds, and among them was the chief's daughter. Then they entered the chief's house. They sat down on the floor; and many had to sit on the posts and beams because there was not enough room on the floor. When the boys saw this, they shook the posts, and the birds flew from one side of the house to the other. The chief made a feast and gave them dry salmon and berries. Then he spoke, "I am old, and unable to split wood. Will not my son-in-law please stay here and help me?" His daughter repeated his speech to her husband, who replied, "Ps, ps, ps, ps!" and the other birds spoke to him in the same manner. Then the chief's daughter said that the birds would go and split wood on the following morning.

On the following morning the chief opened the smoke-hole of his house. Then his son-in-law delivered a speech, and flew out, followed by all the birds. When they had gone, the chief's daughter swept the house. About noon the noise of the birds was heard again.

The chief had a fire in his house, and the birds reentered through the smoke-hole. Each threw some fat into the fire, so that it blazed up high. They brought a long pole as high as a mountain, which was covered with fat. The chief of the birds gave this pole to his father-in-law, who divided it among his tribe. Then the chief and his people in return gave presents to the chief of the Grouses. They gave him a feast, after which the birds left. The chief's daughter and her children went back with them to the town of the Grouses.

TSEGU′KSK^u

In the town Lax-anʟ̂ôE, below G·iʟwunksî′ʟk, was a shaman who owned a rattle and a carved squirrel, which became alive as soon as it was dark. There was a village on the opposite side of the river, whose inhabitants were enemies of the shaman. One night he sent his squirrel across the river to kill his enemies. It obeyed and killed all the people, with the exception of a few men, among them a shaman, whose name was TsEgu′ksk^u. After the squirrel had killed all the people, TsEgu′ksk^u and three other men got into a canoe and descended the river. He had a long board in his canoe which was painted red. They landed near Cape Fox. There TsEgu′ksk^u lay down on the plank and covered himself with a mat made of cedar bark. Then his friends made a small fire on the end of the plank and burnt meat, tallow, and berries in the fire. They turned their faces away from the plank, and when they looked again the plank with the fire and TsEgu′ksk^u had disappeared. They heard a noise from the depths of the sea. TsEgu′ksk^u had been taken into the house of the chief G·itk·staqʟ, who lives at the bottom of the sea. The chief sent for a box drum. The three men heard the following song coming from the deep:

> Wudē′, wudē′, wudē′, hē′yi, wudē, wudō′.
> Hwîl nE-gEbgā′bEl pʟô′ôn qanʟ näqʟ, iē′,
> Hwîl g'ōʟ-qalgâ′l qabâ′q iē′.
> Hwîl g'ōʟ-diē′qat wī-Ts'egä′uks ts'äuʟ wī-hwî′lpsqat G·îtk·tsEm wâ′ôpElē′.

That is, "Fastened together are sea otter and killer-whale; scattered are the cockles where TsEgu′ksk^u walks about in his great house at Wâ′ôpEl."[1]

Then G·itk·staqʟ gave TsEgu′ksk^u a club in shape of a land otter and a small box, the lid of which was carved in the shape of a fin of a whale. Furthermore, he gave him a chamber-pot made of wood. He said to him, "The river is frozen now. Take this, it will break the ice for you." Then TsEgu′ksk^u was sent back. All of a sudden he was seen again in the canoe, and by him were the presents of the chief from

---

[1] A place near China Hat.

below. He threw the club into the water. It swam up the river and
cut the ice. After some time the club became tired. He took it into
the canoe and put the box on the ice. The box assumed the shape of
a killer-whale and moved over the ice, thus cutting it. Then he told
it to go to the house of the shaman who had killed his friends. The
latter had a daughter, whose name was ʟgo-yī′yuk (Little-worker).
Tsɛgu′ksk^u commanded the whale to break the ice when he saw the
girl on the river and to bring her to him. Soon the girl came down
to the river to fetch water. Then the whale rose and carried her away
to where his master was staying, and the latter sang:

Next he ordered the whale to watch and whenever a woman went to
fetch water to take her away. The inhabitants were therefore in great
want of water. Finally Tsɛgu′ksk^u sent his otter club to kill all the
people. The club swam across the river and killed every one. Only
one man, who happened to be out hunting, was saved.

At this time the Haida used to make war upon the villages of
Observatory inlet. Tsɛgu′ksk^u happened to be there with his friends
when the Haida made an attack on the village, and he and all his companions were killed. The Haida cut off the heads of the slain to take
them along as trophies. Tsɛgu′ksk^u's head was placed in the bow of
the canoe. When the Haida had gone some little distance, his head
rolled overboard and swam back to where the body lay. Head and
trunk were joined again, and Tsɛgu′ksk^u rose hale and well. He
returned to Nass river.

The man who had been absent hunting while Tsɛgu′ksk^u's otter-
club had killed all his friends resolved to take revenge. He invited
Tsɛgu′ksk^u to a feast. He was going to give him dried human flesh
mixed with poison to eat. One of Tsɛgu′ksk^u's supernatural helpers
had warned him, however, and had told him to take out his intestines after the feast, and to replace them with dogs' intestines, then the
poison would do him no harm. Tsɛgu′ksk^u put on a bearskin for his
blanket, placed a ring of red cedar bark around his neck, and strewed
eagle-down on his head. Then he went across. He entered the house
of his enemy and sat down. When the food was ready for him, he
remarked, "This is human carrion," but he ate it nevertheless. At
night he became sick. Then he said to the people, "I am going to die.
When I am dead, open my stomach, and take out the intestines. Then
kill a dog, take its intestines, and put them in place of mine. Then

you must sew up my stomach." They obeyed, and after four days TsEgu'ksk^u was alive and well. They placed his intestines in a canoe, which was pushed into the river. It sank at once, and his intestines are still at the bottom of the river. They cause the noise of the rapids.

Once upon a time TsEgu'ksk^u traveled down the river in his canoe. The canoe capsized, and when he was about to be drowned a great number of gulls came to his rescue. They took him on their backs and carried him up the river to his village, singing:

Hâ de-k·å'etnĕ hagun-dE-hwî'lĕʟ qĕ'wundeʟ an-dā'x·ʟ lax-ha'.

That is, "I am taken along on the water, I am taken around the world by gulls."

After a short time an epidemic of smallpox visited the villages. TsEgu'ksk^u placed a pole, which he had painted red, in front of his house to ward off the disease. But, nevertheless, he became sick. He called all the great shamans of his village, and asked them if he would recover. Finally one of them replied that he would not recover. Then he made a bow and four arrows, which he painted red. He ordered one of his friends to shoot the arrows up to the sun. His friend did so, and the arrows did not return; but every time he shot, blood began to flow from TsEgu'ksk^u's forehead and from his cheeks. When TsEgu'ksk^u felt the blood, he said, "I shall not remain dead." He took his rattle and went around the fire twice, following the course of the sun. Then he asked for a coffin box. He crawled into it and died. Then the people took the skin of a mountain-goat, cut ropes out of it, and tied the box tightly. Then they placed it on a large bowlder behind the village. On the fourth night after the burial a noise was heard proceeding from the box. When the people went out to see what it was, they saw that TsEgu'ksk^u had broken the thongs, and that he was sitting on the box. He had assumed the shape of a white owl. One man tried to catch him; but as the owl flew away, he became afraid and returned. Then a second man, whose name was Lō-gwisgwâ's, tried. He did not succeed. After four men had tried, the owl suddenly fell back into the box, and the thongs were replaced by magic. The staff which TsEgu'ksk^u had raised in front of his house fell to pieces and was seen to be rotten all through. Before the owl fell back into the box, it said, "Wuʟ dEmā'ndē;" that is, "Nobody will be left." The epidemic continued for some time, and all the people died. This was the first visitation of smallpox.

ROTTEN-FEATHERS

[The continuation of this story from page 100, line 6, was told by Chief Mountain, as follows:]

Twice she tried to cut it, then the feather snapped and the boys all fell down. The eldest one kept the feather and received the name Rotten-feathers. At the same time when the boys fell down a great many bones fell down from heaven. Rotten-feathers moved the feather over them four times and the bones became again living people.

Then the brothers went to Skeena river. Little-grindstone ate of the berries that were growing there and was transformed into a mountain that may be seen to this day. The brothers traveled on and reached a mountain which they were unable to pass. Rotten-feathers moved his feather over it and the mountain melted down. The molten rock may still be seen.

Finally they came to a canyon. They saw a town on the other side of the river and a bridge leading across to it. Here they met a woman named Great-goose (Wī-ksᴇm-ha′x), who warned them. She said, "You can not cross this bridge. If you try to do so, it will break and you will be drowned. On the other side lives Chieftainess Knife-hand (Haq′ôlᴇm-an′o′n), who has a beautiful daughter. She cuts off with her hands the heads of all her daughter's suitors." Rotten-feathers thought he could overcome her by means of his magic feather. He crossed the bridge in safety and entered the house. The old woman laughed when she saw him, and immediately asked her daughter to spread the bed. At night he lay down with the young woman. He had his hair tied in a bunch on top of his head and in it he had hidden his feather. As soon as the young woman was fast asleep he arranged his own hair like that of a woman and tied the young woman's hair in a topknot. Then he pretended to be asleep. Soon the old woman came. She felt of the heads of the sleepers. She believed her daughter to be the stranger and cut off her head. Then Rotten-feathers tied up his hair again and put the feather on top. He took the labret of the dead woman. Therefore he received the name Labret. The feather carried him back across the river. Great-goose greeted him, saying, "My son, did you come back safely?" He told her what had happened. On the following morning Knife-hand came across the river wailing, "My child! my child! Sister Great-goose, how did it happen that your child became a great supernatural being?" Great-goose replied, "The heavens were clear when my child was born, therefore she has become a great supernatural being, sister." Then Knife-hand said, "O, yes, sister Great-goose." ("ʟgō′uʟguē, ʟgō′uʟguē, g·axgō′dēsg·at ʟgō′uʟgun, g·īkᵘ Wī-ksᴇm-ha′x, qan wī-nᴇxnô′qt."—"ʟda wī-ʟā′nʟ lax-ha′ desg·a′t ʟgō′uʟguē, nᴇʟ qan wī-nᴇxnô′qt, g·īkᵘ."—"Hâ, net, g·īkᵘ Wī-ksᴇm-ha′x.")

Rotten-feathers, who had now the name Labret, heard that a supernatural being named Sleep had a beautiful wife. He desired to abduct her, and, notwithstanding Great-goose's warning, he set out. He reached the house and found Sleep fast asleep. He told Sleep's wife that he had come to abduct her. She was willing to elope with him. She told him that Sleep had a very fast canoe, which traveled by itself. They went aboard this canoe and escaped. Sleep had a chamber-pot whose office it was to wake him if any danger approached. The pot knocked him on the head and the urine ran over his face, but he did not awake. Then a wooden maul, whose office it was also to wake him, knocked him on the head until he awoke. The maul said, "Labret abducted your wife." Immediately Sleep launched a canoe and set out to pursue the fugitives. Soon he descried them. He shouted, "Stop, Labret, else I shall raise rocks in front of you." When the couple paddled on Sleep raised a mountain right in front of them, but Labret moved his feather against it and thus opened a passage. Sleep continued his pursuit. When he approached he ordered Labret to stop, threatening to put his comb in front of him. When Labret paddled on, Sleep threw the comb ahead and thus made a dense forest in front of the fugitives. Labret, however, moved his feather against the woods and so made a passage through it. Thus the couple escaped safely. The mask of Sleep is used up to this day by the G·ispawaduwɛ'da.

ABSTRACTS

Txä′msEm and Lôg̣ôbolā

A chief's wife pretends to be dead and is buried on a tree. Her lover goes to see her in the grave box. They are discovered and killed by the chief. The dead woman gives birth to a boy who lives by sucking his mother's intestines. He takes away the arrows of some playing children, and is discovered and taken to the house of the chief, who raises him. The boy and one of his friends kill two birds, put on their skins and fly through a hole in the heavens. The boy goes on alone, assumes the shape of a cedar leaf, drops into a well, and is swallowed by the daughter of the chief in heaven. She gives birth to a boy, who cries for the box in which the sun is kept. The chief sends for it. The boy steals it and becomes Txä′msEm, the Raven. He puts his cap into a cliff. He goes up Nass river and returns because ghosts whistle in front of him. Therefore the water of the river turns back. He then asks the ghosts, who are fishing olachen, for fish. He is refused and makes it daylight, thus driving away the ghosts. Finally Txä′msEm meets his brother, Lôg̣ôbolā′, who takes off his hat, thus causing a fog in which Txä′msEm is lost. Lôg̣ôbolā′ causes all fresh water to disappear. They have a shooting match and stake the Nass river against the Skeena river. Txä′msEm orders the crows to put his arrow into the goal and to remove Lôg̣ôbolā′′s. Thus he wins by fraud. They divide the stakes and make the olachen go up Nass river and the salmon up Skeena river. They separate.

Txä′msEm

Txä′msEm visits a chief who owns fresh water. He pretends that the chief soiled his bed, and by threatening to tell on him he gets permission to take a drink of water. He takes all the water and flies away. The water runs out of his blanket and forms rivers. He meets the ghosts and turns back, therefore the waters of Nass river turn back. He makes a gull vomit olachen, then he rubs its spawn over his canoe and goes to a chief who owns the olachen. He pretends to have caught many olachen, showing the spawn in his canoe. The chief is annoyed and releases the olachen from his house. Txä′msEm catches olachen and roasts them. Gulls steal them. He throws the gulls into a fire and the tips of their wings become black. He assumes the shape

236

of a deer, ties pitchwood to his tail, and steals fire. He strikes the butts of the trees with his burning tail, and therefore the wood burns. Txä′msEm then marries a salmon woman and thus obtains salmon. She makes his hair grow long. He scolds her, and all the salmon and his long hair disappear.

Txä′msEm

Txä′msEm is born, but can not be induced to eat. Two old men chew salmon for him, and put a scab into it. Then he becomes voracious and is deserted. He tries to catch a bullhead but can not, so he curses it and makes its tail thin. Believing that he sees a beautiful dancing-blanket in the woods, he tears his raven blanket and finds that what he believed to be a blanket is moss. Then he takes a slave. They reach a chief's house. The slave says that Txä′msEm does not like food that has been offered, and eats it all himself. Txä′msEm induces his slave to cross a canyon on a bridge made of the stalk of a skunk cabbage. The bridge breaks, the slave falls down, his belly bursts, and Txä′msEm eats the contents of his stomach. He finds children playing ball with a slice of blubber, and eats it. The children tell him that they obtain blubber by throwing themselves down from a tree and shouting "Piles of blubber!" He does so and kills himself. He comes to life again and goes fishing with Cormorant, takes a louse from his neck, and pretends that he wants to put it on his tongue. He tears out Cormorant's tongue and steals the fish that Cormorant has caught. He exchanges the chief's club for one of rotten wood, and induces the chief to strike him with the club, but in an ensuing fight he kills the chief with his own club. Seal invites Txä′msEm into his house and lets grease drip from his hands into a dish. A bird strikes its ankle and pulls out fish roe. Another bird makes salmon berries by his song. Txä′msEm tries in vain to imitate his hosts. He steals bait of the fishermen from their hooks. His jaw is caught and torn off, but he recovers it. He calls a salmon and kills it. He is advised by his excrements to steam the salmon in a hole. A stump sits down on the hole and eats the salmon. Txä′msEm then invites Grizzly Bear to go fishing with him. He pretends to use his own testicles for bait and induces the bear to cut off his testicles for bait, thus killing himself. He makes the wife of Grizzly Bear swallow red-hot stones to secure good luck for her husband, and thus kills her. He asks Pitch to go fishing and lets him melt in the hot sun. Pitch runs over a halibut and makes one side black. When he reaches the town of the air, he tries to steal provisions, but is beaten off by invisible hands. He asks Deer to accompany him and split wood. He kills Deer by striking his head with a hammer. He then enters the house of smoke-hole, who prevents his escape by ordering the door and the smoke-hole to close. Txä′msEm, caught in the smoke-hole, puts his voice as an echo into a cliff and scolds the chief, who allows the smoke-hole to open again. Txä′msɛm flies away in the shape of a raven. He catches seals and steams them. A stump eats them. Txä′msɛm makes the stump his slave, and finally he calls all the fish ashore and kills them.

THE STONE AND THE ELDERBERRY BUSH

The Stone and the Elderberry Bush gave birth nearly at the same time, but the children of Elderberry Bush were born first. Therefore man is mortal.

THE PORCUPINE AND THE BEAVER

The Beaver invites the Porcupine to his house, carries him over the water, and gives him sticks to eat. They agree to play together. The Beaver carries the Porcupine through the water and almost drowns him. The Porcupine then invites the Beaver to visit him and takes him over slippery ice to a tree which he climbs and lets himself fall down. He carries the Beaver up. The Porcupine lets go of the tree and shouts "Space!" and is not hurt when he strikes the ground; but the Beaver shouts "Rock!" and his belly bursts when he lands on the ground.

THE WOLVES AND THE DEER

The Wolves and the Deer have a feast. They play laughing at each other. The Wolves laugh first. The Deer fear the large teeth of the Wolves. The Deer are told to laugh aloud. When the Wolves see that the Deer have no teeth, they devour them.

THE STARS

A boy ridicules a Star and is taken up by it to the sky where he is tied to the smoke-hole of the Star's house. The boy's father is told by a woman how to recover his boy. He shoots arrows up to the sky, making a chain, which he climbs. He sees a man, to whom he gives tobacco, red paint, and slingstones in return for advice. The father then carves figures in the shape of his son, of different kinds of wood, finally of yellow cedar. He ties this figure on the roof in the place of his son. The figure cries when sparks fall on it. The father escapes with his son. Finally the figure stops crying, and the escape of the boy is discovered. The Stars pursue the fugitives, who throw away the tobacco, paint, and slingstones. The Stars stop and paint their faces. Therefore the Stars are red and blue. The man who had given advice swells on receiving more paint and tobacco and obstructs the way of the Stars. The father and his son safely descend the chain of arrows.

ROTTEN-FEATHERS

Children play ball and make much noise, which annoys Heaven, who sends feathers down. One boy puts them on his head and they lift him up. Others try to hold him and all are taken up. One menstruating girl and her grandmother, who were in a small hut, are the only ones left. The girl puts wedges of various kinds of wood, a grindstone, a knife, and some mucus into her blanket and soon gives birth to five boys and one girl, who are these objects personified. The children annoy Heaven by their noise. The feathers come down again and take them up, though they transform themselves into trees, mountains, and mucus. The knife girl climbs her brothers' bodies and cuts off the feather. Then the boys fall down. The feathers remain on the head of the eldest, who is called Rotten-feathers. The bones of those who had been taken up before fall down. They are revived. Grindstone eats berries and is transformed into a mountain. Rotten-feathers cuts passage through the mountains with a feather and reaches Great-goose, who advises them. He marries the daughter of a chieftainess, who tries to cut off his head with her sharp hands. He changes his own and his wife's headdress and the young woman is killed in his place. He abducts the wife of Sleep and escapes in a self-moving canoe. Sleep is awakened by his watchmen, Chamber-pot and Wooden Maul. He creates a mountain in front of Rotten-feathers and his wife, which is cut by the feathers. Then he throws a comb ahead of them, which is transformed into a thicket. Again Rotten-feathers cuts a passage and escapes with the woman.

K·'ĒLKᵘ

Children are playing in a hollow log of driftwood on the beach. They are carried out to sea by the tide. They strike their noses until they bleed and smear the outside of the log with the blood. Gulls that alight on the log are glued to it by the blood. The boys kill them and subsist on them. The log drifts into a large whirlpool and is pulled out by a one-legged person who lives near by, hunting seals in the whirlpool. He takes care of the boys. His neighbor, Hard-instep, envies him. The boys are homesick and are sent to look for One-leg's canoe, which they can not find because it looks like a rotten log. Finally he uncovers it and it proves to be a self-moving canoe with a head of Wâse at each end. These heads eat whatever crosses the bow or the stern of the canoe. The boys feed each end with five seals and the canoe takes them home.

THE SEALION HUNTERS

One of four sealion hunters finds no sealions on his rock and steals those of his companion. The latter makes an artificial sealion, which, when harpooned by the thief, pulls him with his crew across the ocean.

He is unable to let go the harpoon line. Finally they reach the land of the dwarfs. One of these appears in a canoe, jumps into the sea, clubs halibut under water, and puts them into the canoe. When he jumps into the sea again, one man steals two halibut. The dwarf notices it, finds the men, and knocks the thief to the ground so that he dies. The survivors are invited in by the chief of the dwarfs. Some birds arrive and a battle ensues in which many dwarfs are killed. On the following day the men attack the birds and kill them by twisting their necks. The men are sent home by the dwarfs.

SMOKE-HOLE

A man attains supernatural strength by always sleeping at the edge of his smoke-hole.

TS'AK·

A boy named Ts'ak· catches fish, which are stolen by the Grizzly Bear. He scolds the Grizzly Bear, who snuffs him in. Ts'ak· kills the bear by starting a fire in his stomach, and then comes out and asks his grandmother to cut open the bear. At first she refuses to believe him, but finally accompanies him and finds the bear. He visits the village of the Wolves across the river. They tie him, go to his house, and steal the bear meat. On being released he finds his grandmother asleep, cuts out her vulva, roasts it, and gives it to her to eat. She turns him out of the house. A supernatural being tells him how to take revenge on the Wolves. Through a hollow bone he blows sickness into the daughter of the chief of the Wolves. The shamans can not cure her. He offers to do so, and when he is successful he receives the girl in marriage, and is given much property and a slave named Drum-belly. He desires to get another wife, and starts with his slave Drum-belly and several birds. He comes to a burning mountain, which he tries unsuccessfully to cross by assuming the shape of various birds. He lies down, and is called by a Mouse, whose house is under a bunch of grass. He gains her good will by burning his earrings. She shows him the trail under the mountain. He reaches another Mouse at the far end of the trail, who gives him a carving of crystal for protection, and tells him what to do. He reaches a chief's house with a snapping door. He puts the crystal in so that it can not close, and enters safely. He takes the chief's daughter for his wife. The father-in-law spreads a bearskin with sharp hair in order to kill him, but Ts'ak· breaks the hair with his crystal. Then the father-in-law tries to boil him in a box, and though Ts'ak· seems to be boiled he rises unharmed. He is then thrown into the crack of a split cedar, which closes over him when the wedges are knocked out, but he kicks the tree apart and comes out. The chief orders his slave to throw Ts'ak· into the whirlpool while they are hunting seals, but instead the slave is drowned. He returns with his wife by the same way by which he came.

GROWING-UP-LIKE-ONE-WHO-HAS-A-GRANDMOTHER

A chief's nephew is a poor orphan. A light comes down from heaven and hangs at the end of a branch. It proves to be copper. The chief promises his daughter to the one who will knock it down. The orphan boy receives from a supernatural being stones of four different colors, and with the last stone knocks it down, but the young men take the copper away from him, and claim to have hit it. The next day a white bear is heard behind the village, and the chief's daughter is promised to him who kills it. The orphan boy kills it with his arrow. The other youths claim to have killed it, but the youth's arrow is found, and thus the chief learns that his nephew has killed the bear. The chief is ashamed and deserts his nephew, his daughter, and their grandmother. The boy goes to a pond and shouts. A giant frog, the guardian of the pond, emerges and pursues the boy. The boy makes a trap and catches the frog in it. He skins it and goes into the pond, where he catches a trout. He puts the trout on the beach. In the morning a raven finds it and begins to croak. The princess sends the boy to look, and he brings the trout. Every night he goes out and catches in succession trout, salmon, halibut, bullheads, seals, porpoises, sealions, and whales. Finally the princess discovers that he catches them and asks him to marry her. They have two children. The chief's people are starving, and the chief sends a man and some slaves to see if his nephew, his daughter, and their grandmother are dead. The boy gives them to eat, and they report what they have seen. The people return, and he sells his provisions for slaves and elk skins, gives a potlatch, and becomes a chief. Finally he is unable to take off his frog blanket, and stays in the sea, whence he provides his wife and children with food.

LITTLE-EAGLE

A chief's son, instead of catching salmon, feeds eagles and pulls out their feathers for his arrows. In winter, when provisions run short, the boy, his grandmother, and a slave are deserted. The boy's mother hides some fish in a clam shell. Every morning the eagles bring them food; first a trout, then bullheads, salmon, halibut, seals, porpoises, sealions, and whales. The boy puts on a gull skin and flies to look at his people, whom he finds starving. He drops a piece of seal meat into a canoe. The chief sends a man and several slaves to see if his son is dead. They find him alive and he feeds them, but forbids them to take food along. One slave hides some seal meat under his shirt. At home he gives the meat to his child. The child bolts it and is almost suffocated. The chief's wife pulls out the seal meat, and thus they learn that the prince has plenty of provisions. The people move back, and one of the prince's uncles gives him his daughter in marriage. The prince sells provisions for elk skins and slaves, gives a potlatch, and becomes a chief.

She-who-has-a-Labret-on-one-Side

A scabby slave girl appears on the street of a village. A prince marries her. When his mother feeds her, she puts into the empty dish a scab, which is transformed into an abalone shell. In the evening the girl's mother, Evening Sky, comes and announces that her people will come and give the prince much property. Next day they arrive. The prince and his people go inland to trade. His wife is angry because he does not take her along. She bathes the awkward brother of the prince, gives him red paint, and sends him to the inlanders to trade for weasel skins. He becomes beautiful and rich, and she marries him. Her mother comes again and brings much property, which she gives to her new husband.

The Grizzly Bear

The eldest of four brothers goes hunting with his two dogs. He comes to a glacier, which he crosses, and suddenly finds himself in front of the den of a Grizzly Bear, who kills him and his dogs. The second and third brothers meet the same fate. The youngest, on reaching the den, falls into it and strikes with his hand the Bear's vulva. She marries him. After some time he gets homesick and returns, accompanied by his bear wife. They live with his parents and the Bear makes friends with the man's child and with his former wife, whom she allows to return to him. The Bear and this woman go berrying, the Bear keeping the berries in her stomach. On their return they invite the people in. The Bear defecates the berries into a dish, but the people are afraid to eat them. The Bear robs a man's salmon weir, taking out the fish before daylight. She gives the fish to the people. The owner of the weir scolds her and she kills him. She goes back to the mountains, and tells her husband, who tries to follow her, to go home. When he does not obey, she kills him.

The Squirrel

A young man has killed many squirrels. One day he sees a white squirrel climbing a spruce tree. He goes around the tree to get a shot and finds that the squirrel is the daughter of the chief of the squirrels. He is called into the house. The chief asks him to burn the meat and bones of the squirrels whom he has killed and thus to restore the squirrel people to life. In return he promises to make the hunter a shaman and gives him a dance and a song. After some time the youth's dried-up body is found on the tree. It is taken to his father's house and placed on a mat, and during the mourning ceremony he revives. The squirrel meat is burned and the youth becomes a great shaman.

The Origin of the G·ispawaduwe'da

There are two towns on opposite sides of Nass river. The eldest of four brothers from one of these towns is killed while hunting. The reason for his accident is the faithlessness of his wife, whose lover is the son of the chief of the other village. The surviving brothers find the lover with their sister-in-law. They cut off his head and hang it over the doorway. When the young chief is missing his people send a slave girl across the river to look for him, under the pretext that their fire has gone out. She finds his head, and a battle ensues in which all the people of the first village are killed except the woman whose lover had been slain and her daughter. They hide in a hole under ground while the town is being burned. When all is quiet, the mother shouts, "Who will marry my daughter?" Various animals come, but she refuses them because they are too weak. Finally a supernatural being from heaven comes and is accepted. He tries to carry both women up to heaven, but is compelled to leave the mother behind because, against his orders, she opens her eyes on the way. He puts her into the branch of a tree, where she remains and causes the noise produced by the wind. The daughter has several children, who receive supernatural gifts and are sent back to earth. Among these gifts is a club which, when turned, causes the earth to turn over and bury the owner's enemies. The children come down at the old village site. In a battle with their old enemies the brothers are victorious by using their magical club. Not satisfied with taking revenge, they continue to make war and thus excite the anger of the chief in heaven, who makes them lose their club.

Asi-hwî'l

The people in two villages are starving. Two sisters who live in these villages start to visit each other and meet half-way. They make a small hut, and a supernatural being, "Good-luck," appears and marries the younger sister. Their son is named Asi-hwî'l. He receives from his father magic snowshoes, with which he can climb the steepest mountains, and two small dogs which can be made to grow large and to throw mountain goats down precipices. The boy goes hunting and meets a supernatural being who kills mountain goats by clapping his hands. The sisters, with their son, rejoin their people and become very rich. Asi-hwî'l tries in vain to kill a supernatural white bear which disappears in a cliff. He marries a Tsimshian girl. Her brothers become jealous of him on account of his prowess and desert him on a sealion rock.   When the tide rises he puts his staff in a crevice and sits down on top of it.   When the tide recedes, he lies down and is called by a Mouse, which he observes through a hole in his blanket.   He finds the house of the Sealions under a bunch of grass and cures their chief whom he himself had wounded.   The Sealions send him back in a sealion stomach.   He makes two artificial killer-whales, which kill his brothers-in-law.

THE GROUSES

A chief's daughter elopes with the chief of the Grouses, who appears as a man in fox skins.   Their four children cross the river on the ice, intending to visit their grandfather.   The children chase them away, but finally they enter the house of the chief, who suspects that they are his grandchildren and issues an invitation to the Grouse tribe to visit him.   They all come, among them the lost woman. They bring as a present a pole covered with grease.   The woman returns with them.

TSEGU'KSKᵘ

A shaman has a carved squirrel, which comes to life and kills all the people of a village except TsEgu'ksk".   He lies down on a painted board in a canoe, sings, sacrifices, and is taken down to the bottom of the sea, where he receives a box in the form of a killer-whale and a magical club.   The box, by his orders, becomes a live whale, which breaks the ice and takes away all the women of his enemy's village when they come down to get water.   Eventually the club and the box kill all these people.   The Haida make war on the Nass river villages and kill TsEgu'ksk".   His head is cut off and taken along, but it swims back to the body and joins it, and TsEgu'ksk" revives.   He is invited to a feast.   He knows that he is to be poisoned and tells his friends to take out his intestines when he seems to be dead and to replace them with those of a dog.   This is done and he revives.   Another time he capsizes in his canoe, but is rescued by gulls, which carry him to the shore.   An epidemic of smallpox visits the villages.   He becomes sick.   Four arrows are shot up to the sky, which do not return, and with each shot blood flows from TsEgu'ksk"'s cheek.   This shows that he will die, but will afterward revive.   He dies.   His body is tied in a box, but revives and sits on the grave box in the shape of an owl.   A painted pole which he has erected in front of his house falls over and is seen to be rotten.   At the same time the owl falls back into the box dead.

O

Reprint Publishing

FOR PEOPLE WHO GO FOR ORIGINALS.

This book is a facsimile reprint of the original edition. The term refers to the facsimile with an original in size and design exactly matching simulation as photographic or scanned reproduction.

Facsimile editions offer us the chance to join in the library of historical, cultural and scientific history of mankind, and to rediscover.

The books of the facsimile edition may have marks, notations and other marginalia and pages with errors contained in the original volume. These traces of the past refers to the historical journey that has covered the book.

ISBN 978-3-95940-198-2

Facsimile reprint of the original edition
Copyright © 2016 Reprint Publishing
All rights reserved.

www.reprintpublishing.com

www.ingramcontent.com/pod-product-compliance
Lightning Source LLC
Chambersburg PA
CBHW080821020726

47501CB00009B/2359